A NICE BURGHER GIRL

Jean Arasanayagam

A NICE BURGHER GIRL

Jean Arasanayagam

Social Scientists' Association

2006

ISBN 955-9102-90-7

Published by

Social Scientists' Association
No. 12, Sulaiman Terrace
Colombo 05, Sri Lanka.

Cover: Prof. Albert Dharmasiri

Printed by

Karunaratne & Sons Ltd
67, UDA Industrial Estate
Katuwana Road
Homagama, Sri Lanka.

Dedication

In memory of my parents, brothers, aunts, uncles, cousins, and
nephew Roger Solomons,

for all my cousins, nieces, grandnephews, grandnieces,
for my sister Rosemary,
for Miriam and Iona,
and for Arasa, Parvathi, Devi

Contents

Acknowledgements   i
'Burgher' - *Left Behinder*   iii
'A Nice Burgher Girl'   xi

I   NATIVE KNOCKING ON THE DOOR
     1.   Diary Entries   1
        The Native Knocking on the Door (poem)   4
     2.   The Unbarred Door   9
     3.   That Eden Garden   13
     4.   The Garden Invaded: Shooting the Floricans   17
        Revelations   20
        The Credenza   21
     5.   Dum, Spiro, Spero (While I breathe, I hope)   22

II   TANGLED ROOTS: A QUEST BACK-WARD
        Journey   35
     1.   The Search   37
        For Mungo   51
     2.   The Return   54
        Ancestral Maps   56
     3.   All Flesh is Grass   58

III   THE SEED: LULLABIES IN THE WIND
     1.   The Beginnings – Kandy   75
     2.   The Changeling Bud   80
     3.   The Earthquake in the Garden   84
     4.   The Father – *Visible Reminders*   91
     5.   Flight   95
     6.   Storm on the Lagoon   98

IV   THE FIRST BRANCH: WORLD OF SCHOOL &
KADUGANNAWA HILLS
     1.   Early Kindergarten Days   103
     2.   Aggression   107
     3.   Personae   111

4. Provincial Parties 115
5. Picnics 126
6. Nilame 129
7. Zondare 135
8. Shorn of My Locks 138
9. A Memory 140

V COLONIZER/COLONIZED
Martial Routes 141
1. Colonial Connections 144
2. Living with the Colonials 147
3. The Walk 152
4. The Gift 158
5. The Christmas Cake (& recipe) 164
6. Mrs. Cramer 171
7. Buttons & Bows: Colonial Roles & Assumed 174
Disguises "Chinese Connections," Arlis the
Hairdresser
Borrowed Plumes 190

VI THE WIDER WORLD
1. The Bombay Dancers 191
2. The Jolly Joussen Jollyman 197
In a Colonial Classroom 199
3. Nymphs and Shepherds 202
A Missionary Lady 218
4. A Wider World 219
5. The Day-Scholar 225
6. The Family Doctors 234

VII MOTHER'S RECIPES & GROWING-UP TALES
My Mother 237
1. Doopvisch & Karbonadje (& recipes) 241
2. Christmas Breakfast and Church – Kandy 257
3. Tea and Cakes at Elephant House 264
Puberty Rites 270
4. Attaining Age 273

VIII THE AGE WHEN ROMANCE BLOSSOMS
 1. Parties and Mating Games 275
 2. In Pursuit of Love and Romance 281
   A Different Question 292

IX TRAVELLING & TRAVELLERS
 1. Yogis and Yoginis on the Train 295
 2. Holidays Up-country 299
 3. A Holiday Northwards 308
 4. My Cousin's Guest House Up-country 310

X THE COLONIAL GAMEBOARD
 1. Colonial Extensions 321
 2. The Colonial Gameboard - *The Vision* 326
 3. Later Colonials 342

XI REBEL AUNTS & GENTEEL LADIES
 1. Auntie Tommy's Boarding House 347
 2. Aunt Daisy Was a Saint 363
 3. Aunt Girlie's Banquets 370
 4. Sunnyside Aunts – Aunt Maud - Bertanell 373
 5. Uncle Bertie and His Gallery of Dreams 381
 6. Aunt Elsie: Family Missions & Free Masons 387
 7. Memories of Sunnyside Garden 405

XII MIGRATIONS
   Migrations 411
 1. Diasporic Travellers 415
 2. Early Migrants 420
 3. Emigrant Voices: Evangeline 424
 4. Let's Go Down Under 432
 5. Hoe Lang is Eeuigheyt (How Long is Eternity) 437
   Postscript 446
 6. Patterns of Migration 448
   Colonizer/Colonized 456

Acknowledgements

Thanks to all who were and are a part of the journey:

The Social Scientists' Association and Kumari Jayawardena for helping me to realize my dream to publish *A Nice Burgher Girl* in Sri Lanka, where I felt my works had the greatest significance in relation to my identity search. May Yee for her sensitive and perceptive editing, searching out the connections and helping to weave a flowing narrative out of varied strands of a personal, childhood saga. Also for being amenable to changes whenever new experiences needed to be inserted. Our discussions yielded new insights. She was with me all along the way on this complex journey of self-investigation and self-discovery. Indrakanthi Perera for her insightful reading of the script and her innovative suggestions. Also at SSA: Quintus Fernando for his invaluable help, infinite patience, impeccable work and relaxed good humour in working on the typescript of NBG with its many stages; and Rasika Chandrasekera for all her assistance in the formatting and preparation of the book.

For their support early on: Shamila Joshua with whom I shared a wonderful relationship in the initial typing up of the manuscript; and Rajitha Gunawardena for working on segments of NBG during its genesis.

Prof. Albert Dharmasiri and his creative imagination in designing the cover.

The University of Exeter where I was Visiting Fellow and International Writer-in-Residence, South-West Arts; Alastair Niven, Keith Cameron, Josephine McDonagh, Peter Faulkner, Ingrid and Ron Squirrel, Sally Tonge, Rosemary Goad, Arthur

Bowker, and numerous others who were part of my life at the University, Reed Hall, and in Cornwall and London. Many discoveries, on the colonial background of my inheritance viewed from a post-colonial stance, had their genesis during this period of gestation.

Villa Serbelloni of the Rockefeller Foundation, in Bellagio, where I was writer-in-residence, and experienced vital connectives in writing this autobiography. Susan Garfield, Gianna Celli, Harriet and Sheldon Segal and Patricia Mckenna were all a great inspirational force in my work, in an environment congenial and conducive to thinking and creative work linked with my inheritance journey.

Some excerpts have appeared in: *A Colonial Inheritance, Unbecoming Daughters of the Empire* (Anna Rutherford, Dangeroo Press), *Channels*, *Samyukta* G. S. Jayasree (Kerala), *Lanka* (Peter Schalk, University of Uppsala).

Ananda and Chandika Perera of Mallika Digital Lab and Studio, Kandy, for their careful restoration of many family photographs; some taken in the past by famous, talented local photographers like Conrad Felsingher, Hereward Walbeoff Jansz, as well as unknown photographers. Finally, my thanks to artists Tharaswin and Sonia for their imaginative representations of the Burgher lifestyle.

Jean Arasanayagam
(lives and writes in Kandy; also travels extensively with her alter ego and her diverse personae adopted along the way)

'Burgher'

The word 'Burgher' is derived from the Dutch word that means a citizen of a burgh, borough or town. Article 9 of the Articles of Capitulation by the Portuguese to the Dutch, concluded on the 11th of May 1656, refers to the Portugesche Burgeren (28[1]). The expression, which was first used in the country by the Dutch, referred to a civil status:

> There were two different classes of Hollanders in Ceylon during Dutch times. One was the Dutch Company's servants who were like Government officials today, and served under the Company and received their salary from the V.O.C. coffers. Even the Dutch padres at the time were in this category. The other type was the 'freelancer' who came out on their own perhaps for private business and trade in Ceylon. Most of them had shops and ran such establishments as bakeries, inns, taverns, etc. They were called by the term 'Burghers' or 'Free Burghers' (vrijburger) as distinct from the Company's servants who received official acts of appointment from the V.O.C. in respect of the posts they held respectively (28).

A retired Company servant if he remained in Ceylon joined the class of Burghers. The Company's Servants and Burghers together formed socially the Hollandsche Natie or Dutch community (29). (The word 'lansi' is derived from the Dutch word 'Hollandsche'). Originally, therefore the term 'Burgher' or 'Free-Burgher' had nothing to do with race, but had only a civic significance...

> (Percy Colin-Thome, "The Portuguese Burghers and the Dutch Burghers in Ceylon," excerpt from revised version of lecture, "The Cultural Minorities of Ceylon," Centre for Ethnic Studies, Colombo, 13 October 1984, *Journal of the Dutch Burgher Union of Ceylon*, Vol. LXII, 1985)

1 Volume of DBU journal.

A very large proportion of the servants of the Company and many others who settled here, were drawn from the States of Germany, from Denmark, Sweden, France and even from the British Isles. They came out as subjects of the United Provinces speaking the Dutch language and were here all classed together under one designation – Hollanders or Hollandsche Natie or Dutch community. The Sinhala word 'lansi' is derived from this term.

(from a lecture delivered by R.G. Anthonisz, 1905, in aid of the Building Fund of the Pettah Library)

"the individual Burgher..." a binder together of diverse races, having the blood of both the "stranger within the gates" and "the son of the soil" in his veins and able to "put himself in the place of each – that essential requisite of a peacemaker."

(William Digby, on Sir Richard Morgan)

Family Tree

Grenier

David Grenier de Cauville (ennobled by Louis XIV Lord & patron of Ernemont, Cantepie, Thibouville, Cauville, Raimbertot, St Ouen, Montevillette, in Normandy) d.1759 at Battle of Minden. Son Antoine Jacques Grenier de Cauville m. Catherine Chatillon Jean Francois Grenier, son, (Boekhouder in Sea Customs, Jaffna) m.1800 (30 Nov.) Charlotta Pietersz – 9 children William Jacob Grenier m. Susan Ann de Wolf; 2nd son Bernard Edward Grenier (Sec. District Court Batticaloa) m. (19 May) Elizabeth Dorothea Bartholomeusz – had 8 children.

1stborn Charlotte Camilla Camilla m. Joseph Ed Jansz (son of Adriaan Jansz & Susan Johnston)

Jansz

Adriaan Jansz, VOC Galle, m.1794 Elazabet de Seilve (16 Feb, Dutch Reformed Church, Galle) – had 4 sons

4th son Adriaan m.1828 (16 May) Susan Johnston

7th son Joseph Edward m.1876 (25 Oct, in Batticaloa) Charlotte Camilla Grenier – had 13 children (Aunts Nellie Maud, Uncle Bertie, Hugh)

9th daughter Charlotte Camille m.1921 Henry Daniel Solomons (30th March at Holy Trinity Church, Colombo)

Johnston

Lieut. Col. Arthur Johnston b.1778 d.1824, married a Dutch lady, had one daughter

Daughter Susan m.1828 Adriaan Jansz – had 8 children

Solomons

Fredrick Solomons m.1843 Charlotte Elizabeth Greve – had 5 children

William Henry m.1887 Emilia Sophia Pereira – had 7 children (Aunts Girlie, Ila, Elsie, Uncle Elmer Uncle Bonnie

2nd son Henry Daniel m.1921 Charlotte Camille Grenier Jansz

Had 4 children Henry (Pat), Arthur (Budgie), Rosemary, Jean.

What do memories amount to except for self-discovery,

to resume the exile of childhood, stepping

inside a boat which takes you back to that island

where you thought all was safe.

("Exiled Childhood")

I write my own histories

Time's memorialist bearing the backpack

Of a questioned inheritance.

("The Memorialist")

Jean Arasanayagam

Left Behinder

Sadness fills me. It is oppressive.
Betrayal is corrosive. The violence that gapes
Wide-open its gargoyle mouth, the words that
Squirt their acid to wound the innocent skin.

What do I do? Open out a file in which I keep
Old recipes from the past, descriptions of tiffins,
Birthday parties, dinners, recipes allied to a genealogy.
It is soothing to read of what women did with their
Lives a century or two ago, perhaps.

What a vocabulary of lexicals with all their
Connotations, translated into tastes and flavours
Contrived out of those newly discovered indigenous
Ingredients, recipes that sound to our finely attuned
Ears, esoteric, the tongue exotic, forgotten now
Only to be resurrected as part of an inheritance
History looks askance at.

I retrieve those retrospective names,
Rose koekjes, that cake shaped like the heraldic
Flower; dendeng, strips of meat dried in the sun,
Fried in oil, sugar syrup soaked golden poffertjes,
Allerlei, those mixed pickles resembling our own
Historical breed and countless others, 'toothsome
Delicacies' conjured up by those ingenious women
Who lived in and loved the good life of the Tropics.

Words that now belong to the reminiscences of the
Past, material for the indefatigable identity researchers.

And there are the memories of emigrants
Who set out on their own voyages in this century,
Emigrants who started out from those early genealogies.

They have gone away, all of them, left me behind,
Still write to me of lamprais, love cake and breudhers,
Making merry in those distant antipodes even though
Says Romaine, "Aunty Yvonne had undergone major
Heart Surgery (triple by-pass) only three months ago,"
So, she continues, "Christmas was all eating, drinking and
Being perhaps a little too merry!"

I do not know when I last knew
The meaning of that word 'merry'
Belonging as it does to all those lost annals
Including nativities, proselytization, ballads and lyrics.

No, the word has lost all meaning for me,
I do not make merry any longer
Not with thoughts of blood-sodden battlefields
With their unrecognizable dead, revolutions,
Torture or burning tyre-piles and the weight
Of fear my daughter still expresses of that
Terrifying past inscribed in the minutiae
Of her psyche.

For the moment, it is comforting to read of
The personal reminiscences of others and the
Painstaking process of those time-consuming
Preparations of meats, cakes, fritters,
Burgitter soup and milk ponce, all closely guarded
Family secrets handed down the generations by word
Of mouth, narrating the personal histories of their
Lives, through anecdotal recitals of their culinary
Skills, to enhance those inherited names for a
Fast vanishing, now almost effaced posterity.
Their hands, fingers heavy with gold bands engraved
With bonded initials, kneading pastry dough, beating up
Hundreds of eggs before the centuries cracked apart
In fragments. No more, the perfect shell remaining
To protect the embryos.

No one then thought those people alien?
Not belonging. Were they not accepted just as
They were, for themselves and not as the stranger,
Or did they think their lives a private enclave
Inhabited by a different genus?

The questions are open-ended,
The answers, individual, helped occasionally
By turning over the pages of documented
Histories, while still writing one's own.

What use to others then, are my own memories?
Memories that were and are, although now

x

Faded, part of the warp and weft of that
Tapestry of life, many hands wove together.

I re-read the letters of my immigrant niece,
Piece together the scattered leaves of her
Own memoirs, her family wapenheraut,
Before those pages, in that distant country
Will have no place in any archives.

While she lives together with her people
Displaced from their historical heritages,
She survives on carefully preserved
Ancestral memories before the somnolent eyes
Of the past close in death, recreates, retrieves
Along with remembered childhoods, her past.

What do I possess? I am the lost cipher
Rediscovered, the pointer in that reading
Of a history that is now ruthlessly scrutinized,
Leaving no room for redress.

What is there left to retrieve?
In a room, antiquated artefacts locked away
While I still remain, groping with a rusted key
That reveals in a cobwebbed trunk,
The vital clues, in diaries, letters, time preserved,
Of a fragmented identity,
That has meaning not only to myself
But for our collective histories.   (1 July 1997)

'A Nice Burgher Girl'

"Do you remember me?" I asked an acquaintance from the past. It was an unexpected encounter. I stood before the Supreme Court Judge, Justice Percy Colin Thomé, at the British Council in Colombo. The latter part of the 1980s. I had recently returned from Scotland where I had been engaged in post-graduate studies at the University of Strathclyde, Glasgow. I was now married and had twin grown-up daughters. Many years had elapsed since our last meeting when I was an undergraduate of the University of Ceylon, Peradeniya, and the Judge, at that time a young Burgher lawyer. We were rehearsing Kapek's *The Insect Play* which was being directed by Jubal, a famous figure in the world of theatre from Europe. The rehearsals took place at King George's Hall, which was part of the University of Ceylon in Colombo. Carefree days, long sleepy afternoons, exploring the new roles we were to assume both on the stage and off. "We were young, we were merry, we were very, very wise." Someone told me, "You remind me of Anna Magnani" – the fiery and temperamental Italian actress. We saw ourselves adopting dramatic personae, rehearsing the lines that provided reality to our new discoveries. Years and years before my several metamorphoses had taken place.

"Do you remember me?" The question was also self-interrogative. Did we need to remember the people who had passed through our lives 'like ships that passed in the night?' What of ourselves did we want remembered. What of ourselves did we want to remember, even record for history, for posterity? Who would want to remember us and why? The question was asked in all innocence, but the ramifications within the context in which it was asked, bore its own complexities. There could be no straight answer to so searching a question which entailed a delving back into an almost forgotten past.

What circumstances had brought us together in this time and place? Earlier on in the evening I had presented the keynote address. An internationally famous British writer was to be present on that occasion. He was on tour organized by the British Council and was in India before he embarked on the next stage of his passage to the island. The situation in the country was fraught with risk. Bombs had gone off in the city of Colombo. No one knew when and where the next bombs would be detonated. The political chaos prevalent would not ensure safety to that writer who was of great importance in the literary world of Commonwealth and post-colonial writing. My paper was on, "The Minority Writer in a Plural Society." After the rest of the panel had spoken and the subsequent discussion on the theme of the paper had ensued, Richard de Zoysa read my saga poem, "Nallur." His exceptional voice with its rich timbre preserved forever, after his early and tragic death. Both of us were videoed by World Vision.

And so we met at the Reception which followed, the Judge and I.

"Yes, I remember you..."
The Judge paused, surveying the persona who stood before him. And then weighing his words pronounced his judgement:
"But then, you were a 'Nice Burgher Girl.'"

What then was I now, that he appeared to be as reluctant to acknowledge the person I was? Changed beyond recognition in the new roles I had assumed? Rather, compelled to assume. I was now a writer dealing with a variety of themes, among which were those of ethnicity and identity. I was married to a Tamil and had moved away from the Burgher enclave into that of a traditional, tightly structured, hierarchical order of a society with a religion, language and culture, which I needed to explore. New bastions of power which I entered into boldly, allowing myself to roam at will within that Kailasa. An investigative journey. New landmarks and destinations. How did I reconcile that lifestyle with the strands of my own genealogy and lineage? Suffer a sea change or what? Outwardly, I conformed. I wore the traditional saree and jewellery. I had adopted my husband's name. I tried to understand the new ties and bonds that had been forged. And found that I had to create my own welcome. The hospitality of my parents' abode had to be dispensed by myself in a new environment.

I had noted a tone of profound regret in the words of the Judge. To him and to my own kind, being 'a Nice Burgher Girl' signified the icons preserved through an inheritance, the legacies of the blood, a distinctive lineage, traditions, a way of life. I had not migrated to other countries like my relations, those numerous cousins, nieces, my own sister, aunts… who had been so much a part of my childhood and growing up. Friends too, whom I would never see again 'in the land of the living' to use a favourite phrase of my mother's. I was one of the 'left-behinders,' yet one who occupied and inhabited a familiar, well-known terrain. I made my own forays into the wide-open spaces, I became my own scout and my own guide. It was not just the words of the Judge that made me think of the diverse elements which were part of my psyche as a Burgher girl. There were other forces too which made me go back in time and memory to make my self-discoveries. The unexpected shock of suddenly feeling myself a person apart, not because of my own hybrid birth but because of marriage into a different ethnic minority. My sojourn with my husband and family in a Refugee Camp in the violent eras of the eighties made me aware of barriers and boundaries. I had to know who I really was and find the rationales for asserting an identity. I had to question that identity too engendered by those ancestors and progenitors of mine. Colonial forebears. The justification for their acts of conquest and invasion needed to be scrutinized. Weighed in the historical scales. I was often struck by the ironies which prevailed among my people. The going away, the emigration, the voluntary exile that took them far away from the home which they need never have left.

Oftentimes my exploration made me bitter at rejection. I longed for anonymity, camouflage, acceptance and belonging, but those were the desires of one who wanted to go unnoticed. I realized it would never be, and so I began with boldness to examine an identity and proclaim it together with all its accretions and additions as something distinctive, unique, significant. There were so many facets and interpretations to what 'a Nice Burgher Girl' should be. There was power in the very innocuousness of the epithet. It could imply so many things. Was being non-conformist or radical included? What would be the expected qualities of 'a Nice Burgher Girl'? Would they be concealed beneath the garments of so many disguises, the garments pulled 'out of history's cupboard,' to enact role after role? Would people search for aberrations, deviations, sexual or otherwise, to be considered part and parcel of a hybrid inheritance? In writing of so personal a history is it necessary to make it a confessional, self-revelatory, an expiation of the penitent for 'the sins of our forefathers'? It is for the reader to interpret those myriad signifiers of language. Perhaps a reading between the lines will reveal many an untold secret, the opening of cupboards where skeletons come tumbling out.

For me these chapters of an unfinished personal history also began as a search for my parents. We do not really know our parents when we are young. They were seen as guardians, providers. As we grow older we need to know how much of themselves were/are within us. My father always held me, as a child, high up on the perch of his shoulders so that I would have many views of the world. My mother was the great narrator of fictions which at times embodied historical truth with fantasy, even magical reality. She was also the singer of songs. Spun riddles - Riddles? "Come, riddle-me-ree," she would often say, and we would sit together while she teased me into wild, unimagined attempts at answers. I had to realize that no riddle would ever have a straight answer. Yes, both my mother and father led lives which were in themselves filled with adventure. At the same time with the human emotions of love so overwhelming that it could even lead to tragedy. Yet they survived. Helped us to survive. Made tremendous sacrifices of their own desires, time, energies. And then, gave us our freedom to hurtle headlong into danger. We learned to survive. 'Nice' was part of that survival kit. Part of it being the ability to cajole or laugh at the human predicament.

Sometimes it was necessary to take that quantum leap from past to present. To link up encounters. To continue the journeys. To take the traveller and explorer beyond the boundaries of time.

The search was a long and painful one, belonging as I did to that community which had first spelt safety. Stepping outside of that enclave into conflict and violence. The search still continues. Lasts till the end of time.

Cousin Joyce told me a story of her husband, Colonel George Martenstyn, who had gone with his friends on a fishing expedition somewhere in the Knuckles Range. Colonel George, a vintage hero, Customs Collector, man of property, friend of Lord Louis Mountbatten. He and his friends had come upon a fish, a fish of a variety unknown and unfamiliar. A fish unique in every aspect. Since Col. George had discovered it, it became 'a fish called Martenstyn.' It survives in the freshwater streams of the Knuckles Massif even today, one of the three varieties found only there. Martenstyn's barb (*Pontius Martenstyni*). A survivor together with Phillips garra (*Garra Phillipi*), and the blotched filamented barb (*Pontius Lankankensie*).

We would remain. Adapt ourselves. Make ourselves at home wherever we found ourselves. The Burgher fish in the indigenous freshwater streams of Time and History.

I

NATIVE KNOCKING ON THE DOOR

Reed Hall, Streatham Drive, University of Exeter, where I lived as a writer-in-residence, 1994.

Diary Entries

(London, January 1994)

Waterloo Bridge. The air is chill. A cold winter. Young men cracking wood for fire for warmth. A man juggling with skittles. A world of the homeless beneath the bridge. A young man with gaunt frame, pallid, whey-faced and expressionless, sits on a folded blanket in a corner of the bridge. Huddled in a greatcoat sizes too large for him.

I have just stepped off the plane at Heathrow to begin my journey to the south-west of England: Exeter, Devon, Cornwall. I am still in transit. In London, I have been met by Ingrid and her husband Ben. Ingrid is the Literature Supervisor for the programme I've been invited for. I will grow to know them closely and forge lasting bonds with them as time passes. Now I am rather perplexed as to why I am not taken directly to the place where after a brief stopover I shall prepare for the next lap of my journey. I am feeling the effects of jet-lag. But then, I won't be occupying an impersonal hotel room, making phone calls, reading maps, watching old films on TV. No, I am to go to the home of Rosemary, one of the readers for Faber and Faber. I have to wait until she is ready to welcome me. Until it is time to arrive there, Ingrid takes me to Festival Hall. We wander through a gallery of posters and reach the Poetry Library. I could spend hours there. Time passes. We sip hot coffee. I make phone calls to a cousin, to a friend, and then it's time to set out for Rosemary's flat in London.

Rosemary is a lovely person, warm, friendly. I don't feel that we are strangers. She is going to be another lifelong friend. I have a hot bath. I am to become famous for these hot baths later on. I have a reputation for soaking in the frothy foam. It's a way

I've learnt of taking the chill off frozen limbs and warming up winter-chilled blood when far from my home in the tropics.

Rosemary has baked a marvellous casserole for lunch. We begin one of our unending conversations. A friend of Rosemary's, Heather, is visiting from Edinburgh. We speak of many things. Paintings. Pre-Raphaelite paintings. Dante Gabriel Rossetti, Ceylon, the colonial past. Memories of my missionary school and the missionary principals.

I had attended a private school founded by Methodist missionaries. Heather and I talked of the impressions formed in my mind by the environment created for us in those colonial classrooms. Day in, day out, year after year, at School Assembly which was held in the big school hall with its platform where the principal and the teachers formed an august presence, my eyes had gazed on three paintings hanging on the wall. The central portrait was that of a former principal, Constance Mallet, a classic portrait of those times painted by an Estonian artist Karl Kassman. (Karl was married to our music teacher, Doris Karlenberg, and lived a Bohemian lifestyle, played gypsy Tsiganne music on his violin tempestuously – we used to watch fascinated the Kassman drawing room at "West End" from our house on Peradeniya Road, as he swayed beneath the softly glowing lights with his poised bow, the notes resonating from his Stradivarius, lost in a world of his own.

My eyes used to be always drawn to the two glass-framed prints flanking the portrait: one was of Eve in the Garden of Eden after the Fall; the other was a painting of Christ holding aloft a lighted lantern that shed its soft, luminous rays around him, standing beside a massive wooden door, locked and barred, covered with thorny creepers and brambles. The two paintings belonged to the Pre-Raphaelite School of painting. Both were painted by Dante Gabriel Rossetti. My eyes veered between the three paintings, which dominated my vision while we sang hymns from the Methodist hymnal, listened to psalms, readings from the Bible and announcements about school affairs.

I described to Heather the painting of Christ standing beside that locked, barred door. She ventured an interpretation that Christ was waiting to open the door to the insistent and importunate knocking of the 'native,' pleading for entrance to the spiritual kingdom, ordained by temporal colonial strands of experience. Revelations from the past that made me think of my identity against that background. What I was concerned with was the opening of that door, to have knowledge of myself and of where I belonged. Heather's interpretation remained in my mind. What relevance did it have to my own life, my past, my colonial ancestors, those psychic, unknown tongues that swirled about in my head? I had to search for those beginnings.

Heather was full of amusing, irony-filled stories. She described a wedding she had heard of, celebrated in Ceylon. In the south of the island, in Galle, which had seen three centuries of European colonization. The groom had been a famous English literary critic. His bride a beautiful aristocratic society woman. A wedding remembered for its elephants and champagne. The women, all of them English, wore long evening gowns and were hatted and gloved for the occasion. The men were in full dress suit. It was a steaming hot, humid day. Anglican and Methodist hymns were sung at the wedding service. The service was conducted by an English Chaplain who delivered the homily. At the reception that followed, which was more like a garden party, champagne flowed, but there was no ice to chill it. The champagne was lukewarm. Who knows what happened to the marriage. The names of the bride and groom are to me, unknown or forgotten. I thought of the marriages of three of my ancestors: the Dutchman Adriaan Jansz, the Frenchman Francois Grenier, and the Irishman Captain Arthur Johnston. Staid marriage ceremonies performed in colonial churches. They were not exotic affairs but matters that dealt with the beginnings of my own hybrid inheritance. The European bloodlines began there, at that point in history.

I jot down lines of poetry that begin to form in my mind before I settle down to sleep in this quiet apartment where I am a guest. It is snowing, the white snowflakes are soft, feathery. Heather's mystery story. The native knocking on the door.

The Native Knocking

The native knocking on the door
Is me
Invading that celestial kingdom
With my importunate cries,

Pleading for sin's reprieve
Willing to pay penance.

My forefathers carried arms /
Musket, flintlock, sabre,
Trundled cannon through jungles,
Marched with their regiments of
Mercenaries. Yet the door opened
For them with so much ease.

Why then do I lurk outside
Skulking in the dark,
Flailing upon a door with my clenched
Fists?
I, the native knocking on the door
Inhabitant of the true paradise
Now ambushed by history.

Donhead: "Colonial Missions"

After one of my poetry readings, we go to the home of Muir and Gillian in Donhead. Muir was a poet too. Sipping Armagnac and elderberry wine before a blazing woodfire, Muir, narrator of histories, settled himself comfortably in the drawing room, feet on footstool, and began his recital of the tales of that Imperial ascendancy of the Raj and its aftermath:

"In the latter part of the eighteenth century, my grandfather was the Commander of the British fleet in the Indian Ocean. We had a long tradition in the East. 'Nabobs,' they called us – Anglo-Indians but not in the sense of half-caste. My grandfather had plantations in Mauritius, a big bungalow, slaves. Fortunes dwindled. The plantations abandoned. My people became lawyers, judges, scholars, military men."

As Muir continued his narration, I observed the portraits of ancestors on the walls, ancestors who belonged to the era of Empire building. How would I have been seen by them? If I had lived in that past? *The native knocking on the door*. Justification may be sought by empires for the role of the colonizer by assumptions of that imperial mission, but deeply imprinted in the consciousness were also the hard facts of imperialism and conquest. Now we question that mission, theirs as well as ours. We too carry arms, but less archaic, to detonate the past, to sort out from the debris and rubble of history, remnants of our harlequin garments of hybrid identities. Examine the causes that determined power and aggrandizement before the shots were fired to quell rebellion.

Muir's wife explained that once-held view of colonialism: "They were doing a service, that's what they felt was their duty."

What was the reality then of that mission, that historical mission? Was it not politically expressed in the accumulation and acquisition of territory and commodities? Even the missionaries were involved ultimately in that global enterprise to 'civilize the native,' along with proselytization and evangelization.

And what about the women who came out with the bureaucrats and the administrators? What were their lives like? Gillian had a grandmother who had lived in Kandy, in the latter part of the nineteenth century perhaps. We were separated in time by a hundred years or more. The house, Gillian told me, stood by the Kandy lake – a house with thick-girthed pillars, wide verandas, tiled roof, and enormous, cavernous rooms. The forest sanctuary teeming with deer, elephant, leopard and wanderoo monkeys was the backdrop of the colonial structure where Gillian's grandfather, the British Engineer, lived.

What were the memories of the wife of the Civil Engineer, while he was engaged in his bureaucratic duties?

"The elephants would come out of the forest and show their babies to her. The gem sellers brought their baskets with their packets of sapphires, topaz and moonstones, spread their wares on the wide, cement-floored veranda while she sat regally, leaning against cotton-filled cushions covered with cretonne on the cane chair." Gillian has heirlooms of inherited moonstones from that century.

"She could never, that grandmother of mine, efface Ceylon from her mind. Even after she had suffered a stroke, her garbled words would speak of that island." In her myth-ridden imagination, moonstones of memory still glowed in the gathering dusk of her mind.

My thoughts went back to the prison in the township of Kandy, built during the period of the British Raj. It stood like a medieval fortress, turreted, washed in red, a picture out of an old history book. Prisoners of time peered out of those narrow barred windows. In 1983 I had watched the prisoners in the courtyard of the jail exercising, running round and round in a circular movement. I watched them from the bungalow of the DIG (Deputy Inspector General) up in the pine forest at a time when I was a prisoner of my own fear, a refugee during the ethnic disturbances.

Ingrid, who had accompanied me to Donhead, watched me amusedly as I ruminated, standing, back to the fire. It was chilly. The logs burned steadily, warmth crept into my limbs.

"Victorian men would stand like that," she commented. "Didn't you have an ancestor, Captain Arthur Johnston, who fought in the Kandyan Wars?" He of course, was no Victorian when he started out on his career, which began during the reign of the Hanovarian kings. However, Ingrid had jolted my memory. I was still shackled to that century. Bloodlines noose memory, and bear traces of a faraway aggressor. The experience grew immediate. In my mind the ghostly semblance of heirlooms settled their lassoes round our throats.

Among other things, Muir recounted how during the Second World War the Tommies were sold rubies. "They were sometimes made out of the red ground glass of headlamps," he said. We changed the topics of conversation. Donhead, where Muir and Gillian lived, was to me a strange village. It had no shop, no village green, only a church that went back to the Doomesday Book, turnpike toll roads built with private capital. Dick Turpin the highwayman had lived there too. As I was enveloped in the warmth of generous hospitality and friendship, I felt the continuity of history in a different way. I was no longer the native knocking on the door. We now talked on equal terms.

Muir and Gillian had worked with hospices in Eastern Europe. Thus they continued their individual and personal humane missions. I read Muir's collections of poems in celebration of his 80th birthday:

These heaps of ashes of empires past,
Each more divisive than the last,
Can be kicked into the flame
By frontier, a name –
Old feuds exploding a lethal blast.

(Muir Hunter, *Ashes of Empire*, Wiltshire)

And my own poem:

I observe the portraits of their ancestors
Belonging to that era of Empire Building,
Generals, admirals, Viceroys of the Raj

Looking out upon a changed world
Enclosed within those ornate frames.

Yet I too come within the purview of history's scrutiny.
We discuss, my hosts and I, the prerogatives
Of that Imperial ascendancy. Words, phrases, ring
The empire's Death-knell in my brain.

Transculturation. Hybridity. Slavery,
Sexual exploitation.
Colonialism was a global enterprise for the Empire
Builders
It was an historical mission, thought some.

My hostess says, "They believed they were doing a
service."
It was a gesture that demanded subservience
Yet it's one that's still expected from one's own,
The masters have merely changed.

The bent head. The folded palms.
Supplication.
Submission.
Yes, history repeats itself, here and now…

(1994)

The Unbarred Door

What do I remember of my father? His stories from his own life. From the memories he never wrote down. Stories, yarns, as he called them, from those railway journeys. He was proud of the fact that he was always called upon to be on the engine with his assistant engine driver and fireman on those special CGR trains, which carried the colonial governors on their missions through the island.

"I was chosen because the train ran smoothly under my guidance. There were no jolts and jerks, and I was able to stop the train at the exact spot where the Governor could step onto the red carpet laid for him on the station platform."

There were other stories too. Stories that racked him with grief. Orders were given to carry regiments of sepoys in the trains brought to quell the disturbances that spread over the island as a result of the Sinhala-Muslim Riots in 1915. The Riots had begun as a result of an order given that the perahera should not sound its drums or play musical instruments within a hundred yards of the mosque in Gampola. The disturbances that broke out soon spread to the Sabaragamuwa, Western and North-Western provinces. The British government proclaimed martial law and armed patrols were sent to quell the unrest. A number of people were shot without semblance of trial. It was a harrowing experience, my father recollected, for the men manning the trains to see troops opening fire on the villagers who surged onto the tracks with their rough implements. The soldiers were fully armed. The villagers were mown down under the onslaught of bullets as the troops opened fire. The men on the trains had no alternative except to carry out the orders issued by the colonial government they worked under. There were court martials and the tragic execution of William Pedris. The aftermath of the Riots was agitation for political reform initiated by remarkable nationalists like E.W. Perera, Sir Ponnambalam Ramanathan, Sir James Peries, Baron Jayatilleka, and others.

My father was himself an ardent Nationalist, and to him it was important that Ceylonese leaders founded the Ceylon Reform League in 1917 and the Ceylon National Congress in 1919. All this would appear in the chapters on constitutional reform in the history books later on. When I read of the various Commissions for constitutional change I remembered how my father had been in the thick of the fray, had indeed been a part of the history of those colonial eras. The better part of his life had been spent on those trains, which carried him on those routes that were being pioneered by the Imperial British Government throughout the island, taking him not only on those journeys but also on transfers to remote areas, until he settled into the administrative department in the Railways.

It was during the perahera days that he would carry me through the crowds on his shoulders…way above the heads of the perahera crowds milling on the pavements, the bright lights sparkling in my eyes. We had come to Kandy in cars from Kadugannawa, Uncle Alroy, Aunt Gladys, the Schofields, and all the railway friends. The whole jing-bang would go upstairs at the Muslim Hotel for biriyani, roast chicken and wattalappan.

The dignified waiters wore crimson fezzes with long tassels, and my father, to me a great pasha, would persuade one of them to let him try on the fez as he sat at the head of the long tables pushed together to give all of us room.

Mrs Rulach, another railway man's wife, a friend of the family, would chuckle as she related some of the escapades of my father. After a big 'do' at a social evening in the Railway Reading Room, my father, upon downing several whiskies, would make violent patriotic speeches and challenge the colonial railwaymen for a fight – a real boxing bout – Mrs Rulach said. The hall would rapidly empty, with all of them taking refuge under the billiard table and the card tables until he calmed down… My mother was sometimes a long-suffering woman, yet they remained together for almost half a century.

In his youth my father had been a fine boxer. He was, when young, a bantam-weight champion. The bridge of his fine Roman nose had been broken in a boxing bout. He was never afraid to take on any opponent. Dr Vachel Anthonisz once told me the story of a foreign boxing champion who had come out to Ceylon. No one wanted to get into the ring with him except young Solomons who came forward – my father always stood up to the challenge whether he won or lost.

And then there were my fathers' jungle adventures in Maho. Walking through the jungle on his way to the wewa, a tank which helped to irrigate his paddy fields and those of the village folk, he saw a huge sparrow hawk swoop down on a python that was in the process of ingesting a deer. The antlers protruded from its jaws. The sparrow hawk had soared up into the sky carrying both python and its prey…

Yes, on that coconut estate in Maho he lived in a house without doors with half-walls to let in the cool breeze and birdcalls. The house was surrounded by hundreds of mango trees of different varieties, the smallest variety, mee amba, was never plucked but left for the bats, the flying foxes, the birds of the air to feast on. My father created a sanctuary on those acres for bird, beast and reptile. No reptile harmed him although serpents abounded everywhere, the deadly mapila, the tic-polonga, the cobra, the python. I never saw the green eye-peckers of my childhood there. Once there was a mapila coiled beneath the mattress of his bed. The days of his colonial adventures were then over and my father was close to the people of the village who were part of his life on the estate. He shared their rituals and the house was filled with those intricately woven devale offerings of the first fruits of the harvest. Long tassels of paddy hung from the woven squares that were put up on the walls, and the sparrows would fly in to peck the grain. Thalagoyas crawled into the garden from the jungles. There were brilliantly plumaged jungle fowl, Ash doves, Batagoyas, wild duck, teal… and storks. This was the life he loved, that father of mine, playing his bamboo flute, noting down his observations of nature in his journals together with old proverbial village sayings and folklore.

When the Che Guevarist movement broke out in 1971 he was alone on the estate. The young radicals left him alone. They did not even care to ask for his guns. He was never a part of quelling the movement. Many of the insurgents were shot and buried in the teak grove close to the estate after they had been rounded up and arrested. It was a cause of great grief to him that their youth was so abruptly brought to an end. Yet death did not destroy their ideologies which would always remain. Perhaps he thought back in memory of those troop-laden trains, filled with sepoys who were brought to quell the Riots of 1915. All that was over and done with. Now his preoccupations were with sanctuaries and gardens of life, of nature, a natural world where the notes of his flutes traveled through the dusk to reach the jungle and the wilderness.

That Eden Garden

The bee-hives in my childhood garden were full of honeycombs. My father prepared to smoke out the bees. The honeycombs were brimming. The bees had busied themselves collecting pollen and nectar from our garden during those long, sun-filled days. I would move the little window-shutters and watch them at work. A glimpse into a different universe, the industrious bees scurrying among the waxy combs. The bees flew in and out, in and out of the narrow apertures of the hives, searching for pollen, bringing in the yellow powdery substance from the anthers of flowers, and the nectar secreted within the blossoms. I too would sip that ambrosial wine from deep within those flowers.

My father said that he was immune to bee-stings, yet he wore a khaki-topi covered with a net which soon became thickly sprinkled with bees swarming all over him. I too would get a sting or two embedded in my flesh. My father would first, with delicate skill, remove the sting, and then with white chunam paint over the swelling. Sometimes the bee-swarms clung to the branches of the anodha tree, buzzing about the leaves until they formed a new swarm, suspended pendant-shaped from the branch.

It was a garden with bowers of flowers of thumbergia and honeysuckle, the curving beaks of the honey-peckers and honeysuckers buried deep within the honey-filled throats of the blossoms, bird and flower gently swinging together in their mobiles. Green eye-pecker snakes curled round the grenadilla vine and leaf-nests of red dimiya ants hung suspended from the jak tree.

There were trees laden with anodha, mulberry bushes, a grenadilla creeper, jak trees, mango, and chow-chow vines twining in arbours.

My father had created this garden, primeval in its innocence, a sanctuary for birds and for all living creatures. At the same time it was the garden of his grief. He would ask me not to touch the stems of roses on the bushes he had planted. He did not want me to feel the pain of that stabbing thorn. Nor would he allow me to pluck a single flower from that garden. The flowers bloomed and shed their petals in their natural season. But I plucked his flowers notwithstanding. Surely he would not miss a flower or two, but he did and upbraided me. There were certain rules that must not be transgressed. That garden was his Eden. The earth awoke and became a cradle in which he nurtured his roses, the Holy Ghost orchids, the hollyhocks and the mugerine bush. At dusk the glow-worms shone through the leaves in a nimbus of green phosphorescent light. Fireflies glimmered as they flashed their tiny star-like lanterns among the masses of dark leaves. Green chameleons impaled insects on their sticky tongues. The grey cickanellas were watchful among the flowerbeds. As dusk fell the praying mantis and cicadas crept into the house when the oil lamps were lit.

Strong winds which blew across the valley were held at bay by the clustering vines, bowers, bushes, creepers and the tall eramudu tree with its red blossoms, the fallen petals crushed on a flat stone, the meat of my play-food. The thin-skinned grenadillas ripened on the creeper, translucent, a pale greeny-gold with filigree patterns of light and shade. Millipedes and snails crawled on the earth in their slow uninterrupted passage through my growing years. The birds and squirrels fed from my father's hands, they were so tame, so familiar with and unafraid of his presence. When I crept out into the garden early in the morning I would put out a tentative finger to shake the tiny dew-diamonds that reflected an iridescent firmament within those tremulous oval mirrors. The colour of a fresh rose bled within it, droplets of blood flickering as the wind breathed on each dewdrop. A tracery of lacy light and shade lay on the leaves. The garden seemed jewelled with light and colour. Even at noon the garden was green and cool under the bowers. In the flowerbeds petals opened into the sun, like myriads of fluttering butterflies. I touched the nidikumba plant, which instantly folded itself up drawing feathery fringes together. When would the plant open itself to be seen again? When my footsteps had receded and I had gone away?

The garden tempered the vast, dynamic energies of my father's temperament. His silences sometimes weighed heavily on us when a hidden sense of melancholy filled his heart and mind. How was I to know that my brother Budgie's death, before my birth, would become the source of my father's unceasing sorrow?

At times he sang joyfully when Beryl Schofield played his favourite songs on the piano. Sometimes he tuned his bamboo flute until he began to form his melodies one after another: Handel's "Largo" and his favourite Scottish songs, "Annie Laurie," "You Take the High Road," "All the Flowers of the Forest." He would drink with his railway friends, talk for hours with them, spinning yarn after yarn. "Have you heard this one?" Even if all of us had, we would shake our heads and give ear to his tales again. And of an evening he would sometimes sit reading quietly hour by hour, autobiographies, jungle adventures, memoirs, with my mother beside me reading from a storybook, skipping pages and chapters. She preferred to tell me her own narratives by day. The spiders spun their webs among the tiles.

The insects whirled crazily about the heated globe. The geckos scaling the wall pursued the hidden insects, stalking them stealthily, and the bali drums started up from the village tucked away in the hillside.

I had another garden too. A secret world. Within a bower of thumbergia, a grenadilla creeper with mysteriously shaped fruit hammocked within intertwining leaves. At night the owl called from the anodha tree. Holy Ghost orchids, hollyhocks, and bushes of my father's special white and cream petalled thornless roses grew there. I could run my fingers along that reddish-green stalk which was as smooth as silk and had no snags or sharp thorns. It was a magical setting for a changeling child. But later there were also roses with thorns among the flowers, and my flesh was torn by sharpened stalks. The wound grew infected and its poison almost reached to the bone, encircled with a yellow frill of pus. It grew like a strange flower, its bud opening below my ankle. It began to heal after it was raked out and swabbed with cotton wool impregnated with peroxide. I now knew pain, deep in my flesh. The peroxide stung and burned. So did the iodine. I bear the scar to this day, the skin as fine as a sere leaf.

I spent many years of my childhood in that magical garden. Honeysuckers dipped their beaks into the crimson and saffron-yellow thumbergia bells. Bees crept out of their blue painted hives to gather nectar and pollen. The honey, thick, amber, brimmed over in their waxy cups in the serrations of honeycombs. I pressed the dewdrops quivering on the matt surface of rose petals to my lips still fresh from night sleep and unfinished dreams. It was in this garden that I played with my ayah Mungo for timeless hours; we played with innocent pebbles, contrived our games with leaves, ferns, flowers.

The Garden Invaded: Shooting the Floricans

I was wholly fascinated by the Credenza, the enormous sixteenth century food-server that stood outside my room, in the passage at Reed Hall. I had also discovered the Floricans in 1993 when I had been a guest at Reed Hall, invited to give a poetry reading at the University of Exeter. In 1994 I was a Visiting Fellow of the Department of English and American Studies at Exeter, and International Writer-in-Residence for South West Arts. In my diary I had jotted down notes from the framed nineteenth century magazine *Country Life*, later to be explored in a poem, "Shooting the Floricans." In that poem I was to draw the analogy between the hunter/colonizer, and the hunted, the colonized. I would explore colonialism through that now extinct bird, the Florican. The epigraph to this poem was the description of the Floricans.

The details of the appearance of the bird showed that it possessed a rare beauty. The writer, one of the Empire-building members of the Reed family, had noted it all down minutely in his reminiscences:

> The Florican belongs to the bustard family (otidiae).
> Bears much resemblance to the great Indian bustard
> (Eupodotis bustardis). The ooli more grass peacock in-
> habits the dyaras, the heavy tiger grass jungle. The land-
> scape is like a vast sea, light, silvery with filmy reeds in
> flower. The dyaras are the habitat of the Florican, the
> tiger, the hog deer.
> The male in breeding dress, long loose black feathers
> that hung in front of the neck, a plume or crest of black

feathers from the back of the head to nearly the lower part of the neck. Breast feathers and those of the neck elongated, wings and wing coverts white, general plumage a rich buff most beautifully marked and variegated with black and brown.

The female is devoid of plumes and of white or dark plumage but is most beautifully ornamented with black arrow-headed markings and vermiculated on a pale fulvous ground all over the back and wing coverts. A most delicious bird for the table, superior to pheasant, grouse, partridge.

The guns are put away. Ancestral portraits hang on the wall. I try to read, to interpret the expressions on those faces. To me they bear that imperial air, the expressions, those I was familiar with from childhood, on the faces of the representatives of the British Raj. Empire Builders of the past. I write a few lines in my mind of their biographies.

Will I have time to make a journey to Shalden, in Hampshire, where my great-great-grandfather Lt Colonel Arthur Johnston retired to when his imperial destinies were over in the island of Ceylon? He had left a military narrative of the Expedition to Kandy in 1804. He had also left behind his only child, Susan, my great-grandmother. He was never to see her again after he embarked for England on that sailing vessel in the year 1811 on 11th May. He became Professor in the Royal Military College, finally settled down in Shalden, married Martha Smith, and died on 7th June 1824. In the village churchyard remains the memorial set up by his second wife, Martha Smith. They lived in Shalden Lodge.

Martha was the eldest daughter of Thomas and Martha Smith. The Smith family had once lived in the Manor House at Shalden.

Had Arthur Johnston longed to see his daughter Susan again, or were there bitter memories after the death of her mother, his first wife? I was not here to follow that particular historical trail. I had other missions to fulfil.

I look out of a window, my eyes encompassing part of the extensive acres of Reed Hall, Streatham Drive. Watch university students passing over the horizon among the trees.

> *The window is my view of the world*
> *Nature screens off the horrendous deeds*
> *Of warring people.*
> *Do the squirrels devour the birds?*
> *No, it is not their nature.*
> *Is there promiscuity among the birds?*
> *Excess is not permitted.*
>
> *The view from this one window*
> *Is not a limitation*
> *History stares back at me*
> *Not with hostility.*
> *I am not the invader.*

At Reed Hall, where I spend almost three months in the year 1994, I stand in the foyer beneath an ancient wrought-iron hanging lamp suspended from the ceiling. I am waiting to be taken on some unknown journey to some unknown place to read my poetry. While I wait, I take out my diary and write these lines:

Revelations

So, history weaves its cobwebs
Round this lamp
Yet cannot dim its light
For centuries still to come.

My hands sweep back those clinging
Veils to clearer sight
It is now my dawn
My sun's rays that fall
Upon the empire on which the sun
Has long since set
Imperial dynasties gone to dust.

What are those symbols?
Now so faintly discerned
Their esoteric meanings
Puzzled over in my mind
Those florid lines
Those metal curlicues
Colours of gold and amber
Glowing behind glass frames
Reveal to me in this diminishing
Light, lines too faint, too obscure
To be deciphered, of vanished epochs
Lost in time.

The Credenza

Embellished. Carved out. Mythophilia.
The animal kingdom abundant. Fecund, yet dead.
Half beast. Half bird. The lion. The predator eagle.
Somewhere concealed is the hunter.
Creeping through coverts. Fern moist. The woods smoking.
With fiery leaves. Everything's russet. Setting traps.

The woman looks down upon the rubble of death.
The orgy of the hunt. Does she fulfil her ordained roles
Here? Again and yet again.
Who will release her from her histories,
Unchain her from her legends. Her rituals?
What new progeny will she bring forth?
Sired by whom? Her offspring. This woman's.
When will she free herself from the lion and the eagle
Cease to wallow in this gluttonous slaughter?

(Reed Hall
University of Exeter 1994)

Dum Spiro, Spero (While I breathe, I hope)

Every morning I walk out of my room at Reed Hall in Exeter onto the carpeted corridor where the enormous food server, the Credenza, stands. Who was that man from Sienna, Bertolacci his name, who designed this Credenza with its detailed and intricate carvings on those great hewn slabs of oak, giving himself, along with Count Pecci and Leo III, immortality? I imagine the artisans crouched over their work with their practised craft, shaping, moulding, gouging out those forms both realistic and fantastical. To me it's like a great ark and every day my eyes are drawn to some new aspect of it. The other day I observed Paula polishing it carefully with a soft wad of cloth. Every bird, animal, fish and half-human figure carved into the wood coming alive.

"Be careful, watch out," I felt like warning Paula, "Those lobsters with their enormous claws will grip those delicate, succulent fingers of yours, and the fish all agape have pretty sharp teeth that will clamp down on your little finger, which will vanish into their maws together with all the other sea creatures and plankton and what-not gulped down." The hounds look terrifying, used for hunting game, the fur bristling, sharp pointed fangs bared, slavering over the vulnerable throats of deer, pheasant, wild hare, birds of the air slung in trussed coveys with torn and bloodied throats. So much flesh. Impregnated with blood from the slits and slashes, all being readied for the great banqueting tables. But first the fur must be scraped off the still- steaming pelts, the feathers plucked, fish scales deftly stripped, fins sliced off, the kitchen knives' sharp blades gashing the flesh. What if they were to find a coelacanth? But I see nothing like that here, among the carvings, only fish with spiky tails and fins, with mouths gaping in the rigours of death, soon to fill the cookpots with boiling water or pans sizzling with fat, and served by the aproned servers staggering under the weight of the enormous silver salwers.

After those great gargantuan feasts, who scrubbed all those cookpots and salwers? Maidservants, their hands roughened and reddened with their labour, hands scored with the scrapes of sharp fishbones and slivers of bone from the roasted game. What was there left for them to eat? Perhaps merely scraps and giblets.

Sarah, who generally serves breakfast at Reed Hall, washes up everything in near-boiling water that flows copiously from the taps, especially the plates with the congealing fat from bacon and eggs adhering thickly to the surfaces. She never wears gloves to protect her shapely hands. "I just can't get used to them, " she tells me.

During those Victorian eras, when the Reed ancestors held sway, the cooks, the scullery maids and the kitchen skivvies must have been kept pretty busy. Andrew tells me of the wooden panels with innumerable bells which were rung to summon the servants who were at the beck and call of those lords and ladies of the manor. Now, all those bells are silent. There is no one they could summon at will to cater to their needs. Times have changed.

Going back to the Credenza, I thought of the aching arms and backs, the roaring fires that had to be stoked up, skimming off the thick scum from the pots of boiling meats. I felt a sense of great sadness for those dead animals and birds. Not a chance for any of them, with the baying packs of hounds. Glazed eyes, lolling tongues, torn flesh. Carving those great joints of meats was a skilled job with sharp knives and pronged forks, finely sliced and served onto individual platters carried to the diners, by silent maids and butlers.

In my own three-month sojourn at Reed Hall I made fresh discoveries with Paula every day as she prepared to strip the sheets off the beds in the guest rooms, scrubbed the washbasins and huge Victorian-style baths, replaced reams and reams of toilet paper daily, so much of it that one could begin and complete poems, novels, plays on those spotless white surfaces. Or even make sketches and line drawings.

Paula is a beautiful woman, living with her boyfriend and their young son, who is all in all to them both. She told me of the different jobs she has held to make a living, not to make a permanent career of, however. Once, she was a child-minder and looked after children in her own home while the parents were at work, often the children of single mothers or single fathers. And something even more difficult, spending long, wakeful night hours with children who were restless, fractious, up all night, unable to sleep or even allow their parents to sleep. Paula would probably change jobs whenever she felt like it. With the story of her own life she could probably create a bestseller or create story after story out of the lives of the guests who gathered together at various times at Reed Hall. Or she could become a great stage performer, an iconic actress or a model of haute couture. She had beauty, the beautiful colouring and grace of a Reynold painting of an English country lady of aristocratic birth, but sometimes the onlooker passes these paintings by, turns to other portraits, distorts their reality, recreates images more true to a surreal world. Her stories were colourful.

A famous Black American writer had also been at Reed Hall; like myself, she too had been Writer-in-Residence at Exeter University. "Oh, she had a wonderful personality. She towered over you both physically and mentally and had a rich, vibrant, deeply resonant voice. What a voice it was," Paula told me, "It was a voice that gripped your innermost being and reached into your very soul with its power." Unlike me who took pleasure in pure Evion and Strathclyde water, a vintage port or chilled white wine, the American writer preferred a choice of the very best from age-old cellars stocked with vintage wine. She also loved gin.

Arthur-at-the-bar too had his stories. He told me of another great Latin American writer. "He had a variety of tantalizing 'ladies of the night,' come in from the town of Exeter to entertain him in bed and keep him company in those lonely, silent hours at Reed Hall. Once he had done with them, he threw them out of his room onto the waiting Victorian chairs lining the walls of the corridor, where they had to sit up all night until the great doors at the entrance were opened at daybreak. They didn't have the private keys to open the doors. He had quite a selection coming in from the city every night."

Arthur Bowker, who serves at the University bar in Reed Hall has many tales to tell of the times he was stationed in India during the Second World War, 1939-1945. He describes the dharzi wallahs who washed the British Army uniforms and what-nots, and the women darning, darning away with their flashing needles threaded with strong thread so that the stitches lasted long after the cloth grew threadbare with time. They darned as if they were doing embroidery stitches, mending the big holes in the socks and the rents in Arthur's pants, breeches and shirts. Was it in his imagination that all those women belonged to the Nizam's palace, women flashing with gold and silver zari work and starry sequins with gauzy veils covering their heads and drifting like nebulous clouds about their shoulders? I too entered that vanished era as Arthur Bowker described those women who had made such an impression on him during that faraway-in-time expedition to the East, a transit point on his way to battlefields in the desert or to the jungles of Burma.

Arthur, now the Reed Hall bartender, could have been one of those soldiers, anonymous, that I had seen as a child in huge convoys of army trucks passing along the streets of Kandy, the officers commandeering houses as billets. They were the soldiers who were trundled about in rickshaws or who crowded the Pink Elephant Pub in the heart of the township. It was not only Arthur, but I met others too on journeys to England, soldiers who remembered that stopover in Kandy, with memories of the Kandy Lake and the Queen's Hotel, some of those veterans, now teachers of geography, drawing maps of a world in which the Empire had changed hands.

Gaping tears had appeared in the khaki uniforms after all those journeys hundreds and hundreds of miles away from Bombay, Calcutta, to Chittagong, to the desert broiling in the heat, dust and sand. "You could pour the bully beef out of the tins and the tins were heated metal that burned our hands, metal shining in the brazen sun." As Arthur-at-the-bar spoke, he too was then one of the colonizers with all those ideas of preserving imperial power. I saw in my mind's eye those sweepers and cleaners of the Empire, with their swirling brooms sweeping away the dust that piled up from the tread of heavy army boots, sweeping away layers of dust and brittle sand, debris and old knotted castaway lives like the crumpled, discarded khaki uniforms not needed anymore after the war was over. Those polished buttons, leather sergeant-major straps, the Sam Brownes that lay athwart the chest, the insignia of rank and power, the medals and ribbons of the great hierarchy of colonels, brigadiers, and the lesser beings, the subalterns, the privates and corporals, all the chessmen on that imperial gameboard, vanished.

For me, Arthur-at-the-bar's narratives were more interesting than the history books that documented the events of the Second World War. Arthur Bowker was able to survive like many others I met along the way. Frank Copplestone was another, whom I met in Fowey in the south-west of England, and who recounted the landing at Dunkirk. Many of the others, the soldiers who visited my childhood home had disappeared from our lives: English, American, Australian, Irish, South African, Scotsmen too.

Yes, Arthur Bowker survived that war which was an imperial adventure to him and here he was, my friend, pouring out Lovage and port wine for me. Sadly enough, he told me, when he arrived home after being demobilized, his wife had died. The voyage back to England had taken three months by sea. His two children were in different country villages. He married for a second time, a "Land Girl," Ella, with whom he now lives happily ever after, and he says they keep "a very good table." I thought to myself, of the millions who had died in that war, including the men who enlisted in the Forces from the colonies. As children we had heard of the Allied Powers and the Axis Powers, of great victories, of tremendous defeats, and I had to free a mind shackled to the history of a colonized country that I grew up in. And here now was Arthur, indeed all those others too whom I met at Reed Hall, where we ate and drank without any constraints between one who once belonged to the ranks of the British Empire and one who was once colonized. Looking at the portraits on the walls I had to acknowledge my own hybridity as a result of those colonial ancestors. I had to make the most of my life and survive.

Arthur-at-the-bar and I met every evening, when he prepared a platter of food for supper for me, hungry and tired when I returned from my readings all over the south-west country. A drink of port, salads, chicken, smoked mackerel, whatever there was. We were equals without hierarchical divisions. I was this Asian woman with a different identity to the women in the Nizam's palace whom he remembered. I wore no veil, my gaze was unabashed and open. I subjected the portraits of the Empire builders on the walls to my frank and candid scrutiny. I was one of the Floricans that had survived extinction. The colonizers had once been the Governors, the Judges of the Supreme Court, the Priests, and the Constitution-makers. They had occupied all the high places in Government. The garden party was now over. The King's Pavilion, the perfectly tended lawn, the tea tables set beneath the great tulip-coloured umbrellas, and Governor Caldecott, the Governor's lady and his daughter moving among the guests, had all gone into the past. A tinge of pity assails me. Forgotten histories. The oblivion of past Empires. Where were the heirs and what did they inherit after the period of office was over? I remember that portrait. Was it Governor Caldecott's daughter? A beautiful young woman in white gauzy gown and white wide-brimmed organza hat, a painting of her by some unknown artist hanging at an exhibition on the walls of a School Hall in Kandy, Dharmaraja College. The present portraits hanging in Reed Hall; the memories of past portraits are all historical pointers on this journey of mine.

Arthur-at-the-bar and I share a different kind of equality. He waits on me, not in an impersonal way, but as a friend would. He does not look upon this lonely woman with the eyes of the colonizer. That history is long over and done with for him.

"And what would you like to drink, young lady?"

"Oh Arthur, I'm not young anymore."

"Ah yes, you are, in comparison to me. I'm seventy-five years old. Would you like a little port wine… Yes, that's a nice sipping wine, or what about some apple cider?

I have to prepare for my inaugural lecture at Queen's Hall. I'm going to talk of the role of the post-colonial writer in contemporary Sri Lankan society.

While I chat to Arthur Bowker, Professor Cameron comes to the bar and we begin chatting as Arthur prepares the Professor's fruit platter.

"What do you want me to say?" I ask the Professor.

"Well, well, in "media res" [Latin for 'middle way', i.e. 'not too radical'], you know. Satire, yes, satire and yes, the naivety, the little ah's and ooh's of the encounter with the marvelous, the experiences of the Third World writer."

At lunch in the refectory of Reed Hall, where the academics of Exeter University eat, an elaborate daily menu put up on a board, I sit at my table looking out through glass panes at the gardens, the lawns, the birds and squirrels. The sun is hot. The air golden. The grass a brilliant emerald and jade. The trees suffused with topaz light, golden, the leaves a tender zircon blue. I think of the jewels my mother wore. Of the jewels of my own youth. Turquoise. Zircon. Sapphires. Birthstones. My mother's topaz brooch. Her engagement ring of rubies and sapphires. Strands of Ciro pearls. I look at a jewelled landscape, reminded of my mother. Almost all those jewels are lost, but not her memory. The inheritance she gave me.

Some stranger generally comes and sits at my table. I am different. A visitant. They are aware of it in my whole aspect. I talk with a Professor of History one day, and while we talk a young woman comes and sits at our table and tells us of an adventure she had in my country one night. She had kept the windows of her room open and swarm after swarm of winged creatures had flown in. She had been terrified. She had felt herself under attack. "Meroes," I said, "Winged ants." For her it was the unknown; she had felt helpless and vulnerable. For me, the meroes were a reminder of my childhood and of everyday things. Brevity of life. Transiency too. The meroes shed their wings and squirmed on the floor or drowned in basins of water. Meroes flying in from the garden. Their mating game. The garden at home was filled with birds, insects, reptiles. None of them harmed us.

"I was so terrified," she kept telling me.

"They would not have harmed you," I assured her.

Once at lunchtime while I was eating my platter of vegetables, a weather-beaten man in tweed coat came and sat at my table. "I was at Bremen University," he told me, "Germany. My grandfather was sent out to Australia. Accused of treason. He died there, a disappointed man. He was an Irishman." So was my own great-great-grandfather, Lt. Col. Arthur Johnston.

"Bill's my name." I did not take down his address. We will never speak with each other again. I hear his voice as he continues the conversation. "I sat with you because you looked interesting."

I carry a different identity from a different world among the English folk. Am I one of those meroes that flocked into the room of a stranger? Who would identify me here? I was alien, that was obvious. But Dutch Burgher? What was that? Had to be explained through a personal, historical narrative. Here, on the extensive grounds of Reed Hall, where I was staying, I passed the carved stone entrance and entered the formidable country house. The heraldic arms and the motto of the family were engraved on a stone slab.

"*Dum spiro spero*"– While I breathe, I hope. Yes, I look different enough to appear 'interesting.' To make people curious about who I am. We look at each other with unabashed gazes. Assessing each other's histories. The owner of Reed Hall had preserved his colonial memories of the tropics in that artificially created garden. The tropical garden in the midst of trees and foliage of a temperate climate with a parapet wall of carved stone pineapples. In the garden there were palm trees, but it was a garden that time had neglected. For those who remained there was no need to preserve those memories of dyaras and Floricans, the hunters and the prey. It was only I, who had emerged from that colonial distance, who would try to interpret the importance of those symbols, because I too had lived in one of those gardens. I could understand those memories. I could also understand their neglect and abandonment. On the extensive acres of Reed Hall, this tropical garden, contrived and artificial, distinct from oak, beech and yew, was a piece torn off a map of the East, India or Ceylon, where the British Raj had once existed.

Once those British bureaucrats had served their term of office and ended their tenure, the members of the Reed family like countless others of their kind retired to their country seats. There were no dyaras here, only clipped lawns, pruned hedges, pollarded elms or trees with branches lopped off.

In the past, playing their roles as representatives of the Crown, ownership of those vast diverse colonies was merely symbolic. The administrators of the Empire were mere representatives, not hereditary owners of colonial territories. Here, in Exeter, the Reed family were the owners of all this land, but one perceived how colonization had left its mark in the garden that preserved the memory of the landscape and vegetation of those colonies they had administered in the name of the Crown.

Was there regret, sadness, that no longer the Florican's cry could be heard among the deer, the tigers, in those Indian grasslands? The tropical garden was one of the last remaining memories of the Empire.

It was a place I loved to linger in. Wherever I went, wherever I would go in future, I would explore gardens, not only for the representations of nature I would find there, but because in them I found a continuous historical narrative with intimations of man's will to trammel, prune, clip and introduce hybrid breeds, transferring the genes and species of rare plants in a different climate. Rare plants brought from the colonies had flourished in my childhood gardens, but nothing could stifle the natural growth of that which had always existed and would always exist.

* * *

Today like every day the headlines in the British tabloids blazon forth the most intimate secrets of the lives of the great football stars, the ones who perform such magnificent feats on the field. Women and drugs, enormous quantities of both. Cocaine, women, women, the most beautiful, the most desirable. Power. Power over body and soul. Is it some kind of catharsis, some purgation too? And here I am, asking myself, why I take life and literature so seriously. The great mythology at the base of my life, which I am scrutinizing so closely, is it a kind of hobnobbing with all the deities from Kailasa and the great surround of that supernatural world?

Does the Credenza help in some of the answers? Does Paula help too in extending a different kind of search in the world of the one-time colonizers?

Dum spiro, spero. While I live, I hope. The motto of the Reed family, the one-time colonizers of the great British Empire, might also provide some of the answers to my migrant soul… And now perhaps it is time to take my own journey backwards, in search of the tangled roots of my own garden, through my childhood into a world that was full of discovery, exploration and a gradually growing knowledge of myself.

I remember myself as a child burrowing into a huge barrel filled with fluffy white cotton collected from the pod-filled tree that grew in our garden at Kadugannawa. Our pillows would be soft and plump with that cotton. The cotton still had little black seeds and there was a special pronged stick that would be twirled in that fleecy mass. The cotton was sun warmed. I was small enough to stand in that barrel, the fluff up to my neck and shoulders. A world that cocooned me, where no thorns grazed my skin, no stone hurtled through the void to hurt me. I closed my eyes and felt the warmth and heat seep through me and then I woke up, broke the filmy webs of that cocoon and began to find new trails and footpaths that led me into the wider world I was yet to discover.

My parents wedding: Harry Solomons and Charlotte Camila Grenier Jansz.

II

TANGLED ROOTS:
A QUEST BACK - WARD

Original drawing by Tharaswin, 2006: Mungo, "Lulled in the hammock of her body…" (Women All Women," Jean Arasanayagam).

Journey

I discovered solitude on the hills
the language of silence among the roots of earth.
Above me walking into its own stillness
steps of hills climbed reaching into a sky
stripped clear of feather clouds
the moulting bird of childhood's seasons.
No wound to practise pain rehearsed the
flight that winged me through the leafy
branches crowded with bird and fruit;
on the high rock where agile goats leaped wild
myself shut in within the hard green pod
yet to be seared by sun
curled round its seed, tight in the teeth of core.

I lay like marrow in close bone
buried in earth that slept
until the earthquake of that sudden
night heaved within the garden's veins and arteries
waking our bodies to violent nativity,
slanting like sharp moonbeams against the dark,
joined in the dance of phantoms
the bone spoke, we gave it eyes to reach the distance
of our flesh and breath to speak its auguries,
against the trembling rock we stood
rushing down waterfalls of dark,
earth whispered through each stone
tree branches fell crashing with slivered moon and sky
the obscure nest with its first younglings retched out
upon the quaking earth, uttered strange squawks
and sibilant whisperings.

The country of our fear through which we sped
as yet possessed no name, its inhabitants unknown,
we were its primeval root, its bone, the structure
of our living flesh.

Where first we walked wild flowers and leaves
were fragrant nerves touched with green fever of child growing,
the wounds that throbbed were not mine yet
nor that of seeping blood of tear or sigh.

Walking within his garden my father drank in
with rain, fresh odours of those dews and flowers
blazing or muted twining against his thighs,
swinging against his cheeks like crimson pendulums of birds,
sheared of sharp thorn the stalk grew smooth
silken against his green touch, elsewhere he grafted
their blood-tipped poison, from his own flesh drew pain
his arms swarming with birds and squirrels,
his lips plucked flutes from wind and air,
green snakes watched and writhed, coiled
within nests of grenadilla creepers.
He was our tree and we its fruit and seed, yet buried beneath
the earth which he so often trod, lay, watered
by his tears, both grief and death.

I touched with eyes the language of my parents' lips
and felt the pollen of its pod or bud burst out,
roots grew and tendrils spread from my unclenching fist.
I watched their grief and love grow or abate
as yet unmoved, until from my own private cache
the outwrung seed flew through the air, drifted, sank down
upon the earth tightened with drought
waiting for monsoons of new rain, to sprout.

The Search

Childhood often etches remembered episodes of the past in memory, episodes without strategy, which often in the long periods of time during which we grow, shape themselves into the completeness of the explorer's discovery, whereby we recognize those landmarks we have journeyed through. We set up our habitations and go back to them, retracing our steps, often searching through tangled roots that wrap themselves about our feet, yet beneath that questing tread we search through aeons and aeons. From that buried seed the tender shoots of memory emerge and fill that edenic garden. We follow a path, a signpost, whether of face, rock or stream, plant or tree, hill or tower, and find ourselves traversing a landscape in which those once familiar figures encounter ours, their faces still recognizable, although we knew them in a different clime, a different season. Time has taken them away from us, but we do not speak of them as the dead. They are still there, inhabiting the landscapes of the mind, that vast terrain in which we are often alone wandering over those solitary or crowded places. We glimpse the past as in that glint of silver that appears through a gap in the mountain, to tell us that a restless ocean lies beyond it. My aunt Nellie had once given me a book, beautifully illustrated, called *Beyond the Blue Mountains*, and this became that imaginary and fabled land that I had to reach someday.

From the garden of the house where we lived in Kadugannawa, the view of Dawson's Tower with its gleaming whiteness stood out starkly against the blue green hills of Belungala. Within its dark interior, a narrow spiral stairway with broken steps wound up to a circular platform with railings. From this vantge point, the view offered you an all-embracing landscape, both close and distant, of lush foliage fed by trickling streams and steep precipices dropping into valleys, with a checkerboard of paddy fields, houses and temples, with never a person to be seen. The green pelt lay spread beneath the blue hills, across which passed shadows of light and dark, and the eye searched for the path that descended beneath its terraces and trees, where those truly ancient roots delved into the past of some forgotten beginning.

Inside Dawson's Tower it was always fusty and gloom-filled, the atmosphere fetid with bats and their droppings, but my brother and sister with their intrepid friends had dared to climb to the top of the tower, through the almost choking darkness, till they reached the light and drank in the fresh, pure air. Below them was the world of mosque minarets, church spires, rubber and tea estates. Then there was the vast circle of the railway turntable with its shunting steam engine slowly revolving–it was an experience we sometimes enjoyed, climbing onto the engine and feeling the blast of heat from the inferno of stoked fires, the coal shovelled in with great metal scoops. To wipe out the grease and grime my father, then an engine driver, gave us wads of coloured threads – my greatest joy was to try to unravel those coloured strands of red and green, tangled with blue, white and yellow, smoothen them out, try to thread them through the needle to embroider impossible and fanciful designs on fine muslin and cambric.

I remained always below the tower. My brother and sister felt I was too young to go through the suffocating darkness. So very often I was left alone when they went on their explorations.

My view was hazy, as I dreamed in the garden, thinking of my brother's and sister's bold ascent. As they walked round the summit of the tower they carried the view visually with them – perhaps they could even see as far as Bible Rock. I had to wait till my father led me up the summit of Belungala, to lift me high on his shoulders and show me his vision of the ocean, so distant, so beyond reach, through a haze of blue.

My brother and sister meanwhile were also old enough to escape adult sanctions, to explore their own freedoms. They could take any road they wanted, appear or disappear at will, climb tall mango trees, perch on a branch, and eat half-ripe mangoes. My brother taught me a delicious secret of taking a ripe yellow lime, making a small hollow in the skin and filling it with salt crystals and finely sifted chilli powder, which we sucked as we sat on a rock overlooking the railway lines, away from my mother's watchful eyes. I had a treasured Kodak snapshot of my brother camouflaged in a world of fruit and leaves, with a felt hat perched on his head, on the mango tree above our house... Lost, lost with time that image of his youth.

So many years later, I walked up the steps curving up the hillside that led to the house accompanied by my two young daughters and a friend of their's. Kadugannawa. A place, a location where my awareness of myself was to be gradually realized. It was here that I began to be conscious of a landscape that allowed for discovery and exploration. My steps took me wherever I willed.

But now, I was coming in search, in memory, of those with whom I had lived here. My father. My mother. My sister. My brother. My companion, Mungo. Through this search, I wanted to know them more completely, through the remembrance of utterances, happenings, events, narrations. The dawning of sorrow. The joyful grasping of a transitory rainbow. I had hoped that one particular person would be still alive, to greet me, if not recognize me (for I had altered beyond all things, growing away from the child I had been within that garden – where Mungo, my companion, had spent endless hours with me).

My starting point, my investigation would begin from here. The retracing of the route that led from this house on the hill. But there was no one left to greet me, no familiar figure from the past, friends, neighbours who had lived in those railway bungalows clustering about the station. The railway lines still ran from Kandy to Colombo on unalterable routes. The signal cabin, the overhead bridge arching over the platform, the platform itself, were all unchanged. But the old friends had all departed. First, their fathers' transfers to other railway stations in the island. Then migration. Finally death. All those Burgher families who had worked in the railways, whose lives had been so close to ours, were no more. The colonials too. Not a trace of them was left. My eyes glanced at the Railway Reading Room. Yes, the tennis courts still remained, but were overgrown with grass. And the swing which had been my delight was static. The giant turntable was no longer in use. I had so often been on the huge steam engine with my father as it revolved slowly, ponderously round, being readied for the direction it would take. My first journeys had been on the trains powered by those steam engines, flying cinders prickling my eyes as I passed through tunnels, stopped temporarily, alighted at stations. Embarking. Disembarking. But later there had been other journeys too. Wholly unpredicted ones.

On this journey back, did I really expect to find Mungo still living? Was it only because I had become vulnerable, inevitably, to all that she had tried to protect me from, that I still clung to the memory of the safety she had once given me and the knowledge she had within her, sharing her life with me? As for Mungo herself, I had never known her to go on any journeys on those trains that passed through day after day, night after night. Her route was: from her home, in the interior of that village where her hut was, mud walled, thatch roofed, growing out of its earth, to my home. It was through her that my awareness grew of another way of life, the life in the village with its myths, folklore, legends and rituals. Of her way of looking at good and evil. All this existed beneath the layers and layers of my parents' way of life. The inheritance, the heritage which was what I had been born into but which would change with time and circumstance.

It was Mungo who took me to her home, where the rituals of the Bali ceremonies were enacted whenever there was illness or misfortune in the family. My early childhood was greatly enriched by Mungo, who shared her folklore and legends with me (perhaps reliving a childhood she had never had a chance to enjoy) in those endless and timeless hours of leisure we spent together in the garden or within the rooms of our house. Her mythology, her deeply ingrained beliefs in Buddhist philosophy, her protection from the evil she tried to avert from my life, exerted a deep influence. At the same time she imparted intimations that evil did exist even in the natural world we inhabited. Before I entered the kindergarten of my missionary school, I had already experienced the other life, versed in the rituals, the rites of exorcism, and the incantatory chants of play derived from ancient memory.

It was Mungo who would take me on those early morning walks through a mist-covered pathway with its dense foliage of plants, flowers and trees growing on either side, to her village home, where on the previous night the rites and rituals of exorcism had been enacted. Her brother was the Kattadiya, who in his trance slit the throat of the sacrificial cock-bird, sliced hundreds of limes, swallowed fire, and then spewed out the flames which shot forth in funnels, flowing liquid and molten into the night air.

Mungo had taken me into the room where her child, Menike, lay wrapped up in a white cloth on a woven reed mat, on the floor. The ceremony had been held to cure her of some malady, some affliction.

Outside, in Mungo's garden the huge effigies of the demons, the yakkas, had been lifted down and lay among the scattered offerings of brilliant yellow marigolds, red hibiscus, yellow-white, pink, orange and red-tinged araliya. I had wanted to pick up the flowers. "No, bebi. Do not touch. The evil is in them. You too will be harmed." Her hand had been protective, restraining, on mine. What were those intimations of evil she had showed me? By word, by utterance. Vas. Dos. Evil inherent even in the seemingly peaceful landscape that we inhabited. She had parted that screen to the other life concealed from those with whom I lived the accustomed ways: my parents, their friends, and later my teachers in the missionary school.

I lay awake, often, on the four-poster, wrapped in the fleecy folds of a woollen English blanket, the shadows playing on the white frilled cotton valance, glancing at the whitewashed walls with their chiaroscuro of light and shade. Listening. Listening to the *thud, thud, thud* of the hollow-sounding drums which reached through the dark tree-crowded silence, until the sombre echo filled the entire space of the bedroom, throbbing in my ears with the insistence of a relentless rhythm. I would lie awake for hours in silence, my sister beside me, my mother on the French bed against the other wall, my head hidden in the folds of the blanket. At night it was the sound of the drums that kept me awake. At dawn the mist-dispersing machine sounded its dirge-like siren on the Englishman's rubber estate across the railway tracks. Its long-drawn, monotonous wail filled me with an inexplicable sense of melancholy. I felt myself in a spaceless vacuum being sucked in, a vacuum shimmering with brilliant pointillist specks of colour from which I could never struggle out, until I woke startled out of its disturbing dream.

And in those nightly dreams I was always falling off that bridge onto the railway track, the shrill whistle of the steam engine echoing, re-echoing through a dense, opaque dark. Only the thought of the signal lamp that my father flashed with its sliding glass shades of changing colour gave me any sense of comfort.

And then, there was a different kind of terror, the tales that Mungo would relate to me, remembered from her own childhood. The rakshasi could entice you with those delicious honey-seeping kewun, the cakes which she hung on a tree so that you would be tempted to pluck them and then become captive through her ruses. This is one of the stories I remember that belonged to that ancient oral tradition of the village. I sat cradled in Mungo's lap and she began to narrate the story. I searched for this story in later years and found it in a collection of folktales published by the Englishman Parker, in the year 1910. I relate it now in my own words:

In a certain country there lived a Gamarala who had seven children. The six elder children woke up at daybreak to work in the rice field. The youngest went to school. Together with the other children, the whole party of them used to go near the dwelling of a rakshasi who lived nearby. The rakshasi saw them and from that day onward, decided to eat them. But she was afraid of the men in the village and was kept from seizing the children. She craved for them and so decided that she would use her daughter to catch them. She broke off the leaves of a tree which stood on the road which the children passed by on their way to school and hung plantains and kewun on strips of white cloth which she had bound the branches with. The children were enchanted by the cake tree and plucked the kewun and plantains which they ate. The rakshasi hid in the jungle. She was afraid that the children would scuttle off when they saw her and tell the men of the village who would kill her. So she bided her time. One morning the Gamarala's son came earlier than the others, climbed the tree and began plucking the fruit and cakes. The rakshasi suddenly appeared with a bag. She stood at the bottom of the tree with the bag and spoke to him. 'Here you! Son, pluck a cake for me,' she said. He plucked one for her, but she threw it on the sand. 'Pluck another,' she said, 'I can't eat this because it is covered with sand.' As he plucked and threw the kewun down, she kept dropping them.

'I cannot catch the cakes you are dropping. I will tell you an easy way to do it. Pluck as many as you can and jump into the bag. Jumping is easier than climbing down the tree.'

The foolish child thought to himself, 'Yes, what the rakshasi tells me is easy,' and he plucked as many kewuns with both hands, filled his pockets and jumped into the rakshasi's bag.

The rakshasi tied the mouth of the bag and, concealing him inside, took him stealthily to her house and told her daughter: 'Daughter, today I must eat something flavoursome. There is some tasty meat in the bag that I have carried over my shoulder. Boil the meat for me.'

The rakshasi gave the bag to her daughter and went about her business. The daughter opened the bag and found the boy inside. When she was about to take him out to prepare the meat, the boy said, 'Aney, akka, sister, there are lice on your head.'

'If you can catch them, do so,' she told him and sat down. The Gamarala's son parted the strands of hair as if searching for lice. And then suddenly took up the axe that had been brought to kill him and struck off her head. After killing her he put her into the cauldron of water, placed the pot on the hearth, and boiled her. He then prepared her for the rakshasi to eat. He collected the rice mortar, the pestle and a great number of knives that were in the house. He then climbed a palmyrah palm that stood at the doorway and lay in wait for the rakshasi.

When she returned after her bath she called out to the daughter, 'Has the tasty food been prepared today? It must be done secretly or the men of the village would kill us.'

When she came into the house she found that the boiled meat was there for her to eat but there was no sign of the daughter. She called out to her, but there was no answer. While the rakshasi was searching for her, the youth on the palm tree began to beat the rabana, and said,tan, tun, their own flesh they themselves will eat. On the palmyrah tree at the doorway, tan, tun.'

The rakshasi saw him and came running to seize him, when he threw down the pestle and mortar which struck her. She died at the bottom of the tree. Then the boy climbed down, went home and told the rest of his family the whole story. They came with him and took away all the rakshasi's possessions. They returned home and lived happily together.

Those were the stories Mungo would tell me in her gentle ruminating way. The stories themselves were frightening. In my imagination the cake tree grew in my garden, but it was the anodha tree with its ripening fruit and the owl that nightly gave its melancholy omen-filled cry beside the green tats of the verandah that haunted my dreams.

I would be advised by both Mungo and my mother of the spells and the enchantments that would bind me if I left nail parings or hair clippings about the place. They could be used to make 'charms' which would perhaps be harmful to me, so when my hair was cut every strand of hair was gathered up and taken away, who knows where, but hidden from the gaze of anyone who might bury it after 'charming' it. Nail clippings too were carried away in folds of newspaper. Would those charms bring unhappiness, illnesses? Or would I even be kidnapped, taken away by a stranger, lost forever to my family?

The power of memory assails my senses as I think of Mungo - her skin fragrant as paddy stalks ripening in the sun, the smell of the coconut oil in her hair, and of her cotton camboya washed with Sunlight soap, pervading my senses as I lay on her outstretched knees being lulled to sleep. She was crooning her lullabies to me, the words which I would seek later in order to better understand those dream-induced, hypnotic words that soothed me with their gently rhythms:

'*Doiyi, doiyi, doiya, doiya babo*'

For me that moment, the rocking motion of her knees, the lulling tones of her voice, the feel of her hands lifting the pillow beneath my head, were enough to give me a sense of peace. Those were her inherited lullabies, from her own childhood in the village, heard from her mother and her grandmother. Lullabies which she shared with her own children and with me whom she now nurtured. In my half sleep I knew she was crooning words that I recognized, of familiar flowers that grew in my garden. Saman pitcha, jasmine; of fruit, veralu and dodang (the olive and orange); of the green parakeet; and of the spilt milk flowing in the river, of the deep hum and throb of the bakamuna, the night owl that I heard on the anodha tree growing beside the thumbergia bower.

My eyes, their lids becoming heavy, weighed with drowsiness and oncoming sleep, observed fragments of her face and body, the ruddy sheen of her golden skin, the white cotton jacket with the little silver knobs like drops of coalesced mercury fallen from a shattered thermometer, the safety pins attached to the neckline. Those safety pins served so many functions, picking out those thorns as she trod the earth barefooted, or passing tapes and elastics through the hems of sundry garments. The tiny gold safety pins were used to pin on that pleated arrangement of a fan-like handkerchief on the front of the printed chintz dresses my sister and I wore. My eyes were mesmerized by the silver bracelet coiled round Mungo's wrist, her chain with the suraya, the amulet, the earrings, silver cylinders thrust through her elongated earlobes. The landscape of the village flashed in the mirrors of her lullabies; the fields, the flowers, the fruit trees, the birds, the streams, that poignant story of the pot of milk that had slipped from the grasp of the mother carried away along the current of the stream, the milk all spilt. Did the mother too slip off the stones as she forded that stream, was she drowned, did the baby waiting for her in the rocking cradle, cry endlessly, hungrily, for the comfort of that bosom? A hungry child for whom a mother's milk did not suffice?

In the garden Mungo and I played for hours within a world that no one else shared. In the afternoons, beneath the mara tree, a carpet of red petals covering the earth, we crushed juices on stones to make play-food. She taught me how to twist the dried jak leaves, secure them with ekels and send them whizzing in the air above the thornless roses on their missions high, high above the mugerine bush and the Holy Ghost orchids. Facing each other we sat, the two of us, playing "Athuru mithuru, Dambadiva thuru, Rajakapuru Hettiya," placing the tiny stones and pebbles on the back of the hand, dexterously flipping them over to fill the palm. We shooed away the crows, both real and imaginary, lifting our hands and crying out: "Goraka dain, goraka dain, dain, dain," like the refrain of the ancient ballads. I collected orange-red sapu seeds strewn all over the garden. The selalihini in the cage could talk, imitating our human language. Laughter gurgled in my throat as we exchanged our formal greetings, the bird and I. My father had taught the bird human language. I would stand at the barred cage and offer it sapu seeds from the garden, coral red seeds:

"*Good morning, Sally. Hello, Sally! Good morning.*"
"*Good morning, good morning,*" *sang out Sally.*

Sally hopped about on the bars pecking at ripe papaw and taking tiny sips of water. Salelihinis are rare, my father told me, mynahs are more common. To me, bird language was what I sought to understand. It was the language I wished to speak to them in, not that of the human tongue. We inhabited the same garden of my childhood. My father taught me the language of birds, for he too listened to every bird call.

Mungo crushed anguru, or charcoal, from our woodfire, and filled the empty pots of the Pond's vanishing cream bottles with the fine black powder. She would place some of it on my palm. I would dip into it with my finger and rub it gently on my teeth leaving them white and sparkling or we would use tooth-paste which for me was less exciting than using Mungo's finely crushed charcoal. The cool bathroom with it half- green painted walls had little spider sacs as soft and powdery-yellow as pollen set in the window niches, fragile spider webs that trapped motes of sunlight in their delicate mesh. There were wooden boxes of sawdust with wooden scoops. There were also the adobe dwell-ings of the orange and black potter wasps, with their mazes and tunnels. It was here I mused in the privacy of this cool, shadowy room of the orange tree sprouting within me from the careless seed I had swallowed, imagining the branches thrusting out of each orifice of my body. Love for Mungo was also a growing thing. Its full intent was felt so many years later in recollection, in re-membrance of that nurturing woman, the woman in whose pres-ence I never spilt a tear, the woman who was the very embodi-ment of that landscape I was growing up in.

But why, why did I once pursue her as she carried the night lamp to the bedroom at dusk? She who spread her woven reed mat with its green and red designs on the floor beside the high four-poster to sleep beside me. Her hand shielded the wa-vering flame as she stepped along the veranda. "Mungo," I called, "Mungo," and I tried to hold her back from leaving me, going away from me, but she went firmly on ahead. I wanted to keep her by me, prolong the conscious hours of hearing her voice, feel-ing the touch of those firm hands, and I began a chase.

"Stop, bebi," she called. "Stop!"

"No, no, wait, " I cried out.

"Stop, don't be a naughty girl, stop!" My mother called out as I pursued Mungo, ran behind her, as fast as I could. My feet were nimble. We ran through the dining room, through the hall, along the back veranda. Mungo ahead of me, I behind her, almost upon her, my hand outstretched to grasp whatever of her I could hold onto, and then she fell. The night lamp shattered into fragments, the flame went out. I was pulled away, punished, smacked. And Mungo? Was she angered? Did she upbraid me? Perhaps she did. It was a dangerous game. The flame could have spread. Mungo could have been hurt. Feelings and emotions that were unbridled. A wildness that was almost primordial. Who would explain it all? Instincts. Urges. Language, words had to grow to fit those images in my mind.

I knew what the consequences would be. I would not escape. And now the next chase began. My mother complained to my father of my behaviour. Now it was she who came behind me. I fled from them all and sought out my brother, who was in one of the rooms going about his own business. Wordlessly I ran up to him, clasped his waist from behind and used him as a shield to protect me. We swayed to and fro together, but my mother grasped me, pulled me away. I remember my brother's strange smile, almost as if he understood an act of mischief for its own sake. But he had to allow justice to be meted out. And Mungo? She said, I think, "Bebi, you are very naughty, very danga – very mischievous." I could not get protection from any quarter. I learnt that day that I would have to take the consequences of any act that caused hurt or pain to someone else. I could not control my emotion, my feelings, amorphous as a threatening grey cloud. Nor could I hide away from aggression. I had to articulate those feelings with words I was still to learn.

Lullabies in the Wind
(For Mungo)

Lulling the child beginning to sleep
she beguiles her with tales of rakshasas,
charmed fingernails tearing apart the sapling
forest of demons, outstretched feet rocking
she croons her incantations taking me through
the evenings of her lullabies where the white cranes
flew over a river overhung with dusk whose source
lay, where?

A river flowing through the dark, a shattered
pot of milk floats then sinks, the milk all
spilt swept away in the water, white cranes flew
overhead, but where, where is my mother?

Lifting gently, rocking on her outstretched knees
sleep is a syllable to me resting on Mungo's
tongue as she croons, her shadow hunched,
her image embedded in my drowsing eyes.

Night outside pitch dark,
in the garden firesmells,
wood crackling, brands smouldering,
daylight, sun-dried noon leaves
swept up with sharp ekel spears,
flames, wind-sifted ashes and leaf wraiths.

Within the house
cicada vibrato boring the eardrum
hollow cave echoes from ancient lullabies,
until sleep overcomes the flickering lids
to close into a falling sightlessness
and I clutch onto waking as I feel,
feel myself dropping into a pointillist
vacuum off the station bridge
spanning the railway lines, the signals down,
the train rushing through dark rock-close tunnels,
the child fears whether daylight will ever emerge.

Who was it gave her to me are my now thoughts,
this woman, Mungo?

Yet I had a mother too, to lean breast to,
to feel the candle-warmth of flesh
snuggling in the soft, soap fragrant body
that I stretched my arms round to hold close.

Hours spent in the garden caught up in the
magical spells Mungo wove round me
sharing the folklore of her own childhood
before she orphaned me,
leaving me alone, quite alone,
the garden growing darker, darker
with late evening, dusk, time and age.

Years afterwards
I go in search of her
but she had gone away.

I sought her hut
to me that sacred abode,
it too had vanished,
the walls that once echoed
with her crooning lullabies, vanished,
lost, the stories of the village folk,
the enchantresses, the spellbinders who captured
my thoughts imprisoning my childhood for ever
and ever within the web where escape
spelt danger,

I who lay on her outstretched legs once,
her limbs gaunt to the bone,
rocking, rocking me to sleep
being lulled, being crooned to by her keening
lullabies, her eyes, my own too, encountering visions
that no one else shared in our dreams.

Lulled in the hammock of her body,
feeling myself swing, swing within its
fleece-wrapped cradle, seeking the warmth
of her generous heart.

The Return

"Where is Mungo now? Can I find her? Is she still alive?" I asked the people from the village, who had come to welcome and greet me, accepting me, not as an outsider but as a guest.

For a moment we were all silent. "Mungo passed away a few years ago. Peacefully. She had looked after the children in another family."

I could no longer ask Mungo that question that was so important to me: "Do you remember me? I did not forget you all these years but I thought time would stay for me, that you would still be here when I returned… You who had shown so much kindness to me… Without you, Mungo, I would never have known of the village, of your people, of your beliefs… but it was a secret between us, no one knew how much you had shared with me of your knowledge. You were not always there to protect me, but when I went away, so far away from you, I carried your knowledge with me… Like that talisman you wore round your neck - your memory. With that talisman that protected you, you would have wanted to protect me too."

My journey was more than an identity search. It was a search for self. That self that lay buried within a pod, and once it burst open, the seed enclosed within a diaphanous gauzy casing was released in the air, flew over the garden, borne by the wind to fall who knows where. There were landscapes real and imaginary and a wilderness which led to exploration and discovery. In our garden I played those childhood games which Mungo shared with me.

My father had tended the garden with tender care, tying up the weaker stalks to the stronger, grafting roses. "Touch," he would say - not a single thorn grazed my skin or pricked the flesh. He had created a thornless rose I was never to encounter anywhere else in the world. Glow-worms, fireflies, millipedes, centipedes, dragonflies, bees, red ants, black ants, golden orioles, abounded in the garden. Mynahs, and sellalihinias fed on the coral-coloured sapu seeds strewn in that garden. Dewdrops quivered on leaves as I walked among the trees and flowering bushes, searching for newly opened buds early in the morning, peering at chrysalises, waiting for the moth or butterfly to emerge. I had grown adroit at the pebble game, yet sometimes the outflung pebbles scattered in the air and fell on the earth perhaps bruising some innocent creature.

In 1983 that childish experience was transposed to the present. Within my open palm had lain those pebbles, clenched pebbles because they were part of skills that were being acquired. Tiny, rounded, of different shapes sizes and colours. Buried time. Awakened by memory. Pebbles which grew into stones, rocks hurled at a man of a different ethnic group. The whole scene runs like a film unreeling in my mind. The man running, fleeing from his pursuers. Clambers up a tree clumsily, hastily, clinging onto branches which dip and wave with his weight. His pursuers halt. Stand beneath the tree, hurl the stones and rocks at him until his grip on the branches gives way. He falls. Is trampled to death. But how am I involved? Why does this scene have so much significance in my life? I must turn the pages of my collection of poems *Apocalypse '83* to trace that route from childhood to maturity in a different era.

Routes. Journeys. Landscapes. Railway tracks. Flight. Escape. Searches. Discoveries. Games. A game that I played with the pebbles in the garden of that railway bungalow on that hill in Kadugannawa a long time ago.

Ancestral Maps
(For my great-great-grandfather, Lt Col. Arthur Johnston)

I arrived with them
The memoirs of their missions became mine
Inherited through retrieval of their past.

I read through their narratives
Became a cipher in that imperial code
Explore those ruses that enable
This outsider to assume those several
Identities in conspiratorial collusion with history.

Scrutinize their maps, their secret routes,
Read the landscape of unfamiliar terrain
Sambapelly, Kieratavally, Pangaram
Landmarks in their individual histories.

Those maps have changed together with the
Memory of the invader, their footprints
Now long obliterated, burial places
In the wilderness, forgotten, unrecognizable,
Individual biographies unrecorded,
No totems, no monuments, no tombstones,
Only hidden graves, shreds of cloth
The tarnished emblems of buried insignia.
A few of them survived
"Emaciated, sallow, debilitated,"
Limped back footsore, tattered and unkempt

One of them lived to start this bloodline,
I am lassoed by that birthright
Captive to his history, compelled to surmise
On that life, follow him to his final
Burial place, a rural enclave in Shalden,
A graveyard, a church with its memorial
In that country village where no heirs remain.
I read his martial ideologies
In a different context
Retrace my steps, the ruined landmarks
Now distinct, clear of all ambiguities
Read the final memorials to that life
"Sacred to the Memory of Lieutenant Col. Arthur
Johnston."
That history was no fairy tale,
I can still smell the trampled grass
Of those blood sodden patches,
Hear the tearing blast of cannon, musket,
Gingals.

Those were their times,
They lived within those limits,
Fragments which we piece together
Falling apart the parchment of their recorded
Sagas, allow the blinding light of revelation
To illuminate in this harsh naked light
The pages of those narratives.

Share in an equal guilt
But bear alone its expiation.

All Flesh is Grass

I was searching through archival memory. Listening in my childhood to those ancestor stories that my mother related to me, almost as if engaged in a monologue of her thoughts. I was insatia-
ble for stories, and my mother spent hours and hours feeding the
mind and imagination with her tales. Who else could she unfold
those narratives to? Perhaps she needed a listener like myself.
Perhaps she needed to dramatize her own life and so she filled
those hours we spent together with true stories from her life.
Where that Irish captain, Arthur Johnston, was concerned, she
possessed no written narrative of his military expedition to Kandy.
Family papers were with an uncle of her's, but my mother and
most of her brothers and sisters would have known their grandmother who had died in the year 1897, Susan Johnston, the daughter of Captain Arthur.

All the knowledge my mother imparted to me was by word
of mouth. To this day the words she spoke to me are as clear and
vivid as when I first heard them years and years ago. Those
ancestors began to be familiar and were then summoned when
the need to know more arose. In a sense, it all remained a hidden
narrative, part of a personal history, but the Irish Captain remained
in that mental niche until one day I discovered his portrait in a
history book and the details of that expedition described, recorded
and commented on by historians.

The early words uttered by my mother were to emerge with
profound significance as the years passed. What did she tell me
that made such an impression on my mind: "Your great-great-
grandfather was Captain Johnston. He led his regiment into the

Kandyan Kingdom in 1804, occupied it for three days and was then forced to retreat from Kandy, back to Batticaloa. It was a courageous retreat." But a retreat meant defeat, the aftermath of war, of invasion and conquest.

I later learned:

He married a Dutch Burgher lady and had an only daughter, Susan, who became my paternal great-grandmother. Susan married Adriaan Jansz, bringing in another colonial strand into our genealogy, had eight children, the eight grandchildren of Captain Arthur. My mother left me with those first stirrings of curiosity, which as time passed I needed to investigate and later, interrogate. Her mother, Charlotte Camille, was the great-granddaughter of the French Lieutenant Francois Grenier, and there were cousins, aunts and uncles who were still around and carried the name Grenier together with that of Jansz.

I remember that house and the room where I first heard of the Irish captain. In that bedroom in Kadugannawa, the dazzling sunlight, cloudy with minute motes, slanted through the skylight set among the tiles. A room which led to our hall and dining room.

My mother would sit at her Singer sewing machine with its heavy silver wheel, a giant ring I loved to turn round and round clasping it by its handle. Watching her give it a last twirl with the flat of her palm in that pause before snipping off the thread. She was always hem-stitching sheets and tablecloths.

"Your Aunt Nellie used to make me do a lot of hand-stitching, embroidery and drawn-thread work. I really got tired of sewing a fine seam and decided never to do that kind of sewing again. It tries my patience."

Marriage gave her freedom from certain duties, and she had the time to read. Even as a young girl she had spent hours reading.

I listened to the stories she had read. One was especially poignant and filled me with sadness, "Ships that Pass in the Night." But she was never filled with melancholy for long, although the songs she sang were full of the emotions of lost love and partings. She would spin riddles that teased the imagination as we laughed together.

I would try on her silver thimble as she hand-sewed sundry garments or darned the dhoby tears in sheets. I would help her to thread the needles too. "You have young eyes," she would tell me.

While we went about our often varying pastimes, Captain Arthur grew into a kind of flesh-and-blood figure who inserted his presence into that room. Who was he, that legendary figure? Someone of whom my mother had heard of from the eldest sister, Aunt Nellie, who remembered clearly her grandmother, the Captain's daughter. My mother needed someone to talk to of her own life. It wasn't important then, that I should understand everything she said. Her words were like secret cabalistic signs that were to be interpreted later. I absorbed everything.

The seed implanted gestated within the consciousness. Seeds sprung from the narratives of the mother, entering through the apertures of a hidden inner room. Echoes from those distant monologues still reach me, and it is necessary for me to understand why she had to spin those narratives. My mother never had the time to write her own fictions or memoirs. I was the parchment on which those indelible marks, those signifiers, became manifest. The people she spoke of had inhabited the terrain on which she lived - they were, to her, not mythic, not historical characters that fleshed out her genealogies, but people who had been part of her inheritance. Perhaps she sought to entertain me, create adventure out of the mundane in the provincial town of Kadugannawa. Her escape into another life into which she drew me too.

They were not known to me, and never would be, those men who fathered bloodlines. But what of the women? Some of their names were known, others unrecorded but they were the links to our histories and genealogies. They had brought forth sons and daughters who put their roots down deep into the soil, not as conquerors but as ordinary people, laying their bones ultimately in the long sleep of death, yet with hope in an afterlife. And those who went away in their migrations set out on different voyages many years later, their exploration different, seeking homes rather than the territory of conquest. I had then, no prediction that I would excavate the past, unearth the shards and artefacts left by a colonial patriarchy. My revelations did not occur overnight. Realization grew with time and self-interrogation, when I would recognize the sword, the cannon and the flintlock as symbols of aggrandizement. As a child, I merely listened. Words and images embedded in my mind. Susan Johnston. The marriage of Adriaan and Susan had taken place in Colombo, at the Wesleyan Church in Dam Street on 3 December 1828. Adriaan was one of the four sons of that first Dutch ancestor. Years later I would discover who those protagonists were in my mother's theatre of recollections.

I grew up and one day I opened a history book that dealt with Western conquest in the island, the invasions of the Portuguese, Dutch and British. "Captain Arthur Johnston"– the name stared me in the face. Together with his portrait. "Here he is, here's the portrait of your great grandfather," I told my mother. We both pored over the picture of the officer in the uniform of his regiment. I thought I saw the strong resemblance between his face with its clear-cut features and that of my mother. I traced the shape of eyes, nose, lips, the breadth of forehead. "You resemble him," I told her.

And beneath the portrait, I wrote in my childish handwriting "Great great grand dad." There was no one to dispute the truth. No one at that time would have cared to do so. The blood of the colonizers ran in your veins and was not then allied to that identity search. He was just one of the forebears. I had planted a tiny flag on the route of my discoveries. I was pleased to come across by chance, the verification of my mother's words. She had not been creating fictions. She was a truthful woman. Was this then the truth? I needed more information. I would find it all out. Those were the first beginnings.

I was from time to time to read whatever was available about Capt. Arthur and the military expeditions to Kandy. I kept searching. One day my daughter found the military narratives in the Ceylon Room of the University of Peradeniya. His journals of the march to Kandy, the occupation, the retreat and what took place later in his life. I read over and over again the details of his family of which I was a descendant:

Lieutenant Colonel Arthur Johnston was the eldest son of the late John Johnston of Clare, in the County of Tyrone, Esq., whose ancestor (of the ancient house of Loverhay, a branch of the Annandale family) left Dumfrisshire in the beginning of the seventeenth century, and purchased considerable estates in the counties of Tyrone and Fermanagh. Colonel Johnston, the subject of this narrative, was born in 1778 and when very young received his Ensign's and Lieutenant's commissions in the 19th Regiment and accompanied that corps to Ceylon where he early attracted the attention of the Governor of the island, and was placed on his staff.

Those were the details of the family history that interested me where my personal feelings about him lay. But there were also the other stories, the experiences of the Bombardiers and the Sub-alterns during that invasion of the Kandyan Kingdom in the year 1804. One of the stories that caught my attention most was that of the weeping boy, the distraught woman, and the white rat. My mother was no longer alive when I began reading through account after account many years later. If it had been discovered earlier, we would have read through the narrative together with all its details including Bombardier Alexander's story.

Until I came upon this narrative, I was constructing fragments from the different historians like Davy, Tennent, Father S.G. Perera, and others – the details of the foray, its outcome and what the historians thought and felt about the man, Captain Arthur Johnston.

Where were the connections? Approximately 180 years later, in the year 1983, in the month of July, I was living close at hand to the ferry of Watapologa, where two crossings by the British troops of the river Mahaweli during those early years of the nineteenth century, had been attempted in the conquest of the Kandyan Kingdom. The crossings had taken place during the period of the early Kandyan Wars before the signing of the Kandyan Convention of 1815.

Davy's crossing in 1803 was a disaster, the men massacred before they could get across. Captain Johnston succeeded in fording the river. He and his men got onto the nether bank and the other retreat from 'Candy' (as Kandy was spelt in those days) began.

In the year 1983, escape became a reality in my life too. I too, secretly, had to attempt escape from Watapologa – now renamed Watapuluwa. I had to cross a metaphorical river in full spate on a frail craft. I took the road that Davy had taken, mortally wounded, after the massacre of the British troops. My journey was to a refugee camp, my mind battered and bruised. The events of the epoch in which I lived had plunged me into that newest maelstrom of upheaval. With my family, we had to find individual routes that would lead us out of danger. It was then that I thought of the historical routes of that past and the backdrop to my own search of the road that would lead me to safety.

This then was the self-same city, 'Candy,' where that distant ancestor found himself when he marched into the territory of the Kandyan Kingdom in 1804. He had no legitimate right to be there, neither he nor his men. Soon afterwards, three days racked by anxiety, for he knew that the expedition had failed, he began his retreat. There was no welcome for the new invader in territory where the European invaders, Portuguese, Dutch and British, had been kept out for so long. They had made inroads that would lead to subjugation. But it was all a matter of time. The British invaders ultimately entrenched themselves in Candy, and the churches, the schools and the prison were built. I was baptized and christened in one of the churches, from the font of the Methodist Church in Kandy. Captain Arthur had left his enigmatic shadow behind.

In 1804 Captain Arthur's journey back to the garrison of Batticaloa began. He would have plenty of time too, to think, yes, to think over, retrace, and re-assess every step that had brought him here. For what vain purpose? There is never justification for the sufferings and mutilations of war and for those violent expeditions into other people's territory, those intrusions where a people are not allowed to conduct their affairs according to their own inherited and traditional ways. History is then rewritten time and time again, reviewed through the interpretations of the successive centuries by its recorders. The context changes, seen through the eyes of the so-called conqueror and the yet-to-be conquered at the destined place, at that period in time. The dichotomy exists between the subjugator and the to-be-subjugated. History is also enacted through hierarchies as well as through the lower ranks. There are the commanders, the generals and the captains at the top. Next come the bombardiers, the corporals, the sepoys, the jemilders, the hevilders, the coolies, and those in charge of the commissariat. The truth is found in varying degrees among the ranks. Each one has a different version, and we listen to their discourse. Captain Arthur leaves behind a narrative. That of Bombardier Alexander is yet another. We have read the narratives both of the Captains and the Bombardier. The 'subaltern' discourse of the sepoy is yet to be heard.

Within the context of conquest there is no room for valorization. Through the tremendous quakes and upheavals of historical decades, I assume the role of the recorder and the witness in time. To record all narratives that will give us a glimpse of the truth. In that period of colonial conquest, or of any conquest, the ordinary soldier carries out orders with blind and implicit obedience, until he becomes the survivor in the jungle. Then rank is broken, as the Bombardier's narrative shows in his account of the retreat:

As the distress increased, discipline became more and more lax, and the men often refused to obey their officers. This was the case amongst the white troops, the stoutest of whom were much inclined to separate and urge on right forward, every one only taken up with himself. To stop this destructive tendency in the men, required the utmost efforts of the officers, as non-commissioned officers were as bad as the private men more especially a Sergeant Baird of the 19th. At one period they fairly refused to obey command, replying to their officers, 'what is the use of our stopping to be lost for a few'. They turned deaf ear to those in the rear, and the effecting appeals of their officers, who every now and then placed themselves in front, calling out, 'My God! My God! Stop men – do stop. Will you not obey command? If we do not, we must all inevitably perish, the front as well as the rear': while Captain Johnston was almost driven to a distraction by their refractory conduct. It was only by reasoning and arguing the point, that anything was done even, for the safety of all.

(Bombardier Alexander's Account of Captain
Arthur Johnston's Expedition)

The Captain himself carries out the orders of the High Command. In that respect too there must be obedience. So the march to the interior begins. It began from the coast, from Batticaloa. I construct the fictional descriptions of the march of the invader through my own historical imagination. The march of Arthur Johnston. The year is 1804:

The march begins at dawn. We leave the fort, that safe place, so well fortified with its twenty-four guns, its barracks, granary, magazine and commandant's mansion. As we march in formation and proceed along the coastline we see the last of the mountain Friar's Hood dwindling in the distance. We go past the tall talipot palms, the coconut trees and the scattered hamlets. Some of them have been ravaged by elephants, the roofs stripped of straw, the dwellings razed to the ground, trees wrenched off by their roots, cooking vessels scattered about after the last epidemic of small pox. Cheetahs have not left the poor victims alone either.

Ours is a small force but we will meet the columns that will converge on the capital, Candy.

The landscape begins to change after a march of several days. We pass through thick jungle. The wild wanderoo swing on the strong rope-like lianas. They are like mast ropes. At night they are sinuous and serpentine, sinister, threatening. Our fires lit with jungle sticks flicker. I listen to the murmurous voices of the sepoys. The sentries are awake. Watchful. This is a campaign into unknown terrain. Invasion may be comparatively easy, but not conquest. How long will we remain in Candy? Will our mission be accomplished?

We camp out in a cleared patch of jungle. The dark is resonant with a myriad shrill insect sounds. The fires flicker and gleam. Wild cheetah, leopard, elephant, bear, deer, reptiles abound in these jungles. We rest. I am alone with my thoughts. The fort of Batticaloa was home to me. I am a seasoned campaigner. I am now in unfamiliar territory. New strategies will have to be planned. We are the invaders. The maritime forts are in our hands. We now move towards the interior of the island.

In Candy, we will be an army of occupation if we succeed. We cannot expect an easy capitulation nor a hospitable welcome. I wait for news from my countrymen who will converge on Candy from the other parts of the island.

The jungle is thick and impenetrable. We have to hack our way through. It is difficult to trundle the gun carriages and cannon along the rutted paths. No roadways in this inaccessible terrain, no trodden *ways, hardly any human habitation for mile upon desolate mile. The gradient changes. The air is less humid. Cool, grey columns of trees. Green shade of leafy arbours. I follow the route on the map. We march to a destined end. Food, water – we are constantly in need of replenishing our commissariat. Yet we have to reach our destination. That assignment together with the fate of the invader.*

Towering mountain barriers stretching from Uva to Matale. Backdrop to the mighty river, the Mahaweli viewed from the Bintenne plains. Natural fortifications for the Candyan kings. We begin our ascent of the Pass of a thousand steps – Gal-padi-hella Pass. Steep. Precipitous. Horses an encumbrance. Ascent and descent all the way to Candy.

Hills, mountains, paddy fields. White domes of temples, dagobas. It is all so green and pleasant. The coast is left far behind, according to my maps. We have marched, as it seems, for aeons in time. We come to the river. We must ferry across it at this point. It is wide, a smooth, shining expanse of water. We are here. We have arrived. The long march is over. The columns from the other parts of the island should already be awaiting us.

I see no sign of a single column. We alone, myself and my troops, stand in the midst of a silent and deserted township. Plans have miscarried. We cannot remain here. No, we cannot remain for long, alone and isolated. We rest for a brief space of time, replenish our depleted stocks, and turn the hands of the compass in the direction from which we set out. The retreat will have even greater hazards and dangers. That is the only alternative left us...

The narrative is then taken over by recorded history.

Kandy had withstood all conquest (except for the occasion on which it had been annexed to the Kingdom of Sitawaka by Rajasinghe II in 1582). No European power had been able to conquer the Udarata. Frederick North was the new General of the British maritime possessions after their capture from the Dutch. Conspiracies of the Kandyan chiefs were rife against the Nayakkar Dynasty. There were opportunities not to be missed. Troops were brought from Bengal – they were pouring in; thus there were the sepoys, the jemilders, and the hevilders in Captain Arthur's regiment. At the end of the expedition he had learned the lessons of defeat. The eternal truth that all men learn when they engage in guerrilla warfare: the unseen enemy cannot be engaged in open battle. There were other lessons to be learned. Lessons that were necessary for any conqueror in new terrain. History repeats itself. Captain Arthur's advice ranged on how to tackle the cautious, how to protect the powder for the firearms, the necessity of learning the language of the people thus dispensing with the use of interpreters. He learnt of ways of handling the commissariat and the correct dress in a tropical climate for the troops. There was no way in which the conqueror could win according to European methods of warfare in guerrilla terrain. The important questions to be asked, however, were never asked for these are not questions for the invader: 'Why are we here, where we do not belong?'

At the end of the war Captain Arthur is experienced enough to become Advisor on Military Affairs and eventually join a military academy in England. He had already spent nearly twelve years in Ceylon, the greater part of that time employed in active military service or in the discharge of civil duties: "I had frequent opportunities of observing the nature of the country, and making myself acquainted with the character and customs of its inhabitants and their mode of warfare" ("Narrative of an expedition to Candy" Captain Arthur Johnston).

There were others too who had recorded their experiences here. How much did Captain Arthur know of that other life? – as Knox had recorded it, as D'Oyly had in his diaries, as Cordiner, Turnour, and later Tennent, Marshall, and many others. How much did he know of the complex structure of kingship and governments, of caste hierarchies, of the daily lives of the people, the villagers, the self-sufficiency of those lives? There was the deeper structure; there was the surface structure. Of how much were people like Captain Arthur aware? While his narrative was important for the stark bare statement of historical facts and events, it was important too for the gaps and spaces to be filled in. From that point onwards, we ask questions – and here, the personal stakes make the interrogation more searching: Who said what? Why did they say so? How much was said? The gaps are filled in this instance by the Bombardier's disclosures, unromanticized, the account of the survivor. He is the ordinary soldier. Together with Bombardier Alexander is Lieutenant Virgo. His name intrigues me – the connotations of such a name, Virgo – unsullied, inviolate, virginal, maiden, a man exceptional for his times: "he read and thought much, ultimately he was 'hardly' dealt with, wounded and lost an eye on the retreat" (*Life of Bombardier Alexander*, Vol.1, p.149).

How did those men view the city in which they found themselves? Surrounded by impressive mountains, thickly wooded, full no doubt of all manner of game, fat on the food of the jungle. Leopard and wild boar, deer in plenty, herds of elephant. Monkeys swarming all over the trees laden with wild mangoes. There was a temple of the Buddha within the city beside an islanded lake. The city had been in flames before. The

Portuguese captured Kandy in 1592, and they burned it in 1627 (Ribeyro); and again in 1637 (Faria Y. Souza). The Dutch occupied the city after its destruction by its own inhabitants in 1764, and it was partially burnt by the king on the approach of the English in 1803. When the kingdom of Cotta had lost its power and territory, it became 'Candy,' stronghold of the Kingdom of Candy and the capital of the hill country. Portuguese labour, captive Portuguese prisoners, were used by King Wimaladharma Suriya to build the palace. In 1602, Admiral Spilbergen visited Candy, and described the place thus, "un magnifique palais."

Sir James Emerson Tennent records many descriptions left by the Dutch Admiral Spilbergen of the Candyan Kingdom. The admiral had left behind him both his secretary as well as two musicians at the request of the Kandyan King. The admiral had also enjoyed the wine served him in the Candyan Court. The grapes were grown in Candy. The wine, according to Spilbergen, was excellent. Spilbergen was a wily man. He also captured a Portuguese galliot, which he presented to the Candyan King, Wimaladharma. The galliot was laden with spices and manned by a crew of forty men. This was a significant act, a testimony to his obligations to the Candyans and his hostile attitude to the enemies of the King of Candy.

And the dwellings of the inhabitants of the people, once more as reported by Tennent:

Lime and whitewash could only be used on the walls of the kings' palaces. The roof tiles, set in a perfect design of diamond patterning, were only for the palace roofs. There was a broad street where the first British ambassador, Boyd, described the elephant fights held there for entertainment. Flights of steps led up to the houses to prevent the elephants charging into them.

Entering the city of Candy, Captain Arthur's first encounter had been significant. Bombardier Alexander records it:

> Captain Johnston and his army... reached the capital in safety, without opposition and found it deserted. All they saw was a little boy weeping, a woman over whose fate humanity forces me to draw a veil, and a white rat. The poor boy was allowed to escape, the rat was taken prisoner. Captain Johnston was so much pleased with it, he resolved to have great care taken of it as he meant to have it carried home to Ireland as a present to his mother, but, flushed with success, one of the nineteenth wantonly exclaimed: 'All flesh is grass,' and killed it, for which the Captain confined him, but his confinement was of short duration.
>
> (Bombardier Alexander's "Account of
> Captain Johnston's Expedition")

Why did these men look upon an unknown people as their foe? For the greater part the Kandyans were invisible during this expedition. What is constant in my thoughts now is what happened on the other side–the capture of a Sinhala prisoner of war, the death and burial of a chieftain as a result of this expedition, the burning of a great house on the banks of a river, in Kundasale, and the fate of the distraught woman who was taken away by the men, possibly raped and put to death.

Bombardier Alexander says of her: "A woman over whose fate humanity forces me to draw a veil." How was this lone woman left behind in this township? – wailing, her knot of hair undone streaming down her back, in the tussle, as the men dragged her away. She could offer little resistance. She had no protector. Her jacket was unfastened and showed her plump, golden flesh. Her eyes were wide with terror and her tongue uttered words that were incoherent in their babbling. The little boy with tears coursing down his cheeks. A very small boy. Compassion was shown him and he was allowed to run away.

The white rat had scurried out of one of the buildings, an albino rat perhaps. So rare a find that the captain had wanted to preserve its life. Ironic indeed for the invader.

But how can any living thing avoid its destined fate? That anonymous man from the 19th Regiment had not been able to restrain himself from using his sabre to lop off the white rat's head, uttering the words "All flesh is grass." But we are filled with a sense of foreboding, the fate of the white rat reminding us of the destiny of all of us mortals: "All flesh is grass."

Are we not intended to take note of that utterance? The white rat that was first taken prisoner and its death by the sword? (The woman on whom 'humanity has drawn a veil...") War is a great reminder of human mortality.

Lieutenant Colonel Arthur Johnston, 18th-19th centuries: my great-great-grandfather (his only child Susan M. Jansz, was my great-grandmother; at one time of the 19th Regiment of Foot, 2nd Ceylon Battalion, of his Majesty's Royal Corsican Regiment (Portrait in the Colombo National Museum).

III

THE SEED:
LULLABIES IN THE WIND

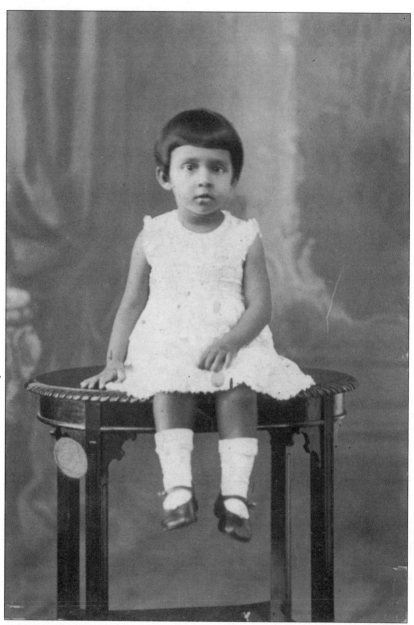

Jean Solomons, three years old.

The Beginnings – Kandy

The map is a blank where my name should be. My birth is its first landmark. An unformed map without routes. Where is the forest? Where is the desert? The roadways, the waterways, rivers and oceans? Where will the land be cleared for the setting up of the first of the dwelling places? The blood predicts that there will be several. The final one, in the wilderness. The going back, after the discovery of the Canaan land, to the locusts and manna of the wilderness.

Surrounded by tea estates and forested hills, the valley in which I was born. The hill slopes of Hantane with burning beacons flaring and sparking off flames when the mana grass, tall sharp-bladed stalks so harsh and abrasive, was set on fire on the tea estate. The tea pluckers seemed like static butterflies that had alighted on those distant tea bushes. The temple stood by the lake with the king's palace and the bathing pavilion of the queen. The forest sanctuary was the backdrop with its hoary trees, vines, creepers, and ferns. Tribes of monkeys, reptiles and animals concealed themselves within those dark coverts. Churches, and schools, built by missionaries filled the valley, Roman Catholic, Anglican, Methodist, Baptist. A turreted, high-walled gaol painted a deep rose-red lay in the heart of the township. In the centre of the township, lay a marketplace with mazes of corridors and small shops. Pyramids of fruit. Baskets piled up with an overspill of mangoes, passion fruit, avocado pears, and pineapples. Bunches of ripening plantains. Buckets filled with gladioli, carnations, Lady's Lace, hydrangeas which had come wrapped in fir branches, from up-country. Fish laid out on slabs, the last gasp and quiver, stilled. Great carcasses of meat suspended from iron hooks. A wooden block for chopping the sirloin and joints of beef. Buckets with boiling water seething with folds of blanket tripe scraped clean and readied for the pot. Goat flesh, hair clotted with blood. Bloodied heads with glazed eyes. The sherbet vendors. Bottles and tumblers of orange, sunset pink, red sherbet poured out into clear glass tumblers afloat with a nimbus of kasa kasa. And the street cameraman, his camera set on a tripod outside the market-place.

The map already bore its invisible tracery webbed with its criss-cross of routes explored by earlier discoverers. My own life map was an opaque sheet of parchment, clear and unsmudged, with its territory and boundaries yet to be marked out.

Katukellewatte. Acres and acres of land that belonged to Colonel Piachaud. His wife, Lilian, was my grandmother Charlotte Grenier's cousin. Colonel Piachaud was the chief attesting witness at my birth. He would never live to see what I would grow up to be. Nor would he have approved my rebellion against the customary mould of tradition. His wife Lily outlived him, a gracious and beautiful woman who also lived to see my own children.

"Mother would love to see your daughters," Marguerite, Lily's daughter told me one day. That meeting was an historical event. Equivalent to being presented to the Queen Mother. Her gifts to her cousin Dolly's children were two kapok-stuffed, striped cloth balls which she had sewn herself. And the two Victorian highchairs that my sister and I had inherited from the Piachaud bungalow were part of her gifts, now bequeathed to my children. The variegated colours of those hand-sewn balls, looking back, provide the metaphors for a genealogical hybridity. Lily Piachaud was like many of the Burgher ladies of a past generation who were never to change their style and fashion of dress from Edwardian times. Ankle-length gowns, lace ruffles, high-necked collars pinned with cameo brooches, long sleeves with buttoned cuffs, stockings, court shoes. Their hair still worn long, knotted or braided. And hats to church.

The Piachaud family lived in a house named "The Retreat" with spacious rooms and a sprawling verandah. Two lofty, leaf-crowned mangosteen trees stood sentinel before the house. A stone birdbath was sunk into the earth. There was an emerald green, grass-trimmed lawn with an arbour of bougainvillea. My parents lived in one of the Colonel's houses. Gowanlea. A name which emerged out of someone else's mythic dream of a mythic place in a mythic country. Someone else's imagined landscape. Someone else's map. Years later I sought out its meaning. A Celtic, a Gaelic, a Teutonic dream. Gowan, the wild daisy. Celtic. Guyan, bud, daisy, Gaelic. Lea, ley, lay, a meadow, grassland, pasturage. *Loke*, *loh* - German. Transposed from across the seas and planted in a tropical landscape. The Colonel was of French descent, settled in this island, but his naming of the houses he constructed was plucked from some mystical memory of landscapes he had perhaps encountered in a world of books and the remembrance of an idyllic pastorale. As for his own house – it was his imagined haven. So distant from the warlike antecedents of those soldiers of fortune, his ancestors. Katukellewatte abounded in fruit trees, birds, bowers of bougainvillea, fern banks, hibiscus and frangipani. The Colonel had an estate in Kadugannawa too, just below the point at which the hollowed-out rock tunnel marked the Pass which led to Kandy. Rising from the valley, the tea estate spread and covered the hill slopes. My mother as a young girl spent holidays with the Piachaud children from time to time. She read to them, narrated her stories, and was their young companion whom they loved dearly.

Where was the house? I searched for it as I passed through during all those growing years, but could never see it. Was it still there, hidden away in some sheltered copse? What I wanted to know, what I wanted to see, was some imagined part of my mother's early youth of which no photograph remained. To share her view of a hidden valley and mountains wrapped in a blue, distanced haze beyond her vision and yet, part of it.

Who was it who had named me at my baptismal font? In the Methodist Church on Brownrigg Street, where John Wesley's hymns were sung together with hymns translated from Latin and German, the walls covered with historical plaques in copper and marble.

His Excellency Lieutenant-General Robert Brownrigg, Governor and Commander-in-Chief in and over the British settlements and territories in the island of Ceylon, in the year 1815, had issued the Proclamation whereby the Kandyan Convention was signed and the whole island had become a part of the British Empire. The Convention contained twelve clauses. The fourth stated that the dominion of the Kandyan provinces would be vested in the sovereign of the British Empire.

My names then were inspired by the readings into a colonial text, the Bible and the canonical literature of those times. Those names swam round, imprisoned within the baptismal font, netted and flung from that ocean fringed by subjugated territory, gliding in those shallow depths, without a channel of escape. Silvery shapes, luminous in the clear, fresh water shafted with green and violet light glancing from the circular stained-glass window above the carved pulpit from which a succession of English missionaries delivered their sermons every Sunday morning and evening to a fervent congregation filling the pews.

Names embedded in my mind: Lansdowne, Nelson, Beven, Middlehurst, Jackson, Small, Cartman, Tattersall, Nodder, Robinson...

Was that first baptismal font ever replaced during the passage of the years? In my imagination there still remains the rainbow touch of glinting fish scales within those ever replenished blessed waters that touched each infant forehead with the chill of presagement. My names remain but their significance needs a new interpretation. The need to be translated using new codes and ciphers. I begin, then, here, at this point of time, with my entrance into the world of Katukellewatte, to define myself, an iridescent speck against the moving, shifting glaciers of history. I go backwards into the past, my birth, which lies within the pre-history of the ice age. The speck appears on the blank map and begins, but very gradually, to assume a shape and form.

My birth, then, was located on that map. It had its own mysteries. I had to construct, piece together those memoried fragments and spin each thread to weave its unending tapestry. My mother had planned an earlier arrival. She had miscalculated the dates. Perhaps, subconsciously, she may have wanted it all over and done with, to get back to the ordinary business of living. Her doctor, Dr Vachel Anthonisz, had tried to coax me out into the world three months earlier than I was due to emerge and face its vicissitudes. I refused to budge, snug in my foetal position, lulled in ripples of amniotic fluid. When the time was ripe I came out into the world to unpredictable greetings.

The Changeling Bud

"Tell them you are my son."

Why was my father asking me to be a changeling? I did not want to be what someone else compelled me to be. My face grew hot, my cheeks flushed, but how could I gainsay my father's command? Tall, towering over me, the Father. There were certain unspoken, unuttered signals of authority which we followed. Black sashes, of ribbon, worn on Christmas day to church. My mother reluctant to spoil the frilled organdy dresses. We wore silver hairbands too. The air had been filled with the tensions of latent conflict. My father had slipped the black mourning band on the arm of his coat. We had to wear the visible symbols of mourning to remind ourselves, remind others too, of Budgie's death before I was born. The grieving would never cease, lasting till the end of my father's life, (but by then I would understand). All that time, a child of age five, I could not. Nor would anyone explain to me. I had only one or two clues to guide me to that signpost.

"Your father was disappointed that you were a girl. He wanted another son."

How could my birth have heralded any such substitution? I could never be the son he wanted. I would always be myself growing up the way I wanted, moving away from the curbs of dominance and of submission.   .

When my father asked me to wear my blue drill shorts – we had shorts for play – and a white shirt (was it one of Budgie's old shirts, I now wonder), with a summons to come to the Railway

Running Shed where he was with his friends, I could neither refuse nor protest. Would I look like a son? I had my hair cut short in an Eton crop too. "Wear your pair of blue shorts. Say that you have brought me a message. When the men ask me who you are, you must answer them, tell them that you are my son."

It was a lonely walk along the main Colombo-Kandy road, past all the familiar shops: Cunjimoosa's with the bottles of gold-covered chocolates; the Barber's Salon with the men wrapped in white togas sitting on swivelling chairs before the mirrored walls; Podi Mahattaya's shop with the green and amber bead curtains. I walked on and on until I recognized my father standing in a group with all his khaki-clad railway cronies laughing and talking together.

I gave my father the message he had requested. What was that message? The words are now lost. I must have stammered out those words with burning cheeks. Those railway men were either credulous or playful. At any rate, a very small child with stiff, straight hair, wearing boy's clothes, could confound those bluff adults. Perhaps some of them had never set eyes on me before. My gender must have appeared indeterminate at that stage. Not even a hint of being girlish in my guise of a little boy. Was this play acting an expression of my father's complex emotions, this subterfuge of transforming my persona, using the magic wand of his will, to create the illusion of my being the son he had loved so dearly but had lost? Those railway men accepted me easily, but I remembered some of their words: "Harry Sol, we didn't know you had another son." I learned then that one could retreat into different landscapes and planes of reality, through disguise.

My father longed for another younger son to take the place of the one he had lost. Arthur, 'Budgie.' Was he like a pet

budgerigar that he was named thus? He was eight years old when
he died. My mother told me how my father had taken his shotgun
to first shoot the doctor who had made the wrong diagnosis of
his illness, and then to shoot himself. The entire hospital staff had
had to wrestle with this strong, muscular man, who had been a
boxer in his early youth, to prevent his carrying out his own form
of justice. Budgie was also supposed to have had the same brand
of courage as my father, and would be the first to come to the
defence–with fisticuffs–of the unjustly wronged.

How had my brother died? The death was shrouded in
mystery. Once my mother said, as if in warning to me, that he had
had a fall, hurt his head, told no one about it and had been given
a bath. That had been one explanation. Once she said that he had
fallen off the swing in our back garden in Kadugannawa and that
was why I should not go on that tall swing. But Budgie had died
in Kandy. So that story was meant as a warning to repress my
unruly energy… Those were some of the stories. Yet another was
that he had had high fever. The doctor had treated him for typhoid.
It was meningitis.

Oh, he could have lived. He could have been saved. I
would have had another brother. I must have another brother. Or
another sister. All my life I longed for a second brother or sister. A
playmate to mitigate my loneliness when my elder sister was sent
to the hostel at Girls' High School.

If Budgie had lived, my mother said sadly, he would
perhaps have been a "vegetable." She could not have borne it.
His nature was mercurial, like quicksilver I was told. But I know
she carried a load of guilt in her mind. Did my father blame her
for not being careful enough, watchful enough? They were both
broken with a shared grief, but it was my mother who had to bear

the brunt of a corrosive feeling of guilt, of somehow being the person partly responsible for that loss and bereavement. It was something she carried till the end of her days. Felt in the silence that lay heavy on my father, my mother, Budgie's name never mentioned when they were together.

My father was bitterly disappointed at my birth. I became the changeling through the magical transformation in his imagination.

My father grew to accept me. Only once had he contrived that I should assume the role of that lost son. That I should appear before his railway friends as the younger son whom he wanted his world to acknowledge. Perhaps it was something that led to my wilful rebellion later on. But by then my father and I had gained enough knowledge of each other to accept ourselves for what we were.

The Earthquake in the Garden

What were the upheavals in my childhood? Halfway up the hill to that house in Kadugannawa, by the curving steps leading up to it, lay a disused well buried in the earth, its secret spring of water silent beneath the tumbled clods, that part of the hillside overgrown with wild flowers, heavy seeded grass stalks, ferns. Ferns that left an impress on the skin, a silver damascened pattern embossing the tender flesh; fern pressing gently laid upon fern patterning every inch of the bared arms and wrists. But first the jewelled ladybirds gently lifted off, scarabs that threaded beads of red, gold, orange on the leaves with their perfect, minute pointillist specks of black embedded on enamelled surfaces.

Upheaval? In a garden without boundaries as if childhood itself extended beyond those demesnes reaching to the summit of the tea estate on the hill behind the house. There were no maps, only a child's discovery and exploration of individual and significant landmarks: the rocky ledge overlooking the railway, where my voice would call out messages across the railway lines to the Foreman Platelayers' house where the Salvages lived; the covert of closely growing wild breadfruit trees with dew-drenched grasses growing knee-high and, nestling at their roots, the breadfruit seeds and tiny cones of bright-red wild strawberries; the two railway houses where the Amits, a Malay family, lived, and adjoining it a closed and shuttered house where a young pregnant wife slept the silent hours away; the tea estate which spread over the hill-top into nowhere.

A reckless, haphazardous childhood, where I wandered at will, everywhere, with my secret discoveries of a world where few human voices reached. My feet followed paths of my own devising where the grass and wild plants tangled, the snakes uncoiled their sinuousities and wove their own passage through the undergrowth. I watched the cobra dance before me, swaying with its flaring hood, and passed on my way leaving it undisturbed.

No one came in search of me. This was not the freedom of the fugitive. I was not in flight from fear or danger. I was not running away from anyone who threatened to harm me. Vulnerability was something not yet understood. I lived in a world that did not need sentinels. My mother, my father, Mungo my ayah, aunts, uncles, cousins, friends were always there or came and went at will. They poured out their narratives into my open ears. I listened. I questioned the mysterious, the unknown. Their idiosyncrasies were part of a normal world. I had to find my own world to belong to, and then it was a world in which language was rarely needed. Utterances. Magical words and incantations. In the ordinary world words had to explain themselves over and over again to those who did not know you. If there were the intimations of language, they were first apprehended in mutations of colour, light and shade; the fragrance of flower, leaf, grass, bark, resin; textures too–the rough, harsh and abrasive, the smoothly silky; the transparent and diaphanous feel of leaf, petal, fruit, seed, serpent shards. It was my finger that shook the dew globules that quivered on the grass blade, shattering the iridescence into fragments, destroying the image that mirrored itself within, a minuscule landscape.

Upheaval. I could cause it by my careless stampede through the natural world, but I didn't. My foot-tread was careful. I stepped aside to watch the glittering millipedes scurrying with golden

feathery feet through the grasses and carefully avoided the phalanxes of stinging red ants swarming over the over-ripe fallen jak
fruits. The leeches clung to my flesh, and swelled into Chinese
lanterns of transparent skin, glowing with blood. Flowers I clipped
onto my ears like my mother's pearl earrings. There were dangers, but I knew no fear in this world that opened itself up to me,
a world without gates or frontiers. Perhaps, then, this was one of
the reasons for a false trust in what would later lead to treachery,
betrayal, the threat of death, and change with time and circumstance. Wings shed their gloss. Magical transformations led to the
distortions of reality.

The signals and signposts were there. When I went into the
outside world there were clearly demarcated boundaries. I stepped
into, went deep into, the very hinterland of new dangers, but I
would have not wished it to be any other way than that. I had
watched from my rocky ledge the railway lines with their criss-
cross of snarled-up silver that dazzled the eyes in the white sunlight–lines which at those given signals straightened out to provide the clear routes for journeys that were sometimes unpredictable. My father had guided those enormous steam engines on so
many rail tracks, taking thousands of anonymous people to their
destinies, people who knew nothing of his life, who never perhaps remembered his face–as I his child would till the end of time.
The trains he guided had never been derailed, but he described
those derailments he had seen to me, derailments when those
coaches had just gone off the track and toppled over, all awry.
Sometimes, a herd of wild buffalo in some remote area, or a wild
elephant in 'musth' had blazed onto those manmade tracks. In
that confrontation there were always the victims.

Death and upheaval. But the journeys had to continue. As they would in my own life, years and years later. The coaches would be righted up, the shambles restored to a seeming normalcy, and the destruction effaced and forgotten.

But those first intimations of that natural world which I moved through, where no one imposed sanctions on me, had its own dangers on the night of the earthquake. I was asleep on the four-poster, my sister beside me. The bed lurched crazily, the canopy billowed out. The flame in the nightlamp flared up, flickering, and then went out leaving us in darkness. My mother was bending over us, "Wake up, wake up." How urgent her tones were - she who was always so easygoing. "Come with me to the garden. There's a sudden earthquake."

An earthquake? We slipped our feet into the swansdowne slippers beside our beds and crept out of the house and down the side steps into that part of the garden where the hollyhock beds were. There was a tall flowering tree in the centre of the lawn. The hill on which the house perched began to heave, and a shuddering movement reached us from the greater hill above the house which sent its tremors down to us. Our long white nightgowns billowed about our bodies. We held onto our mother's hands and allowed ourselves in our imaginations to be rocked on the heaving deck of a vessel ploughing through the earth-ocean. I looked up as the sky tilted down at me, my gaze clutching at the edge of darkness as the cavernous night enveloped and engulfed me.

A dazzling fireworks display. I held my face up to the swinging constellations. Adrift on a turbulent ocean. Swathes of tumultuous waves dashed against the plants, against our bodies. We were swimming among the stars. Our bodies metamorphosed into starbodies. The garden was no longer a safe place. Trees were crashing down around us. The forest was being uprooted.

"Your father... will he be safe?" My mother spoke her thoughts out aloud.

"Why, why?" we asked.

"He is on the night mail - it's dangerous on the Balana Pass. Huge rocks can come tumbling down. Crushing the train, the carriages... what if they are derailed?"

Long dark tunnels, coal-soot, damp-smelling. Hollow echoes with haunting eerie rumblings through the wounded rock, moisture trickling down the rock face. Like being buried deep within a mine. Womb rock. Precipitous inclines. Falling, falling into the valley below. Where our great-grandfather's coffee plantations once stood. Where the ancient temple was embedded in the earth surrounded by a patchwork of fields green as the wings of parrots. Forested mountains. Bible Rock. Far away.

If my father did not return, where would we go?
Leaving the house on the hill? Where?

I feel the fissures opening out of earth. Plants uprooted and tangled in the garden. Branches crashing down. Alarms of shrill bird-calls. The moon tossed crazily in the dark, billowing clouds.

I abandon myself to the swinging, up and down movement of the heaving earth. Earth is a hammock. Earth is a cradle. But growing more violent in its rocking movement. Quicksilver mounting in the fragile glass thermometer placed under the tongue. The fever is rising. Dreams become delirious.

Dark hours in the garden. Three figures, apocryphal almost in white nightgowns, revealing their hidden inspirations. Was it for us to interpret it as truth? It is important to feel that here perhaps is that revelation, and in the years to come we need to write our own apocrypha.

Stones that have long been buried hurtle out of the subterranean mineral world. In the sky candelabras of light dazzle,
swinging among the constellations of stars. The house still stands.
My mother peers through a nimbus of light at the house. Tiles are
being dislodged by a high wind. *Crash, thud*–the clay tiles fall and
splinter. The houses we live in cannot last for all eternity. Cracks
will appear, the rafters give way. We must be ready to seek shelter
anywhere. Here, it is safer beneath the stars.

Our bodies settle into the rhythm of the tilting, heaving
earth. We share its pulsating tremors. Then, very gradually, the
earth settles, but so very gradually. The silence and stillness are
palpable against our bodies.

My father returns the next morning. The train had shuddered its
way through the night, completing its journey.

"I brought the train to a halt. We were just out of a long
tunnel. I had felt the tremors when we were inside. The train
was on the very edge of Sensation Rock. All around us, rocks
were tumbling down, water gushed with force, I felt the
spray from the waterfalls, great stones lay on the tracks…"

The signal lamp flashed about my eyes. Red. Green. Gold.
White. The Call-boy summoned my father in the darkness before
dawn. He would guide the trains again for travellers to reach their
destinations.

We had begun new journeys. Nothing would ever be safe
or predictable again.

What would I do without my father? A man who would
lapse into deep profound silence, brooding over the death of his

son. His silent accusations oppressive in the house. Taking to his bed, his head buried in a book. Refusing to come to the dining table. My mother, unhappy, uneasy. The unspoken silence of guilt I could never understand creating a vast chasm between them.
"Go and call your father to the table."
I obeyed her, getting off obediently from that high chair.
The bedroom was enveloped in a brooding silence.
I delivered the summons to him.
"I will come later," he tells me. "Tell your mother to carry on with lunch."

A child is often a guileless and innocent courier.
The pigeon with the missive held within its beak.
Flying over unknown country.

The Father

If my father had not returned from the earthquake, what would I have to remember him by?

The newly minted coins pouring out of their cylinder-cases onto our palms.

The coloured threads in the wads of yarn from the mills and factories of Lancashire. Fine, unravelled, threads vari-coloured to wipe off the coal dust from his hands, on board those huge steam engines, the fireman raking the blazing infernos of the furnaces.

The signal lamp with its glass shades sliding to reveal the coloured lights, to indicate safety or danger. His curious tales, his yarns, his life a travelogue of history. A passage through colonial times, drawing a sterling salary from the Empire.

The memory of honeycombs filled with royal bee jelly and dripping honey taken out from the beehives. His flute on which he played his own compositions to beguile my growing years.

The naming of the birds. Honey-peckers, honey-suckers, golden orioles, selalihinis, mynahs, kingfishers, woodpeckers, sparrows, the Loten sunbird…

Black and white terriers from his whiskey bottles.
His cherry-wood pipe. The meerschaum pipe. The empty boxes of light wood with colourful lettering and labels where his Havana cigars had reposed.

His collection of walking sticks. Some of them with carved handles, or stout, hard, whittled walking sticks designed by him, made of varieties of wood, wood that he found in the stations he was posted to. His special snake-protecting walking stick with its carved snake head, which would ward off any snake, he used to say.

His huge cabin trunk with its marbled colours. His boxing gloves, his silver boxing trophies, some of them only replicas. He had sold the silver cups or pawned them, never to be retrieved, in those slender years, my mother told me.

His thick gold ring with the grey-green cat's eye gem set in its cusp. His sun helmet, pith hat, stylish felt hat, khaki cap, beret.

His stopwatch that reposed in his coat pocket spelling out time, spelling out the hours. I thought my father would live for ever, read time to me whenever the summons came to me to prepare for some event.

His books overflowed from the shelves, Chambers Journals, biographies, autobiographies of Generals, Commanders, Empire Builders, explorers, adventurers, hunters. Travel sagas. We were both travellers. We were always discovering routes, climbing hills, looking beyond into boundless horizons.

Visible Reminders

And not so visible if I think of the history
Of my life,
Of what I want to remember.

I do not know what I will be remembered
By but recollect other memories.

Shadows on the walls, my father's hands,
Delicate yet strong fingers creating the animals
Which my childhood had still to encounter
Far from the jungle he had walked through.

Shadows.
The crocodile on the tank bund,
The wild hare leaping through the dark
Grasses of the night, the arching body of
The lithe leopard readying for its spring
Where the deer timidly feed.

Remember.
His topaz ring set in heavy gold, lost,
Plundered, his cast aside cobwebbed boxing
Gloves, his sculptured hands hidden within
Those iron fists in his youth.

His walking sticks, ebony, lacquered,
One of them snake-headed, of special
Wood to ward off reptiles on his path
Through wilderness on his jungle walks.

Where is that signal lamp with safety
Colours, warnings of danger,
Signposts, signifiers of arrival or departure.

In my mind's recesses
The haunting echoes of the call-boy's voice
Summoning him at dawn to begin
His journeys taking those mapped out
Routes, that imperial network with its
Complex web of interconnections.

Remember.
My father's blue and vermilion tattoos
Incised upon the skin of memory.
Tattoos on his arms, wrists, chest,
Cupid with the heart transfixed
By arrows, ocean waves with leaping
Fish, mermaids, sailing vessels, anchors,
My father, the navigator of my childhood's
Beginning voyages.

Clear, pigmented etchings
The first illustrations of his unwritten
Books leading me through his own
Discoveries and explorations which I
Now interpret to continue his unfinished
Journeys into the hinterland of his life,
Our sagas merging after those alternate
Odysseys we had pursued through our
Disparate fates and destinies.

Flight

I was with her on that day. That was important to me.

"I had to carry you in my arms as I fled that night. The man followed us with his gun." Where did it happen and when? My mother was always, it seemed to me, speaking out her thoughts aloud when we were together. Where was this country she was speaking of, and why was she always drawing me into danger, escape, flight, fear? What was she running away from? Pursued for what deadly purpose?

"It was getting darker and darker. I had ventured out alone with you that evening."

Her voice fills my consciousness. I listen silently, but at the same time I have filled a transparent glass fingerbowl with water, and carefully taking out from the tissue wrapping the pressed flowers and leaves, Japanese water plants, I drop their wavering strands within the shallow bowl. The plants unfold and spread out, brilliant-hued tendrils and petals vermilion, viridian, saffron yellow, an aqua-world that was strange, entrancing.

My mother preferred to relate her own stories, rather than read the stories from books. Her stories were seldom children's stories. They interwove their narrative through passages of darkness, shadows drawing their webs to enclose my own imaginings.

"Tell me how you escaped," I whispered. Her face wore that inward expression that told me that she was far away in that other country, her story-country. She prepares me for the dangers I will myself meet with years later. Flight. Being hunted. Being pursued. Running away from my pursuers. In actuality and in dreams.

"I was taking a late evening walk with you one day." When? Does my memory give me the slightest nudge? Remember even faintly the thudding of that staunch heart?

"All of a sudden this man appeared out of the shadows of the trees. He had a gun in his hand. He appeared to be stalking his prey in the dense thicket. For a moment I thought he was out hunting alone. A pastime of his. I did not recognize his face. He was a complete stranger but he looked at me as if… as if he had seen me before. I wonder whether he was a visitor spending a holiday on one of the tea or rubber estates. He didn't belong here. In the half-light my eyes rapidly scanned his face, his clothes. Tawny-coloured eyes, wildcat eyes, dark moustache and beard. His eyes had that intent, deep concentration of the hunter-predator."

Did my mother expect me to understand her ruminative words? Words I had not heard before. Words that did not belong to my world. My finger stirred the water plants in the bowl of water. The coloured shapes contained within their petals a tantalizing mystery, but only if they remained in the water.

"… he wore a deerstalker hat, a brown tweed coat, thick khaki shorts, grey hose and creased leather boots. What was strange was that the gun was pointed in my direction. He kept a distance from me, but I felt his eyes intent on my progress as I began to walk faster. He did not increase his speed but kept me within sight. You were in my arms. I knew that I had become the prey he was stalking. I was filled with terror. My fear was instinctual. Yes, I was sure the gun was pointing at me. It was growing darker but his presence was palpable. I knew the terrain better than this stranger, so I was able to take a sudden detour across a paddy field and along a jungle path. For him the place was unknown. Oh, he could have shot me and disappeared. No one would have known until the next day…"

"There was a small wattle-and-daub hut, an old couple sat inside beside the faint light of a bottle lamp. They sheltered me the whole night long. Until the faintest flicker of light and dawn."

Flight. I can now see the stranger's face in my mind's eye. His presence will always be there, in my past, in my childhood, in my life.

Did my father know?

"He was very jealous of me. Afraid he would lose me. Very strong, very violent passions. I had to be careful of even the friends I made among women, of spending time away from him."

I know now that she would never have told my father.

"He would have sought out that stranger and killed him."

My father too had a gun at home.

Storm on the Lagoon

My mother always dramatized her experiences, brought risk, danger, and excitement closer home, involving me in many of those happenings. Her narratives began anywhere, at anytime when we were together, alone. Was she talking to me or were her words reaching somewhere else, someone else? I now think to myself, "Why did you never write all this in your journals, record your own past?" My father, my mother, were always reaching back into their own lives delving into the experiences that had significance on their personal journeys. Somehow the message reached me, and after those years they are there within my own secret mind-cache, to retrieve.

I hear her voice, my mother's voice recalling the storm on the lagoon. I was with her, that evening "A babe in arms," as she told me, "when I went boating on the Batticaloa lagoon and the boat capsized. It was so hot, so very hot here on the eastern coast and I wanted to feel the cool breeze that blew over the stretch of water. It was so inviting, and as I stood with you on the shore I had this sudden urge to take a boat ride. Your father was at work. He was stationed in Batticaloa. I had remained behind in Kandy at Auntie Tommy's. Your father hated being separated from us, but after Budgie's death and your birth there had been a period of disturbance in our lives. I felt you were too young to be taken so far away. Perhaps it was a sense of reluctance to leave the familiar things, the comfort of the known place and friends... I had come here on a holiday."

"We were sailing in the boat. I sat cradling you comfortably in my arms. The waters were calm like crushed silk, gently ruffled by the breeze that touched each wave. Suddenly a high wind rose. The air grew dark. The boat first tossed violently from side to side, tilting dangerously into the turbulence... the waves were rising high..."

I listened, my play suspended. I feel a thrill of excitement run through my body. My mother's story of the danger we had shared was more exciting than my solitary game... maybe a jigsaw puzzle I was carefully setting like a mosaic before me.

It was a story about myself too, and I wanted, with every fibre of my being, to experience that sense of danger, of near-drowning, even of being so close to death. The lagoon waters had drenched us when the boat capsized and in those moments when my mother kept afloat. "I swam," she told me, "I swam against those turbulent currents, it seemed for ages, but it could not have been so long before the boatmen righted the craft and plucked us both from those waters that swirled so about our bodies..." And I? What did I know of that underworld of fish and water plants, being watched by the secret eyes of scuttling crabs, fins touching the skin, fish sliding against the bodies...

We did not go under even once... you had to be safe... your father could not lose a second child so soon." She was telling me how she had wanted to escape from the heat, the ennui of that holiday. What was she reminding herself of? Days, snatched from a calendar, times in her life that were never predictable? Her mind seemed to be recreating her own imagined role.

I had held you high in my arms but the water inundated us. The lagoon was so alive as seething waves, fish leaping above the water, the chill currents touched us... Yes, you had to live... I was reminded of the time of your birth... you were like a tiny fish clinging so tenaciously to the womb, swimming in that amniotic fluid that protected you..."

"A little mermaid?" I asked.

"Yes, if you like to think of your life as being one," she smiled.

I must have felt the turbulence within that miniature storm of birth. Did that upheaval toss me about?

"Oh, you clung tenaciously. Refused to emerge. You bided your time and curbed my impatience too."

My mother must have wanted to be over and done with that birthing. And perhaps she had decided she had had enough. No more children. Had she willed it somehow? For there were no more born after I had emerged out of the ocean of her womb. Had dreamed those months away in darkness. I now grasped those brilliant shafts of light to give myself new sighting.

I would always feel the bonding of those nine months. "Feel the hair at the top head, have I got a whirlpool...?" My mother had said so often, "If you have a suli, a whirlpool, you will have to be careful of water, of being drowned."

I wanted there to be a whirlpool. I wanted to feel the danger that surrounded me in unknown oceans. Her fingers probed among the clusters of my hair. She merely said, "You will always have to be careful of water, oceans, rivers." But I would always walk into the sea as deep as I could and then float on my back with the sun striking my eyes, or swim out as far as I could but keeping the lighthouse in sight.

But one day, many years later, I went under ridges of tall, sweeping waves which dragged me far out into the sea. It was at Closenberg, in Galle. Batticaloa, Galle, landmarks in my mother's family histories. Those forts had known the presence of my ancestors. I couldn't surface from the salt-tasting waves, stinging my eyes and face, blinding me. I couldn't breathe, I was carried,

farther and farther out until there was only the blue, turquoise-
blue, sea-green expanse of water... Suddenly I was pinioned by
the strong arms of a swimmer who had seen me disappearing
beneath the waves. My head was lifted above the spume and I
took a breath of air. It was the third time I had come to the surface,
my gills furiously taking the life-giving draught, shaking off as I
tossed my hair, the tiny starfish and mollusks clinging on, with
tendrils of seaweed amongst my wet strands. And again, later,
the gold wedding ring I had but newly donned, my engagement
ring of blue sapphires, the bracelet around my wrist, had all
slipped off, swept away by the waves, small recompense for the
life that had been given back to me. Gold sinking deep into an
ocean bed, with treasure of innumerable shipwrecks, while the
plankton, mollusks and smaller fish floated in opaque depths
among the drowned bodies of those long-lost human cargoes.

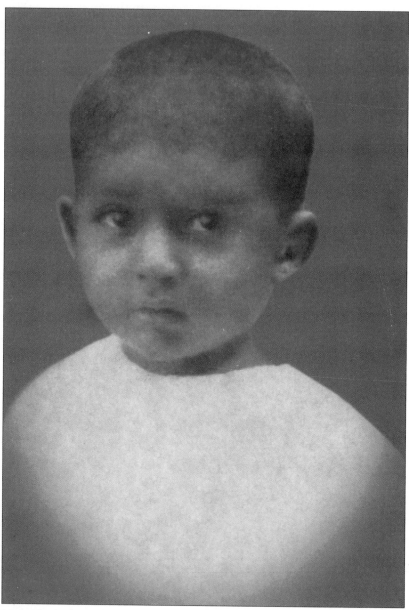

My brother Arthur (Budgie).

IV

THE FIRST BRANCH:
WORLD OF SCHOOL
&
KADUGANNAWA HILLS

The railway scenario in colonial Ceylon during the days of steam engines: my father is seated 2nd from right, beside the English General Manager of Railways. A historic photograph of the CGR (Ceylon Government Railways) with the engine, a powerful symbol of domination in the background (Photograph taken during the late 1920s or early 1930s).

Early Kindergarten Days

I was not to know the world of school until I was almost past the age of being admitted to the Kindergarten or 'Baby Class' at the Girls' High School in Kandy. My mother kept me at home, seemingly reluctant to allow the separation that would inevitably happen. I was her youngest and provided her with companionship, although there were times when I left her to make my own explorations. I hovered on the fringes of her life, listening to her own childhood tales. She had spent her early years with her grandmother Elizabeth Grenier and her young aunt Constance, probably to lessen her own mother's burden of looking after a large and growing family.

Who would listen to her and the narratives of her own childhood once I went to school? I think she could not bear the thought of those long, lonely daytime hours in Kadugannawa. When I was not making my own solitary excursions on the hill and the tea estate, I followed her like a shadow, playing beside her or giving ear to the songs she sang to me and the stories from her own life. We shared our freedom together, but the time came when I would have to leave her. From that point onwards my route began to branch off on its own. There were spaces and gaps when I needed her but could not find her. That independence was to carry greater hazards but also the risks and dangers necessary to my growing. I would lose gradually the illusions of life being an idyll in the safe garden, realize that the world outside had its dark passages when the shadow of the real giants would fall across my path...

Sometimes I would go to school by train, sometimes by bus, leaving Kadugannawa early in the morning. It was usually cold and dark, the garden still mist-covered, the birds beginning their first tentative calls, a summons to light and to the day. In my half-sleep, I was lifted off the four-poster bed and, still in my nightgown, seated on a small bench before a large enamel basin of hot water. Mungo soaped me, washed me, and gently wiped me with a large fluffy bath towel, my white school uniform starched and crisp, transforming me into a new changeling. I drank a glass of hot milk or supped from a bowl of Quaker oats, bread and milk or soft-boiled egg, nibbled toast and butter, and was then ready to go down the stone steps onto the two roads that would take me to the station or bus-stand.

What struck me greatly in my kindergarten classroom was the large glass-framed picture of Jesus Christ. Jesus had blue eyes, wavy brown shoulder-length hair, and a golden-brown beard. Clustered around him were children of various hues and racial characteristics, children who provided, as I was to realize later, a microcosmic picture of the British Empire. As we sang, skipped, galloped, hopped and simulated the actions of bird and beast, the presence of the glass-framed picture made me feel there was a greater force than that of the gentle self-effacing teacher Ethel Wijewardena at the upright piano. A constant presence in our lives in this missionary school – wherever we turned, the picture of Jesus Christ looked down upon us watching generation after generation pass through the classroom. Leaving an indelible impression on the mind of each child. This was yet another insight into the map of the world, which lay outside the accustomed and familiar one of Kadugannawa.

One day I found myself on the school platform which had been transformed into a stage. We were engaged in rehearsals of Maeterlinck's *The Blue Bird*. I was an Unborn Child, dressed in a blue vest and blue bloomers. All the Unborn Children were dressed completely in blue. I was one of the special children, for I had to sit throughout several scenes blowing bubbles from a small bowl of soapy water. In between acting their roles, the Big Girls came and sat beside me, begging for a chance to blow bubbles. I was told that the bubbles must emerge in perfect rounded shapes like the iridescent baubles on the Christmas tree. They floated upwards, tiny bubbles surrounding the larger bubbles, rose in the air and shimmered for a moment, until they burst fragmenting into faint wisps of froth before they vanished. At home too I would sit in the garden with a small enamel bowl on my lap in which slivers of soap had been dissolved, blowing bubbles through a hollow papaw stalk. Within each bubble I caught the reflection of the real world around me. I caught its magic as well as its transience. The colours of the sky, leaves, flowers, sunlight. So brief the captured iridescence of rainbow colours before they vanished leaving the faintest taste of fragrant soap on the tongue and lips.

While I sat among the characters on the stage and followed the story of Tytil and Mytil, I longed to step out of my unreal role. I was a child who already knew something of the world.

This was an imaginary role, the idyllic world that adults imagined 'unborn children' inhabited. The disguise then seemed necessary. The unborn child lived within a paradisal other world where the wolves were kept at bay. A world which Mungo's rakshasas could not reach. My mother, anxious about the gathering evening chill, hovered on the verandah outside the school hall with a cardigan. The teachers were amused at my being fussed over. On stage I enjoyed the freedom of having minimal clothes on my body. There was no feeling of being self-conscious either. Tytil and Mytil were garbed in clothes that belonged to a world we knew nothing of, Maeterlinck's world which had travelled across unimaginably vast and unknown oceans to reach this island.

Phyllis Orloff choreographed our childhood as if it were a ballet. She draped us in diaphanous folds of blue gauze for the "Faery Dance," with great gauzy wings pinned onto our delicate gauze-covered garments. We danced on pointed toes, silver hairbands glittering in our hair, our limbs sprinkled with silver stardust, our faces made up with lipstick, powder, rouge, all from Miss Orloff's mirrored compact and make-up case (she had a more elaborate make-up case too that contained her own magic palette). We learned English country-dances, "Hunstan House" and "Gathering Peascods." We twisted multi-coloured ribbons round the pole, weaving them in a complex pattern in the Maypole Dance.

One morning a climbing frame and mat-slide appeared on the verandah outside the Hall. Miss Elsie Shire christened the mat-slide. White-haired, serious of mien, she consented to slide down the smooth slide. She whizzed down with a valiant expression, while we crowded round and clapped our hands. Elsie Shire, the Irish missionary Principal, became a child along with us. "Poor Miss Shire," we heard later, "she developed a terrible headache and ended up with migraine." What did any of us know of those lives hidden away in the loneliness of the Principal's bungalow which we seldom went close to. There were boundaries that we could not cross.

Aggression

What are little girls made of?
What are little girls made of?
Sugar and spice and all that's nice
And that's what little girls are made of.

What are little boys made of?
What are little boys made of?
Frogs and snails and puppy dogs' tails
And that's what little boys are made of.

Was this ditty first learned at my missionary school? Was it meant to be a deterrent to the early awakenings of sexuality, or was it meant to use the imagery of confectionery to titillate the imagination of the little boys we teased in school. Swooping down upon them with our arms twined around each other's waists, during recess, as our ten-minute tea interval was named on our printed timetables. Was it the early transformation of the feminine image into an icon? We were, as girls, taught to think of ourselves as special. Little boys were made to stir the sense of distaste within us. That was the message that reached us in translation. But that's not what we felt at all – we played joyfully with them and sat next to them in the classroom, until they grew older and were banished into the missionary colleges for boys. Of the three boys in our class I remember, one became a Buddhist monk and died young. Another published pamphlets on Islam later on in life; he too died before his time. Only one of them remains.

Were puppy dogs' tails unintentionally or intentionally a corroboration of the incipient phallic image? Who knows? There was always the dark side of the things that went on in the minds of adults, while sometimes they were unaware of what went on under their very noses. We were careful to hide most of our secrets away from them.

I cannot remember whether I told anyone of how a very young playmate in Kadugannawa called me out to play one evening. My mother was visiting his family in one of those railway bungalows by the rail track and had taken me along too. There were two boys in the family, and not only were our two families very friendly with each other but we as children were playmates, travelled by train to school in Kandy, played with the Meccano sets and Hornby trains in their drawing room.

Renny led me to one of those secret places our parents knew nothing of. Behind his house, at the foot of the tea estate, was a deep ditch, more a huge crevice in the earth with its tangle of wild plants, alakola, sunflower bushes, vines and creepers in which serpents coiled in the cool thickets. Here, when we had clambered down into the deepest part of the ditch, instead of playing one of the exciting games which we devised, getting lost on our adventurous journey into the jungle, Renny suddenly turned on me, his expression inscrutable but determined, and began to punch me black and blue, pummel my body, giving it thumping blow after blow. I could not protect myself from him. His grip on me was so firm. He tore my hair and pinched my cheeks. His hands were round my neck, tightening, choking me. My chintz dress was in shreds. I felt the bitter taste of sunflower petals in my mouth. My feet slipped among the rocks as I tried to break away from him. He hit me repeatedly, almost strangled me to finish me off. He had lost all control of himself. We were both silent. I pushed him away finally, though the blows and thumps I could not ward off. I left him in the ditch alone, spent out. I escaped.

Escaped from my friend and playmate Renny, clambered up the rocky footholds and ran back to his home where my mother was chatting peacefully to his mother. I had learned, early, the ploys and strategies of defence and escape. Resistance I offered. Tears I did not shed. In the vulnerability of childhood there were hidden strengths, in which adult interference was not needed. But I would never forget that the jungle was everywhere, even in the most idyllic landscape.

We were given books on magical myths, where you were supposed to take a morsel of wedding cake after the marriage ceremonies, tie it up in a corner of a handkerchief, pass it through a wedding ring, place it under your pillow - then you would dream of your future bridegroom that night. I wonder how many virgins resorted to those nebulous dreams of romantic embraces with their mystical heroes. The fairytales we heard? How could we interpret them? The magical kiss that would awaken the Sleeping Beauty from a centuries-old sleep, by the prince who would thrust himself through the forest of brambles and thorns that formed its impregnable barriers against all other suitors. The transformations of the Frog Prince, the Prince and the Swineherd, which showed the sin of pride and arrogance humbled, and all these legendary and mythical beings clothed in sweeping skirts and robes of velvet lined with ermine – where was the peasant who brought the wheaten cakes and loaves of bread to the table? On what ships were these fairy stories brought to an island which had its own rich store of folklore?

Who then was the 'other' in our childhood – with the golden curls, the blue eyes, living in castles and palaces? We had first to change the landscape and seek the hovel, the ogre, the witch, the cruel stepmother, and ultimately discover the reality behind the magical pumpkin carriage and the glass slipper. The fairy wand was meant to delude us from realities on which our very existence rested. It was the Little Match Girl perhaps then that told us the true story, because the little match girl dwelt on our own doorstep. Life would never be all chocolate and barley sugar houses. "Watch out!" says history. "Be on the alert." Consumed by your own delusions, you will be left shelterless beneath the stars one day.

Personae

The smell of iodine-soaked cotton wool rubbed on the cut tails of puppies still fills my nostrils. The puppies used to be taken to the Vet in Peradeniya, where their tails were cut short, and iodine applied on the stubs, which were carefully bandaged until they healed.

I played with our Airedale dogs, Jock and Belle, and the cocker spaniel, Timmy. Timmy with the black silky coat, long ears, who had just littered but had to be put to sleep with all her pups after being bitten by a rabid dog. Jock was huge, and in the storeroom, with the wooden door closed, my sister and I mounted on that mild Airedale's back. Round and round the room, we rode him like a pony.

. One day, Belle died. She was my father's favourite Airedale. I saw him carrying her up the hill in his arms, covered in a gunnysack, to be buried. It was the first time I saw my father shed tears. He showed very little emotion – he had gone through it all before, with the death of his younger son, Budgie – the brother whom I never knew.

I felt that compelling need to be several personae, in that world with the fantasy people I created. I was the adult in the child. The world I imitated was the world of adults whom I observed so closely, watching them as they amused themselves with amours, peccadilloes, their own pursuits of love, of life, which entailed happiness, sadness and loss. I viewed their betrayals and their grief in that microcosmic world of provincial society. They swayed together in couples, on the smooth cement floors of the verandah sprinkled lavishly with talcum powder, to the strains of the HMV gramophone records; some small partner and myself gravely and sedately moved among them dancing the two-step: the first elemental steps in that whirling and ecstatic dance, which we ourselves were to experience years and years later with all its savage and uncompromising rites – the mating dance in which all natural beings are involved.

As we danced, we sometimes got in the way of the adults, for we lacked the adroitness of sidestepping to avoid the clumsy collision of bodies. How wide that veranda seemed to stretch, so wide that those couples were a whole universe of men, women, young and old, who felt themselves urged on and on by the compulsion of some internal rhythm to which the gramophone music provided the leit-motif to the courtship dance. The women were suave, svelte, with plucked eyebrows, brilliant tinted hair, Marcel waves; garbed in the fashion of the late 1930s, draped in crepe-de-chine, chiffon, georgette. The men wore flannels, tweeds, tussore. A tropical mélange concocted out of those offshoots of colonialism, yet so real, so alive with a vibrant language that spoke through familiar guitar melodies, mandolin strings, banjo chords, and the harmonica with its plaintive and plangent notes. And we made our own music on those tissue paper-covered combs; a soft, sibilant, whispering music as we breathed into it melodies of our creation. A wind-music that whispered through the rustling leaves of the anodha tree in our front garden. From its branches nightly the owl's melancholy hoot was heard, the frightening bakamuna of our childhood with its yellow eyes shining like lanterns and its predatory beak.

I used to go up on the swing at the Reading Rooms, or play for hours in the ditch, building waterways and dams, constructing my own tributaries and estuaries, the safe bay and the brimming pond. The carter's daughter brought a plateful of kewuns covered with a white cloth. My mother said "no" to the kewun. "Not today," and the child prepared to go away. I stood at the top of the steps, and ran to call my mother. "Please," I say, "she says it is a gift." The girl on the first step stood holding the covered plate, and we looked at each other. I wanted to take the proffered plate in my hands, the kewuns made by her mother, but adult sanctions remained firm. She went away. When we visited the carter's house, the mother showed us where the children slept. For the youngest, two chairs were placed together. When I went home, I tried it out with the straight-backed dining-room chairs. Two would not do for me. I was growing tall. To be comfortable, I needed four. I stretched myself out on the rattan and closed my eyes. It was difficult to turn, to stretch out my limbs to their full length on the rattan-covered chairs. I felt the sharp edges bite into my flesh. I missed the cotton-filled mattress on the big bed.

I loved to draw on walls, always human figures, protagonists of stories I created in my mind, a harkening back to those early primeval urges of cave paintings. My conception of ideal beauty was then neatness and precision, of locating sight, sound, smell, and hearing. The whole body inclined itself to the speaking air, so I did not draw ears. Two dots for eyes, a dot for the nose, and a dot for the lips. And curly hair in waves and ringlets. Later, those eyes grew wide open, windows that surveyed the world and saw adults at their pastimes.

Those were enchanted hours in Kadugannawa. We sat in each other's homes, railway bungalows which were happily blessed with verandas, playing for hours and hours. There was a large oval wooden gameboard with little enclosures closely set with small nails and little gateways – you tilted the board at different angles so that the tiny marbles could slip through the entrance and score marks for you – there were numbers in each round enclosure. And 'Snakes and Ladders' with coloured sinuous reptiles crawling through brilliant squares of red, yellow, green. Draughts, carrom, Lexicon for us children. For the elders, there used to be Bridge, Whist Drives and tennis tournaments at the Railway Reading Room.

One day we went to Nawalapitiya for a celebration at the Railway Reading Room. I watched fascinated as an Englishmen one of the railway men, as "they" were described made a dramatic entrance with his wife, as they swooped down upon the gathering in a Strauss waltz, she in wide skirts billowing, in an ankle-length gown. They danced on and on. A lovely couple. As the gramophone was wound and rewound, the waltz seemed to last forever. They had first stood at the open doorway and compelled all others to make way for them..., and held the floor to an audience enthralled as the hours of that epoch sped by.

Sonia's line drawing that accompanied my article "Those were the Days when we went visiting," in *The Daily News*, 1980s.

Provincial Parties

What else was there to do in this provincial town of an evening except to go visiting or celebrate birthdays and anniversaries? I was never left behind at home while my parents went to parties or when they dined out. I was always taken along with them on those visits. Party games – passing the cushion or the parcel and of course everybody tried to escape being caught, so there was wild excitement when the music stopped, with a flurry of dropped cushions and flung parcels. Once you were caught with the parcel in your hands, you had to sing or dance or imitate something or someone. Anyway you had to do something quite outrageous and be prepared to provoke laughter at your antics. Self-consciousness and inhibitions were dropped. What was wanted was clowning or even a display of talent for singing; solo or tap-dancing or the acting out of a role or reciting poetry. There were prizes for the winner: a box of Pyramid handkerchiefs for the men, embroidered Chinese handkerchiefs for the women, or perfume. I can still sniff the fragrance of Evening in Paris in its dark blue flagon with a sprinkle of silver stars, a very heady, make-your-senses-swoon kind of fragrance.

Gathered round the piano, the sing-songs took place. My father would sing in his strong bass, "Loch Lomond," "Annie Laurie," "Danny Boy," "Drink to Me Only," and "You Take the High Road and I'll Take the Low Road." For years and years I carried those words and melodies in my mind, trying to understand what they meant in terms of love, friendships, parting, death – a search that still continues along different routes. As for dancing, the young people glided along the polished floors to gramophone music, but there also came a stage when the elders would dance the "Kafferinjha" with its elaborate and stately steps, while my father would burst out into its repertoire of songs. I was so fascinated by one special song because it conjured up a whole picture in my mind of a young girl, bound by the constraints of propriety, waiting for a suitor to come along, surrounded by the gossipy neighbours. How then did seductions take place? It was also a period of 'long engagements' where the engagement would first be announced formally in the newspapers. 'Calling the banns' was the announcement in church. There was a particular baila that had its own colourful argot, snatches of which I heard sung here and there:

> Peeping through the window darling,
> What will people say,
> If you want to marry me darling,
> Come the proper way.

What was the proper way? Courtship was a formal arrangement. Permission sought from the parents. Sitting in the veranda or hall with a chaperone at hand. No going out alone except to church. But 'improper' things went on too, which was human, and natural and liaisons and affairs of the heart flourished even between married individuals, while girls were jilted or stood up at the altar, driving some of them to become Miss Havishams bemoaning their spectral lovers.

The Railway Reading Room was the hub of life for the railway families. There were children's parties organized by Reverend Benson Fernando. All of us sat around the room while Rev. Benson had a competition, Question Answering and Spelling Bees. The winners were given prizes of 'Eskimo' dolls. I was left out of the game as I was thought to be too young. My mother explained my sense of hurt to the kindly priest, who then brought home a peace offering of an 'Eskimo' doll for me too. There were Christmas parties for all the railway children and a Christmas tree laden with gifts of storybooks, sleeping dolls, tea sets, cricket balls, bats, mecanno sets, Hornby train sets. I recall a beautiful doll's pram, woven out of cerise-coloured reed, with a tiny doll in it – my very own gift.

My first remembered parties were in Kadugannawa, not only in the railway enclave but also at Royden, as well as in my own home. Royden, was Uncle Alroy and Gladys' house, while just beyond Royden, Paradise View was owned by Uncle Henry. Two houses that were not part of the Kadugannawa railway enclave but enveloped and embraced our presence with a gracious warmth and generous-hearted hospitality.

As a child I watched and observed from the outskirts of adult experience, but the elders knew that I heard things that I shouldn't hear and saw things that I wasn't supposed to see. "Walls have ears and potatoes have eyes," my mother would say, lowering her gaze when I circled about the elders as they chatted on the veranda or while I sat sprawled on my mother's lap. But I heard many things – that Sylvia's marriage was arranged by her father, old Mr Craighlaw to marry Bubsy Direckze, who in my eyes was a delightful jovial man, kind and gentle with us children. Railway society was too circumscribed for someone who was as beautifully enigmatic as herself. Bubsy, with his azure blue eyes and ruddy cheeks, lived on the hill with the pini jambu tree laden with fruit, which we were forbidden to eat. The Direckze children were young, still in rompers, but it was in the veranda of their house that those evenings would be spent, adults and children, doing the Lambeth Walk, the Palaise Glide and Boomps-a-daisy, bumping each others backs with great verve and vigour – especially Beryl Schofield. Beryl was vibrant with energy and high spirits, dancing, bending over the keys of the piano and 'playing' with her nose to amuse us with her syncopated music. She and Artie Schofield were childless. She had an affair, it was whispered, with the Englishman Jem Smith. We sang, we danced. The famous song "Any Umbrella," became popular, so that we would sing it at parties. We pronounced it as "um-be-rella," dragging out the syllables.

I heard "South of the Border" for the first time in the Jones' drawing room, while trains thundered down the lines to Colombo and the rhythmic shunting of engines on the turn-table filled our ears. It was on the veranda of the Jones' house that the minstrel shows were held with the young men all tricked out in black and white with red bow-ties and top-hats serenading us with "Shenandoah," "Old Folks at Home," "Swanee River" and "Polly Wolly Doodle," while we sat and listened to them singing, strumming banjos and mandolins and playing the mouth organ. There were many parties at our house too, especially at Christmastime.

Auntie Gladys' dinner parties at Royden were elaborately planned. Every evening Sylvia and Thelma played duets on the piano or strummed on their Hawaiian guitars. They sang sentimental romantic songs like "Harbour Lights," "When my Dreamboat Comes Home," the harmonizing of their voices, alto and soprano, blending so beautifully together. "Blue Hawaii," "On the Beach of Waikiki" were also songs they sang. Where did those places exist? Where were the South Seas? Where was Hawaii? Where were the girls with their leis of flowers and their grass skirts who swayed to the music? All of us knew how to do the hula-hula, those Hawaiian dances, swaying our hips and arms with delicate motion. We learned by watching Sylvia and Thelma. Tap-dancing too was part of the repertoire, the boys with their steel-tipped shoes so adept at it, dancing like Fred Astaire and Ginger Rogers. The windows of the drawing room opened out onto a garden with two jambu trees, where I had once stood when I was three years old and called out over and over again, "I can see Uncle Henny, Uncle Henny, Uncle Henny," as he walked up the road from his house at Paradise View. When Uncle Henry died I remember the permanent expression of grief on his widow's face. Their daughter Thelma, with her dimples and delicate cleft chin, was one of the most beautiful girls I had ever seen, with her satin smooth skin and almond-shaped eyes. She was a wonderful pianist too.

The Royden house was filled with comfortable cretonne-covered furniture, the dining room was decorated with blue willow-pattern wall plates. The garden behind the house was terraced, leading down to the paddy fields, which lay beside the railway lines. The terraces were steep, covered with flowers, forbidden to us to climb down lest we fall. Somewhere down there, hidden among the thickets of jak and breadfruit trees, was the house with its tiled roof where postmaster Rheimers and his wife and family lived.

At the Royden dinner parties we children were served our food early. We would sit, with our chairs carefully drawn up to the table, starched white serviettes tucked round our necks - those serviettes were always carefully arranged in this manner until we grew old enough to be careful not to spill our food down the front of our clothes, graduating to having them placed on our laps. We sat sedately at the beautifully arranged dining table with its damask cloth, snowy serviettes, gleaming silver cutlery and cut-glass tumblers. The water jug was always covered with a circle of tasseled net hung with tiny coloured beads. In the center of the table stood a glass bowl with flowers and ferns from Auntie Gladys' garden. What did we have for that formal dinner? We ate the same food as the adults were to have after their drinks, exchanging of yarns and singing of songs. Here was a moment encapsulated in time as we sat sedately, tilting our soup spoons half-filled with consommé delicately away from the soup plate without spilling a drop in its passage, inclining our heads ever so slightly as if to receive a benediction. Then a fish course followed, seer fish in a sauce of fish stock, tempered with Bombay onions in butter and thickened with flour; roast chicken - we always looked for the wishbone to make our innocent and impossible wishes – served with boiled potatoes, green peas (most probably the tinned variety from England), a salad of crisp green lettuce – from the Kandy market because I do not recollect lettuce at the Kadugannawa Sunday pola – sliced tomatoes with a delicate vinaigrette; and a dessert of caramel pudding or stewed fruit, apples, apricots, peaches or pears, with custard and a quivering red moss jelly. Yes, we children always ate first, wisely enough since it saved us from becoming querulous or falling asleep before the elders felt inclined to sit down to their meal.

Auntie Gladys was my adopted godmother. I wanted her to be so. She was all that I would find so difficult to become as I grew up. Gentle. Never volatile or hurtful in utterance. It was care and attention to our needs that I always associate with Auntie Gladys, together with her gentle ways, her comfortable body in its well-tailored clothes, court shoes and stockings. To me she never changed, never appeared even to grow old or fragile, her shingled hair smoothly brushed, every strand in place. She knew so much, how to make delicious homemade ginger beer in big earthenware crocks, fat plums, floating on the surface, impregnated with the sweet, gingery syrup, the ginger leaving the aftermath of its sting in our throats. It had that slightly fermented taste and was not fizzy like the bottled variety of aerated waters, and once it was chilled with chips of ice, it set the throat tingling. The ice used to be kept in those huge zinc and aluminum bathtubs, the ice blocks covered with gunnysacks and sawdust to keep from melting. Bottles of lemonade, ginger ale, kola and orange crush, with glass stoppers, were chilled in those tubs. Auntie Gladys also had a wooden ice-cream churner. The custard, a rich one with lots of yellow-yolk eggs and fresh milk, was stirred smoothly over the fire to prevent curdling, flavoured with vanilla and packed into the ice-cream churn, the metal container surrounded with ice and salt, and then the churning would begin with its metal crank. The ice cream was served with a red cherry placed on top, and a crisp wafer slipped in with which we would take tiny scoops of ice cream. Auntie Gladys' parties were memorable because so many things happened within the ambience of those rooms at Royden, in Kadugannawa and then later at Inbastan in Kandy, where we were close neighbours, with evening visits, Christmas visits, and once more, a repetition of those parties.

Auntie Gladys had a beautiful collection of party dresses for Sylvia too – yellow organdy with frills was one of them. We had party dresses of taffeta, organdy, silk for parties because we always dressed up for the occasion. Her parties were special, a kind of initiation into a special world, that spacious world of entertaining and being entertained. Was it a special characteristic of the Burghers? Who knows? We never questioned it at that time but accepted those long hours of sharing the happiness of being together, laughing at Noel's jokes about "Victoria the Dreat" – imagine talking about a queen who lived in an epoch that was so alien to us in that provincial society of Kadugannawa. We would get Noel to repeat "Victoria the Dreat" over and over again. The epithet 'Dreat' intrigued us. We were all unaware of the ironies inherent in that epithet – what were the differences between 'Great' and 'Dreat'? Linguistically, 'Great' signified grandeur to us children, it was a qualifier for very special personages, not for us ordinary mortals! Royalty had connotations almost of divinity. But, 'Dreat'? Was it an unconscious combination of 'dread' and 'great?

Music entered our psyches with the singing of Sylvia and Thelma and their piano duets. The metaphors of dreamboats, harbour lights, blue Hawaii and the beaches of Waikiki that would one day change and take on a new reality. We overheard conversations, intimate and otherwise, from that adult world of Burgher family members and friends. It was the physical location of those houses too that helped, situated in the environs of the railway station of Kadugannawa, each house within walking distance of each other, with people who shared things in common - the engine drivers, the district mechanical inspectors, the foreman platelayers, the guards, the stationmaster. It was an enclave dominated mainly by the Burghers, their social events taking place not only in each other's homes but also in the Railway Reading Room.

But there were the others too, not the Burghers alone, who were part of that enclave: Mr Manikam, Mr Amith, who were respectively Jaffna Tamil and Malay, and our Sinhalese friends, including Baby Uncle, who came from a very prominent Sinhala family in Kadugannawa and who married late in life. Then there were the Aluvihares. Mr Aluvihare had married an attractive Burgher lady. Dr Pethiyagoda and his family lived in the upstairs house beside the police station at the foot of Belungala. He had lovely daughters. There was another set of Pereiras too, the family of Dr Pereira with the old family house and tea estate on the hill behind it which belonged to them. It was on this tea estate that I used to wander alone or where the Trinity College scouts would come with Jock Young, their scoutmaster, on hikes. I had another friend too, Beatrice Weerasekera, and the Swans and Willigs family, all family friends.

There were also the Englishmen Mr Cowie, Jem Smith, and the Scots family of the Murdochs. And there were the people from the village who were a part of our lives, like Hurathala and Sekera, his son who would take us by train to our school in Kandy, a slim, gentle-faced young man with hair tied back in a knot (neither Hurathala nor Sekera cut their hair). Sekera had infinite patience with the rumbustious spirits of my sister Rosemary and myself. I remember myself as being very naughty, impeding peoples passage along the corridors of the train with my legs stretched out from the inner windows to the outer ledges, making the passengers beg to be allowed to pass, or leaning with our bodies half out of the windows, with the wind tearing our hair and cinders blowing into our eyes, almost blinding us, while Sekera pulled us back from falling on the lines.

A pretty young teacher, Laetitia Kotigala, travelled in the same train when we later started school in Kandy. She was teaching at Girls' High School: "I remember you as a quiet child who used to give me a shy, sweet smile. You were reading books all the time." So there were dual aspects to my personality even then. Getting off at the Kandy station Sekera would put us into rickshaws and send us off to the Girls' High School, where we were restrained in our classrooms until interval time when we formed small bands of girls with our arms entwined around each others waists, teasing the little boys with our ditties. We were girls, privileged, all sugar and spice, preening ourselves before them, our words the mimicry of another tongue. The mirrors of childhood did not reflect any distortions then. The grotesqueness would emerge later.

My brother Pat wrote to me from Melbourne, long, long afterwards:

"I was able to meet Noel and Sylvia and had a long chat with them. They remember the happy days we spent when we too lived in Kadugannawa and the holiday we spent with Uncle Alroy and Auntie Gladys when we moved to Kandy. They remember the evenings of dance and song at our place and the music and part-singing by Sylvia, Noel and Thelma, at Royden, with Thelma taking turns on the piano and guitar. They also remember many pleasant evenings at the Railway Recreation Club and the occasional parties and dancing there. And also the Christmas celebrations at the club with people like the Jones, Willigs, Craggs and Sylvie (nee Craighlaw) who was married to Bupsy Direcksze and left him for a soldier; the Schumarchers, Sonna Rosairo, and the Schofields of whom Beryl was delightful, roly-poly and sizzling with energy. They also remember a picnic we had at the Peradeniya Gardens and the fun we had at the old suspension bridge. They recollect dad's flute playing and Sylvia and Thelma who accompanied him with great pleasure. They all agreed that it is a really wonderful friendship we share and were most nostalgic about the days. We had even proceeded on a visit to

Pilimatalawa where the Alagalla road, on which Paradise View stands, leads to, and Sylvia remembers being woken up by the carters song and jingling bells of the bulls which pulled their carts laden with vegetables and coconut and firewood for sale at the fair. She says she used to look forward to hearing them."

"Gengivre" Bier

> 1/2 lb. roots of fresh ginger
> 2 lbs. sugar
> 10 bottles water
> 1 tumblerful sweet toddy
> 1 wineglassful bees' honey
> 1 lemon
> 1 nutmeg
> a bit of cinnamon and mace lemon or orange rind
> 2 eggs

Stir the sugar with a wooden spoon, throwing in the whites and the shells of the 2 eggs; add while stirring the 10 bottles of water, also the ginger well sliced, the nutmeg, cinnamon, and mace, all 3 crushed (but not ground) in a mortar, also the lemon or orange peel rings. Boil the whole for an hour, but do not stir the mixture. When taken off the fire, set it aside to cool and strain through some folds of muslin. After an hour or 2, when it is perfectly cool, add the toddy and the bees' honey (and a pinch of cream of tartar if desired). Last of all add the piece of lemon. Bottle in champagne bottles, and tie the cork down with twine.

Picnics

We would pile into those canvas-hooded cars with rubber horns that went *'pompa-pompa-poomp'* and head toward the Peradeniya Gardens with Uncle Alroy, Auntie Gladys, Noel, Sylvia, Thelma, and the Schofields. We carried wicker hampers of food and drink, lamprais wrapped in plantain leaves, sandwiches, biscuits, cakes and bottles of homemade ginger beer. Fords, Austins, sounding carnival trumpets as we drove, setting out on a sunny day from Kadugannawa. Ladies in linen and silk gowns, patent leather handbags, pearl clip-on earrings and necklaces, and the men in flannels and tussore white shirts with sleek pomades, perfumed green vaseline and , white Brylcream, sleeking down their well-trimmed hair.

The sunlight bathed the Gardens. Was this Xanadu or Tartary? We sought out our favourite summer house, the sugar-white-plastered domed one set like some marvelous confection among the green lawns. Reminding me of heavily iced, tiered cakes sculptured in sugar with twining garlands and silver beads displayed in the glass showcases of shops; rich cakes filled with plums and sultanas within, covered with the shimmering white glacé icing on the outside. The gramophone had been brought along too and the strains of familiar melodies filled the summer house. Looking back, my mind becomes filled with the pictures from Kodak cameras that captured those fleeting moments of joy, of pleasure in our lives.

Running wild on the grassy expanses, we clambered up the looping tangled roots of the Banyan tree, swinging on low overhanging branches. Searching for seeds strewn among the fallen fruit. The smooth lacquer red-black of maditchi, the speckled wild rubber, the coral-coloured sapu. And lovi-lovi, sour on the tongue, dark purply crimson, which the gardeners brought us. The lovi-lovi fruits were large as the plums that Joy Salvage, my English playmate, shared with me.

Then there was the Suspension Bridge that drew us again and again to the swift flowing river.

Those picnics were our idylls where adults and children sought out those gardens and grassy lawns. Was it all a dream? The summer house on the riverbank, the impenetrable wall of towering green bamboo overhanging the swirling waters? I had to join the daredevils on the bridge. Not all of us could cross at the same time. It was old, dangerous and shaky, with missing slats, built in the nineteenth century by the British. There were the reckless ones who ventured out first, walking in a gingerly fashion, taking those initial cautious steps. I was tempted to follow them. "We promise, we promise we won't shake the bridge when we get to the middle... come follow us. Do you want us to hold you by your hand...?" No, I wanted to step out on my own, peer down at the river through the missing wooden slats, watching the currents and the driftwood being swept along. One missed step and I would go plummeting down. I remember my mother's words: "The Mahaweli has shifting sands. You feel you are stepping into the riverbed but the sand will give, layer after layer, and you will vanish from sight..., or be sucked into a whirlpool..."

My footsteps were at first tentative, and then I began to increase my speed. The older ones were standing in the centre stamping on the slats, the bridge swinging and swaying violently... "Careful, careful," voices called from the summer house. I slipped. My foot got caught between the missing slats. I felt myself losing my balance, soon I would slip through, one foot dangling already. The whole world was caught up in that violent turmoil… I stretched out a hand, grasped one of the wooden handrails… "Hold on, hold on," someone cried. I felt a violent wrench as someone grasped my body and pulled me up. "Let me cross over, let me cross," I cried out, "I am not afraid now…" That was my first crossing and the danger was exhilarating; fear, an emotion that was necessary to face the challenges of survival.

As we were piling back into the cars to go back to Kadugannawa, someone's voice called out: "Let's go and have pot-luck at Royden tonight." The shutter clicked in my mind, the snapshot was captured in that moment of time for ever.

Nilame

My father often led us off the beaten track to take us along unfamiliar pathways in the hills surrounding Kadugannawa. This was the way we made incursions into the rubber plantation in Balane, which we glimpsed passing through by train on the way to Colombo and back again to Kandy. The winding path began from the verge of the rail tracks and then vanished into the darkness of closely growing trees. This was the way to the home of my father's friend, Wickrema Bandara whom we addressed as 'Nilame.' He had come into my father's life with the trains stopping at the station. It was there that Wickrema Bandara's gunnysacks filled with the produce of his plantations were loaded into the 'goods wagons.' The two men became close friends, a friendship which was to last for years. Although observing that adult world from the fringes of my own childhood, I too became part of it. Wickrema Bandara understood the silence of the unuttered word, the unuttered thought. He would bring his offerings time and time again, the sacks of mangosteens from the laden trees during each season of fruiting.

Wickrema Bandara. A big-built man with glistening cheeks, black drooping moustaches and a sadly sweet smile which gave his face an expression of both happiness and melancholy. He oversaw many hundreds of acres of rubber and coconut in Balane. He must have possessed power and authority. His sons followed him whenever he came home with the mangosteens, hundreds of them, and stood silently in their father's presence while he sat regally on a chair. They deferred to him and remained in the background while he spoke. He had an air of great dignity. His hair black and sleek with coconut oil, was combed smoothly away from his forehead and tied in a small top-knot. A fine ornamental comb of amber-coloured tortoiseshell speckled with brown sat like a crescent curving round the knot of hair. On his visits home he wore a black coat of some thick material, tailored in the European style, together with a checkered silk sarong tied high up his waist, falling in folds over his ample girth and held up by a broad leather belt with a silver buckle. The villagers who accompanied him carried the heavy sacks of mangosteens, and we could hardly wait to taste the fruit, crushing them between our palms, picking out the white segments so honey sweet, prising them out of their maroon-purple shells like smooth pearls.

On every visit he made, we would ask, "Has Nilame brought us mangosteens this time too?" Yes, he had, if they were in season. Their fragrance reached us from the sacks in the storeroom.

"Now you must come to my home," he said, and one day we all went by train with special compartments reserved for just ourselves by my father. We leant out of the windows, tiny cinders from the engine flying into our eyes, which my father carefully cleaned in a very special way he had, with a slight twisting and gentle rotating movement of the eyelid over the eyeball, cleansing out the irritant with our own tears.

Nilame was waiting for us on the platform when we alighted at Balane station. He was beaming and beaming at us, his firm round cheeks almost bursting with smiles. I hoped that the mangosteen trees would be covered with fruit, but my father told me that it wasn't the season. My father greeted the stationmaster in his white starched twill uniform, with the bright brass buttons adorning the front of his coat, his white solar topi perched on his head.

We walked through the pathway leading to the estate. The air was cold, clear. Huge outcrops of rock jutted out over the rubber trees, the great weight of the massive rocks pressing down on the silent air. There was a faint sound of flowing water from behind the thickly growing trees. Streams of silvery water trickled down the glistening surfaces of the thickly piled rocks. Moist ferns clustered freshly green on the banks. The banks were covered with the dark leaves of breadfruit and plantain trees. The terraced paddy fields led gently down into the valley in green steps, patterned in neat diamond shapes, dotted here and there with houses and temples. Ranges of hills rose from the other side of the valley, thickly forested, wilderness teeming with game, deer, wild boar, leopards.

We walked through the rows of rubber trees until we came to Nilame's house. We went to the kitchen to meet Menike, his wife. She was supervising the cooking and also helping the others. One of the women was scraping coconuts on the hiramane; the other women, relations and friends from the village smiled at us as they looked up from their work. The kitchen was large, with wood fires roaring on the hearth; smoke-blackened walls, piles of firewood, and the womenfolk smiling and pleasant, busy at their work. Wickrema Bandara hovered about with his pleased look and his sweetly sad smile, the firelight gleaming on his tortoiseshell comb. The women continued with their work, winnowing rice in woven wheat-coloured kullas, the milky brown kernels rising in a sheet of brown mist, out of the woven sieve. Some of them were cleaning jak fruit, rubbing coconut oil onto their fingers to remove the sticky, milky koholla. The others were washing fish, cutting fresh gotukola leaves and polos, tender jak fruit, for mallun. The black clay chatties simmered on the hearth.

We explored room after room in the old walauwa and climbed up to the attuwa where the rice was stored. We climbed up the steep ladder timorously. It was dark and musty, smelling of stored paddy and ripening fruit.

In the whitewashed room below, long tables were laid with white cloths. Dishes of food covered each table from one end to the other. They were innumerable: brightly coloured palangans piled with ambulas, curried fish, malluns, sambols and hot rice with saucers stacked into the steaming piles. I felt as if my cheek was pressed against Menike's breast, fragrant like a new harvest. There was a pink glow within the heart of the polos ambula, segment after segment falling apart as it crumbled in our fingers. There was alakola ambula, katurumurunga flower badun, jak cooked in coconut milk, fish red with chillies and sharp with goraka and tamarind, salty and pungent dried fish, spicy yet delicate aromas rising in a steam from the brightly coloured plates from Staffordshire.

Nilame was the perfect host. All his kith and kin from the village were gathered there to make us happy. Once the food was prepared and served us, the womenfolk retired into the background, wordlessly, expecting no thanks, no reward. Nilame smiled and smiled proudly at the laden table, pleased that his guests were partaking of his bounty. His round dark cheeks glistened with a proud happiness and he moved with dignity, radiating a spirit of goodwill, smiling his kindly and gracious smile. We ate rice from his fields and fruits from his orchards, as he piled food again and again on our plates.

After lunch the whole group of us gathered together in the meda-midula for entertainment. The gentlemen of the party had all been well primed with arrack. My father, who was always the center of attraction, sat in state over the gathering, while Nilame cavorted about the courtyard unsteadily like a great big strutting peacock. To every outrageous innuendo of my father's suggestion to his friend, Nilame would reply, swaying with bigness and geniality, smiles wreathing his face:

"Can do. Can do."

"Nilame, sing us a song, a song from you, Nilame," we called out.

"Can do. Can do." But beyond one slightly high-pitched wavering note, Nilame proceeded no further.

"Nilame," my father said, "then shall I sing?"

"Can do, Mahatmaya, can do." My father began to sing one of his favourite Scottish songs, "Annie Laurie," in his powerful, vibrant bass.

Although we never went back, 'Can Do' Nilame always remained our friend. Even after we had left Kadugannawa, Nilame would come all the way to Kandy every month to visit us. He always brought with him bags of mangosteens during the season, carried by one of his men. He would sit on the verandah, his big stomach jutting out, his smile growing slightly more weary and sad with the years.

One day he came sick and exhausted, leaning on a stick and supported by his sons, on his way to hospital, dying of diabetes, with carbuncles that would not heal. His face was drawn - instead of his sadly sweet smile he wore a grimace of pain. His lips had a wry twist. His body had shrunk, and the black coat hung loosely on his gaunt frame. My heart felt heavy with sadness, but I could say nothing. There were worlds between us, a sick and ageing man and a lonely almost inarticulate child.

I could only ask my father, "When will Can Do Nilame return?"

My father was silent. We never saw Nilame again. His sons were not like him. For some time they brought us mangosteens, and then we lost touch with them.

I still pass the estate on my way to Colombo. I have to look carefully out of the windows in case I miss it. The rubber trees still stand. The unchanging pathway, which can never lead me to where I want to return still remains, and if I ever were to go back, I am certain I would never find those whom I have known, lost for ever with time, together with that childhood.

Only their memory remains. Will always remain.

Zondare

One evening at one of the socials held in the Railway Reading Room, the young priest, Reverend Amarasekera, was called upon not to deliver a sermon but to entertain us. He was just back from theological studies in England and had taken over the duties of the Anglican parish in Kadugannawa. I hung on his every word as he stood before us in his surplice and black sash.

"And now Zondare, my performing flea, will entertain you," he pronounced in his very anglicized accent.

Reverend Amarasekera slowly released his bunched fist. "Zondare has accompanied me all the way from England." The priest peered into his cupped palm.

"Zondare, no more cold winters for us, eh? Plenty of sunshine. You'll thrive here and grow sleek and glossy. Now, Zondare, I want you to show your skills and amuse all these charming people as you did in England. No, no, don't get restless. It's not sermons you will have to hear. You've been cloistered long enough. I'll give you some moments of freedom to range the air."

Where had Zondare been all this while, I wondered. Was he hidden in the folds of the surplice or in the lining of that broad black sash? How had this tiny speck of life travelled over the seas for months on end? And what a strange, foreign-sounding name he had. Zondare. Was Zondare from a circus? Was he rescued from there? Had been imprisoned by the Grand Master of the circus?

"A performing flea," my mother whispered. "Watch its antics."

How lonely the young theological student must have been in the closed rooms of his lodgings with Zondare, the secret companion of his hours of solitude. It seemed he even rehearsed his sermons for Zondare's ears. I felt sad for Zondare. With that strange-sounding name he would be a stranger here, as he had been in England.

"Where did Zondare first come from?" I whispered back to my mother.

"Spain, Italy, Greece. Who knows? One of those Mediterranean lands or perhaps from Arabia."

Reverend Amarasekera now opened his palms wide. He lifted his arm, spread out his fingers and began issuing his commands.

"Zondare," he said, pointing towards his left, then to his right, "Go there, and there, and there."

Next, the orders to return to base. "Zondare, come here, and here, and here,"

Control. Power. Authority. Obedience. Zondare's freedom to explore the air was regulated by that gesturing finger. How did Zondare spend the rest of its time? Creep back into some dark niche in that fabled world of fleas? Feed on what? How was Zondare nourished? Was it on the food of the imagination?

Could I capture that flea in my palm? I would take it out and release it. No more orders. No more commands.

The voice kept echoing and re-echoing in my ears. Everything was still outside. No sound of trains or shunting engines obtruded. Only the vibration of crickets and night insects whirred in the sunflower hedges behind the Reading Room. The rubber estate on the hill was wrapped in darkness. The English planter must be smoking his pipe, reading, sipping his whiskey, or preparing to dine. His world so separate, so isolated. Dawson's Tower stood, a silent monument to the spirits of those long-dead road builders.

Zondare. A name made immortal, extending beyond time, to be retained in memory. But why immortality? Because Zondare was more than a flea, a speck of life generated out of the deepest recesses in the psyche of humankind where illusion, maya, became the embodiment of a greater reality. And to Zondare, to the child, what may not be visibly apparent, does exist and have shape and form, for such is the transforming power of the imagination. And it is within us all, to overcome the aloneness of the individual being, to create the 'Other' who will fill that void within ourselves, with whom we can have our most intimate sharings of thought and conversation. But there are inherent dangers too in such a relationship, for one exercises control over the creature generated out of our minds and imaginations.

"Zondare, go there and there and there."

"Zondare come here and here and here."

It is the language of authority, of command. 'There' and 'here' are deictically located in place and time. Where then is there freedom to move out and make the solitary and hazardous journey in a different country?

Zondare has earned immortality. Only the name changes. We are the creators of each of those alter egos contained in Zondare.

We create our imaginary companions, even those invisible beings, to fill the void of loneliness. There are inherent dangers in such relationships. We have the power of life and death over those creatures we ourselves have generated. in our minds and imaginations. They disappear, vanish into thin air, and we are left alone once again.

Shorn of My Locks

The barber came up the hill to cut my hair. He worked in the Barbers' Salon in the township, a salon with swinging half-doors of coloured glass. Rows of men sat before the mirrored walls, swathed in white sheets, the atmosphere heavy with an overwhelming fragrance of talcum powder liberally sprinkled over the freshly shaved faces and necks denuded of hair, with sheared-off tufts and clumps lying about their feet. A thick lather of Vinolia Shaving Cream-was scraped off with lethal-looking razor blades.

The little barber with the squint was summoned by my mother to shear the sacrificial lamb that was myself. His clothes were spotless white, laundered to perfection, crisply starched and immaculate. His face was clean-shaven and daubed with white talc, heavily perfumed. My ordeal was about to begin. The Victorian high-chair was placed in a corner of the veranda and I was lifted onto it. A white bed sheet was draped about my shoulders and tucked in at the nape of my neck. My mother would not allow the barber to use his scissors but gave him her own sewing scissors. The click, click of scissors skilfully manipulated by him sounded sharp and grating at my ears. My mother wanted him to pay special attention to the 'ducks' tail at the nape of my neck, while he took it upon himself to trim imaginary sideburns. The scissors nicked the edges of my ears and neck, drawing blood, the grazes to be dabbed with iodine-soaked cotton wool later on. He used a strange miniature mouth-organ-like contraption to scrape off the soft, downy hair that lay close to my ears, tickling the nape of my neck as he applied the buzzing machine up and down, creating goose-flesh. The stubby hair tickled my tender skin, prickling like porcupine quills. My hair, thick, smooth, a sleek cap was invariably cut in an Eton crop or with a fringe of smooth tassels. When it grew unruly and shaggy, falling over my eyes, my mother would decide that the time had come for a close crop. The entire ritual was abominable to me. The icy touch of the steel scissors, the drawing of blood from the swift nicks, the sharp prickle of blunt hairs, the shower of talc choking and suffocating me made me want to escape from the barber's trap. The serrated teeth of the shears bit into my cheeks, and the shorn locks piled round the legs of the chair made me feel I had lost a warm and protective covering.

My mother was insistent. "Your fringe is too long. It's falling over your eyes. You'll become squint-eyed if it's not cut soon."

The barber would not let me out of his clutches easily. "Sit, still, bebi, or you'll get your ears cut off," he threatened. My cheeks felt raw, stinging and sore.

"Stop, stop," I said. "I don't want you to touch my cheeks any more." Little drops of blood appeared on the white sheet. I felt my body violated. His touch intrusive. Hateful.

He would not stop until he had denuded me of most of my hair. And the most agonizing, humiliating moment was when he began to stroke and caress my body, a child's body. Feeling its tiny bud-like nipples, beneath the white sheet that was now forever sullied for me. I flung off the sheet, scrambled off the chair, my face all red and hot, shedding trails of talcum powder like confetti about me, the stubby hair pricking the raw flesh, and shut him out of my life forever.

I told my mother everything, using words I was just beginning to discover. The barber was never brought home again. My hair began to grow thick and smooth again, and my mother cut my straight fringes herself.

A Memory – Early Childhood

I stood holding onto my mother's hand beside the railway tracks in front of the bungalow occupied by the Muller family. I watched curiously as my father together with Vernon Muller and other railway stalwarts carried Beryl Muller seated on a chair, holding firmly onto its arms, across the railway tracks from their house to reach the hiring car parked on the main Colombo-Kandy road. There was no way she could walk across the tracks as she had probably got her labour pains and had to be taken to the Nursing Home in Kandy. Vernon Muller's railway friends had risen to the occasion. At that time I didn't know what it was all about but most probably later on I did question my mother who explained to me what was happening and what would subsequently take place.

Many years later I met Carl Muller, the eminent writer and he told me that he was the baby who was about to be born. That encounter was to take place in Kandy where we both now live and write. Burgher left-behinders. Carl and I were the only Burgher writers to emerge from that railway enclave in Kadugannawa. The houses we lived in still remain, the Muller house beside the railway tracks and the Solomons' house on the hill overlooking the township. Carl and I are the living memorials.

V

COLONIZER/COLONIZED

Star Fort, Matara, where Captain Francois Grenier was in Command of a Regiment, 18th century.

Martial Routes

I am reading the history of the Castle Keep
The history of a different lineage
As if I have no history of my own
But I do have several histories, taken on those
Of my ancestors too, although they did not have
To take on mine.

Histories compounded of fact, conjecture, musings
On ancestor stratagems and machinations
Nothing new in the politics of unchanging eras,
The plots, the conspiracies are all unearthed
Motives analysed, those imperial facades
Torn down to reveal the workhouse behind
The palace, the pallid faces of children
Creeping through labyrinths and tunnels.

What a small map my life reveals
Crammed with all kinds of landmarks,
Sea-routes, land routes, constellation guides
To lead me through labyrinths and tunnels.

The ancestor maps were large with great
Unnamed spaces of oceans and landmasses,
Islands and bays where those navigators sighted
Safe havens for themselves, their ships, resting
With towering masts and sails, weather beaten,
Flapping out like brine-crusted wings of the
Ancient albatross with curious emblems branded
On those feathers.

Reaching shores that soon became blood-caked
Where those men, history calls them explorers, discoverers,
Conquistadors, laid their brutal whips scourging
The flesh, their machetes severing the vines
From the tree branches, savaging the jungles.

Now, looking out on Como and Lecco
Birds and sails became one in my mind
Piling up like burnished feathers reflected
In the Alpine sunset floating on the rippling
Lakes, while I am here, stationary, in this villa,
On the lookout for hostile invasions ending in ship wreck.
Muse on those townships and cities my ancestors
Came from, I will not recognize the tongues
They spoke in or used for trade and barter
To carry out the daily commerce of their lives,
Those coins have no purchase value for me,
I cannot claim kinship with strangers nor can
I understand their speech, those unrecognizable
Dialects, the flavour of their food unfamiliar,
The wine raw and rasping emptied from wooden
Casques and leathern pouches.

Didn't they have enough of bloodshed,
Plunging swords into flesh, firing loaded
Muskets and flint-locks into the jungles,
Caught in ambush when the rough boulders
Came crashing down, huge tree trunks laid
Across their paths, not even the swollen rivers,
The starving leeches or the thorn gates
Could keep the invader out.

Now, those bones sing dirges in the pelting rain,
Looking down from my balconies on the Italian
Gardeners wielding their long rush-tufted broomsticks

I think about the complexions of my ancestors'
Cheeks like ruddy apples on the fruit platter
At the breakfast table, those men, strangers, who
When they came to that island let their beards
Grow long, their whiskers, untrimmed swinging against
The cheeks like hairy brushes
Brows wrinkled like parched cirtrus fruits
In the sun...

Fortresses, maps, martial routes,
Their fingers traced conquest paths through
Terrain unexplored on those first forays
Led by secret scouts hacking the way through.

Wasn't it enough, the continents they lived in,
The lakes, the mountains, the wheat fields and
Vineyards or was it famine, drought, wars that made
Of their migrations, conquest.
"So many children, so many sons," explains
my Australian friend Barbara Hocking her tones
matter of fact, realistic.

History adopts the soldiers of fortune,
Names the conquerors,
Their progeny fills the new territories
Changing the landscapes,
The odour, the texture
Of their skin, growing ruddy tanned with copper,
Brought with them new plants,
Fruits, built different structures, filled vast
Gardens with new seed proliferating century
After century branches spreading with newly
Grafted fruits, flowers, leaves invading the territory
Where the earth was still rich, fertile, not time depleted.

Colonial Connections

Who then was that Colonel who had mapped out his territory in that once, unsubjugated Kandyan Kingdom? His existence possessed an historical credibility if not justification. His ancestor who fought in the Seven Years War in 1759 was yet another military officer, yet another Colonel Piachaud. Brother officer in the same regiment as Jean Francois Grenier, my mother's French ancestor. Unlike my mother's great-great-grandfather, however, who had fathered one son and sailed away across the Bay of Bengal never to be seen or heard of again, Colonel Piachaud had served in a regiment of the mercenary army of Colonel de Meuron, one that had fought first on the side of the Dutch and after that capitulation and surrender, on the side of the British. The transfer order was sent in a ball of Dutch cheese of which there must have been a limited stock in Madras. The thick red rind would have protected the document from mildew and briny sea spray. An ingenious ploy among the secret-service agents of the seventeenth century. And what of the Dutch cheese? The British officers of the de Meuron regiment must have consumed it together with the Dutch ethos, the roast country capons and Rhenish wines brought in by their East Indiamen.

Marriage alliances between the Greniers and the Piachauds proliferated throughout the nineteenth century. As for their offspring and the generations to come, there were genealogical tables and records well into the twentieth century. The remaining descendants however, were scattered over the face of the earth, living in different parts of the globe, even Malaya, but they migrated mainly to England, and later, the Grenier Janszs, to both settle down in England and Australia. There did not appear to be any need for those recorded histories, documented to establish links and connections in the exile of death and migration. To whom did it matter any longer that champagne flowed at the wedding of one of the Piachauds and that the bride wore a gown of satin with a long train or that the bridegroom was a famous Cambridge cricketer? What did it matter that the descendants of those two soldiers of fortune should have given birth to officials and dignitaries in the British colonial government, becoming Puisne Judges, Anglican priests, teachers and principals, accountants in the General Treasury, attorney-generals, civil servants seeming to have shed whatever warlike antecedents their ancestors possessed?

After the time of the deaths of James Eugene and Lilian Violet, changes began to appear. Katukellewatte had later been named "Piachaud Gardens." The Colonel had had his own carriage road leading up to the "The Retreat." It was so private a road that even my uncle Hugh Grenier Jansz was not allowed to use it when he built "Friedenham" on my grandfather Jansz's land. So a part of Sunnyside Gardens' land had to provide access to the house (a road which now everybody traverses, with the Lighthouse Church at the end of that road where Friedenham once stood).

My uncle and aunts, all unmarried, lived close by at Sunnyside Gardens. When I grew up, my sister and I were taken on visits where we played among my uncle's flowerbeds. He was a florist and his garden was filled with roses imported from Holland, blue – mauve – pink clusters of hydrangeas, carnations of dark crimson and deep rose, pink-streaked with red, gladioli, dark green ferns. There was a biling tree laden with pale green, translucent, thin-skinned fruit, so sharply-tart it stung the tongue. Biling, mulberries, and China guavas we gorged on. We were like wild birds fluttering in the garden.

By the time I had come to live at Sunnyside, the carriage road was no longer private. The Bhishanaya, the radical movement (of the JVP, Jathika Vimukthi Peramuna) which had begun in 1989 gathered momentum by the early nineties. There was death in the air. Gunshots echoed through the township at night. And on Colonel Piachaud's road, two bodies, splattered with blood from gunshot wounds, and with hands tied behind their backs, blindfolded, were dumped into the drain beside the road and left there, exposed for the whole populace to view until the hearse drove up and bore them off to an oblivion from which they had come. "The Retreat" was sold off. Once it had been a place of refuge for mothers and their babies born out of wedlock. There were other changes too..., but the house still stands, its boundaries marked out, its shrunken garden fenced in.

Living with the Colonials

The Ceylonese railway families and the British mingled freely in Kadugannawa. We were in and out of each other's homes. A special enclave was formed by the railway bungalows and I now often wonder who designed their architecture, which was distinctive in style and resembled almost all the other railway bungalows in the island. In Kadugannawa the bungalows were either perched on hills or stood at the edge of the railway tracks on the line that led from Kandy to Colombo. An important stopover was Kadugannawa. The entire railway complex formed a clear-cut pattern in my mind from the very beginning when my childhood impressions were being formed. The Signal Cabin, the coloured signals, the platform islanded among the lines on either side; the huge tunnel-like building where the steam engine was kept beside the turntable; the Foreman Platelayer's (or FPL's) bungalow looking out upon the station, the houses of the engine drivers, the guards. And for recreation, the Railway Reading Room was an oasis with its tennis courts and swing for the children. The colonial empire and its network of roads and railways were responsible for this pocket of heterogeneous people who lived and worked together, formed friendships out of their shared interests in the passage of those innumerable journeys to places near and distant. The railway warrants took us everywhere, to any corner of the island we wished, and we were able to enjoy the privileges of first-class compartments and sleeping berths for long journeys. My father had earned us those privileges.

I wonder what those colonial families felt about their circumscribed lives in the little township of Kadugannawa? In

England, in Scotland, where would they have belonged? Where would they have lived? What would have been the manner of their lifestyles? There were bachelors among the colonials, as well as the "married bachelors" as my father called them. There were also families where the wives and children had accompanied their menfolk to the island. There existed a relationship of equality between our family and those of the Salvages and the Murdochs, where we children played with each other, where the mothers visited each other. I was curious about those people, looking out for the differences in their ways of doing things. As for the men, Jem Smith became a special person in our lives, spending most of his time with the Burgher families, while Mr Cowie, our next-door neighbour at one time, was quiet and reserved.

The Salvages lived across the railway lines which separated our home on the hill from theirs which was closer to the platform. Mr Salvage was the Foreman Platelayer before Jem Smith took over. From a rocky ledge that jutted out from a part of the hill overlooking the station, I would call out my messages, summoning my friends to play. Ray Salvage, tall and willowy, was the eldest daughter. Her sister Joy was our playmate and companion. One day when I was recovering from some childhood illness that kept me from school, she visited me with fresh plums, English plums. We ate them beneath the thumbergia bower beside the grenadilla creeper, talking of childish things as the juice dripped down our chins. How strange it seems now to think of it, eating plums and apples in a tropical garden, plums that were fresh, ripe, purply dark and crimson-skinned. For Joy it was the taste of home, which was so far away but where interrupting our childish pastimes, eventually she would go back to grow up in.

We exchanged visits very often. The colonials too lived in railway houses like ours. Only the FPL's house was set perhaps hierarchically apart. All the houses had sloping, tiled roofs, white-washed walls lined with a narrow edge of black tar at the bottom to keep out the termites, barred windows, with the kitchen and outhouses a separate entity. Skylights were set in the roofs to let the sunlight and moonlight filter through. There were no ceilings. The rat snakes could sometimes be seen coiling round the rafters as they slithered among the tiles in pursuit of their prey. Our veranda had half-walls, with green bamboo tats that were rolled up and tied with rope during the day, and untied from their tether and let down at dusk.

The Barries lived next door. Mr Barrie, a Scotsman, was married to a Sinhalese lady, who wore long gathered skirts and full-sleeved cotton jackets. She bore him many children; and the grown-up daughters, who were much older than my sister and myself, would often stand at the hedge to talk to my mother.

After Mr Barrie was transferred to another station, Mr Cowie, to us a lonely bachelor, took up his abode there. To look after his needs he had a cook, one of the retinue that had emigrated from South India. The cook was lonely too and fell in love with our maid, Mary. Nothing escaped my eye, and I would see Mary beneath the domba tree (Calophyllum irophyllum) talking to him while my mother was taking her afternoon siesta. Mary and I would pick up the domba seeds for extracting the oil. It could be used for lighting lamps, but she would also pound the seeds, tie them up in a small bundle, which she would use to steam and foment an aching joint.

One day Mary eloped with Mr Cowie's cook. My mother was sad. "He's a married man. I hope he won't abandon Mary," she said. Mary came from a very respectable family in Alagalla where her family owned hereditary land. Mary, beautiful, gentle Mary vanished from our lives. Would I ever see her again? She returned to us briefly when my father had been transferred to Anuradhapura. Mr. Cowie's cook had deserted her and gone back to India. She went back to her village and we never saw the lovely, gentle Mary again.

Mr Murdoch was a close friend of my father. One evening my father took us to visit the Murdochs. I watched Mrs Murdoch preparing to give her daughter Heather an evening wash before bedtime. A basin was filled with hot water and Mrs Murdoch took a piece of flannel, dipped it in the hot water, soaped it and scrubbed Heather's limbs. After Heather was well scrubbed, the flannel was wrung out and then used to remove the lather.

I watched this gravely.

"My mother washes me in a different way," I told her.

"How does she do it then?" Mrs Murdoch asked in an amused manner.

"She fills a big tub with hot water, and I get into it. I sit in the tub and am bathed in it with lots and lots of hot water, and then I'm wrapped in a big towel and wiped dry." Yes, then the censor was lit with live coals and incense sprinkled on it. It was taken into every nook and cranny of the bedrooms. The fragrance of incense permeated the walls. Gold, frankincense and myrrh – the gifts of the magi.

If we climbed the hill facing the railway station, we could see Jem Smith's house. When we knew him, he must have been in his late thirties or early forties. To me he appeared to be very tall, with long supple limbs and brilliant brown eyes. He had brown hair with flecks of gold and a slight, reddish-hued moustache.

Jem was a Foreman Platelayer in the railways during the British Raj. Even today, so many years later a pang of sadness goes through me when I think of Jem – his kindliness and his own need for love, being separated from his wife and son who were far from him in England. In those days it was a long sea journey to and from Ceylon in those great cruisers or 'Liners' as we called them. He was lonely. We felt it. Was it sadness, regret, longing? No, those emotions were not as yet perfectly understood by us children, but a certain query lay in our glances when he showed us photographs, snapshots, of his wife and son. They belonged to that era of the early forties, the years of the Second World War.

The black-and-white snapshot of his wife has always remained in my mind: a portrait of an Englishwoman of that era, a woman with her hair rolled up in the fashion of those times, resting on the nape of her neck, upswept and puffed at the forehead, wearing a twin set and skirt – a blonde-haired woman. Mrs Murdoch and Mrs Salvage both lived out here, but Jem Smith's wife never ever visited him. He missed his son. He lived alone with his servants, like many of the colonials of that time. My sister and I would play with the black and white Scotties that came with the bottles of Black and White Whiskey which my father and Jem drank.

I used to watch my father's friends from my mother's lap as they sat round the jakwood dining table pouring out their drinks and yarning away. Never to be forgotten, those faces, those bodies, recollected through the diffused light of time which half obscures their figures, that now seem half-human, half-phantom.

The Walk

There was a rubber estate behind the Foreman Platelayer's bungalow, a mysterious world which none of us had entered. The English planter who ran the estate lived in a bungalow hidden in the very depths of the rubber trees. We had never seen him. His world did not belong to the world of the railway people.

One evening when we were visiting the FPL's house, Mrs Swan suggested that we should go for a walk through the estate. It was peaceful there and perhaps she was curious about the place herself. Moreover, she was confident that we would be accepted by anyone, anywhere we went. Trespassing, territory, boundaries had not limited us so far. It was unthought of that we should not be welcome, even by the unknown planter.

"My father says that the old English planter doesn't like anyone to come there," I said. "He is supposed to be a very stern man, and the villagers who live on his land are mortally scared of him. What if he's there?"

"No, child, he won't be. I saw his car leaving the estate a while ago."

"Let's go then. There are lots of China guava trees there and I would like to see the old deep well that's there."

"We'll have to be careful. There are lots of leeches too," Mrs Swan said.

We didn't know the planter's name. We didn't know his age. We had never even seen him, although the provincial township we lived in was small and in its close society everybody knew the other, visiting and socializing with friends and neighbours in their homes. Even today, years afterwards I remember who lived in each of the houses clustering on the hills or by the railway lines. Everybody was so friendly and helpful to each other – but the planter was a solitary man. He mixed with no one and lived isolated on his estate enclosed within the darkness of the rubber trees. He had no friends and spoke to no one, burning and withering away in the tropical sun. The trees bled their milk for him, dripping into little coconut shell cups. The Englishman's anonymity was preserved by the villagers, who were afraid of him, and by the Indian labourers who were themselves also exiles. Only the shriek and wail of the sulphur spraying machine borne by phantom-like figures garbed in white, told us that there was some life on the estate. The machine was a thing of gleaming brass moving like a great lethal predator through the trees. Yet there must have been myriads of birds that still nested on the branches although we could not hear their songs. Flowers bloomed in the little gardens of the villagers, and China guavas and pini jumbus hung from the branches. Leeches crawled and inched their way, curving in brown arcs from grass blade to grass blade, waiting to fasten on some living thing to feast on its blood and leave behind a festering sore. They gorged and gorged on blood once they had fastened their suckers in the flesh. Blood was drawn just as the milk from the rubber trees. The leeches seemed to be stalking us invisibly as we walked along the gloomy drive, the silent villagers watching us. My sister and I clung onto Mrs Swan's hands. The darkness, the gloom from the rubber trees began to oppress us, but the China guava trees were laden with fruit that glowed like red lanterns. Pini jumbus, rosily pink, hung in clusters.

The village folk stood in their small compounds, the women carrying their naked babies on their hips, the young children standing still and quiet, clinging to the folds of their clothes. The young men, bare bodied, were resting after work, while the old, old ones with their soft white hair gathered into a knot, coughed and cleared their throats, covering their bodies with shawls against the cold and mist that was beginning to creep in. The shadows of the rubber trees fell like long swords on the earth. The grass was wet with dew. Beneath the undergrowth the sharp moist green blades squirmed with the moving, writhing mass of leeches. In the coconut shell cups the milk was thick, viscous. The guava trees were old, gnarled; ripe fruit hung in shades of orange, red, yellow. Yet, not a fruit had been touched. They fell and rotted in the grass.

"Please pick us some fruit," Mrs Swan told one of the young boys.

"Apoi, nona, we cannot, that we cannot do. What if the sudu mahathmaya (white gentleman) comes suddenly? We are not allowed to pluck these fruits. He will not like to see you all here. No outsider is allowed to come to this estate."

"Pick us just a few. No one eats the fruit. See, how many have fallen on the ground."

They lay blackening in the grass, hard and shrivelled. Rotting among the fallen leaves. Split. Crushed underfoot.

Mrs Swan turned to us: "What is there to be afraid? He won't mind. Uncle Swan is a friend of his. They know each other well."

I said: "But, Auntie, he doesn't know you. Shall we go back? It's his estate. He doesn't like any strangers, outsiders, coming here. Look, these people seem to be so afraid of him."

But by this time one of the old villagers had turned to a young man and said: "Banda, quickly climb onto that tree and pluck some fruit. We'll stand below and warn you if the mahathmaya comes."

Everybody was silent. Through the creeping mist I felt this sense of fear, of oppression. The young boy, moving among the branches, picked the ripest fruit and threw them down. We gathered them in our skirts and pockets. Suddenly we heard the sound of the returning car. It came up the drive. We stood petrified. The car stopped. The door opened. A thin man in khaki shorts, khaki socks, brown leather shoes, brown felt hat, with a sallow face, thin shanks, two brilliant spots of colour flushing his cheeks with anger, stepped out. He was quivering with rage.

Such terrible rage and for what? It was he who was bleeding the trees and collecting all the milk. We had hardly disturbed a stone or pebble in his pathway. It was he who disturbed our early morning sleep with the mourning dirge of the machine. It was he who made the friendly villagers silent and fearful. He was such a little man in such a tremendous rage. He had power and authority. He was the 'sudu mahathmaya' who ruled over these acres of rubber. This was his kingdom. I saw the hidden leeches suddenly creeping out of the grass, thousands of them. One, two, three fastened themselves on my leg above the shoes and socks. But I was rooted to the spot where I stood. I dare not even bend to pluck them out before they got a hold on my flesh. I watched them grow fat and bloated until the transparent skin stretched fluidly and grew into globes incandescent with my blood.

Mrs Swan stood silent. My sister did not utter a word. None of us moved. The Englishman ignored Mrs Swan. He appeared not to see us, or rather he chose not to see us. We were dust beneath his feet. I watched the baggy khaki shorts quivering on his gaunt frame. His leather shoes dug into the earth among the fallen spoilt fruit. His face was contorted with rage. He looked straight at the villagers and shouted at them:

"Haven't I told you that no one is to enter this estate? Haven't I told you many times that no outsider, no stranger should step onto this land without my permission? Who allowed these people to come here!" he ranted, without even looking in our direction. How wry and twisted his thin lips were. One of the leeches, fed to satiety on my blood, fell off in a round ball at my feet. The others still clung and fed off me.

I wasn't afraid for myself any longer. I was afraid for the young boy hidden among the branches of the tree. I began to understand. We were trespassers. We had broken his unwritten rules, transgressed his laws. We were under his authority. He had to remain in the eyes of the villagers a symbol of absolute power and authority. Everybody had to obey him unquestioningly. There were boundaries both visible and invisible

Yet what was he protecting? We were just three human beings, a woman, and two children. I quietly looked up at the guava tree. Not a movement of leaf or creak of branch betrayed the presence of the young boy on it. I shall never forget the pathetic group of villagers; standing huddled together, in their silent fear. Even the babies being dandled on their hips did not utter a cry. The old and the young were all silent. They stood on the bank at a slightly higher elevation. We stood below the bank. So did the Englishman. Not a face gave away the young man on the tree.

The guavas we had gathered began to slide down our skirts where we had bunched them up. They rolled away to fall in the grass. A little boy suddenly urinated out of fear. Mrs Swan did not utter a word but, taking us each by the hand, led us silently away, tears of fear and humiliation pouring down our cheeks. It was only after the planter had got into his car, slammed the door and started up the hill on his lonely drive home, that the boy dared to come down the tree. Not a word of blame or censure passed between the people and ourselves. They were ashamed on behalf of their master.

I began to rub the itching bites. Mrs Swan said at last, "Child, you should never pull off a leech. Let it suck until it bloats and falls."

"But it leaves a sting at any rate," I said. "Then it festers, becomes a sore and takes a long time to heal," I continued.

"You could have waited until we went home. Uncle could have put some cigar ash on it or we could have put some salt and lime," said Mrs Swan.

"I wonder whom the old planter lives with," I asked idly.

"His wife and children are away in England."

"Then he's alone in that big old bungalow, all by himself?" I persisted.

"Perhaps," said Mrs Swan drily.

Such a dry, shrivelled-up man. I thought of him then as being old. But perhaps he was only middle-aged. Friendless too. What was he safeguarding… his private empire? I was never to see him again. He had told Mr Swan later on that he did not know that it was his wife who had come on that ill-fated foray to his estate. Tantamount to an apology perhaps. On behalf of himself or the Empire?

The Gift

As Christmas approached the glossy catalogues began to arrive from the big European shops in Kandy: Cargills, Whiteway and Laidlaw, Millers. Page after page was filled with illustrations of hats, gowns, handbags, shoes, suitcases, umbrellas, perambulators, and toys, toys, toys–baby dolls with porcelain limbs dressed in frilly organdy, delicately smocked dresses, bonnets, straw hats, shoes and socks; dolls-houses, teddy-bears of all sizes, storybooks, bon-bons. My unmarried aunts used to go frequently to England, from where they brought us beautiful gifts on their return. We got readymade pink taffeta frocks with tiered skirts, dolls and tea-sets, books too – Encyclopaedia Britannicas, Christopher Robin books, and a book about the lives of the two young English princesses, Elizabeth and Margaret Rose, which my mother used to read to me by the light of the glass-shaded oil-lamp.

Still, the catalogues always fascinated me. I sat on the floor on the leopard skin and poured over the pictures, turning page after page. I wanted one of those 'sleeping dolls,' as they were called in those days, with eyes that opened and shut with a short click over the transparent blue irises of their glass eyes.

"Can I have one of these dolls?" I asked my mother.

"We will ask your father," she said.

Quite often my father used to give us strange gifts. Not toys. He would bring us shiny, newly minted coins carefully packed, so glittery and rich looking, but children's toys he did not understand. He felt our imaginations were enough to create games for ourselves.

I returned again and again to the catalogues, turning page after glossy page. I longed for one of those sleeping dolls. One morning I was turning over the pages, when Jem Smith's tall shadow fell over them. He sat down beside me on the leopard skin.

"Like to come shopping with me?" he asked. "In Kandy."

My parents gave my sister Rosemary and myself permission, and Jem hired the old Ford car, which had to be cranked several times to start, with the horn which went "pomp, pomp, pomp." To get to Kandy, we had to drive past the mosque, the dispensary, the little boutiques where you could buy rulang biscuits and big round gold-wrapped coin-like chocolates stamped with the insignia of royalty.

In Cunjimoosa's shop there were bottles of confectionary brought from Great Britain – liquorice all-sorts, mint humbugs, hundreds and thousands, toffees and chocolates wrapped in gold foil. The round chocolate discs bore the impress of King Edward in all his regalia. What kind of patriotism was this? Was it a kind of subtle impressing of power and imperialism on a colonized people? The cocoa for the chocolates came from the colonies, yet those flat round discs of chocolate were manufactured in the big English chocolate factories of Cadburys and Nestlés. The gold-wrapped chocolate became a symbol of imperial domination. We were not even as children allowed to forget it. Those chocolates circulated round the world, so it was inevitable to ask the question: "Who is this king, this emperor, this monarch?" Did he also rule the world of Confectionary? The Chocolate Monarch. The Chocolate Emperor. But then, the chocolate did not last. We bit into that chocolate empire, bit by bit until the entire chocolate disappeared. A presagement of what would happen one day to the empire perhaps. The gold foil was preserved for a time, smoothed out with a fingernail and kept within the pages of books with other pieces of gilded chocolate and toffee papers, but the gold grew thin, dull and transparent, and then one day disappeared. The king emperor was no more, the foil disintegrated. All those monarchs were so distant, so aloof from our lives, wearing their crowns and coronets, their ermine-lined velvet robes, sitting ensconced on thrones, coloured lithographs adorning the walls of our homes together with canvas paintings of Scottish landscapes by Landseer. Ours was the real world with real people, whose conversational codes we were learning to interpret, whose manners we absorbed as we did the milk wine and ginger wine that Auntie Gladys made at Christmastime.

In Kandy the big European firms dominated Ward Street at that time. We went to several shops. The salesmen surrounded us. Perhaps they thought that we were the children of some wealthy tea planter from an up-country estate. We were showered with attention. We had only to point out what we fancied, than the toys were immediately taken down from the shelves. The dolls were ranged in their deliciously new-smelling cardboard boxes, their pink and white faces with incredibly blue eyes smiling down at us. Long black, dark brown or golden brown lashes drifted over wide-open eyes, curling ringlets of auburn and gold, attired in crisp pink, blue and white organdy dresses threaded with lace and ribbons. My sister and I each chose a doll. She, being the elder sister, had the first choice, although I had spotted that particular doll first, dressed in blue organdy with blue eyes, brown ringlets. Since I wanted a sleeping doll, I was left with a bare, naked baby doll, with eyes that opened and shut, but no hair. I could move its limbs whichever way I wanted. I looked forward to bathing it, putting it to sleep and dressing it in the fine silk, lace-trimmed christening robe, folded carefully and preserved in a drawer of my mother's almirah.

While the dolls were being packed, we chose an assortment of toys and other interesting things – Japanese dolls in checked gingham rompers, which crawled all over the surface of the glass counters when they were wound with a key; packets of red Chinese crackers; boxes of bon-bons, tins of Rose's chocolate; Japanese paper flowers of crimson, viridian green, ruby red, saffron yellow, which opened out in bowls of water; nuts from the big sacks at Cargills, almond, Brazil, walnut.

"Are these pretty little girls your daughters?" the salesman asked Jem Smith. I looked up at Jem, but he did not deny it. He looked at us instead with such affection as if we belonged to him – two demure little girls in smocked silk dresses, shoes, socks, and silver hairbands. "Say yes," he whispered to us, "Say yes." "Yes," we repeated. He willed us to be his surrogate children. Jem carried a photograph of his son in his pocket. It was wartime in England and Jem felt anxious about his safety – what kind of Christmas would the boy have without his father? We looked into Jem's brilliant shining blue eyes with reciprocal affection; eyes that silently asked us to affirm this relationship between father and child.

At last we went home. The street lamps in the township were being lit by the men who went around with their long poles. In the Queen's Hotel the Europeans were sitting down with their whiskies and sodas.

The evening light was falling on the paddy fields, the oil lamps glimmering in the little wayside houses and boutiques. Jem brought us back home and went on his way. The toys he took away with him. He would bring them back to be put into our Christmas stockings, at midnight on the eve of Christmas. I watched them being taken away with some trepidation. I hoped that he would not forget them when the time came.

On Christmas Eve there was a party at our home. All the railway folk had been invited, including Beryl Schofield who played ragtime and syncopated music on the old German piano. The Christmas cake, rich with fruit and spices, was cut, the tin of Huntley and Palmers Cream Crackers opened and the biscuits served with Edam cheese. Bottles of Scotch whiskey filled tumblers. The men folk sat and talked endlessly, story after story interspersed with humourous anecdotes, smoking pipes and cigars and cigarettes. Red and green velvet streamers decorated the walls. Outside it grew darker and darker. I heard the whistle of the Colombo-Kandy train. A lonely sound. A night sound.

It was time for my sister and myself to go to bed. All day long I had been anticipating the toys but I knew instinctively that Jem had forgotten to bring them.

I could not fall asleep, and I enjoyed, in my self-pity, the sensation of the pillow gradually growing damp with my tears.

My mother appeared at the doors of the bedroom: "What, still not asleep? Why the tears tonight of all nights? You know I'm too busy to be with you until you fall asleep."

Beryl peeped from behind the curtain. Then there was Jem towering tall behind her. He had suddenly remembered.

"God, Harry, the toys," he said turning into the drawing room. "I must go back and fetch them."

"What, at this time of the night? Nonsense, you can't go out now. It's not safe," was my father's rejoinder.

"Jem, not after all that whiskey," Arty Schofield murmured.

"Come on, Artie, you take me," Jem entreated.

My parents were annoyed with me.

"You have the Christmas stocking, the books, the nuts, and the Snowball," my mother said. "The doll can wait till tomorrow."

I heard Jem's footsteps go down the stone steps. Artie flashed his torch in the pitch-black night. I turned my pillow on the other side and fell asleep. The noisy voices disturbed me no longer. In the morning when I awoke, the doll was right at the top of all the other toys.

Jem was still there the next morning. The party continued. The adults lazily danced on the veranda, the pile of gramophone records and the baby doll lying on the canvas deck chair. The doll slipped off and broke. I lost it forever.

Jem Smith, did I lose you too, together with my childhood? I have never forgotten the happiness you gave me, yet this happiness so many years later is like an old wound that hurts. Jem Smith went back to England. Since the Second World War was still raging he was mobilized. My father told me that Jem had died in the blitz. I never wanted to believe him. I hoped that somewhere in that distant part of the globe which he called "home," he was still alive. Almost certainly his son must be alive, perhaps the same age as myself. I wonder whether he ever learned of his father's life in Ceylon.

Jem's house, the Foreman Platelayer's house, still stands in Kadugannawa. Our house too, but it is hidden by trees and bushes. I remember how I could see Jem's house from a certain vantage point on the hill. If I called out, he could hear and answer. Jem was one of the lonely ones, the others had their families with them. He made my sister and myself his family. That bonding remains to this day.

The Christmas Cake

"There's a nip in the air. Christmas is around the corner. It's time to think of making the cake," my mother would announce. December is also the season when the Christmas meroes come. When the lamps are lit in the late evening, when the dusk falls on plants and foliage in the deep purplish gloom, swarms of meroes fly into the hall and whirl madly round the glass globes, their wings singed, their ant-bodies crackling and shrivelling up. They burn within the incandescent glass globe or drown in the basin of water so cruelly placed beneath the hanging lamp. I would fish each one out gingerly as I knelt absorbed beside the basin, place them in the palm of my hand, blow gently on their soaked, bedraggled wings. Thousands of shed-wings, shreds of tissue and gossamer are scattered on the cement floor. The ants crawl waterlogged, limp-bodied on the floor. Geckoes pounce on them and scurry across the walls, glutted with their prey.

Alwin the furniture polisher would come early in the month of December to start varnishing and polishing the furniture with his bottles of turpentine and polish; his fingers stained with orangy brown varnish. First the arduous task of sandpapering, and then the application of coats of polish. The house had to be whitewashed and a fresh line of tar painted at the bottom of the wall to keep off the white ants. New lace curtains were bought, run up on my mother's Singer sewing machine and hung at the doorways. The drawing-room suite, settees and chairs were upholstered in bright cretonnes patterned with flowers and birds, and I would open the Dutch chest and rummage among the green and red Christmas decorations to be draped on the walls.

Sometimes a sprig of mistletoe would hang at the doorway, but that was only for romantic adults. My father bought his stock of Black and White Scotch whiskey and the bottles of aerated water were kept in readiness. Ginger ale, ginger beer, lemonade, cola, soda and cream soda were stocked up. Milk wine and ginger wine were made and bottled to be sipped from wine glasses on Christmas visits. Red wines too were served with cake. Port wines were very popular.

Weeks before Christmas the preparations began for the making of the cake. My mother made her own pumpkin preserve, one of the ingredients of the cake. A large ash-pumpkin was sliced in wedges and pricked all over with a fork for the excess liquid to flow out, then the sugar syrup bubbled in the copper pan over a woodfire, and when it was just right, the pumpkin slices were gently eased in and carefully stirred until the sugar crystallized like sparkling frost on each wedge. The amber flesh must remain firm and sweet. We didn't like too thick a coating of sugar, as we preferred the juiciness of the sugar-impregnated flesh which melted in the mouth. My mother also made cadju aluwa–hundreds of cadjus were chopped up and stirred into a sugar syrup flavoured with rosewater in a large copper preserving pan set on the fire, spread out onto a buttered dish and cut into big pieces. Her milk toffee too was made with bottles of fresh cow's milk. Potato aluwa, fruitcake, rich cake – those were her specialties. My mother never used a written recipe in her life. They were all in her mind, handed down from generation to generation. No, there were very few cookery books at home, so I just had to watch or listen to her casually tossed out instructions to her friends: "Well, you put a pinch of this and a handful of that, a brandy glass or wine glass of something, a teaspoon or tablespoon or dessert spoon of that, temperadu the mixture, broil, roast, fry, curry, sauté, steam, caramelize, simmer, bake..." She had original recipes too like adding bee honey taken from our own beehives into her fruitcake to make it rich and moist.

The whole house was fragrant with essences of rose, almond and vanilla, and the aroma of the powdered spices, cardamoms, cloves, cinnamon and nutmeg spread from room to room.

Unpacking the several parcels of cake ingredients from Cargills and Millers was a fascinating pastime. We used to guess the contents from the different fragrances. There was rulang (semolina), which was first sun-warmed and gently toasted later, packets of soft sugar and pats of butter – butter made by Mrs Tilly, an Englishwoman who lived up-country and had a dairy farm from where my father on his train journeys brought the fresh butter. We never had a refrigerator in my old home, so that the glass butter-dish was always kept in a saucer of cold water to keep it from melting. The butter and soft sugar had to be carefully creamed with a wooden spoon, always swirling it in one direction only, and then the egg yolks carefully lowered into the mixture, one by one with a froth of beaten egg white. There were juicy plums and raisins, which had to be carefully de-seeded, and tiny dried blackcurrants. Then there were Arabian dates to be chopped up with cadju, mixed peels and candied peels, chow-chow and preserved ginger from stone jars with cork lids. The preserved ginger and chow-chow came from China and tasted delectable, not too strong, dark brown, with the right degree of pungency. The honey-sweet ginger-flavoured syrup was delicious too. We had rows and rows of those empty ginger jars and kept them for years to store things in or just to be used as ornaments. Bee honey we had from our own hives so that the nectar from all the flowers in our garden sweetened the cake mixture. There would be a big bowl of frothy egg whites left over, and this was poured onto an iron skillet and made into an enormous meringue-like omelette to be eaten for lunch. But who was hungry for lunch on such a day? We had popped too many cadjunuts and plums into our mouths and tasted the mixture from the leavings of the copper pan; we had lost all appetite for lunch and only waited for a slice from the sample cake baked in the round tin.

Mrs Willig, who was now our neighbour, was coming over to help my mother with the cake.   Mrs Willig had no children of her own, and was always amenable to my requests to be the constant guest at my elaborately arranged tea parties on the veranda. The newly unpacked tea-set of Japanese porcelain, a gift from the Solomons' aunts used to be set out on the teapoy, and the three of us would sit round it, my mother, Mrs Willig and myself engaged in polite conversation. At that stage of my life I was not shy and felt very much at ease with all the adults who surrounded me. When was it that I became 'tongue-tied,' as my mother would describe me, quiet, reserved? Was it when I felt myself being carried through swift currents of change, tossed in that tumultuous flood of newly discovered feelings and emotions?

Mrs Willig would often tell us stories of her nieces Mignonne and Decima, who were talented in music, singing, and playing the guitar. My mother too would sing to me, in her clear soprano voice, but her songs were often poignant and melancholy. They filled me with a sense of sadness. Her favourite songs were "Two Little Girls in Blue, Love" and "After the Ball is Over." The songs had stories which she wove about those words, stories of love, romance, parting, recollection of past happiness. Those were the songs she sang to me. Songs of a bygone era. And she spoke of the days when she danced the polka and the lancers. All that she now had was her memory, for my father never danced nor did he approve of ballroom dancing. But when there were parties and dances at the Railway Reading Room, we would accompany Mrs Willig, in her ankle-length gown of wine-dark crepe silk with the tiny loops at the hips through which she would slip her fingers ever so delicately so that the hem of her skirt would not touch the dusty Colombo-Kandy road along which we walked late in the evening.

The preparations for the cake-making took up hours and hours of the day and my mother decided that on that particular morning it would be best to send me to Mrs Swan's home. I could do whatever I wanted there. I would also be out of my mother's way. Dressed in my chintz dress with its sprigged flowers, and yoke trimmed with ric-rac braid, I was sent across to spend the day with Mrs Swan, the kindliest and most patient of guardians.

I spent almost the whole morning of that day with Mrs Swan. I played in the house, in the garden, watched the trains pass, talked incessantly to her, and at lunchtime insisted on serving myself with more food than I could possibly eat. I left most of it on the plate untouched, and then firmly decided that it was time for me to return home alone and unaccompanied. I crossed the road, then the railway lines, then the main road, went along the path to my home and up the hill, then I burst in on my mother and Mrs Willig who were completely absorbed in stirring the cake, engaged in a private tête à tète.

"I have come back home," I announced, expecting my dramatic entrance to be greeted with praise and pleasure.

"Look who's here," my mother said with consternation.

"And how did you come back? With whom? I wanted you to spend the day with Mrs Swan." Her expression was ruffled.

"I came by myself."

"You crossed the railway lines alone?"

"Yes, Mrs Swan watched from the veranda."

There was nothing that could be done. I wanted to be in the thick of things, in the fray. No one could stop me from the decision I had made. A quiet, firm unshakable determination to have my own way. It would take me into deep waters. A stubborn, obstinate streak that would impel my steps through my life.

"I was not afraid," I said, "The signal was not down. The train was yet to arrive."

I was so used to walking along those railway tracks, stepping across from one wooden sleeper to another, measuring the length of my growing limbs, the cindery smell of coal and coke filling my nostrils. I had learnt to read the signals for my temporary safety. And I had arrived where I wanted to be. I had learnt an early independence from my solitary wanderings on the hills.

"Rita Toussaint Vanlangenberg's Christmas Cake" (sent by her granddaughter Romaine)

1+ lbs Rulang   2+ lbs Soft Sugar   1+ lbs Butter
24 Eggs (24 yolks, and half the amount of white of these eggs)
1+ lbs Raisins   1+ lbs Sultanas
1+ lbs Pumpkin Preserve   2 lbs Cherries
1 lb Mixed Candied Peel   200 Cadjunuts
1 lb Almonds   3 Jars Chow-chow   2 Jars Ginger
2 Bottles each of Vanilla, Almond, Rose Essences
Mixed Spices to taste
2 wine glasses of Bees' Honey
3-4 wine glasses of Brandy   3-4 wine glasses of Sherry

Method
Cut up all dried fruit, cadjunuts and almonds. Mix in essences, spices, syrups from the chow-chow and ginger, liquor, and marinate overnight in a glass bowl covered tightly. Prepare cake trays or tins with two thicknesses each of newspaper and brown paper, and then two layers of greaseproof paper which is brushed liberally with melted butter. Warm the rulang and set aside. Cream butter and sugar in a large ceramic bowl with a wooden spoon, until light and frothy. Add in the 24 egg yolks lightly beaten, beating the mixture well after each addition. When well beaten and bubbles form, gradually add rulang and continue to beat. Fold in marinated fruit mixture. Fold in the stiffly beaten 12 eggwhites. Bake in a very slow oven (130⁰C).
Cake is taken out of the oven while still slightly raw, as it will continue to cook for the heat of the tray. This will give you a very moist cake. When cake is cool, cover well and leave in the tray for 24 hours before turning out. Ice with almond paste, cut into squares and wrap firstly in grease-proof paper and then in the paper of your choice. Store in an air-tight container.

Cameo – Mrs Cramer

I was ill with some childhood ailment and lay propped up in bed against the banked-up pillows of the four-poster. The ice bag shifted about on my forehead as I adjusted it, feeling the tinkling ice cubes move about in the pink rubber sac. When the ice melted, my mother removed the ice bag and touched my cool forehead's damp, ice-touched skin to see whether the fever had gone down.

A glass bowl with vinegar and water was placed close at hand, and my mother would dip the soft, folded strip of linen in it, wring it out, and lay it gently on my forehead, the astringent smell creeping up to the roots of my hair and leaving its faint aftermath lingering on the skin.

I watched the mercury shift up and down in the thermometer. When I was very small, it would be placed under the armpit because my mother felt I might crunch on the fragile glass. As I grew older, it was placed under the tongue with strict instructions not to bite on the glass. Perhaps she knew that I bit the glass rim of the tumblers I drank water from. Standing on the edge of the veranda, I would feel I must explore the texture of that fine, cool-to-the-lips glass with its incised design of ferns and flowers – water and glass were indistinguishable – and I bit with my new sharp milk teeth until my lips bled. I was more careful with the mercury-filled thermometer because of the dire warnings of what would happen to me if the mercury traveled through my bloodstream.

As I lay in bed, my mother brought into the room my visitor, Mrs Cramer. She sat carefully on a chair and spoke to me in a gently, crooning voice. She was a little figure with a black hat skewered with a steel hatpin, and a deep black crepe dress with high collar and full gathered skirt which reached to her ankles. She wore black stockings, black leather shoes, carried a black umbrella and a black cloth bag with wooden handles. I surveyed her from my vantage point, that fairytale figure who was like the kind fairy from my storybooks, as she made her strange, prophetic utterance:

"You will be a queen one day. A queen."

A queen? Myself? But how?

"How can I be a queen one day, royal?" I asked my mother.

She only smiled and said, "Yes, if she says so, you will. Believe her."

I watched those hands, Mrs Cramer's hands, so seamed and brown, so earth-like. I saw the ploughed furrows of the fields in those palms. Hard-working hands. How hard they must have worked, those hands, on that plot of land that was so dear to her. She worried about her son. His marriage. "I must find a good, convent girl for him. An orphan, but from a convent." My mother and she chattered about brides for this cherished son of hers. He needed a helpmate, one who would help to work on their plot of land. Then Mrs Cramer came up to my bed and settled my pillows, taking each one of them and shaking them out, plumping them with her hands till they were soft and comfortable once more, shook out my blanket, a warm and fleecy blanket, smoothed my forehead, and combed out my hair with the large tortoiseshell comb.

Was it whooping cough I had, or just fever? In those tumblers by the bedside there was either lemon-flavoured barley water or a thick sweet syrup of tart, sour oranges, ambul dodang, with tal sukiri – only a teaspoon or two at a time. If it was whooping cough, then my mother said that the cure would be to take me up in an aeroplane, soaring into the pure ether where my cough would cease to bother me. Mrs Cramer, my kind fairy, with her wishes and portents, bound me in her spells that would bewitch my childhood – her beady, brown eyes sparkling like shiny bone - buttons in my memory.

The light filtered through the green glass on the tiled roof and through the white cotton valance to spear me with beams that pierced the sheets and blanket with silver darts. The green tats crackled in the slight wind that blew across the valley, and the bees buzzed as they went in and out of the hive. The bed was my barque against all the storms and threats of an uncertain ocean, the turmoil and welter that lay outside of its safety.

THARASWIN

Tharaswin's line drawing that accompanied my "Buttons and Bows and the Good Things of Life," in *The Daily News*, 1980s.

Buttons and Bows:
Colonial Roles and Assumed Disguises

I was wearing a white smocked dress and standing by my mother in a big room in the Commercial Company. There were two tall barrels before me. While my mother was talking to the manager, I kept standing on tiptoe and peering into one of the barrels filled with a black glittering substance. I dipped my fingers into it and found that they were covered with pitch. My mother was oblivious of what I was doing. I knew it was something I should not have done, and so I tried to rid myself of any signs of guilt by dabbing my white dress with the pitch that clung to my hand, smearing it with tiny splotches of black. My mother turned towards me and discovered the results of my curiosity – it was one of those exquisitely hand-sewn dresses, perhaps ruined forever. Texture, smell, the fascination of something new and unknown was what had enticed me, not just being naughty or mischievous for its own sake. The pitch so opaque and yet so yielding was a dark, forbidden lake which I had wanted to stir and cause whirlpools in, with my fingers, plunging into the deepest recesses. I was then about three years old.

The dresses I wore were the creations of many Burgher seamstresses of those days, whose fingers were skilled in creating the embroidery stitches they gleaned from European journals. I myself learned much later how to do drawn-thread work, cross-stitch, cut-work, herring-bone, lazy-daisy, satin, chain, stem and featherstitch. Hand embroidery embellished almost everything we wore. Aunties Elsie and Ila Solomons were always giving us gifts of dresses sewn by their Colombo seamstresses, including one of white georgette, the whole bodice smocked with rows of herring-bone stitch in shaded blue silk with clusters of pink roses in pink bullion and twining stems and green lazy-daisy leaves. And there were all the organdies sprigged with roses and the pink-tiered taffetas, the tartan plaids, the Czechoslovakian embroideries, and the smart American dresses the aunts brought back from their globe-trotting.

As soon as a young mother 'was expecting' her first baby, the layettes began to be prepared. The finest mull and cambric, lawn, muslin, cotton and flannelette were brought from the millinery stores and were cut and hand sewn. The flannel blankets neatly hemmed and then blanket-stitched. Rompers and sunsuits, bonnets and floppy sunhats, matinee coats, bibs and tuckers, wooly knitted coatees and bootees - overshielded our bodies which should have been allowed to feel the natural air and sunlight. And did all those people have hours and hours to sew, 'to turn a fine seam' and click their knitting needles? For some of them it was a profession, a way of earning a living by staying at home and supplementing the income. It was also a way of giving their imaginations and latent talents for design and creativity, a chance to bloom and flower. Each seamstress who sewed for us was famed for either her smocking, her shadow-work or pin-tucks. Others gave an excellent 'fit.' The Singer sewing machines were part of every home.

It was while my own mother hemmed the linen that I helped turn the heavy silver wheel and listened to the stories of her own childhood. All the trimmings, broderie, ric-rac braid, laces, ribbons, buttons came from England. Brussels lace for wedding dresses, slipper satin, grosgrain, and fabrics like Riverina and slub linen were all imported. Ruching, gathering, tucks, insertions, frills and flounces were imitations of another world, another clime, and another society on whose fringes we lived. We were caught up, in that web, ensnared within the pattern and design of that tapestry, the colours muted, the textures and fibres interweaving and interlocking within that fabulae of colonialism and all its varied enterprises. Handmade crochet laces, tatting, beeralu or pillow-lace were attached to bedsheets, pillowcases, and lingerie. Fervent, dedicated and skilled needlewomen and lace makers crocheted, tatted and wove beeralu lace for the altar cloths and robes in the convents and monasteries.

The thromble man, with his carefully wrapped bundle borne on his head, would walk down the street. He would sit on the veranda of our house and carefully unwrap the folds of his khaki bundle. Everything was meticulously arranged in their different sections with the enormous long-handled pair of scissors and the folding wooden yardstick placed on top of the pile. Everything was carefully lifted and placed aside, until we reached the particular material or matching or trimming we wanted. The thromble karaya was a walking milliners shop. There were cardboard boxes of ribbons and laces, French and English laces of varying widths wound around cards which contained their manufacturers names; buttons, braids, sequins, beads, cards of tightly wound tape and elastics; safety pins and needles, hooks and eyes and press-studs; ribbons of satin and sarcanet; and carefully folded yards and yards of chintz, cotton or cheetha (from Japan), 'Fuji' silk (from China) and English linen. How patiently the thromble man waited until we chose and made our selections. He would then measure out everything meticulously with his golden yellow yardstick and carefully cut out the length while we helped him stretch it out, although he himself was very adept at holding down one end beneath his chin and stretching out the yardage at arms-length.

That bundle of millinery had a special amalgam of smells, the smell of newness; each fabric, each individual button or lace carrying with it the aura of something faraway and distant. The smell of human labouring hands, or of factory machines of different climes and seasons was absent. What was it then? It was the smell of something that did not belong to the country or our own experience - wild flowers, crushed herbs, oils and unguents – no, nothing of those fragrances were there. The smells were already defined for us and it was only when we felt those fabrics against our own skins, our own bodies, did they become part of us. Clothes assumed identities – a dress became the smell of mother, the cotton bib that of the milky smell of babyhood, of a baby brother or sister, the wool and cambric embodying the smells of sleep, dream, awakening. The laundered clothes were impregnated with Sunlight soap, soda, washing blue, water, sunlight and the embers burning in coconut-shell irons. The Dhobi-amma had an enormous pol-kattu iron in her laundry. We used a smaller one at home, putting the smouldering coconut shells into the iron, allowing the natural temperature to adjust to ironing the chintz, cotton, pique, silk.

Chinese vendors of silk, missionaries, outlandish fashions in clothes – we were all shopping from that great caravanserai of colonialism in everything, from what we wore, to language, religion and social mores. Some of the readymade dresses my mother wore 'for the house' were from Podimahathaya's shop in Kadugannawa. Almost all the frocks were of a uniform design and cut: a blue and black print on a white ground, with high neck, straight gored skirt, and buckled belts. Those frocks from Japan were hung in one or two rows in the front section of the shops on the main Colombo-Kandy road. The shop had tinkling curtains of multicoloured glass beads, colours that echoed the shades of peacock plumes. 'Hundreds and thousands,' those minute sweets with their aniseed centres filled the tall glass-stoppered sweet bottles together with liquorice all-sorts, chocolates and mint humbugs, a kind of miniature Cranford, the novel by Emily Gaskell.

We had special roles to play, beginning from childhood. Each role had its special costume. Our day clothes, our home frocks were of chintz and cotton with prints sprigged with rosebuds and tiny flowers, checks, pin dots and stripes. With pockets for playthings; beads, pebbles, seeds, silver coins, sweets. For the evening, for dressing up for visits and visitors; for going-to-church; for parties and festive occasions – we had special dresses. More embellished. More elaborate. Frills. Flounces. 'V' necks, sweetheart necklines. Taffetas and organdies. Gathered and billowing skirts. And of course, shoes and socks. Walking barefooted was a delicious and rare treat on the cool linoleum or cement floors. The garden was dangerous in Kadugannawa, with the centipedes, the scorpions, the tarantulas – my mother told me the only way of getting rid of the lethal effects of the tarantula bite was by dancing the "Tarantella."

Butterfly bows and three-tier frilled taffeta dresses for my sister Rosemary and myself were brought from England. Puffed sleeves, pin-tucked yokes – clothes that belonged to the eras of the mother-country. Were we the historical inheritors of the legacy? An inheritance so assiduously followed era by era? My mother's wedding dress in the latter part of the 1920s mirrored the English and European fashions, together with her silk stockings and white satin-backed, high-heeled shoes – a Burgher bride, with a bouquet of arum lilies, wearing the fashions of those times.

Mrs Alexander was one of our seamstresses. She lived in a little by-lane close to Auntie Tommy's house, with steps leading up to the verandah. Mrs Alexander, who by that time was widowed, wore a black felt hat even indoors. The suede hat was skewered with hatpins, and set firmly on her crown, while her hair had been braided into a neat-coiled knot. She was always trim and natty with her leather court shoes and cotton stockings. She carried a smart black patent leather handbag and another bag filled with spools of thread, needles, thimbles, hooks and eyes, press-studs, scissors, measuring tape. The pins dug into your flesh at the most awkward places during the 'fit-ons.' With all the pins stuck between her pursed lips, Mrs Alexander cautioned: "Be careful now, don't move till I finish... now, now don't struggle. It will be over in a minute... just a little here to be taken in and there... too loose... Ah, now that's right. Too tight under the armpits, I'll let out a little. Dart can come here. Let down hem a little, no? Too long? Then I'll take up again. Only tacking, no..." All her hems were neatly turned down and her hemstitches regular in their alignment. She would come home regularly to take in our sewing.

Mrs Alexander's daughter was married to the Goan tailor Mr Raymond. A very smartly attired man in black coat, waistcoat, tie with gold tiepin, and dark grey pinstriped trousers and polished silver buckled leather belt. He was a master tailor and sewed all my father's best suits, of which he had a wide collection for festive occasions, weddings, anniversaries, Easter and Christmas services too. And at funerals too, with his silver stopwatch peeping out of his coat pocket and his gold cufflinks, my father was an impressive figure. Mrs Alexander was always carrying parcels and packets of food for her innumerable grandchildren in her bag, especially white stringhoppers, which were very popular during the war years.

"What to do, Mrs Solomons, always having children, my poor daughter. Every year a child, no. Poor thing, she's not so strong also. Must take stringhoppers, bread for them. Won't stop having children, no. What to do. All girls also." Sometimes Mrs Alexander would bring her granddaughters home, and my mother would persuade me to gift them with my storybooks, especially the *Bumper Annuals*. These I was taught to share generously with them, as I had such a large collection of books. Till the very end, I did keep one of them: *Mr Papingay and the Little Round House*, the little round house being a postbox. The most distinctive thing that happened in that story was that a cake was made with the strangest ingredients, everybody's favourite everything, including a packet of safety pins. I supposed it harkened back to the Christmas puddings of the past, when silver talismans were also put in with the dried fruit and the traditional ingredients.

Colonial roles – did we not assume them from day to day? Almost everything we wore came from other countries, from England, from the colonies of the British Empire – except for our Kalutara straw hats. Almost every bit of our clothing was of the raw material from one of the possessions of the British Empire, while the finished product came from English mills and factories where there was the exploitation of those mill hands and factory workers by the vast capitalist system. All the big department stores which we patronized in the township of Kandy – Cargills, Millers, Whiteaway and Laidlaw – stocked British goods. We were psychologically ingrained with the superiority of those manufactured products, which went hand in hand with our educational setup in the missionary schools – the language we spoke and read, the entire canon of literature which became part of our psyches. The Book Lists we were given at the beginning of each new school year formed esoteric reading for us. The world we studied was from one point of view, constrained by the vision of the 'Grand Master of the Colonial Circus.' We were trained to obey. We carried out those commands, but the whiplash was so subtle that we did not feel its sting, until we became the lost generation searching relentlessly for the significance of self-identity. But we searched with blindfolds, groping in the dark with our tentative hands outstretched seeking out the substance beyond the shadow of own confusion.

Later when I grew up, I discovered the beautiful handlooms woven in the Dumbara Valley and began to feel my personality changing with the colours and traditional designs of a familiar landscape, with the creative artist's imagination transforming bird, flower, and elephant into stylized patterns. Here, there was room for interpretation. And the Indian fabrics, cottons and silk, with their mythical beings, gods, goddesses, people, birds, beasts and flowers continued the transformations. The textures of these fabrics that now began to clothe my body were kinder to my skin. It was like the smooth river stone that Mungo used, rather than soap, to scrub her body as she bathed. The river became part of her limbs; it embodied her own fragrance, impregnating her very clothes with it. Mungo's smell was natural, compounded of water, sunlight, and air. While we had become the icons of the colonial imagination. We had to find freedom from those images imposed upon the psyche.

"The Chinese Connection"

The Chinese cloth vendor would come to our house on the hill, and disclose to our fascinated eyes the exquisite Chinese hand-embroidered birds of paradise and fabulous dragons, in gold and silk threads, crepe-de-chine blouses with multicoloured smocking encircling the neckline, and the long-sleeved blouses with roses, peonies and chrysanthemums. Black silk kimonos were lined with oyster-coloured satin, heavily embroidered gold dragons sweeping dramatically down the whole length of the back; crepe-de-chine pyjamas in their silk sachets, which we took back to boarding school and placed neatly under the pillow after we made our bed every morning, covering them with Chinese bedspreads; dressing table runners and centrepieces with cut-work flowers and appliqué, white flowers with black hand stitching on sky-blue linen; Fuji silk for garments, especially lingerie. Everything carefully folded and arranged in the khaki pack.

With his long black queue flowing down his back, his smooth, polished almond-shaped fingernails, his ivory skin and his khaki tunic and wide cotton pants, the cloth vendor was the bearer of treasures from Cathay. He walked miles and miles from township to township, thinking his thoughts in Mandarin and Hokkien dialect, yet speaking the language that had become universal in those times, the latter part of the 1930s, the early 1940s – the language which was his passport in the colonies – English, with his own rare and special nuances.

My father used to tell us stories of the Boxer Rebellion and the Opium Wars, of the inventions of gunpowder and the printing press, and of Columbus and his dream of discovering the fabled kingdoms of Cipangu and Cathay. Ceylon had its Chinese dentists who created perfect sets of pearl-white dentures, the restauranteurs, and the silk-shop owners. One day in a future as yet unenvisaged, intermarriage would take place between some of our own family members and members of the Chinese community, and other stories would reach us then. Of how Sempar Tsung's family had first come to the island and set up their textile shops in Trincomalee; how during the Japanese invasions his people would dig deep pits, the wedges of turfed earth, used as lids to cover their places of refuge in China. And of the bricks of Chinese tea they stored in their shops. The Tsung family was close-knit, and the extended family system existed behind the shop in which they carried on their business.

My nephew Roger Solomons married Miriam Sûn whose family originally came from Mainland China. Talking about identity, Miriam tells me, "I am pure Chinese" – so unlike our own 'hybrid' identity. Her mother came from Fujian and belonged to a wealthy family. The family house had thirty rooms which not only housed the extended family but also welcomed English and American missionaries in a special Guest House. Miriam's mother and her sisters used to peep secretly at the "white faces." Miriam's mother (the family name was Teoh) used to travel about in palanquins. When the Maoist movement and the Revolution began the family lost all their property. Fifteen years after the Revolution, owners were asked to come back and claim their properties, but by then, most of the families who could migrate had left for places like Singapore, Burma, and Ceylon. Miriam's family had been in the export-import business, one way in which their wealth had been amassed. The missionaries too had influenced the Teoh family greatly, and Miriam's grandmother used to go out every day to preach and teach the Bible. Only an aunt was finally left in the family house, which is now a Post Office in Fujoiyan.

Miriam's father came from Shantung (Shandong). He had deserted from the army. When he emigrated to Ceylon he engaged in trade and used to go on his bicycle through the streets of Colombo, selling laces and Shantung silks. It was later, after his marriage, that he and his wife began the Chinese Dragon Café on Galle Road. Later on the restaurant was run by my nephew Roger Solomons and his wife Miriam, and is now located on Milagiriya Avenue.

Missionary activity was part of the lives of the Chinese migrants. Faithful Luke, a Singaporean Chinese, was inspired to preach God's word and 'got a 'Call' to come to Ceylon. The converts were baptized in the sea, probably at Galle Face. When faithful Luke went back to Singapore, back to his family, the Chinese converts had no preacher, so Faithful Luke sent "Bible Men" and "Bible Ladies" to teach and preach to the new converts; and that's where Miriam's parents first met, when they gathered together to share the teachings of the Bible, sing hymns and choruses...

Some of the back gardens of the Chinese cafes were filled with enormous vessels in which the soya sauce fermented in the open air to add that wonderful flavour to their food. The American missionaries, friends of my mother's who had spent years in China, told her of how they longed to eat the steamed flour dumplings, which they searched for in vain in some of the Chinese cafés in Ceylon.

Some of the silk-shop Chinese in Kandy were converted to Christianity by a little English missionary who was a neighbour of ours, living at West End, one of George E. de Silva's houses, on Halloluwa Road. There, she would entertain her converts to tea and cake and passages from the gospels. My mother and I too were once entertained to tea by the little missionary, who was told that I loved classical music. At my request she played the whole of the Beethoven "Moonlight Sonata," and I heard later that she had had to take to bed with a violent headache after the crashing chords of the "Appassionato" movement had been played on the gramophone.

Arlis the Hairdresser

Arlis the ladies hairdresser assisted in the creation of those Western modes of fashion. He had his salon at the Queen's Hotel in Kandy. He was patronized both by the English planters wives and the Dutch Burgher ladies who belonged to that colonial era, for perms and trims, for shampooing, setting and styling. His specialty was shoulder-length and short haircuts. He was famous for his pin-curls, each strand of hair dampened with setting lotion twisted into a loop round his delicate fingers and clipped flat against the scalp. Or if you so desired it, steel wavers with their sharp serrations of metal teeth would clamp down the hair till it bristled like a silvery helmet. Under the hair dryer, then the pin curls and wavers would release the hair into ridges and ringlets, which Arlis would brush out with the lingering artistry of his hands. So cool, so chill, those fingers like tiny fish that had slipped out of icy waters to quiver in those white porcelain basins with their gleaming silver taps and foaming water. Kiss curls, too, he could create, the hair first clipped into place on either side and then teased into gentle curves on the forehead. A permanent wave, however, was the epitome of sophistication, but you had first to be a 'young lady' before you were granted parental permission for a perm – tight little curls, plucked eyebrows, cupid-bow lips, a touch of rouge, the sameness of the fashions of those times through which individual beauty or personality still shone out.

Arlis began his profession of hairdressing in the year 1934. In the political background, dominated still by the colonial regime, agitation was going on for constitutional reform. The first elections were held in 1931, the State Council met, Committees formed, and Ministers chosen. There were two minority representatives. They were Mr. Perisunderam and Mohamed Macan Markar, later Sir Mohamed Macan Markar. Sir Baron Jayatileke was leader of the House.

Arlis carried on as hairdresser at the Queen's and then at the Suisse Hotel throughout the period of constitutional reform, the Caldecott Dispatch of 1938, the outbreak of the Second World War, the 1943 Declaration Status, which stated that post-war re-examination of reforms would lead towards the granting of "full responsible government under the Crown in all matters of internal civil administration," the Soulbury Commission, the Soulbury Constitution, and finally Dominion Status. He continued to cut, shear, trim, style, set, perm, within the ambience of hotel salons while the most momentous happening and events took place outside those secure structures.

His uncle, he would tell us, had worked in a salon in the west end of London and on the P&O Lines, the Peninsula Orient Lines. This uncle of his, T. Martinus de Silva, hailed from Galle. Martinus was his mother's brother and had travelled all over the world in the P&O Liners. During the Second World War, Arlis occasionally catered to the needs of all those British ladies and gentlemen. Lady Slim, Lady Park, the wife of the chief of staff of the RAF, Sir Park, Lady Wyndham – all were his patrons. Of the men he remembered, Sir Henry Parnell had his hair cut by him.

Lady Edwina Mountbatten, whose hair he would style when she came up to Kandy, once gave him a certificate which he memorized. To him the words were sheer poetry:

"T.M. Arlis used to do my hair on two or three occasions on my visits to Kandy. I can speak most highly of his work and recommend him strongly."

"No tips," Arlis said. Everything was billed to the Queen's Hotel. Lady Mountbatten's Secretary provided everything from Singapore: shampoo, hair-setting lotions, and hairnets. It was also very difficult to get linen during those days, so towels and sheets all came from Singapore. "One day so many ladies came to my salon," he said. "The ship in which they were travelling had been bombed; the young ladies had been rescued from the lifeboats. They came to me, their hair all bedraggled. They had no money but I attended on them all, free of charge."

He continued his work until the 1960s, though by then he no longer ran a plush salon but visited the homes of quiet, retiring Burgher ladies who reposed reclusively in their homes subsisting often on the meagre pensions of schoolteachers. Some of them, like Mrs Vanderwall, never changed their hairstyles nor the style of their hats. Mrs Vanderwall continued to play the organ, in the Methodist Church on Brownrigg Street, with her hat on. The presence of Miss Bamford the missionary was distinguished by her crimson felt hat, very modish and stylish for one who was so serious and dedicated in her mission. The Smiths and the Jonklass families always wore hats beneath which lay carefully trimmed hair. Some of the ladies continued with their braided knots of hair. Mrs Drieberg always wore a stylish black hat to church or even shopping in town. Beneath those hats those unvarying hairstyles never changed: the coils, the braids, the buns, the rolls, which belonged to individual personalities that did not feel the need to relinquish a familiar era or period of fashion. They felt dignified and fully clothed with their hats on. It completed their turnout, the constraints of whalebone corsets and stays, of bust bodices and sheer silk slips, of high necks and long-cuffed sleeves, buttons, buckles, brooches. Hair sleek and brushed in a side part secured with a tortoise-shell hair slide, never changed but framed Dulcie Vanderstraaten's Madonna-like face till the end, with its perfect chiselled features. Gladys, her elder sister, had tiny clusters of auburn curls kept in place decade after decade by an invisible brown net. Trimming the hair, bobbing the hair, perfect fringes, kiss-curls, together with the readymade dresses, hundreds of Susan Smalls suspended from padded hangers at Cargills, together with band boxes filled with English hats, the Burgher ladies all acted out their seemingly preordained roles

Cousin Joyce described the fashions of the 1950s which the modish Burgher ladies adopted from the colonial models. She had attended a wedding at the Women's International Club in Colombo and had worn a gown made by a very famous Burgher dressmaker during that time. Joyce vividly remembered that dress even after 30 years or more.

"It was green," she told me, "with white stripes, 'off the waist' according to the fashion dictates of the day. I wore a white hat created by an equally famous Burgher milliner, Merle Condelag. It was a beautiful white hat, remodelled. I stood before my husband, George [Martenstyn], preening myself in my fashionable attire. I thought I looked like a Gainsborough painting."

"I asked George his opinion. 'How do I look?' I expected to be showered with compliments. 'You look like Mrs Perrie,' was all he said.

"Mrs Perrie was short of stature, big bosomed. She had two kondes bunched at the ears, her hair being thick and abundant. She usually wore a hat set straight on her head, set at a stylish angle and round her neck were innumerable chains, amber, crystal, lapis lazuli, dazzling, iridescent glass beads. Well, I didn't speak a word. I had fancied myself. I had a slender figure, a flawless complexion and was always well groomed.

"Well, I thought, why should I save and not be even the least bit extravagant when it came to making myself fashionable and smart. I visited the exclusive Yaiyar Tailor and got myself a very special outfit, all in shades of grey – lovely dress, matching grey hat, grey court shoes. I looked like a portrait out of Vogue Journal.

"'Well, how do I look?' I asked George, preening myself once more before him. George was a man of few words but this time he implied that I had a pleasing aspect. 'There's the mirror, you can see for yourself,' was what he said. That was George's way of paying me a compliment. He believed that everything should always be nice. Nice house, nice clothes; and when it wasn't nice he told me so. Didn't mince words".

George himself was such a dapper, handsome man. He had his quirks, never wanted ornaments on the walls.

"Looks like a bloody jail," Joyce once told him and put a nail on the wall.

George made no comment.

George was very high up in the Customs Service. Never accepted gifts and would return whatever he did get. A huge basket of fresh vegetables was once sent from up-country – cabbages, carrots, cauliflowers, leeks, beetroots. He sent it all back with thanks.

Borrowed Plumes

Disguises, part of pretensions to glory
Creating new self images
Taken from the grandeur of historical
Identities other than our own,

Concealing the starveling poverty
Of the cringing flesh frozen in ice-bound
Winters of subjugated centuries and alien
Traditions decked out in the trappings of
Those we think heroic.

Do manners go with textures,
The vari-coloured fibres spinning
Whole tapestries of legends, epics, sagas.

Find them mouldering in odd places,
In old villas, palaces, castles, museums,
Tracing histories of vanished epochs
As we step out of our prison frames
In search of the lost home we left long ago
Territory no longer defined by the boundaries
Of the colonizers.

Conquest gave us new mapmakers
Staking out piece-meal territories, given
Sanctions by the forgeries of history,
Setting the counterfeited seals of monarchies
And empires on those documents, scrolls
Fought for and won by assassins and hired
Mercenaries leaving the invaded body
Wretched, naked, stripped of all camouflage,
Clothed now in borrowed plumes.

(Hyderabad, 2004)

VI

THE WIDER WORLD

"Sunnyside Gardens," Peradeniya Road, Kandy (photograph by Conrad Felsinger).

The Bombay Dancers

At Perahera time everyone sought out the Bombay Dancers. They were not from Bombay as we were to discover but were our own people who performed their own version of Kathakali, Bharatha Natyam or Kandyan dancing on an improvised stage in the marketplace with sarees draped as curtains and bright petromax lamps providing illumination. To the innocent rural folk who had flocked to Kandy from the outlying villages Bombay Dancing was an exotic, spellbinding form of entertainment. The more sophisticated street-wise populace of the township of Kandy also formed an avid audience.

Rows of wooden benches were placed inside the tent. People bought tickets at the entrance to watch the new-fangled dances. A swirl of drums heralded the entrance of the dancers onto the makeshift stage as they emerged from the wings, faces perfectly painted, garbed in dazzling costumes aglitter with sequins, gold and silver embroidery, shimmering satins of orange, red, gold, emerald green, turquoise blue. Their heads bore elaborate gilded crowns and coronets wrought out of cardboard pasted with gold, silver and scintillating coloured foil cutouts that simulated precious stones. Rubies, emeralds, diamonds, glittered against a patina lavishly sprinkled with silver and gold dust. Magical transformations of the ordinary.

The drums, the tabla, the dola, the tambourine, the serapina and flute provided the music and the rhythm, while one man kept the talam as the dancers whirled on the stage in a free and wild abandon. They devised elaborate mudras and adapted the postures of the great classical dancers, most probably learned from the Indian 'talkies' which they had viewed in the cinema. In addition they improvised the steps of the Kandyan dances they had seen from infancy.

One night, after viewing the Perahera, my mother, father, sister and myself drifted into the tent to watch the Bombay Dance. I was perhaps twelve years old and had never yet seen it before. The Boru Kakul men walking on stilts through the streets of Kandy were a common sight during the Perahera time, but the Bombay Dancers were something still never seen or heard of before.

The night of that Bombay Dance was for me, a fateful night. There had been much fanfare as dancer after dancer, some of them impersonating seductive-looking females, performed the mudras and intricate steps. And then I recognized one of the dancers who held the whole stage to himself. It was Simeon, Lily Speldewinde Livera's carpenter. I recognized him beneath the layers of powder and paint and the disguise of the fantastic embodying the exotic, with his shining satin costume, embroidered waistcoat and lavishly embellished crown.

"Look, look, that's Simeon, Auntie Lily's carpenter." I nudged my mother. Didn't she recognize him? I could so easily see through all the concealment of makeup. I was fascinated by his changed appearance. Simeon the epic hero of the Mahabaratha or Ramayana in his glittering clothes, not Simeon the carpenter in his white shirt and white cloth, sober everyday wear. His khajal-darkened eyes blazed in the stark white light shed by the petromax lamps. He twirled and swirled, brandishing a golden sword, his feet beating out the compelling rhythm of the tabla and drums. Passion, abandon, the total relinquishing of his ordinary soft-spoken self intimated those hidden fires. He was Simeon, one of the Puranic heroes. He was also the same Simeon—a man with secret, hidden urges which bordered on the sinister and threatening.

Where had I earlier encountered that seemingly innocuous man? A man whose name revealed nothing about his true identity, his family, the place where he even lived. All we knew was that he was always around at Lily Speldewinde Livera's, the home of one of my mother's greatest friends. He must have been the oddjobber there, a repairman or handyman. Always dressed in white, meek of mien, whose voice was seldom heard. The flamboyance of his alter ego was kept totally concealed.

I remember how when I was about eleven, Simeon had offered to mend the leg of my Shirley Temple doll. An enchanting doll with golden curls and blue eyes that opened and closed. I trustingly gave over my doll. Simeon promised to make a beautiful new wooden leg for her.

On my way to school one morning, Simeon beckoned to me as I passed on the other side of the road. He was obviously lying in wait for me in the shaded gloom of Auntie Lily's wide and spacious veranda. I crossed the road and walked up to the gate. Simeon had my Shirley Temple doll in his hands.

"Bebi, come, I want to take the measurements for the doll's leg." His words sounded strange. After all, the doll still had one leg. "I want to see your leg, I want to see its shape."

"No, Simeon, I have to be in school on time. The bell will ring in a little while. "Where is everybody? Auntie Lily, Margaret, Maisie, Thelma? Where is Uncle Frank and his wife?"

"Frank master and his wife are downstairs. Bebis have all gone to school. The lady is inside the house, sleeping. Only a little while, come," he wheedled.

I was reluctant. I didn't trust this man at all. His suggestions were strange to me, and yet I wanted that doll back. I found myself standing on the veranda quaking with fear. Hypnotized.

He took out a foot ruler and said, "Bebi, show me your right leg."

"Simeon, look at the other leg of the doll," I pleaded. "You don't need to see mine." "Bebi, I can't repair the doll until I see your leg," he insisted.

I had to lift the hem of my school uniform slightly to show him my leg. He placed the foot ruler against its length pressing the straight piece of wood against the calf and passed his wide palmed hand caressingly against the whole of my leg. I hurtled back, impelled by some kind of sixth sense for my safety and fled from Auntie Lily's house, stumbling over the steps, crossing the road, and entering the safe domain of school, that temporary shield against the outside world.

Simeon was untrustworthy. I would never see my doll again. I felt tainted. Sullied. The screen was parting to show me glimpses of the outside world where there was sometimes no one to offer you protection.

Watching Simeon during the Perahera, season, while he performed the Bombay dance in his glittering costume on the stage, I sensed the hollow sham of a world of enchantment and magic. Beneath the disguise charming the eye and imagination were the dark and unknown spectres that spelt the bursting of childhood's bubble illusions.

Simeon would haunt me till the end of my days, but the fear and threat I felt also embodied pity for a lonely man who had to walk unacknowledged on the streets of the world. It was when he mounted the stage that the world would applaud him, make him the centre of attraction and attention until the lights of the petromax lamps were quenched, the stage dismantled and his moment of glory passed, never to be recaptured again. Lonely, lost, forgotten. As for myself, that loss of innocence entailed growing up, and stripping the gaze through rose-coloured spectacles, to inhabit the reality of a murky landscape.

What difference was there between Simeon or the barber of my early childhood, and that doctor, a celebrated physician, the father of a classmate and playmate? Spending the day at their house, waiting for lunch to be served, a special dish being prepared in the kitchen. I sat in a corner of the veranda reading a storybook. My playmates were invisible. Was it a game of hide-and-seek they were playing?

The door of the private consultation room opened, and doctor's genial smiling face peered out. "Come in here for a moment, little girl," he smilingly beckoned me in. The room was at the end of the wide veranda. No one was to be seen.

I went up to him in all innocence. He drew me into the room, began to fondle and caress my child body. "You're such a pretty little girl, so sweet, let me kiss you," he said, enveloping me in a huge embrace, pinioning my body within his arms.

I broke free of him and, pushing him aside, I ran into the house. That lunch was agony for me. My face burned with humiliation. But this was a secret I did not withhold from my mother. I forgave my friend but not her father. It was his daughter whom he had betrayed. He did not wear a mask like Simeon dancing to create magic on an improvised stage. He was the father of my friend with an open, smiling, jovial face. A man who had never impinged on our childhood games, and yet he was the lurking predator in centuries of myth, legend, fairy and folktales with their warning signals of transformations, impersonations and metamorphoses.

There were the glass chewers and flame throwers, the men who performed acrobatics daringly in the centre of the main road with their Houdini acts. There were the "Exhibitionists," as they were named. I once saw this anonymous stranger lurking behind the shoe–flower bushes in the garden of the vicarage of the Anglican priest, intrusive eyes peering out of the interstices of leaves, bushes and flowers; and the man at Wace Park who drew all the Brownies at a picnic to view him. Then there was the Joussen Jollyman who gave us laughter, filling the air with canticles of joy.

In my childhood there existed both the frighteningly real and the imaginary, the real which led to nightmares and fear of the dark, the unknown and the invisible forces. The ritual slaughter of the cockbird in the Bali ceremonies, the winged flames, travelling through the night, the chanting of the exorcists as I lay sleepless in bed. The effigies into whose enormous eyes I gazed the next morning. My world was filled with figures that loomed over the horizon, sometimes growing larger than life.

The Jolly Joussen Jollyman

The Joussen Jollyman, how did that name emerge and from where? It was my mother who announced his arrival at our gate. "Ah, here's the Joussen Jollyman." We would leave our books and gather round, together with other onlookers and bystanders on the street, to hear him. Clicking his improvised castanets, dancing in steps of his own devising, wearing a motley of patched clothes, singing snatches of English songs and nursery rhymes, he enthralled us with his joyous abandon. But entertaining us was also to earn a few coins to keep body and soul together. Listening to his ditties, I caught words and phrase, echoes from all the conquests that had taken place in this island. Echoes from his own lost childhood. Snatches of songs and rhymes from our own childhood. "London Bridge is falling down... Oranges and Lemons... Lavender's blue, dilly dilly... Twinkle, twinkle little star." Sung with his lilting voice in a code which we had to interpret in order to recognize the magic of the Joussen Jollyman with words taken from his own mystical lexicon. A language with its twists and turns translated with our own knowledge of a familiar language. A familiar language yet one which sounded a different tongue with its original inflexions and nuances. Maze-like routes, ant-hill labyrinths.

Often in our secret childhood world, thoughts were unuttered. Inward. Finding words to describe sensations. Actions were often easier. There was the language of parents, friends, adults, in a familiar environment. An inherited language but one allied to that colonial vocabulary and syntax. A language with rules but one which also changed, casual and informal, to fit the milieu in which we lived. For things had to be renamed constantly, even the food we ate, the clothes we wore, the names we bore… There was that other language too, the language of my childhood landscape– rooted in that natural world. In music, in games, in drawings. The lullabies crooned to me were in Mungo's language. She lulled me to sleep and my sleep and dreams were part of the intimacy of her magical utterance.

The Joussen Jollyman was his own one-man theatre. He was everything to us – cabaret artiste, circus performer, court jester, clown, the divine fool – his face transmuted to fit a stage world, white with talcum powder, reddened cheeks, wearing Jacob's coat of many colours. In his hands were jingling bells, castanets and the tambourine. He was full of colour, light, music, riddles and ballads. Unlike the bogeyman or the billa of our nightmare dreams, haunting the darkness of our curtained rooms, the grotesque shadow of our imaginations falling upon the walls from the light of the flickering night lamp. The bogeyman, the billa was there, filling us with the cold chill of fear beneath our beds. He hid behind the clothes humped on the wooden clothes pegs, he stirred the water in the water jug with its covering of tasseled net and fringe of beads. The bogeyman who waited to grab your hand and drag you under the bed into the darkness that swallowed you up for ever; while the Joussen Jollyman embodied light and the dispelling of darkness.

In a Colonial Classroom

I learned my language from the Radiant Way,
I counted beaded years upon a frame,
Blew bubbles in the air to catch the sun
And send their swirling prisms high above my head
Until they burst in scattered fragments like my
Thoughts untenable and transient.

I played their games of sheep and wolves,
I sang their songs, their rhymes I mouthed,
Their verse I mimicked, around the Maypole danced,
On those steamy monsoon days of torrential rains
Gathered peasecods in those English country dances,
Forgot our cloud filled months.
Ate cherries ripe, strawberries and cream while in
My garden, the bats marauded, nightly, the laden
Guava tree, the seed dropping in minute pearls
Rooting in this virgin soil proliferating with both fruit
And flower in this rich humus impregnated with moisture and
Dews natural to our native seasons.

Rhymes of daisies pied and violets blue, lambs and roses,
Daffodils, recited I with fervour and solemnity
In this colonial classroom of the past,
The sunflower in our hedge had lost, within
Our somnolent eyes, its saffron hue,
The blood that streaked the carcass in the butcher's
Stall was pallid, violet-tinged with branded dye,

The offal baked in crenelated pies with lofty
Turrets served in platters willow patterned
Shipped in those Indiamen to far-flung destinations.

The birds whose songs were familiar to my ears
Were those of nightingales and chaffinches,
The peacock in the forest stilled its mating dance,
Silenced, its skewered tongue vanished into dark
Leaving its mourning mate with drooping wing,
Blinded its sight.

Lambs bleated in the meadows, larksong rose high
Mingling with cuckoo cries clothed in Wordsworth's
Pastoral metaphors while Tennysonian eagles from their
Tall cliffside eiries swooped down upon a turquoise
Ocean in our poetic imagination, the faery seas forlorn,
Deserted.

To my ears, the hoot of owl and cry of Devil Bird
Were alien, parrots swore strange sailor's oaths
Their feathers tough, sea-brined and salty,
Wings stiff as sailcloth toughening in the elements.

I took so long to recognize the orioles and the barbuts
Abounding in that innocent garden, feeding on golden
Mango flesh and pomegranates, ripe the fruit, the
Seed so translucent yet so ruby red.

I pored over books of ancient chivalry,
Of knights and ladies, bards and prophets.

My blood too changed by that colonial alchemy.
How then and when would I discover from
Base metals or from gold my life's true elixir?
And in which obscure epoch or century
Make that all-important discovery?

Missals and psalters too and tales of
Pilgrimage, Arthurian legends and that
Sword Excalibur that became a symbol
Of our own division.

Now all the tapestries I once viewed
Are thick with dust, covered with mildew,
In ancient houses, musty with disuse
Tattered memories, the legends lost in time,
The threads fit only for a worn out rug
Or unravelled, re-woven,
Knit into a dunce's cap to fit our uncrowned
Heads.

Nymphs and Shepherds

After spending seven years in Kadugannawa, the time came for my father to be transferred to another station, which was to be Anuradhapura, in the North Central Province. He had also been given a promotion and was now DMI–District Mechanical Inspector in the Ceylon Government Railway. He would be involved in more administrative work and was to spend many hours in the Trans Office, as it was called, next-door to our railway bungalow in Anuradhapura.

The change of place would result in a period of transition in my own life. I was to be separated from my mother for the first time. And I was never to see Mungo again. My mother decided that I too should be boarded in the Kandy Girls' High School hostel, where my sister already was, but before I became 'a boarder,' occupying a narrow iron-bed in the Junior dormitory, my sister and I were to spend a period of time with Auntie Tommy in her Boarding House. From there, my sister and I would travel to school by rickshaw every morning and would return by the same means.

I was wholly and totally unprepared for the experience–school boarding or Auntie Tommy's boarding house. I did not want to be separated from my mother and pleaded with her that I should be a day-scholar in the convent at Anuradhapura run by foreign nuns. My mother, however, was insistent that not only should my education be uninterrupted in the missionary school but also that I should be in Kandy which was considered to have a healthier climate. Anuradhapura was then considered 'a malarial station' and my mother sought to protect me from malaria.

Being a very little girl at that time I was welcomed into the hostel by the bigger girls, who for a short while made a pet of me, but later carried on with their own concerns, which left me free to discover myself. I began to experience a sense of loneliness and separateness. I went through a painful passage of self-discovery. But I was also settling into an unaccustomed but necessary routine of learning, reading, and thinking for myself. What I missed most were the narratives of my mother and Mungo's folklore and the emotional security of my mother's constant presence. I was, however, beginning to form and create my own narratives. I had left the railway enclave of Kadugannawa and bade farewell to a part of my childhood, but I was still to know that I had a long journey before me. My solitary forays and adventures on the hill and the abandoned tea estate had acclimatized me to the unexpected with paths still to be explored. This time it would be on the verge of the precipice or where my foothold was hazardous, treading the narrow rocky ledges in my ascent to the summit of mountains hitherto seen only from a distance.

The figure I was most conscious of, from the very beginning of my entrance into this strange new world of boarding life, was Rita Kaul. She was unmarried. Self-trained like many women of that era to take on responsibilities that many would quail at the thought of, like looking after her charges, both the very young as well as the others who were adolescents or approaching adulthood. Rita Kaul and the ayahs who looked after us were for the most part mother figures, but there was one among them, Elisa, full-bosomed, her thick head of curly black hair saturated with herbal oil, who was different. Those women were in charge of our bodies, washed us, bathed us, and supervised all our bodily functions. Elisa would wash me thoroughly and in the process feel the most private parts of my body. I knew very little, no, I knew nothing of those very private parts of myself. Elisa would catch me alone when I needed to be washed and wiped, and press, but gently, that unyielding unformed part of me. Her face wore a secret, bemused smile. Poor Elisa, brought from some remote village, young and full-blooded. How painful it must have been to spend her days and hours looking after us, filling our enamel wash basins, squeezing the McLean's toothpaste onto our brushes, pouring bowls of water and washing us after even our toilet visits; how she must have craved for the fulfillment of her own instinctual urges...

After a time I lost sight of her, but the nameless curiosity I felt then was to tease my mind years and years later when I searched for the explanation of her experimental probings. Perhaps she herself was no longer a virgin when she came to the hostel. A married woman with children, who needed to work for survival. I remember her satiny skin, her full cheeks with an inner light beneath each cheek, the insidious smell of oil on the rippling waves of hair. Elisa. I could not express in words what I could not understand, but I resented her intrusion of my body. Her invasion of my freedoms so hard won on that lonely hill in Kadugannawa. What was innocence? How could one talk of a lost innocence when that word was not even known or understood in a world of childhood where each new experience signified my own personal and intimate pleasures of discovery. And how could innocence be lost when we did not know we even possessed it? But if we learned its meaning in the realization of its loss, there was also the acquiring of knowledge of self, of others.

I was beginning to learn the importance of individual territory and boundaries in this old two-storeyed building. I now spent my life in the company of others. I watched and in turn I was watched. We observed each other and sought friendship where there was harmony, but the discords could not be kept out. Rita Kaul lived among us, retreating into her little wooden-panelled cubicle at the end of the junior dormitory. At night I glimpsed her fleetingly in her crepe-de-chine silk kimono. This was a world of women and women alone. There was only one single night watchman with his lantern, who kept vigil throughout those long and silent hours when school bells and voices were stilled.

My narrow bed was arranged the way Rita Kaul had taught us. My Fuji silk pajamas reposed beneath the pillows folded within a silk sachet. My mother had bought everything from the Chinese peddler who used to come up the winding steps to our house in Kadugannawa. The dormitory had a little curtained cubicle with a commode and slop-pail. Bandara Menike, her mat spread on the wooden-panelled floor where she slept every night, would lead us behind the white curtains, the night lamp in her hands acting like a camera obscura, whenever we woke her up, tiptoeing into the darkness of the cubicle, the wooden panels of the floor creaking under our tread.

During the day Rita Kaul was impeccably groomed, her wavy black hair arranged in a bun on the nape of her neck, secured with shiny hairpins and a hairnet. She wore tailored dresses of linen or silk, with collars, buttons, buckled belts, buckled court shoes and stockings. At night she wore felt carpet slippers, high-necked, long-sleeved cotton nightgowns. And was swathed in a kimono.

It was the first time I was out of home, living in a hostel. I was one of the 'small girls' and sat beside Rita Kaul for breakfast in order to be initiated into boarding life. Uniformity prevailed in the way the table was laid, and in the shape, size, colour of plates, cups, saucers. Rita Kaul sitting upright in her straight-backed chair pulled up close to the table. On her plate was buttered toast and, I watched fascinated, two varieties of red-hot sambols. She spread pol sambol on one piece of toast, and katta sambol with crushed dried chilies, maldive fish, onions, salt and lime on the other slice. It seemed much more interesting than the soft-boiled egg and toast that was before me. When my mother came to visit me I described this tantalizing breakfast to her, and the next time Miss Kaul smiled amusedly at me and asked, "Would you like some too?" She generously offered both varieties of sambols to me. I said, "Yes, please." We shared our breakfast together amiably. I did not yet know what it was to be self-conscious about being curious about other people's differences.

Wartime rationing was on and there were many substitutes at breakfast. Wheat porridge was one of them. Bowls of wheat porridge with milk and sugar. There was a doctor's daughter who bravely spooned every bit of it down her throat and then, creeping quietly into the study before leaving for school, vomited all the porridge into her suitcase. Rita Kaul discovered it in the process of seeing that we had packed all our books, pencils and erasers. What a to-do there was in the boarding that morning. First of all the mess had to be cleaned up; the exercise books and textbooks were soggy. There were tears too, but I don't remember the doctor's daughter ever eating wheat porridge again.

What our English principal, Ruth Allen, had for breakfast was quite different. I made my secret discovery one morning when

Miss Kaul sent me to her bungalow with a message at breakfast time. Ruth Allen was seated on the lawn beneath a jam-fruit tree thronged with early morning birds twittering in the branches as they pecked at the ripe berries. She sat at her white-linen-spread breakfast table as if it were a summer morning in the English countryside. My eyes quickly took in the silver toast rack and silver butter dish, the Chivers marmalade, and the teapot in its quilted tea-cosy. She was in the act of scooping out a segment of ripe yellow papaw. I stood before her in my starched white uniform and gravely delivered my message. For a moment I forgot that she was the august principal of our school – one of the several missionary principals responsible for the well-being of our souls, kept bright and shining like newly minted coins polished with daily prayers and hymns and Bible readings at morning assembly and Bible classes. But as our eyes met – she being a woman whose senses were alive to the morning freshness of the day – she smiled at me, probably amused at my gravity of mien. Miss Kaul knew I would retain the message clearly in my mind.

The years would also preserve other memories; at that moment I began writing the poem, which took shape and form many years later when my investigative explorations of a past, which I was compelled to retrieve and recall through a difficult passage on stormy seas, began to make sense. Life behind the convolvulus and the hibiscus hedges was a screen from which one day I had to emerge. Was that safety only illusory and temporary? I would remember Ruth Allen all my life. In remembering her I was to know myself as I was then.

One day I fell sick and was isolated in the sickroom downstairs. When I was convalescing, Miss Kaul plied me with books. I read hour after hour, all of Dickens in their old bound first editions. I devoured each book, discovering the writer whose stories I had heard related by my mother. I was now ready to read independently, silently. Meals were brought in on a tray. At night, one of the hostel ayahs spread her mat beside my bed and slept until the bell rang to wake us up. *Little Dorrit, The Old Curiosity Shop, David Copperfield, Hard Times,* I couldn't have enough. I was described as devouring books, and sometime known as a 'bookworm.'

"May I have more books, please?" I asked Miss Kaul. "Have you finished these already? You read too fast." The next time she picked up the books and said, "Have you read all these?" I said, "No, I haven't." I began re-reading them.

Before I was ready to leave the sickroom, a few more patients were brought in. There were four young patients in the room, bored at being cosseted in bed. In between meals we ate the military biscuits, which were part of my father's wartime rations. He as a member of the Volunteer forces. The military biscuits were a kind of hard square cabin biscuit made with coarsely ground wheat and oats. My father told me it could sustain the soldiers on their long marches. I had a good stock of them under my mattress. The evenings were long in the sickroom with all of us boxed up inside. I stopped reading and we would talk instead. We began to unfold our secret thoughts. Curiosity about our growing bodies.

Sheila's eyes were bright. They gleamed with excitement. "What are you like under your nighties?" she asked. The dim bulb of the electric light cast shadows on the walls. "Would you like to see what I look like? I'll show you. Then you next, and you, and you…"

We were all very excited, waiting for some kind of dramatic revelation. A cabaret, I thought. Everybody kicking up their legs or gracefully pirouetting in turn, having learned Eurythmics and ballet from Babe Jonklass in school when we danced in the main hall. The bedsteads were of iron with a base of springs. They creaked as we sat up. We would be the audience and then we would take our turn to be the virtuoso performers, giving our solo items.

Marlene suddenly sprang up. Flung off her cotton nightgown, and like Aurora, appeared before our eyes, her arms moving rhythmically as Babe Jonklass had taught us. She was caught up in steps of her own devising, the movements gathering a wild Bacchic momentum, whirling about, almost falling off the bed. We were all spellbound. Nakedness revealed, stripped of the severity of uniforms. Sameness. Conscious of shape. Not illusion but reality. Suddenly we were aware of an almost imperceptible breathing at the keyhole. This was Saturnalia for us. It never seemed to end. Suddenly the door burst open. Miss Kaul appeared.

"You naughty, naughty girls," she scolded, but not harshly. "I must put you in separate rooms."

None of us had reached puberty yet but we were caught up in what we imagined to be the forbidden pleasures of discovery. Soon, too soon, we would go back to the demure concealment of our bodies in their pleated uniforms and buttoned blazers, until we achieved the freedom of flinging them off for all time, being unashamed of the true image. Those were the discoveries instinctual, that we made in that primeval garden...

In the hostel garden there was a lilac tree with purple flowers and beds of barbeton daisies, asters, Easter lilies, jasmine and dahlias. My father sent me a star tortoise all the way from Anuradhapura. It lived in that garden, and in the evenings when we were sent out to play on the lawn I would seek it out and hold it in my hands. We were each in our own way learning to survive in a different clime.

One morning an Englishwoman was brought to this garden. In her hands she bore a hazel wand. "A water-diviner," Miss Kaul told us. "As she walks with the hazel wand over the lawn, it will quiver wherever there is a hidden spring." She walked up and down the lawn, a slender Englishwoman wearing a patterned linen dress, buckled shoes and stockings, a straw hat with a sarcenet ribbon round its crown, the brim shading her face from the sun. I willed that hazel wand to quiver. A secret spring must surely be there. Perhaps a well would then be dug. A well full of dragonflies and water sprites. At one moment the wand began to move as if the sibilant whispers of the buried spring were summoned by mysterious, unexplainable forces of the hidden subterranean earth depths. At that spot, she stood silent, the Englishwoman, the slender wand quivering in her hand as if she herself felt the ancient blood rhythms move within her own body. Herself the guardian of those ancient sources of nature. Would the wand in anyone else's hands move as it did in hers? What was her special gift to lift those secrets out of the earth, to feel, perhaps to hear the bubbling sound of water as it whispered within its source? "Yes, there is a spring of water at that spot," Miss Kaul told us. Then a well would be dug there? We could peer into that magical mirror which revealed our own secrets then? No, the well was never dug. The water lay undisturbed as it had for aeons and aeons. Everyone would forget. That sunny day and that magical wand would be forgotten, effaced from memory with death and departure.

The lawn remained undisturbed. In the shadow of damp ferns and moss the star tortoise moved stone-like among the grey rocks. The English lady disappeared forever and went back to her country. She would walk over the earth's familiar terrain in some other part of the world or in her own countryside with her sensitive magical hazel wand always by her side. Exploring what ordinary humans could not – the source of inner springs. Subterranean secrets. The beginning of creation. Not any branch from any tree. Only the hazel tree. I would have to make an imaginary tree grow in my own mind and bear its branch in my hands. I had to reach deep down to those buried sources of my own beginnings, listen to the secrets that words would whisper in my blood. Carry that wand throughout with me on an unfinished journey. Standing rooted on that spot on the lawn was that nameless Englishwoman who had metamorphosed into a hazel tree. And so she remained in my memory.

There were two separate worlds within the hostel. The Big Girls formed a distinctive entity presenting a solid bulwark of dignity and aloofness. They inhabited a world of their own, sometimes condescending to talk with the small girls, allowing them to play with their cutout paper dolls with paper wardrobes from English books. It was comforting to me in my homesickness. One night when the township of Kandy was filled with British Tommies, there was a big hubbub in the hostel. Everyone was in bed. Lights were out. Snatches of song echoed up the school drive. There was a banging on the doors. Whistles. Summons to the girls to come out. The big board at the entrance to the school proclaimed that it was certainly a girls' school. The night watchman was helpless to quell the bunch of Tommies.

Well primed at the "Pink Elephant" pub in the heart of the town, the soldiers were homesick and heartsick, preparing to leave for the battlefront somewhere in Burma or some other part of Southeast Asia. Lord Mountbatten was in command of SEAC during this period and was stationed in Kandy.

"Let us in, let us in," they called, out pounding vigorously on the doors.

"Girls, stay where you are." Miss Kaul was guardian and protector with a solid barrier of hostel ayahs. The Big Girls felt a sense of excitement and fear at the same time. The teachers, Miss Nonis, Miss Abayasekera, Miss Kotigala and the others came into the dinner room in their kimonos.

"There'll be blue birds over
The white cliffs of Dover
Just you wait and see..."

Voices echoed in the still night. Songs that belonged to the camaraderie of the doomed with their already lost dreams. Songs that clamoured for a world to be unchanged if and when they ever were to return to Blighty...

Miss Ruth Allen had by then contacted the Military Headquarters, and soon the Military Police roared in on their motorcycles. The soldiers were persuaded – or had they to be compelled, to leave that chaste abode of teenage and very young hostellers? What would have happened if the doors had given way? The Big Girls were in a tizzy. They would embellish the happening and relate with exaggeration everything to the day-scholars the next morning. Somehow it seemed sad when those unknown soldiers stumbled into the dark, leaving as it were an unfinished epoch. The time for the departure of the colonial presence would also take place within the next few years.

Rita Kaul had made a fetish of looking after us, and life was regulated by the daily rituals she devised for our well-being. On a special table were ranged all the tonics that would keep us fit and strong. We were fed with iron tonics, which we sipped through straws so that our teeth would not be stained. Bottles of Panepepton, Waterburys Compound, and Seven Seas Cod Liver Oil from which we were given daily dosages. And there were all the other purgations we went through. Besides nauseous doses of castor oil, we drank Fizzy glasses of Eno's Fruit Salts (Andrew's Liver Salts were for adults). Why did we need all these interior cleansings? Were they meant to curb any rumblings and rebelliousness of volatile, colonial subjects? Miss Kaul filled a little duck-shaped glass with warm salted water and tilted it through the beak into each of my nostrils. Trickling down to my throat I felt as if tiny, briny waves flooded its passage. After dinner each night, the ayahs filled rows of tumblers brimming with salt water for gargling our throats. The night air was filled with our choir of croaking frogs. After the gargle we were fed with tiny comfits compounded of liquorice and sugar to prevent coughs and colds. Our voices were now perfect for singing "Cherry Ripe," "Early One Morning," and Rounds.

Our parents had been instructed to bring us sweets and chocolates for 'afters.' The tins and bottles of confectionary were ranged on the shelves of a locked cupboard. We would stand encircling Miss Kaul after lunch while she doled out our share. Glass containers, of lemon drops, acid drops, spirals of barley sugar were what my mother supplied me with. Miss Kaul poured in hot water to melt the last of the barley sugar, which she prised out with a spoon.

I lived, but not for very long, within this carefully spun cocoon of fragile and transient safety. It was a brief and illusory feeling, for even within this enclave the outside world crept in with its fearful emotions of confusion, perplexity and loneliness.

I experienced a time of intense unhappiness for which Rita Kaul could offer no paregoric. The darkness of being threatened. Isolated. We were living in what appeared to be a haven of female peace and harmony, but the mirage was dissipated into fragments leaving us without the comforts of even that illusion. The fact that I adapted, after a free almost vagabond life in childhood, to an ordering of my hours and days, helped me to be an assiduous student to whom learning was a delight even if it were grounded in an alien ideology. An ideology of which I was still to become conscious. But it caused unhappiness in a playmate and friend of mine – a girl who was a few years older than myself.

It irked this girl that I had turned out to be a student who won prizes, came first in class and in whom the teachers found promise. It was an unrehearsed part of my life. No one had prepared me for what I now had to face, alone. I would in time move out of that tormenting period, but it was the beginning of understanding emotions that would surface years later – betrayal of friendship, cold-shouldering, and the waking thoughts of a sinister presence ever beside you, invading your private space, invading your very being.

Physically bigger, stronger, over-aged for the class, this girl did not shine in her studies. It was my mother who had put me into all this trouble for she had spoken to Miss Kaul and the principal recommending that those two sisters should be given a place in the boarding. The younger sister was as mild and gentle as a kitten. The elder one tormented me. She had that enabling power to instill a corrosive fear through her hard cold silences, and whispered words of contumely: "Favouration, favouration. How could you be absent from school for so long and still come first? The teachers are favouring you." And sometimes she would physically hurt me, push me stealthily from behind or shove me about. I did not as yet have the knowledge to fight back like a wild cat and oppose her. Vulnerability was not a shield. Being left out of private games, conversations, I had still to cultivate the ploys and strategies to contend with an insidious enemy. Time would teach me. The enemy would always be there waiting to undermine, to set off the detonation. It was best to avoid the morass and make oneself invisible, skirting the edges of that dangerous no-man's land. Those were the secrets of childhood. The adults had little knowledge of the dark tunnels in which we moved blindly, stealthily until we reached the light.

When would the holidays arrive? When would my mother come to carry me off from boarding school for even a few brief hours at the home of her friend Lily Livera? I had to escape. To run away. I planned it meticulously. The clothes I needed were packed away. I knew how to unbolt the door downstairs. I had no plan about the route I was to take but it lay on the road outside the convolvulus hedge. Perhaps I would go to Lily Livera's, which was close to the hostel. From there my mother would be summoned – I did not think of the consequences the disruption would cause to my future. I had not relinquished the recklessness that had impelled my footsteps on that lonely hill. I left my bed. Everyone was dead asleep. Having crept down the stairway, avoiding the creaking stairs, I found myself in the parlour before the big door. The key was in the lock. A heavy wooden bar lay across the double door. I could not lift it and step out into a freedom full of unforeseen dangers. I had to return up the stairs. To my bed. It would not be the last time I had to plan escape. The time would come when I would go through the barriers or through the open gates stepping out onto unmapped land. As I lay in bed that night I dreamed of flight. That journey was still to be.

The bullying, subtle and secret, continued. The days were dark, clouded. The sun disappeared behind a cloud but the darkness would not last forever.

I longed for the day when my mother would come to take us back to Anuradhapura. When she came at the end of term she brought my sister and myself each a pair of brand-new tailored navy-blue slacks and white cotton shirts for the long train journey. At Polgahawela station, the transit point for the connecting train, we waited on the platform with our suitcases. On one of the railway tracks was a stationary train, the compartments filled with an excited gaggle of young men leaning out of the windows smiling, waving, giving wolf-whistles at the two of us. We were in for a few boos and cat-calls too. We realized that we did not belong, could not be accepted in these new-fangled garments which marked us out as being different. I felt embarrassed. Singled out for the wrong kind of attention. Being mocked at. I was only too happy when the train arrived at the station and we began our next journey. I had been so proud of my new clothes. I was now conspicuous in the wrong way. We were attired in clothes that were synonymous with a culture at odds with the one we lived in. I needed to be colourless and less conspicuous for my safety. To be exposed on that lonely isolated platform had shown me that the oasis would not shield you from the vast desert beyond

My father was later transferred from Anuradhapura to Colombo, and was involved in more administrative work. My mother decided to set up home in Kandy. Unmarried sisters , brothers, her cousins, her friends all lived there. The family house was still a fortress in Piachaud Gardens. My grandfather had, however, asserted his own independence, and he called his territory "Sunnyside Gardens." My life in the school hostel came to an end. Miss Kaul ceased to be my guardian. In later years she became my friend.

I was growing up. Moving among innumerable aunts, uncles, and cousins. Forming new friendships. Shedding the ordered routine of hostel life, abandoning myself to the exploration of new freedoms. Often I rushed headlong into danger. "You always go where angels fear to tread," my mother would say. She could do nothing to quell my rebellious nature. Those who could not discern what I truly was were perhaps deceived, or was there a certain envious irony when they described me, as the old retired teacher Miss De Vos once uttered tartly: "Ah, you are a paragon of virtue!" What was the point of disputing that contention? I wanted to be and I could be a chameleon. Nature provided me with both camouflage and metamorphosis. I was the sphinx. The enigma. And grew to be Sybillic in utterance. Intuition and prophecy were, I was to discover, protective as well as dangerous. In the costume box of my imagination, I had several changes to fit the roles I assumed from time to time.

A Missionary Lady *(for R.A.)*

In the garden,
Early morning,
The English missionary
Sits eating ripe papaw
Scooped out with a silver spoon.
Already the trees are fruiting
And purple magenta bougainvillea
Cascades into her ordered garden.
Birds sing, marbles of sound
Clinking against each other
And the braids of her auburn-grey hair
Are shell-coiled round her ears,
As if to shut out the noise of birds
And human voices.

I think of you with nostalgia
And pity, single, lonely English lady
With no one to share your bed.
You looked into my submissive brown face
Often, but did you ever remember
The careful regard of my dark eyes
Burning a hole into your existence
Like sun scorched paper.

You made us puritans
You preached a stern morality
And yet you wept, lonely
Over an exile's letters,
The hot sun left your skin dry, mottled,
Your patterned silk gowns
Clung with time, more closely, to your angular limbs,
Your fine-boned hands, sensitive as butterflies,
Yet so impersonal.
Enclosed within a safe garden
Among the lazy tortoises and purple lilac,
It took us centuries to break away
From that alien pattern of living,
Nor can I weep over, or regret
Its final disruption.

A Wider World

Living in Kandy was a moving out into the greater world away from the railway enclaves of Kadugannawa and Anuradhapura. We no longer lived in railway bungalows but had to search for private houses, especially one that would be close to Girls' High School where we would be day-scholars. My life began to change here, and our home became the family oasis where all the cousins, aunts and uncles congregated, together with many of my father's friends who were part of the colonial backdrop. I missed my wanderings on the hill and the freedom I had to make my solitary explorations wherever I found myself. I was, however, to find alternate routes.

The township of Kandy was full of uniformed men and women who belonged to the British Forces and later, the American GIs crowded in. The huge camouflaged trucks conveying troops would pass by our house. Private houses were also commandeered for the officers. Military camps were set up just outside the environs of Kandy. Schools were turned into military hospitals and the classrooms converted into wards for men recuperating from war injuries brought over from the campaigns waged on the South-east Asian battlefront. I was taken into one of those military hospitals by my father who was accompanying one of his soldier companions. It was a sombre scene. A quiet, silent place with rows of British soldiers propped up against pillows, their faces wan with the pallor of pain.

The cinemas screening Gaumont British News and several war films, like the Mrs Miniver series and "In Which We Serve," together with Hollywood movies, were crowded with khaki-clad men and women.

I would even be taken for all the adult films along with my mother and aunts. Looking at me, reminded of children left behind at home in England, a soldier sent a message to the group I was with in the foyer: "May we give the little girl a kiss? She reminds us of a daughter..." I was self-conscious, and embarrassed the soldier whose name we never knew by bursting into a storm of tears and protests. How could I understand those longings, that feeling of homesickness? I had never been in exile, although the fine threads were beginning to separate in my cocoon.

My father was a Regimental Sergeant Major, an RSM, in the Volunteer Forces. He was very smartly accoutred in khaki uniform with badges and gleaming buttons impressed with the regimental insignia, and a well-polished leather Sam Browne belt across his broad chest.

"Will he be sent to the battlefront? Will I ever see him again if he goes?" I asked my mother fearfully. "If he receives orders, yes, he will have to go," was all she said. My mother's friend, Lily Speldewinde Livera, had a daughter by her first husband. Lily's daughter and son-in-law were both prisoners-of-war in Singapore after its Fall and during the occupation by Japanese troops thereafter. The daughter alone survived. A sad woman with a careworn face, dressed in black widow's weeds after the death of her husband in the camp.

English soldiers and occasionally an American, one of the Yankees as they were called, would come home on my father's invitation, joining in the sing-songs, the family gatherings, lunches and dinners.

At the same time there were the old colonials, the travellers over the face of the colonial globe, and the English planters who entered our lives. Where was there a corner for me to study, do my lessons, my homework, with all the people who crowded into that home of ours? I had even more freedom now, as there was no one to supervise my studies. I began to read voraciously, anything that was at hand, but my shyness remained. I was hurled too early into an incomprehensible world of adults, but those early intimations of life with all its conflicts and complexities prevented me from being too cushioned, too protected from turmoil and upheaval. I began to see what effects the war had in that society. Broken marriages, war-babies who were accepted and assimilated into the larger family, war marriages, brief tempestuous love affairs with lonely servicemen, war widows, and everyone having what was termed 'a good time' with the Forces. 'A good time' meant love affairs even while the dance of death was being enacted.

Auntie Gladys and Uncle Alroy had moved to Kandy and were our neighbours. Sylvia was with them too. Thelma would come from wherever she was with her mother. There was no end to the parties and visits. There was a continuous round of them. The parties now had 'soldier boys' and sailors because there was a bevy of young girls with whom to dance the tango and the fox-trot; to sing "White Cliffs of Dover" and "I'll Wait For You" and to have transient, passionate romances with before they departed overnight to 'The Front' never to be seen or heard of again.

There was a big Fancy Dress party one evening at Uncle Alroy's and Auntie Gladys' home. The hall was crowded with guests and family members with the 'soldier boys' in their uniforms and peaked caps, and a few sailors too. Ninny Paulusz, in pink gingham rompers, pranced about among the eighteenth century ladies with their powdered wigs and the veiled 'oriental' houris. Where would she end up one day? Would she migrate, like so many other Burghers, to Australia? Slipping so easily into her role, with her brown credulous eyes wide open behind her spectacles, was that air of innocence a bar to romance? There were so many British soldiers, sailors and airmen, lonely men, far from home, their wallets filled with photographs of girlfriends in

England, wives, children, parents, brothers and sisters. Ninny Paulusz did not appear to have wartime romances with any of them. Jack Kells, Charlie Culbert, Ivor, Nick Carter, names of Irishmen, Englishmen, from London, County Cork, Shoreditch, our minds mapped with landmarks that were so distant to us, visited our home, bringing their gifts of Black Magic chocolates, cigarette cartons and Bully Beef. They left the Burgher boys fuming, taking away their partners – the young nurses like Doris and all the pretty girls, Phyllis, Thelma, Helen, Beryl, who were being courted by the English soldiers. What a party it was with 'passing the cushion' games, Musical Chairs and Musical Arms, Blind Man's Buff, forfeits, dancing. The men disappearing at regular intervals behind the scenes for their whiskeys round the dining table, with toast after toast being proposed, the final 'One for the road' of which there were several roads and several journeys. And who knew where the ultimate destination lay?

I too wanted to be part of that Fancy Dress parade and had turned over the pages of *Weldons Journal* with the coloured plates of Harem Beauty, Pierrot and Pierrette, harlequins, an eighteenth century lady, a Tudor Queen. I wanted to wear the 'Harem' costume, not knowing that I was too young and insouciant for the role that went along with the mysterious yashmak and the satin trousers with the embroidered waistcoat over a long-sleeved blouse. I wish that all those pages had been preserved. My mother had shown the journal to Auntie Gladys who felt it would be the ideal costume for Sylvia. The costume projected the Orientalist dream of the houris described by the European travellers of the nineteenth century, the women who knew all the ways of giving a man the ultimate escapist dreams of pleasure in bed, a sexuality which they imagined had greater freedoms than the West. I was totally unaware of those narratives by European writers who ascribed these qualities to 'the otherness' encountered in those women in their descriptions and encounters, their paintings, their travel diaries and journals. The discoveries were to come later as one explored the historical routes of colonialism and their dominant roles.

I was left without a costume for the fancy-dress party. I had a wide-skirted white organdy dress. I would make myself a symbol of Time, of that age, of that era. I snipped off yards of narrow black velvet ribbon and sewed a clock-face on my skirt. I was 'Times Progeny!' I would set the hands of the clock at midnight. The witching hour. The hour before the break of dawn when that vast and hollow detonation would take place, and the epoch in which we lived lie in shattered fragments before us all. We would not be destined to see those soldiers and sailors again. They would depart for their distant battlefields, to be mown down by bullets, drowned in submarines, becoming prisoners of war, or their planes devastating cities with their bombs. And those who returned would bear their memories back to their countries and homes.

The impact of the war was felt on school life, too. Ruth Allen, our principal, would read, at morning assembly, snippets of news from letters, letters from 'Home,' letters from all parts of the world, even prisoner-of-war camps in Germany. Sometime her guests, soldiers, would be brought along to address us at our formal assembly. Homesick soldiers who were faced with the strange and novel experience of speaking from a school platform in a missionary school. Behind them on the wall loomed a solemn painting of the one-time missionary principal Miss Mallet by Karl Kasmann, the Estonian artist. Miss Mallet, who later became Mrs Gordon, posed in her graduate gown, seated at her desk, a figure of unquestioning authority. Two pre-Raphaelite paintings flanked the portrait.

Ruth Allen had been in the forefront of my life ever since I entered the school hostel. I remember a game we played with her in the hostel one evening. For each question that you answered correctly you could step forward until you passed the others and reached the very front. One of the questions required the answer, "Rule Britannia, Britannia Rules the Waves." We could not forget how we stood at the cinema for "God Save the King"... We collected money for the War Cause. This was done during the Bible Study period every week. We knew nothing of the issues that were being fought for. VE Day marked 'our' victory too. We recited "Hohenlinden" and "The Burial of Sir John Moore at Corunna" with passion, but my mind used to wander with the Cloud Messenger in those Sandesaya poems, over cities so vividly described, closer to my own experience of history and society and landscape. At the same time through the strength and dominance of that other tongue, through a different myth, allegory, metaphor, what was nearer home appeared to be more distant and exotic and what was real lay much further away. Yet there was no time to think of such complexities. Confusions were less, life was more simplistic. The complexities were beneath the surface to be unearthed aeons later. The senses, the ears, eyes, tongue, savoured all the differences until they became a composite amalgam of hearing, sight, taste embodied in the flavour of a different speech of reference. The nightingale's song sounded, even in an imagined landscape, more familiar than any bird that perched on a branch in our own gardens. The changeling feeling was reflected even in my handwriting, dipping into inkwells with G nibs, writing in an alien language, shaping letters, words, sentences, shaping the years and lives with a fastidiousness of trying to achieve a perfection which we strove so hard to attain. We had two languages, two alphabets, the shapes of which were different, contrastive even. We even thought in two languages, spoke in two tongues, slipping into a duality and divisiveness that was engendered thereby.

The Day-Scholar

I became a day-scholar at Girls' High School and sallied forth to school every morning wearing my pith hat pipe-clayed in white or khaki helmet to protect me from the rays of the sun. Did I need that protection? No, I did not, but I submitted to that imposition anyway. Perhaps my mother was following that way of life belonging to the colonial idea where the sun was supposed to cause heatstroke or sunstroke.

I first carried my books arranged on a blue-covered Royal Society drawing book, and later on in a leather satchel filled with boxes of coloured crayons, Grey Hound pastels, Reeves Watercolours, pens, pencils, textbooks and exercises books all imported from England. On my way to school I was observed intently by Lily Speldewinde Livera's grandchildren. They were the daughters of Frank Speldewinde, whose second wife was Sinhalese. The daughters were sent to the Kandy Convent. Their pale moonwhite faces with their watchful eyes followed my progress as I walked confidently along with my brand-new books. They longed to study at Girls' High, where there were no distinctions between the students. At the Convent there were various stratas: the Cottage girls among whom were orphans or foundlings, Eurasian offspring boarded by planter fathers, and the privileged ones – a system which prevailed under the aegis of Roman Catholic nuns. And the skirts of the white uniforms at the convent were much longer in length than those of ours.

Although I was now a day-scholar and had more freedom, it was in many senses a protected way of life behind the thick-leaved convolvulus hedge which screened off the outside world. On the green games field we played endlessly between classes – netball, tennequoits and badminton. We jumped over wooden hurdles, practised zig-zag races adroitly side-stepping between lines of rolled-up coir mats. We ran round and round the pitch as we called it, and at one stage played baseball as a result of the American influence during World War II.

In the big Hall we sang choir songs – "The Lonely Ash-Grove," "Down in the Valley," and Sea Shanties like "What shall we do with the drunken sailor?" We twisted multi-coloured ribbons, skipped round a Maypole, and learned English country-dances like Hunston House and Gathering Peasecods. The older girls donned black frilled gowns and black lace mantillas as they performed elegant Spanish dances on the stage. Others in sailor suits kicked up their heels in "The Sailors Hornpipe." There were kitchen orchestras with the banging of pots and pans. "Riding down from Bangor" was enacted wearing Welsh costumes and aprons and bonnets. Piano solos and duets were performed. The plays of Shakespeare, Marlowe, Sheridan and Shaw were staged. We were yet to discover our true selves emerging from layers and layers of a colonial education. When would we ever get to listen closely to the familiar tongue of the everyday world outside of the convolvulus hedge?

From Standard Five onwards Gladys Vanderstraaten taught us almost every subject under the sun, from those colonial syllabuses that were planned in the Empire, transferred in our Readers and poetry books, while we learned to do sums with pounds, shillings and pence. Gladys was very proud that, as one of her little pupils, I had got the highest marks in the Kandy district for General Intelligence in Standard Five, but she never praised me openly. Only whispered it in my ear with a pleased smile. "Would you like your daughter to have a double promotion?" was the question often asked my mother as I made my exploratory progress in school. My mother, however, preferred that I should go through each stage of my learning at a normal pace. Racing ahead of the subjects taught at school could be done in my own private world: drawing, painting, creating stories, writing poetry, and reading adult books. Access to books was never denied me and my father's library was mine to discover.

Miss Vanderstraaten taught us about those mysterious geometrical calculations. We measured and drew parallelograms, right-angled triangles, rhombuses, colouring them with crayons. We memorized Walter de la Mare's poetry. Recited "Nicholas Nye" with "expression" and the correct English pronunciation – Standard English and RP (Received Pronunciation) as ingrained by her. That was our colonial education in the missionary school. With Gladys Van there could be no pins in belts or at neck openings. Nails must be trimmed and impeccable. And heads too or they could be metaphorically lopped off.

Miss Van's own appearance never varied from day to day. Wearing her neatly tailored linen dresses of a uniform design, collar, buttoned in front and buckled belt, court shoes and stockings. Her hair with its soft brown waves fitted her head like a silken helmet, kept in place by a fine, almost invisible hair-net. "It's a wig," the Big Girls would say. It was a subject we conjectured on endlessly. But it wasn't a wig. It was her very own hair neatly brushed, entrapped in a filmy web. She never aged. In our eyes our teachers never grew old. They had learned the language of children and shared in that private world of our innermost thoughts and feelings.

On a weekday, a Friday afternoon, drowsing in the classroom, Miss Van would open a register, seat each one of us by the open door so that the sunlight glanced on our heads of hair. She would then take up two pencils and gently rake through unbraided plaits and fringes and Eton crops. It could have led to the most delicious sensations creeping over our scalps fragrant with Lux and Palmolive soap, but we were on tenterhooks lest we fell short of her scrupulous standards. Some of those heads were like luxuriant tropical jungles in which lurked 'creatures.' What a mild way of describing those unknown inhabitants of a wilderness of untrammelled black locks. "Head Inspection," it was called. And we earned marks, for the cleanest scalp. 'A' was pure and pristine glory, 'B' denoted a subtle backsliding, 'C' was ignominious, 'D' a catastrophe.

With what infinite patience those teachers performed their duties. What indignities to subject them to. And ourselves generating feelings of fear, trepidation? Was it not an exercise in moral restraint for our teachers to resort to once every week, term after term, year after year? It was to their credit that they never jabbed our scalps with those chopsticks-like pencils, scratching with lead points those indelible commandments of cleanliness on that parchment. Those were the very hands so beautifully manicured that held the whitest chalk tracing equations, sums, phrases, and sentences on the blackboard, taking us along the routes that marked the adventure saga of our learning. We bent our heads in submission like sacrificial lambs while those merciless pencils hunted out their prey. How assiduous the hunter was. There was no escape for the lurking beastie. Yet sometimes that gentle probing was like a caress. There was never hurt. Never pain, for us, but they were not the memories I would want my teachers to carry to the grave.

At the Methodist church we had Harvest Festivals just as you would have in a country church in an English village. The altar was piled with fruit and vegetables. In church, we waved our palm branches as we walked down the aisle crying our Hosannas. And later on when we began studying Latin, Mrs De Mel draped us in Roman togas as we enacted a wedding procession on the stage, singing and chanting the marriage hymn in Latin, "Hymen, O hymenis." What a culture-mix we experienced, eclectic, polyglot and in many instances alien to the indigenous culture of us students. It didn't matter whether you were a Buddhist, a Hindu or a follower of Islam. Such was the strength of that colonial era, and of that missionary zeal, that all the students met for assembly every morning and prayed and sang Christian hymns and bowed their heads in Christian prayer. It was indeed a microcosmic world of the British Empire, and our lives were shaped and formed to a great extent by the missionary principals like Elsie Shire and Ruth Allen, exceptional and indomitable women. With their strong sense of integrity and moral values, they taught their lessons more through their own example than anything else. What they set out to do was dictated by the firm conviction that they had a mission, and part of that mission was to impart an education based on religious values taught in an alien language, that 'other tongue.' Some of those principals were young and beautiful. They founded schools and colleges, dedicating their entire lives to their charges

We were completely immured in the history of the British Empire, its language, its literature, so much so that, when we started writing poetry ourselves as students, the natural forms of expression for us were the forms of English poetry: our models were the Augustans and the Romantics, our verse forms the sonnet, the lyric, heroic couplets. In spite of this, looking at the school magazines from the 1930s to the 1950s one could find real talent and an awareness of our own culture in poems like "The Perahera," "Ante Lucan," "The Muezzin Calls," by Sunethra Wickremasinghe and Fauzynne Sally, both of whom died tragically young.

At that time we did have our own Ceylonese poets – Blazé and Keyt – but it was only anthologies of English poetry we read. This began during our earliest days at school, when Miss Gladys Vanderstraaten read Walter de la Mare to us and asked us to write our own poems on animals and birds. "Nicholas Nye" was one of my favourites and so was "The Scarecrow." I was so influenced at that early age (and all this began in middle-school and kindergarten days) that I decided to be the Scarecrow for a Literary Characters competition between the school Houses. Wearing an old tweed coat, a bashed-in felt hat, a shirt with missing buttons, patched breeches, old boots with a meerschaum pipe clenched between my lips, I won the Lawrence House prize, above all the Cleopatras and Henry the VIIIs and Sigiriya Frescoes.

My Auntie Elsie was the first Ceylonese Inspectress of schools. Miss Westrop was the last Englishwoman to occupy that post. Miss Westrop had to come for school inspection at Girls' High School. I was in the Baby Class. She sat quietly on one of the baby chairs at the back of the room and watched the lessons in progress. It must have been nursery rhymes, counting beads on frames or writing on the slate that day. She was unobtrusive. A quiet presence. Aunt Elsie took over and came very often for school inspection. The teachers were kept on their toes. I was then in Standard Two. She based her inspection one day on a practical Geography lesson. We were to divide the class into groups. Each group was asked to create the habitat and way of life of a particular country: Japan, China, Africa, India, 'Eskimo Land.' We were taught that the 'Eskimos' (now properly known as Inuit) lived in Igloos, dome-shaped structures built out of ice blocks. They were snugly fitted into fur-lined clothes. They lighted their lamps with the oil of seal blubber. They harpooned seals. When I got home I opened my mother's almirah and took out an armful of her white sheets and searched for warm coats in the old Dutch chest. There was my dead brother Budgie's tweed overcoat, sundry fur-collared coats too. I took them all back to school, and we built an igloo with chairs and desks covered with sheets. I constructed a makeshift sled, which was drawn along by the huskies who were my docile, yet enthusiastic classmates. 'Eskimo Land.' Alaska. Greenland. Not yet within our reach, only to be envisaged through our textbook imagination.

Auntie Elsie visited our school again and again. Her pronunciation changed after her sojourn in America. She spoke of "Progress," of her visits to the UN as an observer, of her meetings with Eleanor Roosevelt. She was always globetrotting, often with her sister Ila. They brought back photographs of themselves standing in Trafalgar Square. They had been to the Royal Coronation too, and Auntie Elsie had been to those colonial Garden parties at Buckingham Palace.

School inspection with someone who was my aunt was always an ordeal for me. I had to be formal, distant, apart from her. She addressed us from a platform. We sat on the coir mats and listened to her just as the older students did. But I also felt a sense of pride in her – she was an independent woman. Had made her way through life. Forged a career on her own.

At Sunday School we were given beautifully illustrated picture postcards on our birthdays -- the artist was a famous Englishwoman who painted exquisite pictures of elves and fairies. Whenever I think back on the world of poetry, I remember the innumerable poems on that world of fairies, a fantastical world of the imagination. But that world of the imagination was centred in a temperate clime in England, in Ireland, so that the background was compounded of colours so contrastive with our own tropical world. "Goblin Market," "The Fairy Queen," "Elfin Skates," "The Elfin Artist," "The Death of Puck," "The Lost Elf," "The Leprechaun" or "Fairy Shoemaker," to mention but a few. I still read them with a sense of curiosity, lingering on the names of those poets who wrote them: de la Mare, Nightingale, Hamilton, Allingham Hood, reading that esoteric, archaic language. We learnt those poems off by heart, and then we recited them aloud either in a chorus or individually. Reading out aloud, reciting aloud "with expression" was common in those days and we were given marks for this exercise.

From my poetry book I recited with gusto "Oki poki Chinga Ma Ring, native wife of an African king..." With its racist overtones, it was certainly very different from the translations of African folk verse, with the revelations of each tribal culture, which I was later to read. Africa, in my childhood, was the "Dark Continent," the continent of Stanley and Livingstone, of pygmies, cannibals and the illustrations from *Punch* magazine of missionaries in cookpots. We had much to learn. Several cultures confronted me, but at that stage the history, the language, the literature was from the point of view of the colonizer – during my childhood there were still British governors. I remember Sir Andrew Caldecott, the Governor's lady and their daughter at colonial garden parties at the Governor's residence, the Kings Pavilion. A walled in garden. Imperial territory. While I read and recited English poetry, Florence Paranagama, an excellent teacher, read and translated Sandeseya poetry, and I, to this day, bear in my imagination descriptions of those cities nearer home with their familiar metaphor of swanlike women, their faces radiant as the moon and of their doe eyes; the lotus ponds, the palaces, while we also sang 'kavi,' verses in Sinhala. It was Mrs Weerasiri who introduced Sunil Shantha's songs to us and also brought Sri Jayana as a young dancer to teach Kandyan dancing at the High School, while Noble Paulickpule introduced us to Bharatha natyam.

Adolescence approached. One day I became subtly conscious of soft hands caressing my long plaits braided and tied with black ribbons. We were sitting cross-legged on the rough coir mats listening to the announcements made by the principal. I felt a soft voice murmuring: "Lovely thick plaits. Heavy. What long hair." I turned my head behind and looked into a pair of dark almond-shaped eyes shaded with long lashes beneath finely arched eyebrows. She had a Burgher name. Her father was Dutch Burgher; her mother, it was rumoured, Singaporean Chinese. She was slim. Fine boned. Her face and smile enigmatic. A delicate ivory statuette. Her fingers were long and delicate. We smiled at each other. She was one of the senior girls. Grown-up. The Big Girls lived in a world apart.

I felt Dora's touch on my hair at Assembly whenever she sat behind me. We become aware of each other as individuals. I began to feel those first faint stirrings of emotion. Who else was there to share them with in a school surrounded by girls, the older ones already nubile? There were so few opportunities to meet boys except at school fairs, carnivals or when we acted in plays. The world we lived in, so limited in many ways, became dimensionless. Emissaries carried our messages to each other. Mutual admiration. Love. Eternal friendship. There was a powerful attraction growing between us. We became special to each other. We seldom spoke except through others. "Tell her I like her very much." "Tell her I like her too." Did we notice the word 'love'? I had a black and white snapshot of her. She had none of me. We were like the moth and the flame. And one day she vanished. Did she go to another school in Colombo or back to Singapore? I was never to know. But I was never to forget her either. Our passions could not be contained even within the rigid timetables ordered for our growing. We were able to let loose those trammels and begin the exploration of our latent emotions. Yet no one really knew of that world concealed behind the convolvulus hedge. Our secret world.

The Family Doctors

Dr Vachel Anthonisz brought me into this world. He and then Dr Winn looked after our health and welfare until the end of their lives. They were very much a part of our childhood, adolescence and even adulthood.

I remember Dr Anthonisz taking part in plays that were staged at Trinity College during the days when elaborate backdrops were painted for the stage décor. He had an elaborate wedding for his daughter Irma, who married a very talented, very gifted photographer, Reg Vancuylenberg. The wedding reception was held at the Laza cinema hall, and white pavadai, the traditional white cloths, were laid out for the bride and groom to come up the hill heralded by Kandyan dancers and drummers after the ceremony at St Paul's Anglican Church. The doctor's son Brian was a handsome young man who was sent to Cambridge, but he told us that he couldn't stand the winter cold, loneliness and food rationing after the Second World War and returned to Ceylon without completing his degree. Brian met with a tragic death, knocked down by a three-wheeler.

The two Burgher doctors lived in great style in those days with their well-maintained households and chauffeur-driven cars, played golf, went on safaris to the Eastern province. They were always impeccably and immaculately attired for work every day. They were GPs who in those days specialized in all the ills of humankind. Dr Winn would come driving to our home in either his Morris Minor or Borgward whenever there was some childish illness that needed his diagnosis, and the first thing my mother set out for his arrival was a basin of water, soap and a fresh towel for before and after his examination of the patient. He rinsed his hands out with great care. He used to tell us of his vacations; he would go on safaris and fishing expeditions to the Eastern Province. He had amusing stories, like when he told us of the Italian priest at the Roman Catholic monastery in Ampitiya who paid him with bottles of Italian wine. His diagnoses were excellent; it was he who took over from Dr Anthonisz later on, and it was he who dispatched me forthwith to hospital one day for surgery after he had diagnosed acute appendicitis.

He would listen patiently for hours to all our family problems and could be trusted implicitly with any secret. It was so sad at the end when I used to visit him, seeing him lying on his armchair, breathless with emphysema. Yes, those doctors knew every family secret, they were more than doctors. They were friends, and even father-confessors.

My mother

My sister Rosemary

My brother Pat

VII

MOTHER'S RECIPES
&
GROWING-UP TALES

Self Portrait, Jean Solomons.

My Mother   *(for Charlotte Grenier-Jansz)*

My mother was real, I knew her.
She too was part of the history of conquest
She gave me this hybrid blood
Now I am proud of it.

Her high cheekbones, amber eyes that slipped
Into topaz, gold or tourmaline were jewels that
I wore within my brain.
Her chiseled lips were those of Tutankhaman
Ancient, pharonic, beautiful but lost to time
Until my birth when she was rescued
From the tomb.

I loved her closely and sobbed my tears
Into her eyes,
I lay my sadness like a wreath of flowers
Upon her breast
Felt sorrow seep through pores
Like bitter bile and
Tasted death.

I hurt her, I loved her, spoke into her ear
Using the only language that I knew
Acquired from others, words from psalms and
Prayers and hymns uttered before icons
Inscribed by prophets, visionaries, in their
Imagistic lines, strung with the artifacts of
Unfamiliar metaphor to fill my mind, that cave
In which lay those long-necked jars
Immured for centuries
Which urned my thoughts, those Dead Sea scrolls.

I sometimes lashed her with my own guilt
Cried out my curse at birth
It was my own tongue that whipped me flagellant
To learn that unknown sin which I, guided from
Those thunderous pulpits
Must penitential, expiate and seek.

She fluttered like a bird about my cradle
Her golden wedding ring struck me like a ray
Of frozen sun, cold, bright on her warm flesh
Its touch warmed me with fire and ice
With that strange foreboding of Death's
Marble chill.

She read me fairy tales, their half known morals
Stung my ears like avid bees
Seeking the pollen of her words,
Then it was I knew of my changeling birth
Born old in time
Knew separation from my kind.

Into my room beguiling me she leads that
Ancient crone all dressed in black, disguise of
The raven, enchantress, spell binder, Mistress Cramer
Black hat, black gown of rusty crepe, seamed black
Stockings, black boots laced at the ankles
What Hanseatic blood or Rhenish flowed within her veins
Her tongue brimming with their ancient tales
From the Black Forest of her memoried life.

I'm hot with fever, ice bag melting on my forehead,
Icy ants of moisture dripping from vinegar sponges
Creep within the thickets of my hair roots
She utters her magic spells and incantations,

Weaves within her earth stained fingers
Green with herbs and plants and tubers,
Cats cradles of legends and fables
Swing me in their hammock and knot me in
That womb of string safe from the jagged shafts
Of wounding stars and falling meteorites.

My mother's silver thimble glints,
She darns the nail-torn rents that peer into
My dreams with terror-eyes
The Irish linen of the sheets are fresh
Smelling of earth and grass against my cheeks
The green tats clack their bamboo xylophones
The beaded net that covers the barley-water
Jug tinkles against the glass.

A tiny fly entangled in a frill of lace
Swings like a pendulum and ticks out
Time.

Predictions, portents, prophecies she utters
Mistress Cramer takes from her handsewn bag
Spells and magic potions.
"You will be a queen one day
A queen, a queen one day."

Me, earthling, changeling.
Through our migrant bloodstream swam the
Legendary fish within whose belly lay
To be one day discovered the golden ring
With wishes three,
The throne, the crown, the phantom prince.
Fairy tales.

The valance stirs, its linen billows
The sails plump out, unfurl to swing me out upon
The surf edged ocean.
Shipwreck of dreams stare beyond my barque
A reddening sea crimsons and spills bright as
Cockaded silk and sweeps me out where storms
And dragon winds hurl the wild clouds of the
Medusa's hair and suck me in to spew me out
At century's end, my bones to scatter on the shore
A string of sea-gnawed pearls pitted and coral
White through which the fish swam in and out.

I wake to find the fairy vanished but
Mistress Cramer's face still spins, a silver
Coin within the radiant eddies of this
Well of memory.
It is at night, at dark, the terror starts.
My mother sleeps, my prayers are said
The water in its thin carafe shivers, trembles,
Breaks the petals of the moon's white face
Splinters in strands of ravished death.

The drums creep within my blanketed ear
Exorcists leap through fire over the mountains of
Dark, devour the flames pure demonic power
The night's instinct, alive
The human smell of bodies press rises through
The thick fumes of burning oil
And my ears hear a different speech
These are the living myths that stayed outside
At birth in that alternate, supernatural world
Now entering with their magic words
Where fire and air and water speak
Of latent spirits that live and breathe
Within my neighbourhood.

Doopvisch and Karbonadje

Memory is sometimes the colour of hibiscus and the flavour of tangy lemon. My mother and I culled the red hibiscus flowers from the hedge in our back garden in Kandy where they flourished, their petals fresh with a sheen on them. We had to be careful as we moved among the trees and bushes. By the wall grew a tree with leaves, grey – green, of a sandpapery texture, covered with innumerable grey caterpillars. If a single of the caterpillar's shiny bristling hairs touched the skin it would leave stinging weals.

The red hibiscus petals were steeped in boiling water which tinged the water in the bowl a rose pink. Freshly cut limes were squeezed in for flavour, sugar stirred in, and then the China moss added which helped the jelly to set. Poured into a silver mould, the jelly unmoulded sat transparent and quivering in the cut-glass dish. My thoughts were often the colour of hibiscus. Blancmanges, too, my mother would make, milk-white blancmanges served with red strawberry jam, like snow-covered mountains over which the sunset streamed. And caramel custards. Recipes for epicureans, the burnt sugar spreading its aroma as it steamed in the saucepan of boiling water over the wood fire. My mother created a childhood of colours and flavours together with her stories that grew in my mind into unending fictions.

I was growing up in a world that was being revealed to me day by day, a world in which my mother was the guardian and the custodian of a way of life which she shared with me. Once we came upon mounds and baskets of oysters on the pavements. "Pearls, pearls, let's search for them," my mother told me.

"Perhaps you will find a pearl of great price." We brought the oysters home and filled basins of them, prising open shell after shell. Within them were sometimes minute seed pearls which shimmered on the palm of my hand, but I never collected enough to string them into a necklace.

I would creep into the kitchen to sit by Emilin and Podi Singho while they ate their food. I preferred the white china plates on which they served the rice and curry, with clusters of blue flowers. "Made in Japan" was the trademark. Even their cups and saucers were white with blue flowers. Emilin had now come into our lives. Mungo was my dream of the past. Emilin not only cooked for us with the help of old Ammé, whose back was bent in two and had worked for the Sunnyside aunts, Emilin also ironed our clothes with hot coals smouldering in the pol-katta smoothing iron, brought us steaming bowls of soup on a chilly, rainy evening, watched us at our pastimes and offered the balm of solace to tumultuous feelings.

It was not easy for me to forget Mungo during that transient period of my Kadugannawa childhood. A childhood which I thought would last forever. In that world it had been play among the mugerine bushes, the thornless roses and Holy ghost orchids, but here, in Kandy, I became more curious of a world, a mysterious one, which existed far away from the rest of the house; reached by a flight of stone steps, the kitchen, where hours and hours were spent preparing those repasts that were served up, straight from the earthenware, the steam still rising from the pots on the hearth onto the Johnson and Johnson or Meakins platters. The kitchen was a special preserve, a special world, with Podi Singho, in between polishing the brass and sweeping and dusting, running up and down to the boutique to bring newspaper cones filled with condiments. The cooking went on almost the whole day for the spices were freshly ground on the black-pitted grinding stone. The grinding stone must not be too smooth, so from time to time the old craftsman came to hammer out an intricate design so that it became like some archaic game board and the red chillie filled the tiny pits upon the surface. The chillies crackled and burst like Chinese firecrackers as the stone, cylindrical, crushed them and the pale yellow seeds merged into the smooth red mound of chillie paste.

My mother prepared to make roast beef in which she excelled. She first marinated the beef in pepper, salt and vinegar, tied it up into shape with twine, and set it in the pot where it boiled for hours until the gravy had been reduced to almost an aroma which clung to the earthenware... then it was lifted out and fried in its own fat. The thinnest slices would be carved at dinner time and served with roast potatoes, carrots, and boiled cabbage. What remained would be 'devilled' the next day for lunch. Sathay curry was another favourite, the meat strung on ekel skewers and roasted on the grid iron over the charcoal fire.

The place in the house away from the cretonne-covered furniture and the polished brass and china ornaments, was the kitchen encrusted with rough bark-like dumbutu from the soot, the beams, rafters and tiles blackened with wood smoke from the hearth fires. In the railway bungalow at Kadugannawa there was a big iron stove fed with coke and coal from the railway yard, in which my mother baked cottage loaves, crusty and brown, to be eaten with clover-leaf butter. On the hearth, curries simmered; pots of jak, beef, fish and chicken. The fires on the hearth were fed with jungle wood, coconut shells and coconut husks that the men brought in bullock carts.

My mother excelled in preparing the characteristic recipes that were served at the table, both for ordinary meals as well as meals for the great festive occasions.

When I think back on my mother's prowess and skill, with her delicate hands and wrists, I marvel at all that she accomplished in the serving up of those delicacies which we took for granted and accepted as our daily fare. And she shared all that she made with a most hospitable heart. The aunts and uncles who visited us were given their "share" to take home afterwards. Auntie Maud would come visiting of an evening all dressed up and groomed for a social call. My mother usually had a tin of fried breadfruit chips, one lot dipped in sugar syrup for sweetness, the other savoury and salted. She also made milk toffee, cadju toffee and huge wedges of pumpkin preserve. There again, my mother was never parsimonious with the generous portions she cut. "Dolly's Christmas cake was always in big chunks." She never cut the cake into thin slices or wrapped them in silver paper like wedding cake. Each time the visitors came round, the cake trays were taken out of the almirah. In fact the whole almirah was redolent of its aroma during the season, for it was kept on the bottom shelf of the wardrobe section together with all our very special dresses on hangers, my mother's, my sister's and my own. Those dresses were taken out only on special occasions.

My mother had a huge preserving pan in which she made all the conserves and preserves, especially the pumpkin preserve, which had to be taken off the wood fire at the correct time, the last stages being crucial in getting the correct consistency, not too hard, not too crystallized. Ah, she was such an expert in making her confectionaries, cakes, sweets, savouries too. All the special flavours of childhood were associated with my mother's unwritten recipes for every conceivable dish from love cake to lamprais, handed down from the Jansz and Grenier side of the family. I wonder just how much she must have learned from her maternal grandmother with whom she spent many years during her childhood. On our dining table there was often served the famous beef 'smoore' set on a big china platter for my father to carve. Even the sharpening of the knife blade was done dramatically by my father until it was keen enough to cut and serve the portions onto each plate with their complement of potatoes impregnated with the spicy gravy.

In the kitchen, skills were being practised that I too wanted to master. I would watch the rhythmic movements of those women's hands crushing the dried chillies, the coriander and cumin, the tumeric, on the grinding stone, until everything became a smooth paste in varying shades of yellow, red and brown. Then to be placed in rounded mounds on an aluminium or china plate, pinched off bit by bit and added to the coconut milk in the earthenware vessels with their simmering curries. The chicken, meat and fish cooking slowly on the wood fires the while.

It was always women's hands that performed every task meticulously, skilfully. The Maldive fish was washed and dried and then pounded in the mortar. It flavoured everything, seeni sambol, pol sambol, kiri hodhi, omelettes, vegetable curries. We loved to taste the finely powdered Maldive fish pounded with the wooden pestle, scraping it off the sides of the mortar with a spoon.

There were the traditional ways of doing everything. The women brought their lore from their homes in the village, sharing their skills with my mother's own inherited knowledge. She possessed a rich store of memorized recipes handed down from generation to generation. The kitchen hearth, the roaring wood fires, the clack of the coconuts being cracked and the sound of the coconut halves being grated began the day for us, giving us a sense of security, of order, that a well-known and familiar pattern of life was being resumed.

The hearth was as hard as brick with the fires that burned daily. In our Kandy home we used only the hearth, feeding the fires with wood, coconut husk, dried coconut fronds, coconut shells. The coconut shells, however, were not used for cooking meat, as there was a belief that it would not turn out tender. Through an iron funnel or 'bata,' held close to the mouth, the living breath made the flames rise high as the women blew through it until the brands kindled and were set alight. What an art there was in the kindling of that particular arrangement of firewood sticks, the quick springing to life of the growing flame licking the sides of the soot-blackened chatty pots; the smouldering firebrands drawn out so that while the curries still simmered, the oil would rise to the surface. Chatty pots containing polkiri baduns, the meat cooking and frying in the thick coconut milk itself. There were chatty roasts and mulligatawny, made of beef or chicken stock, tempered and flavoured with cumin and coconut milk.

Before going out for a dance where we wouldn't know at what time we would have supper, we would have bowls of mulligatawny and rice served in soup dishes. Food did not matter very much as we whirled about to the music of Strauss waltzes in the Queen's Hotel ballroom, with Peter Allon playing his repertoire of music with its ripple of chords and arpeggios, his favourite piece being, "In an Eighteenth Century Ballroom." Mulligatawny and rice was the all-in-one meal, sustaining yet not leaving one uncomfortably overfull. Many years later I thought of that meal when I had 'ikanbilisi' cooked specially for me by a Chinese friend, rice boiled in stock and pork chops, spring onions, slivers of ginger and raw egg tipped whole into it so that the egg cooked in bubbling stock. The ikanbilisi, the tiny dried sprats added fillip to it.

There were special cooking vessels, all earthenware and as hard as iron with the preservation of the years, for the roast beef and smoore ('ismore'); large, wide-mouthed chatties with delicately incised designs ornamenting them.

For the 'ismore,' the indigenized meat stew, a special hunk of beef was bought, about four or five pounds in weight. It was lightly washed and pricked all over with a fork to tenderize it and allow the ground spices to impregnate it. Roasted dry chillies were ground into a rounded ball, a 'guliya,' while the condiments, the coriander and cumin were roasted separately and ground into a fine paste. The dark sienna brown, the gamboges, the ochre turmeric and dark red chillies were set on a plate, resembling an artist's palette. The sliced red onions, rampe-karapincha, ground garlic and ginger, cardamon, lemon grass were sautéed, flavours amalgamated in the temperadu which added to the fragrance that emanated from the pot, as the beef cooked for hours on end on a slow fire. Thick coconut milk was spooned over as it simmered. The temperadu was something special. Wasn't it also a compound of our varied personalities? The Burgher characteristics had their similarities to this process, the way I see it, in that special, very special aroma that titillated the senses. A fragrance that awakened the tastebuds, enwrapped in savoury steam, the dish served hot, hot, from the kitchen, straight off the chatty which was left on the fire, simmering till the last moment. The word 'temperadu' derives from the Portuguese and has its specific meanings and connotations. The skill in mixing, the correct timing, of putting in each requisite ingredient into the hot oil until it was correctly browned, carried the secret of its success. The mixture was lightly stirred with the coconut-shell spoon. There were special spoons for special preparations, individual spoons for fish, meat, vegetables, rice, milk, sweets, cake mixing.

What were the other specialties my mother made? Lots of 'devilled' dishes, hot with chillies, vinegar and fried rings of Bombay onions. Dishes which probably made us by temperament even more volatile than we already were. Our food was hardly bland, nor were our natures, but there were the dishes that created a fine balance too. My mother's Karbonadje, the rolled Dutch cutlet of meat, seasoned with pepper and vinegar and cooked in coconut milk, was one of my favourites. The original Dutch Karbonadje was altered to suit my father's taste buds, more pepper and spices added. And there was yet another favourite of mine, Doopvisch: a dish made of slices of seer fish, boiled first, the stock flavoured with tumeric, pepper, karapincha, rampe, lemongrass and peppercorns. The Doopvisch was served with an egg sauce, the raw egg beaten into the fish stock until it was of a creamy consistency to be cooked on a slow fire without curdling. Meat and fish cutlets, what would generally be termed meat or fish cakes, rissoles and rolled cutlets with their fillings of minced beef, or mashed hardboiled eggs, were brought piping hot to the dinner table together with a tureen of mulligatawny. And on long railway journeys as children we would take parcels of cold beef cutlets and slices of bread and butter to still our hunger. Leftover cutlets from the night before were made into a delicious cutlet curry for lunch the next day. 'Frickadela,' 'forced' meatballs, were for special festive occasions when we had ghee rice or yellow rice or lamprais.

What I think back on now is that a special relationship existed between my mother and the women who cooked in our old-fashioned kitchens. They did things together, harmoniously, talking to each other, sharing their knowledge and skills. My mother taught Emilin, Sophy, Pinchiamma, Menike and the others all she knew, and they too revealed their way of doing things. Things which I remember to this day: the way they washed the rice with that rhythmic movement of the two palms holding the circular edges so that the minute stones settled in the patterned grooves of the clay koraha; the way they cut and sliced, and tasted for the adding of more seasoning, a little soupcon of the gravy taken up with the coconut-shell spoon and slipped onto the cupped palm, and then with a delicate lick proclaim, "just a little more salt or lime" to add that extra fillip to the curry.

For some of these women who did not themselves eat chicken, fish or meat, the aroma was sufficient to adjust the correct proportion of seasoning of condiments, spices, salt and lime.

Yes, it was a special world for women in many ways, with their bonding as women. Preparing almost ritualistically the meals for the family. Sharing in the pleasure of the eating of a carefully prepared dish. They too were discerning women, meticulous in their special skills displayed in the way they sliced an onion, a green chilli or even a lime. They were not considered servants in our homes; they were friends, they were companions to us. I learned a way of life from them, their manner of doing things in the way they had learned, just as my own mother had done, from their elders. I used to often ask them questions. How did you learn to cut the mallun leaves like that or how do you know how much chillie or thunapaha to put into the curry, or who told you that coconut oil is the best way to remove the sticky white milk from the jak fruit? Or I would plead with them to teach me how to grind chillies on the grinding stone, or pound rice into flour, or make hoppers or stringhoppers or halapa, with jaggery and coconut and kurakkan flour steamed in that special leaf, the kenda kola. Oh, I wanted to learn so much from them. They possessed so much wisdom, so much women lore, deep recesses of knowledge; of herbs and the qualities of certain fruits and vegetables and how they produced 'heaty' and 'cooling' properties. Their lives they shared with us in every way, yet sometimes they would say, "Ah, it is better to eat salt and rice and be with our families enduring poverty, enduring hardship." It is a phrase that has served me to this day, to create a philosophy that I have evolved from those ancient sayings. To possess a proud sense of independence even with very little of this world's goods. That which suffices to give a sense of contentment even during moments of the greatest duress. Lunu – salt, buth – rice. What more is needed when all craving ceases?

My mother, although she never consulted a recipe book and had everything stored in her head, also had books for social etiquette. Books which she must have consulted in the early days of her marriage to help her in running the house, entertaining guests. Foulsham's *Guest Entertainer* was a book that I have preserved to this day, and the opening quotation from John Blunt in *The Daily Mail* reminds me of the hospitality of our household. Real hospitality, the author said, consists of making other people happy and not just looking after our own interests. The contents of each chapter fascinated me with the detailed descriptions of how to conduct every single event in the calendar, from the giving of a lunch party to a private dance, a garden party, or a "Jolly Children's party." Menus, recipes, letter writing, the duties of host, or aspects of "An Empire Day Luncheon" were described in chapter after chapter. The descriptions of the patriotic lunches, official and private, reviewed within the post-colonial context, revealed a whole mystique of that period. The date of Empire Day was on the 24th of May. The private parties were meant to be specially regarded as a compliment to the colonial friends who happened to be visiting the "Old Country." The menu was to be an "All British One." Everything from wine to dried fruits, from tinned salmon, the flour in the pastry, the joint of beef, the dessert and everything else should come from the "Motherland" or the "Colonies."

The centerpiece would be a large dish of fruit: apples from Tasmania, bananas from the West Indies, oranges from Jamaica, plums from the Cape. The table decorations too had to be special and a tricoloured scheme used, with bows of ribbons in red, white and blue fixed to each dish. Even the flower vases should be filled with blossoms of the same three colours: white, blue violets and red carnations. The menus were to be decorated with little Union Jacks, and scattered around the table small Empire flags should be fixed.

The suitable toasts were as follows:

"Ladies and Gentlemen, the King and Empire."

"The Motherland and her far-flung dominions, Britain and all the British."

"The Empire."

"The United Kingdom and her United Empire."

We never, however, found occasions or necessity to celebrate such a luncheon party. The British Empire was at our table, with the wanderers of the empire appreciating our menus. The toasts that Johnny Walker proposed were, "To Harry Sol,

Harry Boy or Harry Solo and his family"; the whiskey continued to flow as Johnny refilled his glass as an accompaniment to rice and curry.

Where my mother's life was concerned, home, marriage and family with all its concerns dominated the greater part of her life. And that home was kept going with just one man's earnings, my father's salary which he earned from the CGR, the Ceylon Government Railway. Every comfort we enjoyed, we owed to my father's labour. But it was the women who ran the household and created its order and stability. Both of them, my father and mother, were the most self-sacrificing people in the world, and in those days our education in the private missionary schools, boarding fees at Trinity College and Girls' High School were all paid out of that one wage. There was never a complaint or grumble from my parents about those family commitments. Responsibility for offspring was taken for granted and duties carried out. Now it becomes so significant when I think of how my father would bow his head over his plate before and after every meal, and repeat the litany of grace. Before the meal was begun he would bend his head over his plate and say: "for what we are about to receive, the Lord make us truly thankful, Amen."

And after the completion of the meal my father would say: "For what we have received, the Lord make us truly thankful. Amen."

As children we repeated the simple words: "God bless this food. Amen."

My father had moral strictures about how we ate. "Never take more onto your plate than you can finish," he would advise us, and "never grumble at the table." It was his wages that provided everything on that laden table and nothing was ever denied us, but any 'complaints' or faddiness would earn a stern: "Well, if you can't eat what's before you, please leave the table." We were sufficiently warned not to repeat the error. My long-suffering mother, however, endured all things, rebellion in all its forms, both silent and vociferously expressed. What she left behind was the memory of a living example of a mother, friend and companion. She bequeathed a legacy of unwritten stories, which I would record through recollection in later years.

My mother's nature was never a solitary one and she was always accustomed to the companionship of those who were part of our household, intimately so. We had women who were individualistic and allowed to be so, like the old Ammé who was unmarried and centred all her devotion on dogs whom she fed from our kitchen. There was Ampitiya Ammé who earned everything for her grandchildren, kept nothing back for herself, and was self-compelled to scrub, scrub, scrub and swab kitchen floors every day with her bare hands. But Emilin? Emilin was special, as special as Mungo.

Emilin belonged to our lives in Kandy. She was, moreover, not exclusively mine but belonged to the other members of the family, too, for she was responsible for the greater part of the cooking. Other women also came in to help, but Emilin had left her village and lived with us. She was a very pretty, very petite woman with wavy hair, tendrilling about her forehead, soft skin, and a bubbling laugh. She advocated her own kind of beauty treatment like using hot ash as a depilatory and rubbing white sandalwood with milk on a stone, to use on the skin to remove blemishes. She was adept at preparing every dish and, trained by my mother, could prepare rissoles, caramel custard, polkiri badun, ghee rice, hoppers, soups, anything. For afternoon tiffin she had her specialties: soft white laveriyas filled with pani-pol, that delicious jaggery and coconut mixture; halapa, steamed in kenda kola, wide leaves plucked from the back garden; aggala, thala guli; pancakes with a filling of sugar and lime; Bombay toast. But Emilin did more, much more. Not only did she cook for us but she would also iron a frock or skirt in a jiffy, heat water for our baths, comfort us when we were ill or sulky and demanding attention, cosset us and try to restore us into a good mood.

"Shall I bring you a cup of hot soup, bebi? A glass of milk? Ginger tea for your cold?"

She would sit beside the bed telling us stories of her own life and of the people she had worked for, one family being a Sinhala doctor with an English wife. When I had fever and tossed restlessly in bed, Emilin would press my small feet with her equally small hands and I would cling to the feel of her presence in that half-darkened room with the faint light flowing in from the skylight. She never interfered in our quarrels but would detach herself after trying to reason with us, waiting abstracted and patient until the turbulence was naturally quelled. Quarrels left her sad but philosophical. We were growing up and were trying to cope with adolescence, with new awareness, to live with ourselves and our siblings. Our conflicts could often not be resolved.

Emilin stayed with us until she said, she "couldn't eat fire anymore." She used to walk down Peradeniya Road sometimes to the meat stall, and one of the neighbours, who had had an eye on her for sometime, took her on to look after the children. How I missed her. There was never anyone after that to really replace her. I had 'attained age,' reached puberty when she was with us, and she had assisted in all those rituals of bathing, wearing new clothes, having jewellery put on my wrists, fingers and round my neck after my isolation in the bedroom for some days. She took part of my childhood away with her when she left. There was an aching void ever afterwards.

As for Podi Singho. He had lived with us for years and years. He had been with us in Kadugannawa too and had put my brother Pat to sleep, as a baby, rocking him on his knees and singing lullabies to him. Sometimes we called him lovingly, "Old Boy." He was supposed to have come from a tea estate, from the time he was a child brought up by the Jeronis family to whom he would return whenever he felt like it. He helped with the marketing, polishing brass and silver, and washing the dishes after our meals. He lived to a great age, would quarrel with the other servants, flounce out of the house and return when he wished. Laying the table was one of his great artistic efforts, the correct placing of every bit of cutlery and the folding of the serviettes. I suppose in our home, individual talents were always encouraged. And everything he did, especially the painstakingly arranged décor of "The Table" was sheer artistry – creating the origami shapes of those starched damask napkins and placing the arching serving spoons of silver beside the dishes. In his sleep he would still sing snatches of lullabies he had sung to my brother in his babyhood. He was always ready to go to the Muslim Hotel and bring us those luscious triangles of Turkey bread, ice-cream from Elephant House, and bondhi, jalebis and kalu dodol from the market sweatmeat stalls. Ours was his only real home. And all who were part of that home were also part of our family.

Milk Punch/Pons

Take 5 bottles arrack, 3 bottles water, 2 bottles good milk,
+ bottle of lime juice, 3 lbs sugar, + nutmeg, 1 1/2 drams clove,
+ dram mace, 2 drams cinnamon, fresh green peel of 18 limes.

Bruise and soak the lime peel and other aromatics in 1 of
the 5 bottles of arrack for 24 hours, then mix together the infusion
of lime peel, etc., the arrack, the water, the lime juice and sugar,
and pour in the milk when boiling hot. Next stir the mixture well,
colour with burnt sugar, and strain through flannel and bottle.

"Rita Toussaint Vanlangenberg's Love Cake"
(sent by her granddaughter Romaine)

Ingredients

2 lbs Rulang	4 lbs Soft Sugar
400 Cadjunuts	24 Eggs
1 lb Butter	1 oz Rose Water
1 wine glass Bees' Honey	
Mixed Spices to taste	

Method

Toast rulang until pale golden brown in a heavy frying pan over a
low heat, stirring constantly. Remove from pan and allow to cool.
Beat eggs (reserve egg whites) with sugar until light and creamy.
Mix butter with rulang and stir into the creamed mixture. Stir
finely chopped cadjunuts, bees' honey, rose water and mixed
spices, and continue to mix thoroughly. Whip egg whites until
very stiff and fold into mixture. Pour into cake tin prepared with
two thicknesses of brown paper and two thicknesses of grease-
proof paper. Brush paper with melted butter. Bake in a slow oven
(125 degrees C) until cake is cooked through. Cake should have a
nice, moist centre, so do not think it is undercooked.

When cool, wrap and store in an air-tight container. Well wrapped
this cake will keep for weeks.

Christmas Breakfast and Church – Kandy

Everything was laid out on the dining table, the dhoby-washed-and-starched damask tablecloth spread over it: breudher, rich with eggs and plums, a ball of red-rinded Edam cheese, bacon and eggs, bread and butter, a comb of fat kolikuttu plantains. It was not that any of us were particularly hungry at that hour of the morning; we had already had such a surfeit of food during this Christmas season. Moreover, we were dancing impatiently on our toes, looking at the clock, watching the minutes passing by, waiting for Banda tailor to bring our Christmas dresses for church, where everybody would be dressed in brand-new clothes. Banda tailor must have been putting the finishing touches at the last moment to those historical dresses which should have belonged to period museums of that colonial era, with their elegant basques and coatees, ruched yokes and accordion pleats.

When we lived in the little provincial town of Kadugannawa we used to go to church on Christmas day in a hiring car all the way to Kandy. The drivers of the past, men like Hendrick or Simon, were dignified men, dressed in coat and sarong with big silver-buckled leather belts. My sister and I wore our special Christmas dresses with tiers of frills, sashes round our waists, smocking. We wore silver hairbands and English shoes and socks. Yes, everything we wore was from England and so were all the toys we had got on Christmas eve. Our "stockings" (really pillowcases tied to the bedpost) were filled with English toys: snowballs filled with toys, boxes of dolls which were replicas of ourselves except for the colour of hair, eyes, and complexion. Then there were varieties of nuts at the bottom of the pillowcase – almond, hazel, walnuts, Brazil – all bought from Millers or Cargills, where bags and bags reposed against the counter.

For church on Christmas day my mother was decked in silk stockings, court shoes, veiled hat, silk gown buttoned up high at the throat; her jewellery was chaste, a pearl necklace, a topaz brooch, thick gold bracelet with a little chain to hold it together. The hats my mother wore were fascinating – belonging to Bond Street or Regent Street, so fashionably Londonish in style – yet they came from the big shops in our town, Cargills, Millers, Whiteway. They reposed in crisp new bandboxes, which were generally kept on top of the almirah. My sister and I wanted our mother to be as stylish and modish as possible, but my father had such conservative tastes. Her hair was worn long, braided and coiled in a knot at the nape of her neck, since my father would never allow her to bob her hair or have a fashionable shingle. Her ears had never been pierced so she usually wore pearl clips in them.

My mother's hats were generally of black felt with interesting brims – to which you could give a slight manipulative twist so that the eyes (my mother had deep-set amber eyes) would be half hidden in their mysterious shadow. Clusters of waxy flowers nestled in the stiff band of ribbon. Or sometimes a scarlet plume, plucked from the plumage of some exotic bird, or a dyed feather of petunia shade adorned it. A spotted veil of fine-black mesh lay like spume spilling over her forehead, and she was ready for church. Her engagement ring was also brought out of a blue-velvet-lined box – a cluster of rubies and diamonds, worn with her thick band of gold – nothing of which now remains except that portrait that I paint in my mind to hang in the galleries of memory. It is as if even that lingering whiff of perfume, Yardley's English Lavender, still remains as I touch the remembrance of her garments, neatly hung in the wardrobe section of our old jak wood almirah. I remember how I loved to pull open that single drawer and examine its contents: the family christening robe of fine ivory silk with valenciennes lace insertions and minute pin-tucks, my mother's pearl necklace, brooches, the ring, her gold bracelet and her bottle of Yardley's Lavender. There must have been other treasures but this is what I recollect. And in that almirah, on a bottom shelf were also the trays of Christmas cake, brought out for visitors, cut in generous slices to be served to the guests.

My father too was busy dressing up for church: coat, tie, and crisp new shirt worn with gold cuff-links, along with pin-stripe trousers. Good strong leather shoes specially made for him by Peterson, the shoemaker. My father generally polished the shoes himself with Kiwi polish, black and tan. Sharpening his razor on the leather strap, until the blade was lethal, he brushed on a lather from the green Vinolia shaving stick, and carefully shaved himself in front of the small mirror on the back veranda.

At last we heard the sound of Banda tailor's bell, and he would alight from his bicycle with brown paper parcels neatly tied up. Designs had been chosen from the most sophisticated journals like *Vogue*. Sometimes Banda tailor would introduce his own original ideas, but generally the dresses were beautifully turned out, with his young Muslim assistant Hafiz sitting cross-legged on the carpet and stitching away.

Of course, our family was never the earliest at church. We would stand at one of the three doors through which we could enter the Brownrigg Street Methodist Church and survey the backs and heads of the congregation. Our hearts sank: every pew was full – sometimes even the side pews. We would have to march right down the aisle to the front pews with all the curious eyes following us. My father of course always stood out among the others, big and strong in his smart grey pin-striped suit, his gold cuff-links and stop-watch, his gold ring with its cats-eye, and his hair specially trimmed for the service.

What I enjoyed most was to sit where I could watch rather than be watched; for the first time in my life I saw streaked hair on the head of Ena Heyneckker's daughter and was utterly taken up by it. I looked and looked, observing hairstyles: buns, braided telephone coils over the ears, or a coronet of plaits round the head; kondes with jewelled kuras, rolls of hair at the nape of the neck, permed sausage curls, top-knots, Then there was the headgear: suede, felt and straw-brimmed hats; and the silk gowns, chiffon and georgette sarees worn by the Sinhalese ladies. Even when we knelt to pray we would slowly open our eyes to have a better look and sometimes intercept another's gaze too. All the families were known to each other in that small community and so no one was a stranger here. Each year it was interesting to see the new additions – daughters and sons-in-law, grandchildren – while with the years the older generation grew more aged, until one by one they vanished leaving a last survivor like myself to remember. I wondered whether my name, if ever it were to be engraved on one of those copper, brass, bronze or marble plaques, would mean anything to anyone in a church whose congregation had not only diminished but was full of ghosts of the past.

The Christmas sermons were preached year after year by the Methodist Missionary priests – English priests, Irish and Welsh. Reverend Bevan (who I once sought to confound by my new-found, exploratory and hardly comprehended knowledge from my brother's books – *Ethica Nicho-Machea* – and who so fervently tried to answer my naïve and immature intellectualizing, was one of them. Reverend Middlehurst was another youthful, blushful and bespectacled, minister, who ended up by marrying a young missionary lady who taught at Sunday school and who called young men "fellows." There was Reverend Nelson with his beautiful bass-baritone voice, who sang not only hymns but also the famous "Londonderry Air" with great power and feeling. Reverend Nodder gave long and deeply profound sermons based on the Biblical texts, while his pale-faced wife, so faded by the brilliance of this tropical light, sat in the choir listening raptly to his words. Reverend Basil Jackson and his wife were a great Methodist couple. Reverend Jackson was also one of the former principals of the College that in the past belonged to the Methodist and Anglican Missions (I was to become a lecturer at the English Teachers' College many years later). And Reverend Small, gentle, meek, mild, a great scholar, had also been Principal of Richmond College Galle where my own grandfather William Henry Solomons had once been headmaster.

The missionaries, although allied to the Imperial power of the British Empire, owed their allegiance to a different kingdom. The priests and school principals who preached and taught us felt they had a mission. The language they preached in was also my mother tongue, as a Burgher. It was not unfamiliar to me, yet was I not screened off like many others from our natural environment? Were we deluded when we imagined we heard the nightingale and the cuckoo bird rather than the oriole and the parakeet? Did our lives pass through the seasons of spring, summer, autumn and winter, so that our metaphors of growing emerged from that burgeoning of the daffodil and primrose? It took me years to awaken to the realization of who I was, the creating of an identity which took its form, shape, colour and texture from the superimposition of different cultures.

In those days the choir used to be full – this was before most of the Burghers migrated to Australia. I can never forget Miss Dulcie Vanderstraaten singing in her perfect soprano, taking the high notes with such exquisite pitch and modulation that one thought that the stained glass would shatter in splinters as the notes struck the air. Her voice would always be heard above everybody else's – a perfect voice for European opera. Such tal-

262 A Nice Burgher Girl

ent and such rare beauty lay within those sculptured features, alabaster complexion and dark shingled hair. She was 'an old maid,' a spinster, her beauty coffined in chaste morality, buried in time. Who was there to appreciate or record that voice to be played on the gramophones of that era? Perhaps the angels heard her, and perhaps that voice of hers that sang in praise of God, Sunday after Sunday, had assured her of a place in heaven. I knew her till her death, visited her and her sister Gladys, my old fifth-standard teacher at Girls' High School, until she too passed away. Dulcie sat on a cushioned chair, her Helen of Troy beauty diminishing, yet so brave, an ancient sculpture in a ruined classical garden among the pagan gods, Pan, Apollo, Aphrodite. Crochetting lace in patterns that came from memory to keep her mind calm and quiet. Her eyes would sparkle when she saw me. "Ah, it's Jean, isn't it?" she would say. I would always remember her lark-like voice which held me spellbound in my childhood.

Yes, I remember those organ players too, playing that huge pipe organ, like something out of one of those gilded medieval paintings: Lena Vanderstraaten; the Jonklaas', Smiths. A brother, Dr Smith, had married my mother's sister, Norah Jansz, and worked at the Pasteur Institute in India, before the family moved to England. Then there was Mrs Vanderwall who had a son, I remember him as a very handsome man. I used to see him and his wife on Christmas day, the family having come from Colombo to the family home. The wife was an extremely beautiful and talented pianist – Irene Vanderwall – I have heard her playing Beethoven and Bach, Chopin, Handel, Mozart at "piano recitals" as they were called. Ultimately she went to Australia, but Mrs Vanderwall stayed on, living in part of the Piachaud house, "The Retreat," close to Sunnyside Gardens. Later on she shared the Vanderstraaten home. Come rain, come sun, Mrs Vanderwall unfailingly played on that pipe organ while wearing her hat and her ankle-length, high-necked dresses.

The church on Christmas day was beautifully decorated with arum lilies all white and gold in the shining brass vases. My attention was always drawn to the Baptismal font, where I imagined myself in that long, ivory silk christening robe, leading me to wonder about those three names that were given me: Jean (because my father had a Scots friend whose daughter was also named Jean), Lynette, Christine. To my mother, when she felt affectionate towards me, I was "Jeano" or "Babachi"– pet names. On the walls of the Methodist church were pages from history in marble or brass: the names of missionaries and their wives and the native local preachers, lay preachers, and Sunday School teachers who devoted their lives to Evangelism in that austere Methodist set-up. On my mother's side were the Grenier Janszes who belonged to the Church of England and worshipped at St Paul's, the Anglican Church, where they had their special pews. The Solomons were staunch Methodists and pillars of the church. When they sang in church, my Solomons aunts, Elsie, Ila and Elia, always sang alto and contralto, so their voices stood out just as much as they themselves did in their Western clothes brought from England, Europe and America. And my Solomons aunts loved bright colours, they were real Birds of Paradise.

After service was over we would all stand together in the foyer of the church for greetings. Friends and relations were embraced and kissed, or we shook hands. The comments of my mother's friends were invariably, "dear girl, how like your mother you are," or "Dolly, how this child has grown" (my mother's pet name was Dolly, her real names were Charlotte Camille) or yet again, "how like Dolly this child is." I was at any rate supposed to have "taken after the Janszes." I was still to know what complex ancestral strands existed within that inheritance.

Tea and Cakes at Elephant House

With my mother tea and cakes at Elephant House were the usual happenings when we went into Kandy town for shopping at Cargills, Millers, Whiteaway and Laidlaw, Bata's and Cosy's.

The waiters would be at our table with spotlessly white starched napkins draped on their arms, taking out their pencils from behind the ear to jot down our requests in the order book. The waiters were all familiar to us, spending a lifetime there until they grew old, grizzled, and retired from service. For that's what it was, serving us with patience and courtesy.

"Yes, madam, yes bebi, what would you like today?"

My mother would look at the menu, perusing it closely. "Battenberg and cheesecakes. Jam tarts. Iced tea cakes."

"Pot of tea for two, madam?"

"Yes, a freshly brewed pot of tea, with fresh milk..."

"And what would bebi like?"

"Cream buns, chocolate eclairs and vanilla ice-cream, please."

"What about sandwiches, madam? Ham with country mustard? Or anchovy paste?"

"Well, not today, thank you, just cakes and tea, and yes, cream buns too... and ice-cream."

Ice-cream was brought with a red glacé cherry and two crisp wafers because we were old friends and regular customers.

Sandwiches were daintily cut in triangles, the crusts trimmed, buttered, with thin slices of ham or potted fish paste. But it was the cakes, the variety, the flavours of which I had my favourites: Elephant House chocolate cake, deep, dark and rich, sandwiched with cream, topped with a special "chocolate water icing," as it was called; cheesecakes and ribbon cake. Cakes with a sprinkling of desiccated coconut was not something I particularly fancied.

The teapot, milk-jug and sugar-cube bowl with its silver scoop came on a silver tray. The two of us, my mother and myself, would sit at our leisurely pastime taking pleasure in our moments of close intimacy, moments which appeared like the paintings on remembered birthday cards of the past.

On Fridays, the bluff, loud-voiced Ceylonese planters would flood Elephant House, wearing their khaki shorts, white shirts, khaki hose and thick leather boots. They would swagger in with their wives and children and call out to the waiters in their peremptory manner as if they were in their bungalows or at the Club. Cries of "Boy" would summon the waiters to the tables and, the orders taken, steaming platters of food would be brought, piping hot from the kitchens: mixed grills, liver and bacon, grilled seer and French fries, grilled lamb chops, sausages and tomatoes, fruit salad and ice cream for afters.

Sometimes my mother and I would lunch on slices of fresh fried seer with French fries, tomato salad and a slice of lemon perched like a pale green moth on the golden brown fish. Sometimes it was poached eggs on toast or scrambled eggs. Occasionally we ordered a mixed grill which cost rupees four fifty. The platter came filled with a grilled lamb chop, sausage, bacon and liver, beef, chicken, a poached egg, tomatoes and potatoes. The meats were all doused in rich gravies. On the table were silver cruet stands with Worcestershire sauce, ketchups, pepper and salt.

My mother would take out her stylish leather handbag with its gold clasps that clicked shut or clicked open with an adroit flick of the fingers, the fragrance of Yardley's Lavender reaching my nostrils, a fragrance so haunting and yet so alien, from that gold-topped flagon with its picture of a lavender lady on its label. A song we sang in school went:

Lavender's blue dilly, dilly
Lavender's green,
When you are king dilly, dilly
I shall be queen.

The bill was paid with crisp rupee notes and the waiters' tip was placed on one of the side plates.

Out on Ward Street, Mr Mortimer, the one-time planter, would lift his felt hat and bow to my mother. Macintosh Mortimer was a good friend of my father's. Most of the English and Scottish planters were his friends. Toshy had a Sinhalese wife and many children by her. He remained with them till the end. Many of the planters went back home on furlough and brought back English wives. Toshy was faithfully tended by his family until he passed away. He never went back to England. He had lost his billet on the estate as a result of his daredevil ways, his fondness for whiskey, "going native" and riding into august colonial territory – the foyer of the Queen's Hotel – on elephant back, drunk as a lord, at the height of the perahera season.

The "Muslim Hotel" was yet another landmark in Kandy, famous for its biriyani, rich with ghee, enormous joints of roast chicken buried in its fragrance, embellished with hardboiled eggs, and wattalappan. The glass showcases were full of trays of what we called "Turkey bread," with its layers of pastry, dried fruit, plums, raisins, dates, drenched in sugar syrup and flavoured with rosewater. Tandoori chicken red as firecrackers, transparently green wedges of Muscat, kalu-dodol, and intertwisted braids of golden brown sweet bread were set on flowered china platters.

The wattalappan was served in tiny porcelain bowls, rows of them waiting to be lifted out off the glass-fronted showcases and served as an accompaniment to the biriyani and Turkish coffee, hot, spiced and sweet.

The Goan tailor "Raymonds" establishment was adjacent to the "Muslim Hotel." Mr Raymond was always smartly attired in full suit, tie, pin-striped black coat. A handsome man with a Clark Gable moustache. His mother-in-law, Mrs Alexander was our seamstress.

On the pavement sat the man with the red-tasseled fez, a small wooden cabinet before him filled with tiny glass phials of perfume, containing the purest essences of ambergris, jasmine and rose. Just the teeniest drop on a bud of cotton wool would suffice to impregnate every crevice of your body with its dizzying perfume. The men of the Muslim community used to tuck those buds behind their ears. The perfumes, essential oils, were very expensive. I was fascinated by those strong heady fragrances. They were rare and strangely exotic, unlike the flowery colognes and lavenders my mother besprinkled herself with. "Too strong, too strong", she said, as the glass phial was unstoppered for me to take a deep breath to inhale the perfume. The perfume of houris and odalisques. Such tiny phials containing so much fragrance. "Just a drop would do," my mother told me. "Yes, nona," the Magician of Perfumes interjected. "A tiny drop and you will be covered with fragrance." But as children, if ever we used perfume it was April Violets or 4711 Cologne. "Evening in Paris" together with Uncle Bertie's corsages of mauve and purple orchids to be pinned on the shoulders of those ball gowns of lace and organdy when we grew up. Your image reflected in the long pier mirrors at the Queen's. Transforming the ballroom into Impressionist paintings as we waltzed in tulip bells of tulle and taffeta.

Perhaps there would be more shopping before we went home in Hendrick's hiring car, an old Ford. We would go to Millers where my mother would try on hats which she wore to church on Christmas day or buy shoes and socks for me. Dress materials too, for Banda tailor to sew, taffeta, lace, Broderie Anglais, Riverina, Aertex vests, silk stockings, Susan Small model dresses with basques, twin-sets of angora wool, Coty's pink face powder, Icilma, Pond's Cold Cream and Vanishing Cream. At Millers, Mr Kurian would give us red cellophane packets of chocolates with their crunchy aerated centres. Tins of Quality Street and Roses assortments filled the shelves.

There were tins of chocolate too, Cadbury's, Nestlés – my mother would tell me the story of one of the heirs of these great Firms, how he had spent his childhood in Ceylon and had lovingly remembered his old nanny whom he came to visit from England.

English children were always looked after by 'nannies,' as the Burgher, Sinhalese or Tamil ladies were called. Even this word 'nanny' was imported directly from England and remained in use until very recently. 'Nanny' was a very anglicized term, and nannies were supposed to be special, better trained, more responsible and doing things the "English way," so that the term carried with it a complete set of conventions and connotations. Moreover, nannies and governesses were employed among the Ceylonese too, the more westernized and the more affluent. Planters, the English as well as Ceylonese generally, had nannies to look after their children. They spoke in English too. Good nannies were prized possessions and carried many testimonials and references to their character and abilities, which included being able to speak in English to their masters, mistresses and charges. Perhaps there grew a strong sense of bonding which took place as a result of the transference of maternal duties to the nannies and the future Empire builders whose fathers were planters and administrators in the colonies. The ordinary yet important acts of day-to-day life, eating, drinking, washing, bathing, playing, entertaining, putting to bed, were all in the hands of the nannies. In those huge estate bungalows and spacious houses in tree-filled avenues a secure inhabited space was created between nanny and child.

My cousin Diana Albrecht's Indian nanny was always dressed in starched white sarees and spoke only in English. Diana's mother, Lorna, my mother's niece, was always very careful of being "correct" in manners and language – they (Lorna, Myrtle and Ronald, with German Redlich blood plus the Dutch and French variety of Grenier and Jansz) had European-like fair skin, blue eyes and hair that was Titian red, auburn or gold. And there were the Albrechts, also of German extraction. Bert Albrecht worked in a European firm, and had once lived and worked in another British colony, India. Their identification was more with the European strain and the British lifestyle.

Sometimes language too had certain indigenized connotations. 'Bundy,' which referred to stomach, was a word that was used occasionally when adults spoke to children or even when my ayah spoke to me. I do not know how this linguistic term originated but it belonged to childlike language, and wasn't always approved of by those who spoke only 'Standard English.'

With all the inhibitions of language, social manners and alienness of culture imposed upon me, I was truly fortunate to have Mungo, my ayah, a woman from the village who opened my eyes to other worlds. She was a simple country woman who made me aware, even as a child, of forces of good and evil, as I sat with her, played with her or was rocked to sleep on her outstretched knees. We shared a language too. Her language became mine.

Puberty Rites

"You are a big girl," they said
"You have attained age."
The taboo period of seclusion over with ceremonies
Pots of water poured over my head by the reddi nenda
Who came from Deiyangewella – the field of the gods
She of the ruddy skin and long silver-pierced earlobes
The white towel scrubbed on stone
Thrown over her shoulder
She who ironed our clothes, the hot iron
Spitting out its heat with the sprinkled moisture
Pressing the stiff starch into crackling folds
Puffing out gathers, folding the smell of sun
And water into white school uniforms
Pleating our seasons into orderly growing
Arm lengths of sheets squared and folded into shape
The stains of our lives bleached out of Irish linen
Spread on sunned grass and stone to crackle dry.
The iron filled with smouldering coconut shell
Embers taken from the burning hearth.

Reddi nenda who brought carved brass bandesi
Of rasa kaveli for the Aluth Avuruddha
Covered with pure snow-white embroidered cloths
Edged with tatting renda, piled with
China plates of kewun ekeled into honey
Crumbling kondé, palm flat atirasa and
Saffron yellow kokies, finger-pressed seeni

Kema crystallized with sugar syrup and
Asmi streaked with pani

Diamond shapes of aluwa and kiribath
Moulded flowers embedded in the milk-rice
Rich grains, the comb of plantains
Painted with white chunam for ripening.

Poured pot after pot of water on my head
In ritual cleansing of the stains that dreams
Left from wet leaves that brushed and clung
To my new breasts from the thick-knit forest of dark
From the fruit that ripened, split, bared
Its teeth, bit into flesh
My long hair swathed with water
Her hands soothing the turmoil
Of weltering waves dipped with
The richness of irrigated fields
Streaming with rivulets, the earth now silver,
And then her two hands
Broke the pot shattered at my feet.
"Now you are no longer podi-bebi
Now we will call you missy
When you marry you will be called nona."

Days bound in white napkins
As blood sped from my body.
"She has grown up," they said with love
And pride, relatives gave gifts encircling
My fingers with family heirlooms

Telling me that I was now ready
For love and procreation.

The pieces of shattered pot gathered up
Flung no one knows where
The water flowed away
From the body like cut vein.

Red the drooping cockscombs
Of the slaughtered bird that screamed
At dawn
Red the simmering ants that crawled
On the nectar of the spoiled jak fruit fallen
Red the bee stabbed hibiscus
Red the blood of my new wounds.

Repetition of rituals
For my daughters whose bodies
Tremble with the cold of splashing water
Bright the gold on their wrists
Bangles taken from mine
My hands cut in diamond shapes
Legends and myths from the platter
Of milk rice to feed dreams to each other.

Falling into the river the full moon
Bleeds slashed by the blazing chulu
Lights of the nightfishers.

Attaining Age

I had attained age. My entrance into puberty. There are secret smiles on the faces of the adults. My mother tells me that I should have holidays from school for a space of time. I lie in bed and read for hours on end with books piled round me. Voracious reader. Bookworm. Walking encyclopaedia. Paragon of virtue. Strange, the way adults looked at me.

Volumes of John Buchan, Henry James, Jane Austen; Charles Dickens, *David Copperfield*, *Oliver Twist*, *Little Dorrit*, *The Old Curiosity Shop*, O. Douglas, *Penny Plain*; Baroness Orczy; Margaret Mitchell, *Gone with the Wind*; Bernard Shaw... I lie propped up among the cotton-filled pillows, my toes nestling warm under the woolly blanket. The day comes for the purificatory bath.

There are special rituals to be observed. I submit to them. My mother has arranged that the family laundrywoman should carry out all the rites. I love my 'Dhobi-ammé.' She always smells of sun, soap, water. She comes from Deiyangewela – the field of the gods – near the railway station. When you pass by in the train on the way to Colombo, you see the women washing the clothes that have been steeped in the 'wellawa' overnight. There are rows of cement structures filled with water and washing soda. All the most stubborn stains are removed. The clothes are rinsed; for us, Dhobi-ammé uses 'kenda' to starch the clothes, a homemade starch of sago. The garments and the linen are carefully folded and arranged – a bundle which she carries on her head to our house. She has a special starch for our garments made of fine fabrics, organdy, voile, muslin, cambric – a flower-starch she calls, 'Mal kenda.' A fine light, yet crisp, starch. As light as flower petals.

Dhobi-ammé is very much a part of our lives. She comes in like a welcome guest, and massages my limbs. I lie in bed flat on my stomach and she takes a wet towel, wrings it out and rubs my shoulders, gently, caressingly, or with her smooth, scrubbed hands feels my head till my scalp tingles. I am like a cat as she ministers to me. Her parents and grandparents have worked for my mother's family for years. At the New Year festival, Dhobi-ammé brings me the special rasa kavili that I like – asmi, the texture like a dry, crackling bird's nest, creamy white in colour, with honey syrup poured over it.

She knows everything about our family. Now it is time for her to give me my ritual bath. Early in the morning the big enamel bath tub is filled and I am led inside the washroom. She has a new clay pot in her hands, fills it with water and gently pours it over me. My hair clings to my head in thick, wet strands. I shiver with the cold, cold water. She pours innumerable pots – there is a certain magical number – and then I am swathed in a white sheet and led back to my room. My parents, my aunts, shower me with gifts. Heirloom jewellery, gold necklaces, bracelets. My fingers are covered with rings. Blue zircon. Topaz. Sapphires. Turquoise. With time, they will vanish. The jewels that sparkled on my fingers, in my ears, on my wrists. Vanished. Were lost… mostly stolen.

I am now grown up. A young lady. No longer called 'bebi' but 'missy' by Dhobi-ammé, by Emilin who cooks for us, and by "old boy" who sweeps, dusts the furniture and goes to market. "Missy." Grown up. Adult. Nearly.

VIII

THE AGE WHEN
ROMANCE BLOSSOMS

Jean as Julia in Sheridan's *The Rivals,* and bridesmaid at the marriage of Delsie de Niese and Glen Oorloff, 1950s.

Parties and Mating Games

Didn't they all live as if there were no tomorrows in their lives? Dancing, playing parlour games, romancing? Life was not allowed to grow monotonous with entertainment limited. Homes became places where the floors were polished, the chairs pushed back against the walls, and the piles of records arranged on the teapoy beside the gramophone or radiogramme. Those who took the floor would be the centre of attraction for the onlookers, including the mothers and aunts who enjoyed watching the young ones at their incipient mating games. Homemade patties, sandwiches and cakes were served in plenty, together with iced drinks, ginger beer and fruit cordials. Everybody knew each other. Family friends congregated in the homes that were familiar places for friendly visits of an evening.

A letter from one those sparkling young women lies before me in which she recounted her memories of some of those occasions:

"I remember those parties. We called them subscription parties or 'sub parties.' Two rupees per head. Dancing and games, with shorteats, Elephant Brand soft drinks and one round of delicious iced coffee, all for two rupees. The records were lent by Claude Vanderstraaten, brought to the party by him and also removed by him after the last dance. He would watch with an eagle eye to check whether the records were being handled carefully. He had a wonderful selection, all the latest from Cargills Record Department. 'Silver Dollar,' 'If,' 'Near You,' 'My Happiness,' the 'Harry Lyme' theme, 'Blue Skirt Waltz,' 'Always,' 'Brazil,' 'Kentucky Waltz,' 'The Anniversary Waltz,' 'Deep Purple,' were some of the melodies we danced to.

"We had games in between dancing – Bigamy, the Winking Game, Musical Bag with an assortment of garments inside. The bag was sent around while people were dancing and when the music stopped the couple pulled out a garment and wore it. Some of our guests were doctors, lawyers, civil servants who enjoyed those sub parties and used to encourage us young ones to organize them – remember Ellis Grenier and his wife, Norma – (he was a civil servant and Government Agent in Kandy)? Then he used to bring others if they were around. We used to organize parties in his house too and what about your cousin Evangeline's home? We had a lovely party there (two rupees sub). I remember it was August and we had the CR and FC Rugger players turning up. Even Pieter Keuneman attended the party in a red shirt after a political meeting in Kandy. He enjoyed himself so much that he had wanted to be invited again.

"It was the company that was great. The 'big' ones enjoyed themselves too. You remember Ginger Misso and his wife (he was a lawyer)? We also had 'Progressive Parties' at Christmas. We spent two hours in each home. One year we started at Trevor Williams' house next to Cox's, then our own family home and finally, Soujarh's. We used to sing carols and popular songs in between, even along the road, and no one said we were crazy. We had to walk of course.

"When someone couldn't find a partner for the Excuse Me Dance, the one who got caught would shout in mock helplessness, 'save me' and plead to be rescued. Brian Anthonisz used to jump on the furniture when the girls refused to dance with him. Claude used to coo sweet nothings to the young girls but he was considered quite harmless.

"I remember you well. You were chatting merrily to one of the boys (I don't quite remember which one) and he said. "Jean's a friendly girl. She doesn't only talk Shakespeare.' I think you had just entered university." (excerpt from Norma's letter)

Then there was an eminent Burgher surgeon's wife who lived alone in a lovely house in Siebel Place. She was a very elegant sophisticated woman, well made up – pink powder, lipstick, penciled eyebrows – smoking cigarettes from her long-handled cigarette holder. We were fascinated by the stories we heard of her, especially of her extravagance in sprinkling Tosca Cologne all over her immaculate, tiled bathroom. There were lots of parties at the Railway Running Bungalow too, with indoor games and dancing. Musical arms, musical chairs, the parcel game, forfeits and young Cherrington playing on his guitar. We had parties at Sonna Rosairo's home in the railway quarters in Kandy. A spacious house with many rooms and long verandas.

Sonna had two thumbs like a water diviner's twig which would fascinate us. He had married late in life and had a young Sinhalese wife whom he kept in the background while he was often the Master of Ceremonies at the railway parties...

There was always the 'trickster' pastole at the parties. Platters of hot-hot patties were brought straight off the pan from the kitchen where they would be frying. One particular pastole would be filled with 'pol kudu,' the residue of the coconut kernel after the milk had been extracted, and if you were tricked into biting into it there was no way of concealing the fact. Everybody knew you had been caught out. But why this ploy? Who devised it in the first place? It had become a tradition. No one escaped. But did one want to escape? Even for the shy ones, wasn't this a way of drawing attention to oneself? At that moment you become the focus of all attention. Blushing, laughter, not cruel laughter but one of spontaneous delight. Not you this time, but the next time it will be you. To be able to laugh at yourself became a useful lesson to be learned. Anton would always say: "Learn to laugh like your father. He has a wonderful sense of humour and a fund of jokes." There was always so much to be learnt from others, yet we were so intent on our minutest preoccupations and on ourselves. A form of vanity. The trickster pastole made you the 'fool,' but the fool confounded the wise ones time and time again. All wisdom was contained in the laughter, for laughter is a memory of people who loved you, who made all those elaborate plans for an evening of entertainment. All day long we had sat round the dining table and rolled out the dough for those patties, cutting the rounds with the smooth rim of the tumbler, placing the teaspoon of pastole curry in the centre of the circle and sealing the edges with a fork, the pastry moistened with egg-white. Within it was contained something else too, the surprises of life, the expectation of delight and the inevitability of disappointment. Were we not becoming acquainted with the philosophy, not to rave, rant and rail but to turn the unexpected into laughter?

With everyone gathered round the piano, the sing-songs took place. My sister Rosemary could pick up any tune and create a melody with all its variations, although she was equally adept at playing classical music. She had a talent for 'playing by ear' as well as for sight-reading music.

Those parties of the past were a part of our growing up, of shared ties of kinship and friendship with those who were still to experience exile, migration and diasporic journeys.

During the war years some of the young Burgher boys found that the 'Forces' were considered to be more desirable escorts than themselves to partner the young ladies to the dances that were held in Kandy. Even at house parties there would be young English soldiers and sailors who were either beaux or friends of the young ladies. At least we had memorable parties to remember.

I will always remember how we danced to the music of the gramophone or the long-playing records of Claude Vanderstraaten's radiogramme. We foxtrotted and quickstepped to the music of Charlie Kunz and Victor Sylvester's ballroom orchestra. There were the big bands too with their cool music, Glen Miller and Xaviar Cugat. All those parties had chaperones, mothers, aunts and friends who would generally sit round the hall and watch the young people dancing, and of course see that they were on their best behaviour. Sometimes they too would be invited to dance, very courteously by the young gentlemen. You could of course politely and without fuss decline to dance with someone, especially if he was not too adept in his steps and trampled your toes and didn't keep time to the music, colliding into the other couples too.

Claude had parties in his drawing room at Inbastan. After the Alroy Pereiras' had left Kandy, Claude had moved in with his parents. His mother was a Tradigore, half-Italian; his father one of the upper-crust Dutch Burghers, a Vanderstraaten. Claude's mother was a woman who loved life. She was not only a superb cook but a wonderful seamstress too and could turn out any pattern from the dressmaking journals we showed her. She made some memorable gowns for me with yards of brilliant canna-red taffeta, white organdy with appliquéd lace flowers and pearl centres, in which I whirled with my flaring skirts reflected in the huge glass mirrors of the Queen's Hotel ballroom. Banda tailor, I remember, made me a blue watermark taffeta dress as well as the gown I wore for my brother Pat's wedding (when he married Iona Vanlangenberg), a dress which was the replica of Princess Margaret's bridesmaid's outfit. It was of blue lace with a blue net fischu. Mrs Vanderstraaten also made me my 'costume' for the Sheridan play *The Rivals* in which I took part. It was of delicate green muslin with tiny white embossed dots edging the skirt with white organdy frills. I have a photograph of it which I have preserved to this day.

As we danced in the Inbastan hall with our cousins and friends from Colombo, Bertram Wallbeoff Jansz (teaching at Royal

College at that time) being one of them, we would have a very intent audience outside the gates of the house, standing on the main Peradeniya road, pressing against the half-wall and the wooden bars with folded arms as if they were viewing the 'bioscope.' They watched in silent fascination, those young salesmen from the cane furniture shop, the vegetable and grocery shops, the 'sillare kadé,' and sundry passersby, as the 'lansi' people danced sedately circling the room in couples.

On certain evenings Claude would plan a programme of classical music. We would receive a formal invitation and he would come over to our place to invite us. My mother loved classical music. Together with my sister and myself and joined by other like-minded friends, we would gather at Inbastan, arrange ourselves in Claude's drawing room, sinking into his deeply cushioned Chesterfield suite to listen to the "Emperor Concerto," the "Sonata Apassionato," Chopin's "Polonnaises" and "Etudes," Mozart, Rachmaninoff, and the opera singer Melija Korjeous singing "Finiculi"…, her voice reaching the highest pitch, lucid, silver, the notes quivering like diamonds in the air. And sometimes it was cool, cool jazz, something that my mother did not care for much – she loved the Chopin etudes.

No one was allowed to utter a word while Claude played his records. It had to be complete surrender and concentration to his music. We would sit, deeply ensconced in our chairs, eyes half closed, lights lowered, listening to whatever he chose to play to us, whether it was "Moonlight Sonata" or "Going Fishing."

Going fishing
There's a sign upon the door,
Going fishing…

In Pursuit of Love and Romance

Yes, in those days we did have a lot of fun. Once I spent a weekend in Colombo. Kandy was a fairly quiet place, although we did have our parties and moonlight picnics too. I was staying with relations who took me to see films, *La Traviata, Captain Hornblower, Anthony Adverse*. With my friends we would go to the island of San Michele on Bolgoda Lake. It was lovely there at night, with a wooden dais for dancing, the place all lit up, with the dark waters illuminated by coloured electric bulbs. I remember a famous Burgher Communist Party leader dancing away with his partner. His partner was an attractive woman, Minette de Silva, an architect whose mother was Miss Nell and father a UNP stalwart in Kandy. It was nice to see Pieter Keuneman enjoying the simple pleasures of life, taking a break from trade union work and politics.

We had so many friends too, some of them were undergraduates at the University of Colombo. I remember Chandra, who had those strange greeny grey eyes with long curling lashes. I had met him at an SCM Conference in Galle. We used to be part of the Student Christian Movement and go regularly for conferences that were held in different parts of the island. During the holidays we would all pile into cars and explore Colombo. Chandra once had this crazy idea of smuggling me into one of their lectures at the University. He was reading for a degree in English Honours. Well, I was game for it too, and I joined the small group. I was curious, yes, at that time still in school in my first year in the University Entrance class. The professor entered the lecture room. He was a Burgher too. He must have recognized that there was a stranger in their midst, but he didn't bat an eyelid and carried on a lecture on the Metaphysical Poets, whom I had already read. How well I remember those lines, those metaphysical conceits, those images. All to do with love, a major preoccupation in our lives in those days – Suckling, Lovelace, Carew, Marvell, and Donne. We had to discover the reality later for ourselves. We never thought of growing old, we thought youth would last for ever... and so we pursued Romance as if it were the only thing that mattered in life.

*   *   *

(i)   Drama? Plenty of it in our young lives. Like the time I was in Peradeniya University and my friends decided that one of the young men courting me shouldn't be in my life. They took the law into their own hands the next time he came to the Hall of Residence to visit me. Of course all those visits were very formal: we had to sit in the Common Room of the Hall, and the visitors had to leave at 7 o'clock sharp. My friends went downstairs and had a long earnest talk with the young doctor who was in love with me, while I was kept out of the discussion. The young man sat pinned to his seat in the car, while my new friends, two senior undergrads who were more worldly wise than myself, told him among many other things that he was not to pursue the affair as he was not suitable for me. I do not, up to this date, know why they became my self-appointed guardians. Did they want to protect me, knowing the world better than I did? Were there moral strictures involved? He was supposed to have made 'a promise' of marriage to a young lady doctor.

Whatever it was, he had even approached my father with a proposal of marriage which was not acceptable to my parents. I had just entered university. It didn't mean that there would be less space for our passionate, juvenile romancing of which there were many encounters and opportunities with our very own group of friends, some of us belonging to the "Kultur" set as we were named, with our interests in music, both classical and jazz, theatre and drama, poetry writing...

I was so innocent that I didn't even question my two friends, both sophisticated Colombo girls who knew "all about life,"and let them do the talking while I leaned over the balcony of Hilda Obeysekera Hall, silently watching them. The car drove away. My friends came upstairs and said: "You're never to see him again. We heard that he has someone else too." Was that, I wonder now, the only reason why they wanted him to keep away?

That very night when we were either studying or all abed when the whole of Peradeniya campus was shrouded in darkness and stillness, a single car was heard roaring along the deserted main campus driving at breakneck speed, someone's hand pressed unmoving on the blaring trumpet sounding horn while my name was shouted aloud for the whole world to hear, again and again, unendingly. I still hear that resounding echo in my ears. That was the end to that particular affair. There was no heartbreak, no poignant feelings of nostalgia.

How many long years did it take for that screen to be pulled away and raw reality – show the two-faced Janus of our lives, in university and out when we began and continued our search for destinations we often never reached. The poems we wrote about those youthful days, sitting on the banks of the Mahaweli and reading "Ode to Autumn," poems which turned to elegies for those who died young or emigrated, rarely to be even remembered...?

(ii)   A Poem and a Letter: I remember how a romantic poem had been written and dedicated to me: the "Dewdrop," with very convoluted imagery. It was sent to me by a law student at the university. I had inadvertently left the poem in a reference book which I had returned to the university library. The poem was of course discovered by someone, read with relish since the dedication was to me, and then a strange series of events took place. A letter was addressed to me at my Hall of Residence which contained a message embodying subtle forms of blackmail. The gist of the letter was as follows: "We have discovered a poem dedicated to you and are intrigued by the subtle images within the poem. We find the imagery very suggestive in a metaphysical kind of way. Since it's a very personal poem we are sure you would like to have it back which you may under certain conditions. You will have to place a certain sum of money under the stone [the place was indicated as well as the amount] at the entrance to the Arts Faculty entrance. Please enclose it in the envelope. When you have followed the instructions the poem will be posted back to you. If you do not follow the instructions we will circulate the poem throughout the campus."

I found the letter disturbing. I was so young then. Moreover, the letter was unsigned. It was the first and last anonymous letter I was ever to receive. Together with my coterie of friends we decided to take the letter to the Chief University Warden, Mr de Saram. We went to his University quarters, the house with its lovely garden just in front of the Women's Hall of Residence, and I poured out my tale of woe to him. He was most understanding and calmed us all down: "Well, it's an anonymous letter, destroy it, throw it into the wastepaper basket. On the other hand, if you really want to discover who it is you can go ahead with the instructions and then we can nab the lot." Well, after the long discussion – and Mr de Saram knew how to deal with young ladies in the most charming manner – we decided to do nothing about the matter. The letter was probably torn into shreds and destroyed.

I never got the poem back. That was a pity. Juvenilia should sometimes be preserved for their historicity. The young man who wrote the poem, however, remained my friend until his untimely death. He became a district court judge. He remained a writer but began to compose songs and plays rather than poetry. The poem was never circulated as threatened. The imagery must have appeared titillating – conventional imagery of bees, nectar, and dewdrops. Yet there was a darker side to the whole affair; one could be vulnerable, you could offer no defence when such things are cloaked in anonymity.

(iii)   He was going abroad for a space of the time and thought perhaps I would find time hanging on my hands, so he spent a whole evening telling me how I should do "Window Dressing." An artistic pursuit according to him. I think I even took notes on the various suggestions. Looking back now, the whole episode seems so unrealistic and so amusing. Imagine trying to transform the display windows of Cargills and Whiteaway with all the English fashions and European models, using arrangements like Spanish mantillas, toreadors, and models of local fishermen with sailcloth and fishing nets draped all over the woven-straw fisherman's hats to boot... I wish I had preserved those notes.

The suggestion of "window dressing" implied a subtle control of space, of life, of youth which you think unending, during which there are few intimations of mortality. There was also the control of thought and imagination approximating that relationship with deception, the superficiality of surface disguises. It turned out to be a stultifying relationship. The first impassioned verses written during that period together with the fables that were written finally reached an ironic summation in any poem, "The Visit," which was the finale.

Derrick was different. He loved my sister and myself, as he later wrote from Australia where he emigrated, like his very own sisters. He was quite content to spend evenings on the veranda of our house where we spent hours and hours talking together of our lives and pastimes, listening meanwhile to his accounts of a eventful and adventurous life in the navy, which he had joined at the age of sixteen. At twenty-six he was still unmarried. We were schoolgirls. He would ride on his motorbike along Peradeniya Road from his home in Augusta House on the hills of Kandy. We were his avid audience to the tales of his youthful exploits in all the ports and harbours he had been in. Hinted at wild escapades. Later on he took to planting up-country following the traditions of his father's family. He was a blond-haired Burgher boy, and resembled as everyone said, the Duke of Edinburgh, in his youth. A superb rugger player too, who played for the Planters' Clubs at Darawela and other up-country stations. We missed him when he went away, and never saw him again.

(iv)   Nissanka was mad about me, a Sinhalese youth, a lawyer, supposed to be brilliant, won all the Gold medals at Law college. He came from a well-known family, his father a doctor, his mother involved in social service work in Colombo. He saw me on the dance floor while I was whirling about in the "Blue Danube" and wanted an introduction to me. Well, that kind of thing was just not done – we only danced with those within our familiar circle of friends; strangers weren't encouraged to gatecrash. Of course there was the "Paul Jones" where you danced in an inner or outer circle and when the music stopped you didn't know who your partner was going to be; and there was the "Excuse Me dance" too, just a little tap on the shoulder and the polite request, "May I have the pleasure of a dance with you?" It was bad manners to refuse. Of course your own partner would be close at hand to 'rescue' you, so that dancing with a stranger was not prolonged.

Sometimes it happened, somebody caught your eye, someone visiting from Colombo without a partner, a kind of lone wolf not encouraged to join our circle, but this young man knew someone in our party and begged for an introduction to me. Anton didn't care for him really, but he pleaded so much that he gave in. "I'm Nissanka," he said. "I had to get to know you. You're so beautiful," he told me, "How old are you? Sixteen, seventeen? Sweet sixteen, you should already be in the marriage market."

Marriage market? I was so shocked. What did he think of me? I had other thoughts in my head, not just catching a husband. Plenty of time for that, I just loved dancing, enjoying myself, hated the thought of being tied down to anyone. I wanted a career too, not just being housebound. It was really the first time I had heard such a phrase – did he think we Burgher girls went to dances to catch husbands? Such a thought was never on my mind. When the time came I'd make up my mind about settling down – all that was a long way.

Anyway, Nissanka said, "I must see you again."

"You don't know my father," I said, "He's very strict."

"I'll brave it," he said. "I'll visit your home and make a formal proposal."

"Proposal?" I said stunned. "What proposal? I'm still at school."

"A marriage proposal of course," he said.

I was rather amused. I couldn't take him seriously. I supposed I would marry a Burgher boy and settle down to a way of life I was familiar with... oh, but years later.

Then he said, "I have a patrimony of a hundred acres of coconut – that's my inheritance."

"A hundred acres of coconut?" It didn't mean a thing to me. What was he trying to tell me? Did he think that I would be dazzled by the fact that he owned property, that he was wealthy? I just couldn't imagine anyone trying to get round me by saying that he owned property: that didn't attract me at all. I wasn't going to fall for that.

Anyway, true to his word he came visiting one evening, and my parents treated him politely but they were cool towards him. My parents were cool towards anyone pursuing me with romantic interest, since they felt I was too young. So they were very protective towards me.

Well, Nissanka didn't stop at that. He came on a special visit to see my father; unfortunately for him I was taken ill suddenly with acute appendicitis and had to enter the hospital. I think I was scared of the situation I found myself in and wanted to escape from any emotional involvements. I heard the story from my mother later on.

"That young admirer of yours," she said, "approached your father, said he wanted to marry you, and then what do you think he said, that his patrimony was a hundred acres of coconut, as if we care about that kind of thing. When the time comes you'll find a suitable partner, from your own Burgher community... Your father was furious. 'Patrimony of a hundred acres of coconut? You're a cradle snatcher; you're not going to have my daughter... Don't come this way again.'"

Nissanka wrote letter after letter, but I was an obedient daughter. I didn't want to displease my parents after all they had sacrificed for me.

The story ended sadly – Nissanka never found his true love or married. He committed suicide one day with an overdose of sleeping tablets. His patrimony must have gone to his brothers and sisters. I heard later that he had led what in those days was called a"dissolute life." Nissanka's home life had been one of emotional turmoil and insecurity. His parents led separate lives. Each went their own way, while he had affair after affair but nothing filled that gap in his life.

(v)   There were some quite not-so-innocent parties too. I once went to a party where most of the guests were young House Officers serving their internship in the General Hospital Kandy. This was in the early years of the 1950s. (The party was held in the quarters of the Medical Superintendent in the University of Peradeniya.) It was the usual party with music and dancing, and the hostess was the newly married wife of the university doctor. She was a pretty, convent-educated girl, from Chilaw. It had been an arranged marriage. Antoinette had been a charming hostess but, since she didn't dance, she had slipped away to the privacy of her bedroom after supper. I was searching for the bathroom through the strange house and got lost in one of the corridors. I found myself standing before the open door of one of the bedrooms. Lying in bed, like Aphrodite among the billowy white pillows, lay Antoinette, her face turned towards her husband who was gently caressing her and on the point of making love to her. This was their home and the party had palled for them, since they were completely enthralled by each other. I had still to find the bathroom. I quietly moved away until I found myself in the dining room, the kitchen adjoining it.

At the door stood the cook woman with folded arms listening to the sounds of music and merriment in the drawing room. I next found myself watching a different scene arranging itself before my eyes. Two or three of the young doctors were moving towards the kitchen door, and I noticed a tall, extremely handsome man with a cherubic expression on his face, sliding into the kitchen. The woman disappeared. So did the doctor, and the door closed behind them. The others were outside awaiting their turn. The dancing continued. The doctor and his wife did not reappear. After a while the young man reappeared, his smoothly brushed hair ruffled, his tie askew, his habitually beatific smile adorning his pink-tinged lips. The woman in the kitchen, what was her role? Indulgent, accommodating, curious?

I moved back to the drawing room. I sat, very still in a corner, sipping a cool drink of iced passion fruit. A masqued ball, I thought to myself. Two planes of life. One, the apparently carefree and respectable, conformist and conventional on the surface, but behind it the hidden instincts and urges that lurked in the darkness behind the closed door. By midnight each of the bachelors had moved through the labyrinth of darkness and emerged with their dual selves into the world of light and music and repartee. My feelings towards that man underwent a sea change. He was considered to be a most eligible bachelor, good-looking. "A nice Burgher boy," my mother had once commented.

I became conscious of the duality in what I thought was an extremely conservative, conventional young man. There were hidden sources of knowledge, the effervescent, bubbling springs of sensuality we had not yet tasted of how the deeper instinctual urges of sexuality operated. We had neither encountered its language nor that physicality. We read a literature which described those feelings of passion without the awareness of its realities. The entrance into that darkened room opened my eyes to new realities.

(vi) When you are young you can sometimes be quite insensitive about other people's feelings. There was that English poet doing his National Service in Ceylon. He had read my poetry in one of those literary journals of the time and written to me, wanting to meet me. I was just out of university. He called me "Marjorie Morningstar," and that made me want to read the book, which I did… Oh, it was all years and years ago. People were always saying that I resembled the heroine in some novel or other, women in books by Aldous Huxley, Evelyn Waugh, and Emily Brontë. I think it was just that they wanted to romanticize Romance and make me a fictional heroine. Anyway, the English poet formed a romantic attachment to me, wrote letters and wanted to visit me in my home. At the first meeting we walked sedately through the Botanical Gardens at Peradeniya. Well, he did come again, but I decided I didn't want to pursue the relationship. The poor young man had used his leave to come up to Kandy, and I quite callously hid behind the scenes and sent him a message that I wasn't in – quite without compunction. My little niece was with my family at that time. Childish innocence does not resort to subterfuge, so she went running to the door and announced gleefully: "She's in, she's in. She's in the dining room." "You've let the cat out of the bag,." she was told, but by then it was too late. I never met him again, but he did write a long letter and told me how he had looked forward so much to the encounter and I had dodged it… all his precious leave wasted.

I do feel guilty when I think of how careless we were of other people's feelings when we were young. Too late to make amends now. I don't even have a copy of the journal in which our poems appeared. I wonder whether he still lives in Dagenham in England or whether he migrated to Australia or Canada after he had completed his stint at National Service. But I do remember him still…

Looking back on those remembered evenings so many years later. I think how manipulative human relationships can be when you are young, impressionable, naïve.

A Different Question

I walked down the long corridors
Looking into mirrors, seven mirrors
Show me seven faces only my feet sound
Walking the lonely mirrored corridors
Among the pillars.

I mount stairs and descend
Then suddenly run to catch the
Light that seems to evade me
Walk alone on balconies looking out onto
The road, it's almost empty, one or two
Sauntering along, young men with questions
In their files already answered, learned by
Rote, nothing else is allowed to remain
Within their memories, nothing except what
Others have presumed to know about love,
About life, about death.

Stanzas shift in their minds
Lie heavy like stones weighting down
The brain and later perhaps to clack
Like old bones disintegrating in coffins
Of time.

Their faces are all turned away
From the birds, from the flowering trees
From water and cloud.

Turned away from the faces, the young
Bodies that are waiting for them.

The corridors and balconies stretch,
I climb up and down stairs
I watch my seven bodies move through
Glass and in each mirror the eyes ask
A different question, and the lips move
But there is no one to answer those questions
There was only a silence
There was no time to even say 'Goodbye'
To any of them.

They went away rapidly walking
Passing the bend lost to sight,
Already old, old men.

My cousin Joyce Solomons (Masterstyn) with gramophone, wearing her Girl Guide uniform.

IX

TRAVELLING
&
TRAVELLERS

After Recognition service, Methodist Church, Brownrigg St, Kandy; I am 3rd from left, with students from Kandy Girls High School, and our teacher Mrs Bevan, wife of Reverend Bevan.

Yogis and Yoginis on the Train

Those train journeys of the past took us everywhere we wanted. Sometimes the strange and unexpected confronted us, but we emerged unscathed from each new experience and encounter. Was it our own unsuspecting innocence or the thrill of the unknown discovery which gave us a feeling of excitement?

Of course we were always given the familiar warnings: "Don't talk to strangers," "Don't eat anything that's offered you; the food may be 'charmed,' you might eat of it, lose your senses and goodness knows where you'll end..." But here we were, myself and a few of my friends travelling back to Kandy in the evening train, seated comfortably on a wide, plush-covered seat running the length of the first-class compartment. We had got in sedately, at the Fort station and found a virtually empty compartment except for a quiet, innocuous-looking elderly gentleman seated alone, taking up a whole seat for himself.

My friends and I, all schoolmates from our Methodist missionary school, were about fifteen or sixteen years of age and quite intent over our own affairs of which we had much to mull over.

After some time, the elderly gentleman, bespectacled and serious of mien, wearing long khaki shorts and a white shirt – he had, I noticed, a thin, wiry-looking body – introduced himself and began talking to us.

"My name is Mr Mahinda," he said, "and I am a follower of yoga. For many years now I have mastered all the yogic exercises and the special art of breathing – pranayama. If you wish, I could demonstrate these exercises to you."

Various people had tried to instruct us in many and diverse skills, so we were quite adept at western ballet, eurhythmics, turning cartwheels, doing the splits, arching our bodies into bridges beneath which our classmates wiggled through, and of course 'drill' performed according to the timetable in the School Hall, supervised by the 'Drill Mistress.' The gentleman looked harmless, and at any rate we were intrigued by the new experience he promised us. Moreover, nothing much was happening on the journey in this train, chugging away at times or speeding along at others, in the days of the steam engines. The gentleman would at least offer us a diversion. We could always learn and then carry our latest skills back to school. The ticket inspectors were nowhere in sight, and we didn't think it the least unusual that someone was in deadly earnest to teach us to practise yogic breathing and yogic exercises in a railway compartment.

"Breathing correctly," said the gentleman in his calm and gentle voice, "is a source of energy and life. But first you must take up the Lotus Pose. Follow me. It's quite simple. After you have taken the Lotus Pose I will show you how to inhale and exhale."

He adopted the initial pose – he had a whole plush-covered seat to himself – and began to draw his legs up first, sitting in a cross-legged posture. He crossed his ankles, legs drawn wide, proceeding with great ease and agility to place first his right leg on top of one knee, then the left on top of the other, until he looked the picture of serenity.

"Now I will breathe slowly and begin to repeat the mantra. OM," he chanted. "Now you must do the same." The three of us, wearing the modest attire of those times, decided to give the yogic exercises a try.

"You will be the yoginis," said Mr Mahinda to Carmen, Yvonne and myself. "I will be the yogi." We followed each of his moves carefully, as he once again unwrapped his limbs from their serpentine sinuosities and began our initiation into his yogic world. We looked at each other, then at Mr Mahinda and began to follow his movements. So, yoginis we would be. The lights came on in the compartment. Outside, dusk began to darken the glass shutters. Mr Mahinda and the three young schoolgirls were in a world of their own.

First, breathing, pranayama. Then the Half Lotus which we were beginning to master, our young limbs being supple; next, the Full Lotus. After which we chanted "OM, OM, OM," muting our voices till the mantra sounded deep, sonorous, profound, entering the secret recesses of our very being.

There were other exercises, Mr Mahinda explained. He was in his element. We were turning out to be very flexible, very inspired, under his yogic tutelage. Rapidly we executed half, full, half, full... Lotus Pose.

"Good, good," he murmured. "Very good. Now I will tell you all about Hatha Yoga. It is the secret of happiness and well-being... Next, I will show you the 'Salute to the Sun,' the Suryanamaskara."

Mr Mahinda gracefully withdrew his limbs from the Lotus Pose and stood, quite steadily, on the jolting floor of the compartment. So did we. We stood, straight and erect, hands at sides, feet slightly apart. Rose on the tips of our toes and stretched first with one hand and then with the next until we appeared to reach the sun. Finally we lowered our heels and touched the floor, relaxing our bodies.

Another of the exercises, "Knees full bend," resembled one of our physical training exercises that we did in school while Aileen de Silva or Olga Wijewardena blew on their whistles and issued short, sharp commands.

"And now I will show you the Headstand," Mr Mahinda said. "It needs years of practice and much skill."

Carmen, Yvonne and myself could not accomplish perfect headstands in a jolting compartment, but we retired to our Half Lotus pose, breathing pranayama, and observed the clever Mr Mahinda with admiration. What a transformation! The elderly, innocuous-seeming, serious-looking gentleman was so beautifully supple and agile in his movements; no young gentleman had so far impressed us so deeply in their lives, even with their ardent gazes and protestations of eternal love.

"The Headstands brings the blood directly to the Head," explained Mr Mahinda. We were chanting "OM, OM, OM," to encourage him from our eminence on the wide compartment seat.

"It also stimulates brain power. It is one of the asanas I have mastered after years of practice. Watch." Yes, that was all we were prepared to do. Watch. We were at any rate hampered by our attire, however modest it was. We were not in our divided skirts or gym uniforms.

Nothing could have impressed us more. Mr Mahinda, who was most probably a Government Servant of the Old School and a bachelor, had captured his audience of admiring schoolgirls. He maintained the pose on the compartment floor with his legs perfectly aligned to the rest of his body. It lasted for just a few seconds but his control was perfect.

All the while we maintained our Lotus poses feeling quite at peace with the rest of the world. Nobody interrupted us newly initiated yoginis. We had the entire compartment to ourselves for the rest of the journey. Mr Mahinda went his way. We went our ways, but the mantra was to remain in our minds for all time, together with Mr Mahinda's tranquil image. It was then truly the age of innocence.

Holidays Up-country

The trains were a second home to us. We travelled from a very early age along that network of railway tracks, which webbed the island, on journeys long and short. My father was entitled to first-class railway warrants and so we travelled in comfort, often spending the night on the train, occupying sleeping berths all to ourselves.

Whenever we needed a change of scene and air, my mother would pack the cabin trunks and suitcases and we would go on holidays to stay with relatives. We were fortunate that Uncle Bonnie was postmaster in Bandarawela and in Nuwara Eliya, and so we had our up-country holidays in the Post Office quarters.

The trains powered by steam engines took us along those winding routes. From our window seats we gazed upon a changing landscape, the air growing crisp and chill as the train climbed higher and higher, the rhododendron trees twisted and gnarled with their scarlet cockades appearing among the green-blue undulations of hills. The tea-pluckers wrapped in their dark cumblies dotted the tea-bush-covered slopes, planted like tiny flags on a plush green map. We glimpsed the isolated estate bungalows, long low-roofed dwellings with glass-paned windows, green-painted roofs, gardens with well-laid-out green lawns and flowerbeds of gladioli, carnations, hydrangeas, phlox, dahlias, arum lilies and ox-eyed daisies. Huge tree ferns thrust themselves out of the high earth banks. Tea trees, ancient and gnarled, grew wild and un-pruned among the rocky places. Against the horizon a fringe of windbreaker trees crested the hilltops with their feathery wind-swept branches. Tea factories, like white confections thickly encrusted with icing, nestled in the valleys through which running streams of water wound serpentine among the rocks. The dwellings of the plantation workers, the line rooms, had huge rocks and tyres on the roofs to prevent them from being swept off by strong gusts of wind.

We were the historical sightseers of that colonial era viewing those scenic enactments of history unfolding their panorama before our eyes. We were to explore the realities later. My father told us of the valuable topsoil washed away by the rains after the land had been cleared and the forests cut down for the tea plantations; of the erosion of thousands of acres; of the "coolie treks" starting out from Devipatanam and Talaimannar; of the line rooms for whole families of immigrant workers; of the eternal indebtedness of the workers to the Kanganies; of the diseases like cholera, typhoid, small-pox which the men and women succumbed to on the long marches to the interior of the island. Those who couldn't make it were left to die on the fringes of thick jungle, and those who made it often died of chills and pneumonia when they reached the damp, mist-covered up-country regions. All that was screened off from our present view.

The steam engine chugged up the slopes. We climbed to higher altitudes far above the valleys with their miniature landscapes. We took our warm cardigans to ward off the unaccustomed chill, but the air was fresh, exhilarating. The Refreshment Car waiters, in starched white coats with silver or brass buttons and garbed in spotless white cloths with buckled leather belts, came round to the compartments to take the orders from the printed menu. The steward bowed and asked my mother:

"What will Madame have for breakfast?" He spoke in English. He showed her the printed menu.

"Bacon and eggs, toast, butter and marmalade," she ordered, "with a pot of tea," The silver tray was brought with the thick, white railway crockery, the hallmark of the CGR. White cubes of sugar, very fine, filled the sugar bowl. The cream floated on the surface of the milk jug. The teapot was filled to the brim with steaming hot tea. There were tiny silver tongs to lift out the sugar cubes. The sugar, my father told me came from the cane fields of the West Indies. Pure white sugar and Demarara sugar which was brown. I was unaware at the stage that even sugar had the distinctive flavour of colonial history. We had still to read of indentured labour, of those migrations from the Indian sub-continent, of the sagas of the cane cutters and their lives on the plantations of the West Indies. Here the Indian migrations had taken place to labour on the coffee and tea plantations.

Uncle Bonnie's postmaster's quarters faced the park at Nuwara Eliya, where we went for morning and evening walks among the borders of carnations, gladioli, sweet pea and phlox. The nannies sat in the grass gossiping with each other, dressed in their white sarees and blue knitted woolen jerseys, keeping watchful eyes on their charges, small English boys tumbling about in the grass. "Come here, Master Charles"... "Don't go there, Master William"... quite sternly admonished not to stray too far. One day they would be elderly men, who perhaps went on to the task of Empire building and then retired to their country homes to remember, maybe even recollect those days of their childhood in those cool hill stations, and that grassy park. Part of the Empire which their fathers had so strong a stake in.

We passed them by, walking sedately in the long English overcoats which my aunts had brought back from England. Mine was smooth and fawn-coloured with a fur collar. The big buttons had to be moved up to reach my waist as the coat had belonged to the era of a by-gone age. This was in the period of the 1940s, while the coat belonged perhaps to those low-waisted fashions of the twenties or thirties when the aunts had begun their globe-trotting.

We usually took a hiring car from the station to Uncle Bonnie's quarters. He was a quiet, soft-spoken man, yet one who possessed determination and commitment to his work. During the Second World War when Trincomalee was bombed during the Japanese air-raids, Uncle Bonnie, who was stationed there, refused to be evacuated with the other administrative officials. He chose to stay behind to keep the lines of communication going between Trincomalee and Colombo from his Post Office. He, like Uncle Elmer, remained a bachelor, but unlike Uncle Elmer, whose love affairs had an aura of mystery, "Uncle Bonnie had been in love" with Barbara Smith. She had given him "hopes" and then let him down it was said. He was inconsolable, really "heartbroken," so he never married. He was a generous-hearted man, allowing his privacy to be invaded by his sister-in-law, his nieces, his sisters, for spending holidays up-country was a much-looked-forward-to happening in our lives. Especially during the Season when everybody came up to Nuwara Eliya, stayed in guest houses, walked in parks, explored the Maze, ate up-country fruit and vegetables to their hearts' content: pears, peaches, tree tomatoes, fresh cauliflower, carrots, cabbages. Uncle Bonnie ordered all the food for us from one of the wives of his post-office clerks, so we would have cutlets, stews, roast beef, steamed cauliflower for dinner and delicious rice and curry for lunch. Uncle Bonnie did everything for us out of his own salary. We just took it for granted, I suppose, that it was both pleasure and duty for our bachelor uncle to have us as his guests.

The post-office quarters were very spacious in those days, in solid, old colonial buildings. Even in Kandy, Uncle Bonnie would entertain us in the main GPO Headquarters upstairs. The post office had once been an hotel. Auntie Ila stayed with him too for a time in Kandy, when she was teaching at Trinity College, and when we went visiting she would prepare Welsh Rarebit for us, cheese on toast. I never once saw Uncle Bonnie in anything but the best and most cheerful moods, although he had a long illness to bear in the latter days of his life. The saddest day for me was when we received news that he was seriously ill at Durdan's Nursing Home in Colombo. My aunts and my father were beside him till he breathed his last. My mother, my sister and myself stayed out in the garden the whole night through, watching and waiting in the car. The whole scene still remains imprinted in my mind, the room in the nursing home, the doors wide open, my father and my aunts by his bedside or moving about attending to his medications until they came out and announced to us: "The death rattle has started. The end is near."

My sister and I used to spend hours in the pear orchard at the back of the post-office building when Uncle Bonnie was the chief postmaster in Nuwara Eliya. We were given freedom, my sister and I, to eat the ripening fruit, hanging in their clusters from the branches, our teeth biting into the skin, so crisp, crunchy, the flesh with a slightly sandpapery quality yet impregnated with juice at once acrid and sweet. So, childhood was associated with special textures and flavours of fruit and leaf and flower. Colours too. The orchard was a secret place where adults did not venture and here we went about our earnest and exploratory experiences, our private discoveries. Orchards and mazes were habitations of childhood, shelters and labyrinths, cyclic and seasonal in flowering and fruiting. The maze was the dark threat we sought, for we needed to confuse ourselves and feel the fear of not knowing how we could find the aperture to escape, footsteps quickening, yet tentative, the self-game you played. Within the labyrinth with its trimmed fir-tree walls we sought out fear and the unknown as an escape from predictable routes. This was the small island and here the unknown beast dwelt. There were other holiday-makers too at Nuwara Eliya. Friends from Kandy. "Valencia's mother sucked out the venom from a snake bite when she was bitten or stung one day, the venom travelled in her veins and made her nervy." We were told of those snake stones too. We had one, that curious grey stone which I imagined turned agate blue as it absorbed the venom from the deadly bite of the reptile. My sister and I would peer out of the many windows of the upstair quarters at the people and the landscape, the visitors who had come for the Season, taking walks in the crisp air, wearing their warm coats, the glimpses of evergreens, fir trees, well-tended beds of flowers ablaze with colour.

And that young red-haired boy from Colombo left little billet-doux for my sister in the cabbage patch of the post-office garden. My sister was very beautiful, with her fine features and vibrant personality. She attracted many admirers wherever she went. In the evenings we sometimes lit a fire in the fireplace built of red brick in the drawing room and read book after book from Uncle Bonnie's collection: Rupert Brooke, Jeffrey Farnol, Ngaio Marsh, and lots of grown-up novels. We were kept warm as we sat by the fireplace with its burning evergreen wood. Uncle Bonnie never had a cook, never had servants. He was a very self-reliant man.

I was constantly drawn to the Maze. It filled me with a sense of fear and adventure. It was a place apart which I wanted to explore again and yet again. A place where I just wanted to lose myself among those confusing passages, experience that sense of desperate trepidation of not being able to find the way back to the outer world. Those high green walls were much taller than the lost and wandering child. I held my breath in fear. Would I ever be able to find my way out? The Maze was only a part of childhood. I knew that when I grew up and entered it as an adult, I would never find the same thrill of the prisoner finding freedom. Yet the Maze and groping my way through was a rehearsal for that journey through the labyrinth. The Minotaur was there, somewhere, lurking in the shadows. I would have first to contend with those legends and myths, and then confront reality. No one knew of my secret joy when I emerged out of the Maze all on my own. Yet how safe was the world of adults where I found myself once again?

Who were those adults? Some of them were strangers. Some were familiar figures belonging to the world of aunts and uncles. There was Auntie Girlie who would also be holidaying at the same time as ourselves as she too had school holidays, working as she did in the office administration of a missionary school. She was so easy-going, loved food, and was always good-natured. She was an excellent cook who made all the pilaus and the chicken curries, while my intellectual Aunt Elsie was no cook but she always 'ordered' treats for her nieces and later on grand-nieces – tins of fried breadfruit chips, jaggery, pumpkin preserve, sweets, cadju aluwa, potato aluwa, and milk toffee. "Auntie Girlie is Martha of the Bible. Mary is Auntie Elsie."

Her brothers, Uncle Bonnie and my father, always invited Girlie whenever she wanted "a change of air, or scene." She would descend on Uncle Bonnie's quarters, travelling from Colombo with its steamy and humid climate, with a prickly heat rash, a tin of prickly heat talc, and a wooden backscratcher of antique design.

"Now girls," she would summon my sister and myself, "give me a good scratch for my prickly heat. First sprinkle the powder on my back and then gently use the backscratcher."

My mother would bridle at the suggestion and whispered to us softly: "I don't know why Girlie wants you to do this. I don't like it at all. Scrub your hands well with soap and water after you finish."

I thought the backscratcher one of the most fascinating things I had seen and longed to possess one myself. It had a long handle so we didn't need to touch Auntie Girlie's skin. Her bared back was like a map with all its little knolls and hillocks. Ah, it was one of the most sensuous pleasures of Auntie Girlie's life, this back-scratching, as she closed her eyes and guided us with her instructions.

"Just a little towards the middle, there, there..., just there..., the sides..., mmm, a little towards the left directly beneath the shoulder joints..., put more talcum powder..., scratch...scratch," Girlie was enveloped in clouds of airy powder which blew all over her and tickled her nostrils too. She would sneeze. My mother, who was lurking disapprovingly in the background, would whisper, "Move away, move away, don't get the powder all over you now." We knew we would have to have hot baths after the whole exercise was over. Sensuality? All those feelings must have been there, and as spinsters (although Auntie Girlie with her soulful orbs had had her Romance), there must have been a certain amount of repression, of dormant feelings of sexuality.

Sexuality wasn't openly talked of in those days. Even to describe pregnancy there were certain phrases. A newly married young woman was "enceinte," or would be whispered about by adults as "so-so is suffering from morning sickness" or she's expecting." "She's in the family way" was another phrase, and of course a pregnancy out of wedlock meant that the man "had put her in trouble and "they were forced to marry," "a shotgun wedding." There was much that we had to learn, on our own, of life...

So even Auntie Girlie's back-scratching perhaps produced feelings of pleasurable enjoyment that marriage denied her. Being 'on the shelf' or a 'wall-flower at a party' were situations to be avoided. Yet my aunts were all self-made women who made careers for themselves and left, each in their own way, a tremendous impact on the times and in the society they lived in.

A Holiday Northwards

My parents always spoke of plans for a long train journey in India, to visit relatives, but they were always too preoccupied to embark on that route to the subcontinent.

Anyway, it was left to us children to do most of the travelling, both in Ceylon and abroad, and there was yet another memorable holiday that I spent with my Jansz cousins in Paranthan, Jaffna. Uncle Theodore was stationmaster there and the daughter Yvonne had been a classmate of mine at Girls' High School at one stage.

It was a long journey to Paranthan, in a slow train with the steam engine chugging along through changing landscape on that journey to the north of the island. The stationmaster's house was above the offices on the station platform, and we were able to look down on the passing trains and into the railway compartments as they passed through, watching the passengers, sleeping and eating on their long journey, the banana leaves spread out with rice, curd and delicious murunga (drumstick) curry. Yvonne and I used to walk through the peaceful green glades of Paranthan among the shady trees, with bird calls sounding from the leafy branches, making up our own adventure stories. Koinmenike cooked for Auntie Maisie. There were many Sinhalese families living in a row of houses by the side of the railway lines who worked for the CGR, like Koinmenike's husband. How far they had come from their Kandyan villages and from the villages in the south.

We once had a picnic in Killinochchi with another Burgher family – we camped out in a shady arbour and celebrated a birthday party with an enormous Elephant House iced chocolate cake. It was all so peaceful. The little birthday girl was Melanie Ernst. From Paranthan we made a trip to Elephant Pass. I remember the ford once used by the wild elephants for their passage from the mainland during the season when the palmyrah fruits were beginning to ripen, clusters of them, on each flower stem of the palmyrah palm. The elephants used to feed on the fruit fallen on the ground and eat of the sweet pulp. We visited the Elephant Pass Rest House erected from parts of an Old Dutch fort. Elephant Pass, Pass Beschuter and Pass Pyle were erected by the Dutch to accommodate the guards who were stationed at these particular strongholds to check the incursions of the Vanniyars and their followers. In 1803 the Vanniyars had succeeded in seizing the fort at Elephant Pass. At the same time they succeeded in dislodging the garrison at Mullaitivu.

Later on I was to learn that Pass Beschuter obtained its name from Marcellus de Boschouwer or Bosehouder. This Dutchman had played an important part at the beginning of the seventeenth century. At the court of the King of Kandy of Senerath, according to Sir James Emerson Tennent, Boschouwer was made into Prince of Migone. As for Pass Pyl, according to Valentyn, it was named in honour of Lorenzo Van Pyl, Governor of Jaffnapatanam in 1679. It was at Elephant Pass that we were entertained by the Claasz family. Lorna was their delightful daughter and a wonderful cook.

Noel Templar was one of the Burgher engine drivers who worked on the Northern line. The Templars were our neighbours in Kandy and his wife Primrose used to sew beautifully for us. Noel Templar was asked by my father to bring a basket of upcountry vegetables when he went through Paranthan: carrots, cabbages, leeks, lettuce, and tomatoes.

When the holiday was over, my mother came all the way from Kandy to take me back by train. She too spent a few days at Paranthan. After being in a house surrounded by trees and gardens abounding in flowers, it was such a unique experience sleeping upstairs in a railway bungalow with the sound of trains passing through to the peninsula and the dense and uninhabited jungles that spread for acres and acres behind the railway quarters. I was still to go beyond Paranthan, beyond Elephant Pass to the heart of the peninsula.

My Cousin's Guest House Up-country

Cousin Joyce and I sat in her Mill Hill drawing room in London. A huge suitcase lying open before us was filled with photographs, snapshots, and beautifully bound albums all empty. Sheaves of photographs were strewn all over the coffee table and on the upholstered couch. Joyce and her family had left Ceylon in the 1950s "for the sake of the childrens' education." They had chosen to settle down in England.

Joyce was one of the links with the Solomons family. A family scattered all over the world. One of them, Elise Bartholomeusz married Francois Prins, the Verger at St Paul's Cathedral, London. Burghers. Now lost to the annals of our family history. Like so many of the Jansz and Solomons branches after their migrations. Their voluntary exile.

We took up individual snapshots and Joyce recounted her stories as she shuffled them in her hands. A pack of memories in those portraits of grandparents, aunts and uncles, cousins, friends, missionaries in pith hats and sun helmets. Her own wedding photographs. Unwritten chapters, visual mementoes of the past in the island they had left. To which I would always return. Joyce, slim as a wand, sylph-like in her wedding gown. Birthday parties. When would those albums ever be filled? Who would have the time to delve back into that past which had vanished phantom-like? Who would want to remember?

I picked out the photographs I wanted to bring back home, black and white, sepia tinted. Joyce showed me a picture of the guest house her parents once had in Bandarawela. She was lost in its recollection. "What a spacious house it was, and the garden? Daisies, barbetons, gladioli, arum lilies, roses, blue and mauve and pink-tinged hydrangeas. Apple trees – we had different varieties of apples. Peaches. Guavas. Vegetables. We had our special visitors who came regularly to spend holidays with us. The air was so bracing, especially during the hot season in Colombo..."

Guest houses up-country. Walks and well-spread tables. Up-country fruits and fresh vegetables. An English breakfast of bacon and eggs, toast, butter curls, Chivers marmalade. Rice and curry for lunch. Afternoon: tea, cakes, sandwiches, conserves, all homemade, scones, jam-tarts, pancakes flavoured with lemon and sugar. Dinner: soups; 'courses' – of beefsteak, Irish stews, roast beef; Shepherds pie, steak-and-kidney pudding, rissoles, cutlets. Desserts: stewed fruit with custard, bread pudding, caramel custard, blancmanges, and jellies.

Joyce and I together were turning over the leaves from memoirs. Memories of recipes handed down from unwritten cookbooks. Compounded of family secrets. Burgher secrets for love cake, rich cake, breudhers, lamprais... Each family preserved this secret lore, and at times of celebration and festivities the tables literally 'groaned with food.'

Joyce recounted how one of their regular PGs or Paying Guests at their Bandarawela Guest House had been a very well-connected Burgher gentleman, Mr Van Rooyen. Stemmed from some faraway ancestor from the Netherlands. One of those colonial adventurers who settled down in the maritime areas of the island. So many of them in the south. In the northern peninsula too. Joyce's grandparents had had a 'mestizo slave' named Topsy.

What were the two of us now doing together? Mulling over our memories, sharing Joyce's memories in which we had connections and bonds. Here, in our hands we held the documents from those archives preserved for so many years. Documentations of our identities in those quaint, uncontrived tales handed down by word of mouth. We laughed together, Joyce and I, weaving those fictions to give chameleon colour to the greyness and drabness of factual histories.

Who then was Mr Van Rooyen? Individualism and self-preservation, appearing to be characteristics for survival. I heard Joyce's voice intoning.

"He took great pains to avoid catching chills. On the other hand, he was afraid of being affected by the ultra-violet rays of the sun. He always wore a pith helmet, pipe-clayed to a pristine whiteness."

Pith helmets. The colonials wore them. We wore them to school as children too. To protect our heads from the brassy rays of the sun. Pressed down firmly, shielding our unruly heads from the violent elements. Imitations. Khaki helmets too. The elastic snapping under our chins. Imperial followers. Joyce's memories made me recollect my schooldays. The cake of white pipe-clay reposing in its saucer. A dampened piece of rag saturated with the liquid, applied overnight so that it would be dry by morning. Pith hats like iced-cakes dotting the colonial landscapes, with their glazed-sugar surfaces moving in a phalanx through dark forests and vast expanses of desert. At the beginning of every school year the pith hats were renewed and the packets of pipe-clay ranged on the washstand together with the bottles of Milk of Magnesia, Listerine, Dettol, McLeans and Kolynos toothpaste, Palmolive and Knights Castile soap. An old toothbrush was often used to pipe-clay both hats and canvas shoes.

Burgher gentlemen like Mr Van Rooyen were familiar figures in our childhood. Joyce recreated that shadowy figure from the past into life-size dimensions. He had been a part of her irrepressible adolescence.

My curiosity was roused. Did he live to a ripe old age? Did he protect himself from violent passions and emotions? He remained a bachelor till the end of his days, said Joyce, and became a lodger in the home of another old Burgher lady in Colombo.

A Burgher bachelor. He could afford to indulge in quirks and idiosyncratic manners. Whereas in our childhood, we had so much freedom that we could be ourselves without constraint. And so we grew up without that compelling need to demand attention or cultivate foibles.

"And," continued Joyce, "walks."

Walks were part of rejuvenating oneself on those upcountry holidays. Walks. Leisurely. Sauntering along or walking briskly. Very British. Exhilarating air. Hills. Dales. Valleys. Rhododendrons. Trout streams. Fir trees. Pear orchards. Walks in the garden of the guest house too. Spicy scent of carnations. Heady fragrance of roses. Hydrangeas, emptying flagons of fragrance in the air. Senses swooning. Mr Van Rooyen was quite intoxicated with the over brimming pollen-filled craters of nectar. The pollen, the nectar, the fragrance became almost a threat to quiescent emotions. Reminders of bridal banquets. Virgin brides in charmeuse and satin, their arms embracing sheaves of arum lilies and Ladies Lace. Burying your face in those virginal, chaste-looking white bouquets. Mr Van Rooyen promenaded among his dreams and visions. Unrequited.

"He wore that hat indoors as well as outdoors." It had been then a part of his armour. His defence against the elements that threatened to cause his unease or discomfort. In the seventeenth century he would have worn his hair long with a cockhat covering his locks. Now, he lined his hat with a cabbage leaf from the garden, or for coolness with a strip of banana leaf. Wore it on the 'throne,' as the commode in the bathroom was called. The bathroom had a zinc-covered roof; Mr Van Rooyen decided that it was wise to shield his head from the droplets of moisture. And there were those tiny leaks too; the bathroom was a subterranean cave with fine, needle-sharp stalactites dripping from the roof.

The climate was decidedly cold in Bandarawela and the water could be quite icy, so much so that Mr Van Rooyen would be reluctant to bathe too often. As a result he was often teased by the two young daughters of the house, Joyce and her sister Brenda. When the sun came out he decided it was time to have his bath. The big zinc bathtub was filled with hot water and placed on Aunt Etta's well-polished floor which was of smooth green cement. The light in the room had a kind of aqueous quality so that Mr Van Rooyen appeared to be a large, pale, luminous fish that had surfaced up for air as he splashed among the soapy bubbles from the lather foaming about his body.

Aunt Etta had a fetish about floors. They were always well polished with Mansion polish. The shining surface was rigorously maintained with pol-matta and Aunt Etta pushed strenuously up and down with her foot. Only the bathroom floors were of green cement while the rest of the house was of red. Those gleaming floors were Aunt Etta's pride and joy, and to think that the perfect surface of the bathroom floor would be ruined with pools and puddles of slippery, soapy water and the strong aroma of coal-tar soap would have Aunt Etta gritting her teeth.

Joyce was her aunt's most loyal ally. So if Mr Van Rooyen woke up and said, peering at the sky, "Today it looks as if it's going to be a bright day, I think I'll have a bath," Joyce knew and sympathized with Etta's feelings. She would run to the window, part the curtains, glance at the sky, and announce to her expectant audience: "Mr Van Rooyen, I don't think the good weather will last. The skies look grey, what a gloomy day. I'm sure it's going to rain today. There'll be a draught from the roof too" – and so the bath would be postponed indefinitely and the floor saved.

Mr Van Rooyen varied his breakfast with either a soft-boiled egg or a hard-boiled one, but that again depended on the number of visits he made to the toilet. Soft-boiled eggs were meant for normal days, but the egg had to be hard-boiled if there was the slightest variation in the number of times he "went out." He had an implicit belief in the binding properties of hard-boiled yolk and white of egg – but there was never any variation in his wearing of the pith hat with its fresh leaf lining.

Joyce would often observe that Mr Van Rooyen, despite his hesitancy to bathe, was a man of "clean habits." She observed the manner in which he performed his ablutions. "He would," she said, "wash the dial (her colloquialism for its shape) of his face, his hands, up to the arms, waist downwards, and then unfailingly gargle his throat." He had also established his own methods of relaxing – rhythmic massage. Of an evening, the blue dusk falling, the fireflies beginning to flicker in the bushes, he would sit on an easy chair, massaging his knees, every so often giving them a smart slap to activate the sleeping muscles. His evening walks were cautiously taken as he cruised among the flowerbeds, flashing his torch like a searchlight into dark nooks and crannies, suspicious of the unknown, carefully avoiding the serpent and temptation lurking among the ripening fruit in the garden of Eden.

Mr Van Rooyen had once gone on a long sea voyage to South Africa and had brought back mementoes from the ship: apples from the fruit basket and cubes of white sugar from the breakfast or tea table, carefully wrapped up in Bromo toilet paper. He led a leisured life after his retirement and spent tranquil days as privileged PG at the Guest House.

The two girls observed the PGs and their appearance carefully, since life had to provide some kind of fun and stimulation being so far away from the township of Bandarawela. Joyce remembered the little idiosyncrasies, the manner in which they preserved themselves, their little vanities too. Another frequent guest was a District Judge. When he came on holiday, his moustaches were a glossy black. He felt a man was not a man without flourishing, well-groomed black moustaches. It was when his moustaches began to take on a greenish tinge that he felt it was time to pack up and go. This happened when the effects of the dye he used began to wear out.

Mr Van Rooyen and the Judge both left their impress on the lives of Joyce and Brenda who at that time were young schoolgirls in the early 1930s. They were both very observant young misses always on the lookout for the opportune moment to have a little innocent fun. They observed Mr Van Rooyen's allergy to finely ground pepper. If the slightest whiff wafted into his nostrils he would sneeze as much as if he had taken a pinch of snuff. One day while peppering his soft-boiled egg, he unfolded his serviette and began to sneeze without a pause. Frank Solomons, the father, took one look at Brenda's face and pointed sternly to the door. She got up meekly from her seat and walked towards it without protest. Within the folds of the serviette, Brenda had put in a liberal sprinkling of pepper.

Joyce recollected the occasion when there was a great to-do at the stream which ran at the bottom of the garden. A man, who had come for a bath, had had a heart attack, and had died on the spot. She was present when the post-mortem was being carried out. "To me when the knife carefully slit through the corpse it was as if a dark overcoat was being unbuttoned to reveal the pink flesh beneath," she recounted.

The death was a big happening at that time. Willy Prins, with his dark, lustrous eyes and curling black lashes, who was working at the hotel in Bandarawela, came up to the spot where the body lay, solemnly doffed his cap and with a sober expression on his face shook hands with the corpse. "Goodbye, old fellow," he said. "Farewell."

The death had a dramatic effect on the whole village and the funeral was a great event. The people built the pyres on the patna land and set them alight. They blazed away like beacons, heralding the happenings. Buddhist monks were present at the performance of the rituals. Coconuts were thrown into the fires at the point at which the brain would burst within the skull... "Those are my memories of those funerals which were in a sense epic happenings in that remote past," Joyce recounted.

Joyce's grandmother, old Mrs Buttery, was a formidable character in their lives. "You could balance a dish on her bosom," was a saying about her. She was also supposed to be able to see with her eyes closed, so that if she was even lying down in bed to rest or taking an afternoon nap with a pillow across her face, she would be aware of everything that was going on in any part of the house.

During the war years Mrs Buttery hoarded rice to circumvent any shortage or rationing. There were bags of rice in the bedroom, which were put into zinc trunks and covered with appliquéd crepe cloth to match the curtains. The bags ended up lasting not only for the duration of the war but for long afterwards.

"She was given to hoarding." That was Joyce's succinct comment.

Mrs Buttery had been quite a dashing young woman in the early years of her marriage. Her husband had been in the Survey Department, and very often she was left alone in some remote outpost when Mr Buttery went on his surveying expeditions. When they were stationed at Kantalai she had felt bored one day, so she dressed herself up in a contrived disguise, donned her husband's heavy raincoat, put on a papier-mâché mask which had been lying about the house (it could have been a Santa Claus mask or even a Punchinello, at any rate it had ruddy cheeks and blue eyes), and with a hat pulled low over her brow, she took her three children with her and walked to the village. Everytime personable young village women passed by, she would reach out her hand, stroke the women's arms and murmur, "nalla pombalai," "beautiful woman." The women grimaced and frowned at her, shrugged her off and complained to their menfolk that Mr Buttery's brother, who was in the navy, had returned from one of his voyages and was molesting women. Those village women did not know about masks, that kind anyway. The headman came and complained to Mr Buttery about his brother.

Mrs Buttery was so protective of her husband, that when the day arrived for him to collect the salaries for the workers, she would go forth accompanied by the children. She put all the money away carefully in the fold of the hem of her long-skirted gown and draped the gathered skirts over her arm.

Mr Buttery, too, had his adventures when he went surveying the terrain. The cart bull would be blindfolded as it travelled through jungles infested with bear, leopard, wild boar and wild buffalo. The carter would beat with a stick on a kerosene-oil tin to scare any leopards away. The leopard would disappear but only for a short time, and as the cart turned along another path or reached a grassy knoll the leopard would confront them in another part of the jungle.

Joyce recollected yet another story that her grandmother had told her. All these events had taken place in the latter part of the nineteenth century. Kantalai would be periodically flooded during the great monsoonal rains. One day, the headman had a dream that a human sacrifice was necessary to protect the village from famine, so he went to his elder sister and told her that if the village was to be saved from all further vicissitudes, the life of her eldest son would need to be sacrificed. This according to his dream, was the only way to prevent famine and death. The mother consented reluctantly. The boy was first taken to the market, where the uncle bought him sweetmeats, and from thence he was led to the sluice gates where he was made to lie down. While the boy was eating the sweets, the cement and water were mixed together and the mixture poured gradually over the boy's body. When it went into his eyes, blinding him, he called out "Mama, kan" ("Uncle, my eyes") – and ever since, according to the story handed down from generation to generation, the spot where the water passes under the sluice gates near the Kantalai rest house is supposed to be haunted. According to R.L. Brohier *(Seeing Ceylon)* the legend has a different twist: The human sacrifice was a virgin who had to give up her life to satisfy "the lust of the demon." She is also supposed to have shouted "Mama talai" (Uncle, "my head"). The lake came to be called thus "Kantalai" and a portion of the embankment called "Women's Bund." However, Joyce's narrative remains as she told me.

Before Joyce and Brenda were born, their great-grandmother came on a holiday visit to Bandarawela accompanied by a little boy who was staying with her. He was given a dose of castor oil emulsion one day, of which some was left over. Their grandmother did not believe in letting anything "remain." "Ah child, how to waste." She said, and drank the rest of the castor oil. She purged continuously until she fainted from weakness. Yet to her, it had been worth the while: not a drop of the emulsion was wasted.

"Ah child, how to waste" became a favourite maxim in that household ever after.

When nightfall came it was always pitch black as there were no streetlights near the house in Bandarawela. Candlelight, paraffin lights were used, as there was no electricity in the neighbourhood. The household was always well stocked with rice, salt, wine and oil, so that there was no necessity to go in search of these essentials after dark. One day the ayah was chased by a polonga as she went into the house. She had the presence of mind to drop one of the outer cloths tucked round her waist. The polonga was diverted by it and pecked at the cloth, while the woman escaped. Joyce had once been playing and coming home at dusk almost trod on a polonga as she raced up the garden. Danger lurked among these apple trees and flowerbeds. Nightfall and darkness were alive with more palpable forces. The landscape changed. Odours, smells, strong, rank, predominated over the delicate scents of 'hush-n-hana' (queen of the night) and (kiss me quickly): bronze tebia uniflora.

That upcountry home still remains, but no longer the home that belonged to the Solomons family and no longer a Guest House. Whenever Joyce returns to the island she makes it a point to go up to Bandarawela, where she still meets the caretakers and servants from the past. But the PGs and many others have long since vanished from the scene.

X

THE COLONIAL GAMEBOARD

My grand-aunt Solomons, an English woman (top), grandmother and grandfather Solomons.

Colonial Extensions

That jakwood dining table, in childhood memory, always seemed enormous. Right from the beginning I had a place at it, as if my territory had been staked out, laid claim to. It was a square table but somehow it had been established where the head was and that place was always reserved for my father. From his position, sitting on one of those straight-backed chairs, even after the dishes were cleared away, my father would assume the role of the entertainer. There were certain rites and rituals we engaged in, like the "wishbone ritual." After the roast or curried chicken had been relished, from his platter he would hold out 'the wishbone' to us. We would take turns to pull it. He would hold the bone in such a way that one of us would be left with that bit of the bone which allowed us to make our secret wishes. What were those wishes? Wishes that followed us all through that childhood from Kadugannawa to Kandy unvaryingly, on every important, celebratory occasion. That wishbone was a bonding between us, father and children.

At Christmastime, the nutcracker was brought to the table and the nuts piled up before him, each one was carefully cracked, the kernels prised out delicately and handed to us. Or he would fill tumblers to brimming with cool, clear water from the earthenware goblet and with the tips of his fingers circle the rim over and over again creating cascades of liquid crystal sound. Tremulous musical notes. Strange, unearthly chords. Music that sounded like rills of flowing water, the table an enchanted island. And then there was his special brand of magic – swallowing coins and pulling them out of his shirt or drawing them forth from his shirt cuffs. Magic emanated from the very air he breathed. Balancing his glass of water on his head to display his perfect equilibrium. He never drank whiskey after meals. Saying 'grace' over our meal was a special esoteric incantation which blessed the food. A benediction remembered from his staunch Methodist upbringing.

Even the act of sitting round that table in my parents' house provided an entrance into a wider world, one that extended beyond our own view of life. My parents were very hospitable and they shared their largesse with whomsoever entered our home. We were brought in contact from our childhood days with travellers and wanderers engendered out of those colonial peregrinations. That table accommodated many representatives of the race of 'Empire Builders' as well as their off-shoots, people who wanted to be accepted by the colonized. Some of them had strayed away from the mother country and had either succeeded or failed in their individual missions. They were survivors. Possessed of a tremendous vitality and zest for life. Time and time again, as children, we too sat at this same table for lunch or dinner. We never felt left out. At that time the table seemed enormous in its proportions, or how else could it have had so much space not only for our family but also for all the other guests? And how much conversation flowed through the house, the guests sitting on the veranda, exchanging stories, laughing over tall tales, my father pulling out joke after joke from the top-hat of memory. He had books and books of amusing tales, witty and pithy sayings, proverbs and anecdotes which he would bring out, drawing attention to his own powerful and vibrant personality. He had first-hand experience of life and adventure on the railways and in the outstations where he served. He had, as a result, contact with the British planters, especially on the up-country lines with that network of railways for the transport of goods to be exported to England.

The Second World War brought so many heterogeneous elements into our house. Besides friends and relations, there were my father's soldier friends: the Englishman, Ivor, who had been a Music-Hall entertainer with his inexhaustible repertoire of songs and ditties – his favourite being "Widdicombe Fair" where all of us would race through the final lines with their quaint rustic names, ending with "Uncle Tom Cobleigh and all." There was the genial Irishman, Jack Kells singing the haunting strains of "Kathleen Mavourneen" and "The Rose of Tralee" in his Irish brogue. "Cobber" Davidson, the Australian who had worked on a sheep farm of thousands of acres and sang his songs about Kookuburras and "Waltzing Matilda." Rastus was an artist, a South African of Boer extraction; and Charlie Culbert was a Cockney from Shoreditch. Each one of them brought the stories of their lives, snapshots of families, mess-room yarns, tales of desert campaigns, and verses from Rudyard Kipling's "Barrack Room Ballads." There was so much singing and stirring recitals – "Gunga Din" was delivered in dramatic tones by my father. Often they would share their army rations purchased from the canteen in return for my parents hospitality – 'Bully beef' and Black Magic chocolates.

How did these men fare on those far-flung battlefields and how many of them ever returned home? Taking their pegs of whiskey was never done in the presence of ladies and children. "Well, what about another?" my father would say. "Wouldn't mind, Harry," Johnny Walker would reply. They would all troop into the dining room and stand round the table, pouring out their drinks, exchanging their innumerable tales. After a while they would return to the veranda or stand around the piano singing. It was only after 'one for the road' and my father singing his Scottish ballads of parting that they would put down their glasses and prepare to take their leave. Where would Johnny Walker go? And

Mr Bazley the English piano-tuner? We were never to know where they spent that part of their lives. Perhaps it was the Old Empire Hotel, but whenever they visited our homes they were always immaculately attired in full suits of starched twill with coat and tie and felt hat, Johnny Walker twirling an elegant silver-topped walking stick.

Johnny Walker? Was that really his name or one of his colonial nom-de-plumes? What a life of adventure he had lived, according to the sagas he related to us. He had made a fortune gun-running on the China seas, letting the guns out of the gunwhale on the approach of government launches into the high seas. The tragedy of his life was the death of his beautiful Polish wife, a ballet dancer, who had followed him on his trail of adventure, dying of typhoid in some faraway place. He related the epics of the Ramayana and the Mahabharata, which he had seen enacted in the Balinese wayangs, the 'shadow plays,' which he described in great detail. He had made journey after journey through the territories of the Empire, that intrepid Highlander who had now come almost to the end of his search and was left only with memories. He had made and lost his fortune. Never returned to Scotland. Clung to my father's friendship, always welcomed in our home for food, drink, conversation and companionship. In the end the Planters' Association looked after him and he spent his last days in a bungalow on a tea estate in Kadugannawa, to be buried no one knows where. This perhaps is the only living memorial to him.

Mr Bazley made some kind of living out of tuning pianos. His one dream was to return 'home' to England where his mother still lived, and this he accomplished one day. He was a true virtuoso in tuning our old German Nagel, and to me he was a man who had unwritten musical compositions in his mind and soul. I was always hoping that he would play some magnificent opus on the piano when he came to tune the instrument.

He would begin by tuning note by note, the treble clef then the bass, placing his finger on the key that possessed the flatness of tone, and seeking out the dissonance which produced the discords when my sister practiced her classical repertoire for the Royal College Music examinations. I learned to play the piano too but insisted it was only for pleasure, so I didn't sit the exams and was not restricted to the prescribed pieces. My sister played brilliantly, everything from Haydn and Mozart to Bach and Beethoven. I played Debussy, Chaminade, Beethoven, Chopin, Tschaikovsky. Joyce Perera and Mary Samarasinghe taught me anything I fancied in the music books I took with me for my music lessons. Mike Havilland, a planter who visited us, could play the most complex sonatas and etudes, in short, any piece of classical music, entirely by ear. The keys of the piano were of ivory, the ivory from the tusks of African elephants sent all the way back to Germany from one of the European colonies for the manufacture of those antique pianos. Everything during the colonial period appeared to be part of the exploitativeness, which distinguished the great global enterprise of acquiring everything from territory to commodities of trade. No one thought at that time, while the notes cascaded from the keys of the piano, of colonial aggrandizement, of the ivory that embellished the keys together with that valuable forest timber – ebony, which made up the structure of the piano.

After the tuning had been completed, showers and cascades of chords thundered beneath Mr Bazley's hands, waterfalls of sound. He would be lost in the music of a symphony of chords in which I heard an entire orchestra. Mr Bazley spent the war years in Kandy, and then went back to England to spend his retirement in that longed for reunion with his old mother. Those friends were all the global adventurers and colonial wanderers of my childhood world.

The Colonial Gameboard

Don Solomon: The Colonial Entrepreneurs, Missionary Endeavours and Scholars

Frederick Solomon, my great-grandfather, was born in Kollupitiya in 1810. His parents lived in the vicinity opposite the present Temple Trees State Residence. My great-great-grandmother Solomons died in 1831 and was buried in the family vault. Reverend Toyne, Methodist Minister, officiated. Reverend Elijah Toyne (b. 7 April 1805, Sheffield) arrived in Ceylon in 1830. He served in Matara, Galle and Colombo, and again in Galle. He returned to England in 1840, and died in May 1871 at North Shields. The Methodist connection appeared to be strong in the Solomons family from the early part of the nineteenth century. A family that started out with the name Don Solomon, but then added an 's' along the way to become 'Solomons.'

During the period of my great-grandfather Frederick's birth, the Kandyan Convention of 1815 was still to be signed. In 1815, the British deposed Sri Wickrama Rajasinghe, and by the Kandyan Convention the King of England assumed sovereignty according to the Act of Settlement planned by D'Oyly and two Kandyan Chieftains. The cession of the Kingdom of Kandy was followed by the Great Rebellion of 1818. The Rebellion itself was a formidable one, whereby the British felt that the Kandyan Convention was threatened. It was ruthlessly crushed by the British. The Rebellion lasted over a year and the Kandyan Chieftains were either court-martialed or beheaded. Ellepola Nilame was court-martialed and beheaded; Keppetipola, Pilima Talawe and Madugalla were taken into custody by the British. Keppetipola was also beheaded. His cranium ended up at the

Phrenological Institute of Edinburgh. Pilima Talawe and many other chiefs were exiled to Mauritius.

After the British began to establish their rule in the Kandyan Kingdom, pioneer Methodist missionary endeavours were directed towards the interior of the island. In May 1826, Alexander Hume, one of the Methodist missionaries, paid a visit to Kandy, Galagedera and Ginigossa. By 1829 Benjamin Clough, yet another Methodist missionary (whose publications were as follows: *Dictionary English-Sinhalese and Sinhalese-English, Pali Grammar and Vocabulary*; "The Ritual of the Buddhist Priesthood," translated from Pali Kamarachar; *Short Sermons for Schools in Sinhalese; Family Prayers in Sinhalese*), agreed with Hume that the pioneer Methodist missionaries should begin their work in the interior with Kandy as their Headquarters. "We think we should go." Many Methodist soldiers were there and many "country born people, clerks and agents for mercantile firms" wanted a missionary. There were already Colonial Chaplains and CMS missionaries in Kandy – but "there is enough work for a dozen missionaries," was the thought uppermost in the minds of those who wanted to carry out the mission in Ceylon. They determined that "the step must be taken." Clough believed that he would be the most suitable person to take up the task and, more than a younger man, would have the support of the Governor, who was at that time Sir Robert Horton (1831-37). There was by 1834, "a splendid carriage road" to Kandy from Colombo; Ritigala was easier to work from Kandy than from Negombo, and Kurunegala could also be visited. However, since "Clough's services were indispensably necessary" in Colombo for an additional year or so, Spencer Hardy went in his place. He too published many books, ranging from books on English drama in Sinhala and English, to *A Manual on Buddhism and Eastern Monarchism*. Spencer Hardy bought a large house, situated on the esplanade opposite the Dalada Maligawa, which had once belonged to the First Adigar. The small congregation consisted almost entirely of British soldiers, Burghers and low-country Sinhalese who were connected with the Mission. No doubt my great-grandfather, Frederick Solomon, who arrived in Kandy from Colombo on 20 June 1833, as a young man of 23, was also part of that congregation. Frederick was baptized in the Audience Hall in Kandy by a Methodist missionary, so my father told me. As a result, the Solomons family were strongly bound to Methodism for the rest of their lives.

Spencer Hardy, whose sermons my great-grandfather must have listened to, was himself a powerful personality. He had received a request from the inhabitants of Ratnapura (there was no Christian school in the whole district) and he travelled 160 miles on foot, waded through many miles of water, crossed... on "dangerous" bridges and "lost count of the leech bites." Hardy felt that Ratnapura needed a Methodist mission. Hardy's stay in Kandy was only for the space of nine months, as he had to take Clough's place in Colombo. Clough himself left Ceylon in February 1837 because of illness ("a severe fever") and Spencer Hardy took his place in Kollupitiya. J.A. Poulier continued Hardy's work. John Adrian Poulier (b. 13 April 1801, Galle) served in many Methodist stations in Galle, Kandy, Matara, Colombo and Kalutara. He died in Kandy on 2 June 1880. Poulier was a Dutch Burgher and one of the first four Ceylonese ministers.

My great-grandfather Frederick's life continued its connection with Methodism and also became involved with the new entrepreneurship (no longer restricted to the maritime provinces), instituted as a result of the opening up of the Kandyan Kingdom to enterprises connected with the plantation industry. All this was facilitated by the building of roads along which troops and guns could move quickly. Travellers could make easier journeys, since hitherto they had used horses and palanquins. Bullock carts, too, used the Colombo-Kandy road for transporting goods at a cheaper cost. In 1831, a cartload of 1,206 pounds of coffee was taken from Kandy to Colombo for one pound sterling, while earlier an equal load carried by porters used to cost eleven pounds fifteen shillings. The mail coach helped the postal department, too, and post offices were started at Colombo, Trincomalee, Jaffna, Galle, Matara and Mannar. With the taking over of the Kandyan Kingdom, letters were sent to the interior wherever it was possible, but where mail coaches and other means of transport could not be used, the system of runners was still maintained.

Great-grandfather Frederick was one of the first Burgher entrepreneurs to acquire wealth and land in Kandy. He had vast tracts of land under coffee cultivation in Balane. He bought several acres of land in Kandy itself. The property in Kandy was called "Solomonwatte" (Kingswood College now stands in its environs). He used the fortune he acquired from coffee to educate his sons in private missionary schools and colleges, and then sent them on to India and England. He had married at St Peter's Church Colombo (6 January 1843). His wife was Charlotte Elizabeth Greve. Frederick and Charlotte's son William Henry Solomons was educated at St Thomas' College Mt Lavinia.

The founder of St Thomas' College was James Chapman, a scholar of King's College, Cambridge (1819); and in 1821, before he had taken his degree, he was appointed master at Eton. While at Eton he was admitted to Deacon's Orders by the Bishop of Ely, on his Cambridge Fellowship. In 1844 Chapman was asked to become a candidate of Harrow and, ten days later, another letter offered him the bishopric of Colombo.

"You know my principles on such subjects," he wrote to a friend. "I need not therefore tell you that God gave me strength yesterday to renew my dedication of myself to Him, all unworthy as I am, kneeling at His own holy table." Chapman set out to find the men and money for his new diocese, his first object being a Cathedral and a College, "worthy of a prospering colony." At the time of Chapman's arrival in Ceylon, Sir Collin Campbell was Governor of Ceylon, and the coffee industry was prospering. Bishop Chapman's vision was as follows: "Education must be the great work for me to look to, to lay the foundation if I can, and leave others to build hereafter." For him Ceylon was an "Eden of picturesque beauty and loveliness, far surpassing any power of mine to describe." He needed assistance to acquire a property at Mutwal, which would be the site of a Cathedral and College. Then during the period of Governor Torrington's rule, the colony experienced many difficulties – after the last Kandyan Rebellion of 1848, wild speculation resulted in the coffee industry experiencing a period of depression. Nothing daunted the Bishop, sought help from the Society for the Propagation of the Gospel to obtain the funds he needed, and in 1849 the foundations of the school buildings were laid upon a hill at Mutwal.

My grandfather William Henry Solomons, in the first number of the College Magazine, published in 1875, says of the school: "It faintly exhibits in the disposition of its buildings, the desire on the founders part to model it upon Eton, the famous sanctuary of his boyhood." Such were the foundations on which a colonial education was begun together with its close alignment with religion. What race of men were to be engendered out of this system, only time would tell.

By 1872, coffee had greatly prospered and the revenues used to improve the economic conditions of the country. Great-grandfather Frederick was one of the new breed of entrepreneurs bred by colonialism. The scholastic and academic achievements of Frederick's sons were achieved not only through the newly established missionary schools but also by the fact that this education was within their means as a result of the booming coffee industry.

Suddenly, however, the coffee blight, Hemelia Vastatrix, affected the coffee plantations, and with the crash of coffee many planters had to face loss and ruin. The acres of land in Balane and Alagalla still remained in the hands of the family, but no effort was made to either sell the lands or to introduce new crops like cinchona or tea. The land went back to the wilderness. However, Frederick Solomons still had Solomonwatte in Katukelle, though this too was finally sold, most probably to enable his sons to proceed abroad with their education. One of them was the first colonial surgeon in Ceylon, while my grandfather became Headmaster at Richmond College Galle and, later on, a lawyer practising in Anuradhapura and Matale.

Frederick's sons were not entrepreneurs and landed proprietors like their father. My grandfather was a scholar in Greek, Latin and Hebrew and was one of the first Ceylonese graduates of the University of Calcutta. William Henry's ideas of morality were strictly adhered to through the theology he practised. At one stage of his life he gave up the practice of law. There could be no subversion of the truth in any area of his life and thought. William Henry was a writer, his style that of the classicists and of the English writers of that system of education which he imbibed. Reading his essay on the public school system it would be difficult to extricate his style from that of the models he was no doubt so intimately acquainted with, expressed in sentiments such as the following:

"A Public School, as has often been pointed out, is a small commonwealth. The fictitious advantages which birth and fortune confer upon men in the after struggle for position and wealth have here no place. Each person is estimated solely on his own merits whether place be displayed in the cricketing field or in the nobler 'racing grounds of the soul' and not according to those of that ancestors of his, who wore 'chain armour in the 13th century...'"

What then was William Henry's identity? He was both unique and individualistic, this is in spite of the fact that he was moulded, through education and religion, by the colonial set-up at that time. He did things his own way, and of course he had a truly wonderful woman in his wife, who followed him wherever he went. Amelia Sophia Solomons was the daughter of Daniel John Pereira and Susan Bartholomeusz, and through her intrepidity as a pioneering woman, was a strong influence on the lives of her children.

I remember my grandfather in his later years, a quiet, silent and meditative man, after a spent and weary life, albeit one in which he had fulfilled some at least of his life's ambitions, at peace with himself in the house at Karlsrhue Gardens. My brother Pat, who spent some years of his childhood with his unmarried aunts at Morvan, recollects that grandfather William was a quiet and gentle man who spent most of his days reading the Bible. My brother, then about twelve years old, would read the New Testament to him in Greek every day – this discipline enabled him to be a Classics Scholar in the University of Colombo years later. It was here, too, that he learned to play the violin tutored by the famous violinist Wagn.

What about the human side of my grandfather? He would stay with my mother occasionally when she was newly married and living in Colombo. He would go all round the city in a rickshaw along the tree-shaded avenues with their flamboyant blossoms, riding past the colonial-style bungalows, their walled gardens cascading with bougainvillea, flowering bowers, bushes and ornamental palms, breathe in the tang of salt breezes as the rickshaw puller drew his frail old frame. Returning home later he would hardly be aware of how many hours he had spent being carried along the quiet avenues. "Dolly, would you pay the rickshaw fare for me, please?" he would request politely. The practicalities of life were now gradually being left to others. He loved his long cool baths in the Colombo house, using my mother's damask tablecloths to dry himself with. My mother was a most tolerant woman and pandered to the courteous and scholarly old man. He never touched "strong drinks," never smoked cigarettes, cigars or even a pipe. Nor did he approve of card games like Whist and Bridge.

He loved music, Church music, the Gregorian chants especially, and he was well acquainted with the Tonic Solfa method of scales. I, too, would warble out "do re mi fa so la ti do…" in mounting scales as I practised the different tones and pitch. On my grandfather's deathbed, as he lay peacefully breathing his last, his expression became calm, beatific. "Listen," he whispered very, softly, "Listen, can you hear the heavenly choir of angels?" His sons and daughters, who sat beside his bedside, his faithful wife Amelia Sophia and all the other close relations who stood beside him, strained their ears to hear the heavenly music. The voices from some other world reached them too, and my grandfather's eyes closed and his breath stilled, as the heavenly strains of the music of the spheres with all-surpassing harmony reached the watchers by his bedside, the music growing fainter and fainter as he gently slipped away.

The Solomons family never laid claim to the Balane coffee lands. Many emissaries would visit my father, to persuade him to try to reclaim those lost domains, but my father had no interest in them. Acres and acres went back to the wild primeval forest. No vestige was left of that colonial enterprise except the Deeds that perhaps still repose in the archives of the Land Registry Department. My father had no interest in acquiring property. His world was a different world. There was not an inch of the island that he had not travelled through. He knew every forest and wewa in the Dry Zone. He knew the tea country well. He was acquainted with the jungles of the Eastern and North Central provinces and of every bird, beast and reptile that dwelt therein. He was well versed in jungle lore and strongly interested in the politics of the era, a strong supporter of nationalist aspirations. He also had a vast knowledge of indigenous culture and folklore, moving away from the strong classical bias of his own father. He would recite intricate Veddha invocations and chants. He had a tremendous library of travel books, autobiographies and military reminiscences. He read very little fiction and never read novels. He spent hours in his garden with his plants, birds and bees. He loved music and played classical melodies like Handel's "Largo" on his bamboo flutes, of which he had a well-seasoned variety. When he passed the estates that had once belonged to his grandfather, on the train which took him through the Balane Pass with the towering rocks overhanging the rail tracks, he would point out the acres where Frederick Solomons had made his fortune. Whenever I pass through these regions, the deep valleys with their paddy fields, the temples, the dark wooded hills, and beetling crags, a sense of that ancient and primeval past assails me. I try to understand the forces that led my family along those unpredictable routes that were part of the history of a newly developing society. One day my search gave me this poem, "The Vision," in which the changing landscape, after the coffee plantations had been developed on virgin land, took me on an allegorical journey:

> Then it was all unknown,
> The mysteries of this valley in those ancient
> Times, until a finger pointed out landmarks
> In that wilderness.
>
> The totems of mythology changed,
> The spirits fled into different habitations,
> Some, still lurked among the trees and
> Streams.
>
> Tiled roofs sloped upon new dwelling places,
> The forest groaned, branches cracked sharply
> Asunder and slung their bones in graves
> Soon covered by the flowering coffee
> Bushes.
>
> White blossoms made the senses swoon
> With heavy fragrance and the new
> Migrations began to make their inroads.
>
> Now we view depletion of a wilderness
> The lichens cling to archetypal trees,
> The natural springs are dry,
>
> The riven rocks once foaming with their
> Spume are parching tracks where those
> Perennial sources cease to flow
> And stop their crystal courses.

There is a reference to my great-grandfather in *The Story of Kingswood, Kandy*, by L.E. Blazé who was principal from 1891-1923. The Blazés were also close family friends of the Solomons family, and his daughter Ray, whom I remember, was a great friend of my Solomons aunts. The following extract is taken from that book: "The land belonged at one time to the father of W.H. Solomons [my grandfather] and was often visited by the young people of the Seventies and Eighties [19th century] in their morning walks."

The Methodist laymen in England contributed to the purchase of this property and Sir John Randles offered Rs.10,000 to the Wesleyan Missionary Society for the setting up of the school. Sir John expressed the typical colonial sentiments of that period in the following words: "I wanted to do something that would be for the greater glory of God and the good of my fellowmen in some part of the globe where the British flag flew..." And this place happened to be Solomons Gardens, Solomonwatte.

A very long poem of several stanzas titled "Solomons Garden" appeared in *The Story of Kingswood*. This was the garden that was to be the setting of the Royal Sylvan Secret – Kingswood College. The Queen of Sheba's wish, which was granted by the "wise doting learned fool Solomon," was that the garden should be set apart to educate boys not girls and to transport this school to the East and set it "in an isle of state." To be the realization of the colonial dream –"a dream of every fantasy." It was a school that was at that period part of the great 'Wesleyan Missionary Endeavour.' A garden that was in a sense an island within an island, isolated by colonial ideals.

> *"And hedge it in on every side,*
> *To shut out pigs and dogs and noise.*
> *O what a lovely School 't will be,*
> *A dream of every fantasy!"*

This was a school for the Ceylonese Rehoboam, who according to the Queen of Sheba's observations was like the original Rehoboam, a son of Solomon:

> *"a goodly well grown boy,*
> *but a naughty fellow."*

(poem by Reverend W.A. Stone, 1922)

This then was the system of education in the private missionary schools that my ancestors too were part of. There were traditions to be followed which belonged to the colonial experience. Some of these traditions were the school magazine, the prize-giving, the debating class, the cadets, and the House system, which was adopted in June 1922, the houses being named after "Eton, Harrow, Rugby and Winchester." Missionary priests like the Reverends Broadbelt, William Goudie, A.S. Beaty and John Eagle also served at Kingswood.

My uncle W.F.A. Solomons studied at Kingswood from September 1896 to May 1901 and January 1903 to September 1906. Soon after he left school, he died at age 19 in Anuradhapura in 1907, where my grandfather had his legal practice before he went on to being headmaster at Richmond College, Galle. My grandfather's own Wesleyan upbringing insisted on the absolute moral integrity and truthfulness of every utterance he made and so, as my mother told me once, "he gave up being a lawyer and took to education."

Although my grandfather practised law briefly in Anuradhapura, connections remained with Kingswood. My father Harry Daniel Solomons and my brother Pat both began their education there before they went on to other missionary schools.

Time and time again the personal histories of the Solomons family are closely interwoven with the Wesleyan church and missionaries such as Moscrop, Garrett, Triggs, Rigby, Hessen, Bestall, Williams, Jebb, Hartley, Prince, Philpots, Nelson, Beaty, Rowton Lee. Moreover, the family records are also preserved in the histories of private missionary schools such as Kingswood College, Kandy, St Thomas, Mt Lavinia, Wesley College, Colombo, and Trinity College, Kandy, where the Solomons, Grenier and Jansz sons and heirs studied before they continued with their further migrations to other colonies or to British universities.

Proselylitization and colonialism were indicated in their baptismal names – English names – the menfolk favoured with names from British history especially the names of Monarchs: Edward, Richard, Henry, Frederick, Charles, William, Harold; and the womenfolk bore names like Elizabeth, Sophia, Caroline, Mary, Alice, Amelia, Selina, Rosalind, Grace, Henriette, Charlotte, Isabelle.

My grandfather's name, W.H. Solomons, appears in the Honours Panel of St Thomas (STC) 1872 as a winner of the Duke of Edinburgh Scholarship. Sir Joseph Grenier (the Knighthoods were part of the Colonial Honours bestowed on the faithful subjects) mentions that W.H. Solomons, J.L. Perera, C.P. Markus and himself sat together with a few others for the Entrance Examination to STC. The subjects were English, Latin, History, Geography and Mathematics – "All students passed, much to the Warden's gratification" ("Leaves from my life," Joseph Grenier). It is also interesting to note that my grandfather W.H. Solomons is mentioned as the only graduate in the whole of Kandy when he taught for a short time at Trinity College in the latter part of the nineteenth century: "Mr W.H. Solomons was another of our distinguished teachers of this period (the 1880s) though only for a short time, the only Ceylonese Graduate in Kandy" (Trinity College, Kandy, 1872, Centenary Number).

An aunt of mine, Ila Solomons, too, taught in the primary school at Trinity, where among many other things she taught her little charges 'table manners,' as one of them recollected. And while they were eating one mouthful they had to cut up their food for the next. "Elbows off the table too!"

My brother Pat (although he inherited the traditional Solomons' names of Henry Edward William) was thus called because he was born on St Patrick's Day, the Patron Saint of Ireland. To me he lived a mysterious existence as a boarder at Trinity College in Kandy, where my mother would occasionally take me along with her climbing up these innumerable steps when she visited him from Kadugannawa. He had interesting tales of the German lady who was the Matron of the boarding, a large, full-bosomed, comfortable-looking German fraulein who ministered to the Ceylonese hostel boarders. His Latin he learned from yet another German, Miss Valesca Rheiman. Jock Young, the Scots schoolmaster and scoutmaster who lost his life in the Second World War, and the English Chaplains were part of that colonial scenario which I too glimpsed. Sometimes we went to the Trinity Prize-givings where my brother carried off prizes –the Ryde Latin Prize (he was a scholar of classics, of Greek and Latin, like his grandfather) and the W.S. Senior Memorial Distinction and Poetry Prize. He also skippered the College Cricket Eleven and was awarded the esteemed Cricket Lion – emblazoned on the blazer, which he wears to this very day. He was also the Prefect of his House. I only saw my brother when he came home on his vacations. He taught me ballroom dancing in Kadugannawa when I was a very little girl, when the adults danced on that veranda. My brother was at that time a young student wearing his cream flannels and dark blue blazer with his highly polished English shoes (he had shoe-trees to keep them in shape), and glistening hair, dark waves shining with pomade or Vaseline or brilliantine, "Brylcream." The dressing table was covered with his hairbrushes and those jars and bottles with their lemony tang or lavender scent of his hair creams. Writing poetry, studying Latin and Greek from the German teacher, Miss Rheiman, and making us laugh our sides out with the boarding mistress Miss Hoffman's attempt at pronouncing 'pathola'– this vegetable so mundane, indeed tasteless, became 'pashoshes'– far more exotic than anything served up at the refectory table in the college boarding.

I would beg for the chance to wield the cricket bat with which my brother practised his cricket strokes – a tennis ball in a large woollen hose suspended from the lintel of our door, in the house in Kandy. He often had fascinating objects which he brought from University later on: a metal chest expander, textbooks which I pored over trying to understand things that were beyond me, like the Socratic dialogues, Platonic discourse and the Ethica Nichomachea. I read his prize books, a collection of Thomas Hardy novels of the Wessex countryside: *Tess of the D'urbevilles, The Mayor of Casterbridge, The Return of the Native*. I tried to memorize the Greek alphabet too.

We had albums filled with snapshots of the family and of friends, taken with a Kodak camera, photographs which possessed no intimations of the future. There was one of the young Scots schoolmaster Jock Young sitting on a rock and peering at the view through his binoculars. Jock, who once brought the Trinity Scout Troop on a hike to Kadugannawa where the boys built campfires on the abandoned tea estate and boiled water in an iron kettle for tea. What vision of life did he have through those lenses? I watched him all unbeknown as he mingled with his young adolescent charges. He went back to England during the Second World War and was never seen or heard of again. Did he ever envisage the end of the empire? – both his personal as well as the greater one to which he belonged and in which he too had a stake, for he had come out to the colonies to teach in one of the most prestigious missionary schools in Kandy, Trinity College.

The empire meant so many things to so many people who were involved in that missionary enterprise of proselytization and education. For the Germans like Fraulein Hoffman and Dr Rheiman of Trinity College it meant the Third Reich and the rise of Hitler's Germany, but they had played out their individual roles in the British colonies. What did the Third Reich mean to women who had left their country so many years ago? And the British Empire, to Jem Smith, Mr Bazley, Johnny Walker, Jock Young, the old-age pensioners among my father's railway friends, who returned to their Elders Homes writing back long letters full of sadness and loneliness with the furling of the Union Jack. Valesca Rheiman ended up in Australia, and Fraulein Hoffmann came back to spend her last days at Trinity College. The hands of the clock were moving towards the new changes, but English Chaplains still continued to be part of 'the system' together with the annual Christmas Carol Services at Trinity College, Kandy. And today an Englishman is once more the principal of the college.

Later Colonials

I met David Bridges and his wife Doreen in 1994 when I was returning to Sri Lanka from England. He had been a planter from the period of the British Raj in the 1930s. He had also spent the early years of his childhood in Ceylon. Husband and wife visited my home in October 1995. He still lived very much in the past. He was 75 years old. We discovered a very important point of contact. He had been planting on a rubber plantation where my family and I had enjoyed many weeks of hospitality and kindness at the home of friends in 1983, after we had left the refugee camps during those troubled days of the communal upheaval. We spoke of the huge sprawling bungalow, a very typical planter's bungalow perched on its eminence on a hill and looking down into the valley "with its white dagaba in the distance," David recalled. We had crossed that chasm of almost fifty years through our recollections.

"David, what else do you remember of those days?" I asked him.

"Well, I was a young man then, liked playing a game of tennis, taking a drink. There were lovely Burgher girls but you couldn't date them. The parents were very protective about them. You couldn't meet them unless you were here from a long time, then dating meant going for a dance or tea or for a walk, not sleeping with them. Yes, if you were here for years you could eventually take them out for a meal or coffee. They wouldn't come out with you."

"Well," I said, "they probably knew that marriage was not generally in the books. That may have been a reason."

"Perhaps,"he nodded, silently in affirmation.

"At any rate," I continued, "where are the Burgher girls now? They've all emigrated to Australia. There aren't many left, hardly any."

"But that was fifty years ago," Doreen interjected. Our thoughts, our emotions, past and present were interlocked at this moment.

"What do you remember of the Raj, David?" I asked. ""We had all those people who visited our house – the adventurers, wanderers on the face of the earth, they now appear to be. We offered them hospitality, friendship, in my parents' home. They ate and drank with us, spent hours and days in conversation on the veranda. We expected nothing of them. It's what we gave them, in their loneliness, those homeless people. With no fixed abode, unlike the planters. The representatives of the Raj were certainly not the bureaucrats and the administrators alone who extended their paternalistic and the imperial order patronage to the people."

"Well," David ruminated, "I remember the Raj. I myself went to a very exclusive school in England, Millfield. There were two Indian Princes too. So much wealth. They were nice fellows. Adapted to life there. Two brothers from a princely State in India. They died fairly early. Well, some of the members of the Raj were snobbish. Some of the planters, noses up in the air, they were soon tarred and feathered and sent back. Even the way you spoke, it was important not to just issue orders. 'Would you please do that,' rather than 'would you do that,' was acceptable. The periya dorai was king but I believed that you should address people with courtesy. Well, the Raj. Most of it was good, railways, law and order. People mixed more. Sometimes the black sheep of the family was sent to make good in the colonies. You were spoilt here, you didn't do anything, not even clean your shoes."

"Not Mr Bazley and Johnny Walker, my father's English and Scottish friends. They did all that for themselves. And what about your life on the estate?" I asked.

"I wasn't rich. Just five pounds a week."

"And food?"

"The local meat was five cents a pound. Boiled gradually it was soft and delicious. The imported beef cost a little more but the local beef was excellent. And cheese, cheddar with Port wine. I tasted it all at Pitiakande, the cheese steeped in wine for a month. And short-eats. Petals from the flowers that grew on the vines of the vegetable marrow with butter on toast. Crisply fried. I tasted them first at Moratenna. Since we had no fridges in the old days we used to cool our drinks by filling a sack with straw and hanging it in a draughty position on the verandah, then dousing it with water periodically. The drinks were quite cold. Wild coffee grew at the edge of the jungle. The coffee beans were gathered, dried, pounded and roasted. I loved the brew. In 1935, since there was no refrigeration, I never ate prawns or shellfish. They would go bad by the time they reached the estate. And at the clubs the planters would 'take tea' in rotation. Afternoon tea with cakes and sandwiches. I visited the Bandarawela Hotel in 1981. The last time I was there had been in 1935: morning breakfast, scrambled eggs, toast, marmalade, fruit salad all cut by hand, tea, coffee; dinner, pork chops, roast beef steaks, mulligatawny, fruit salad. And in 1981 when we returned it was the same and double and treble rooms just for 25 pounds.

"At the outbreak of the war, I went back to England. That was in 1940. We used to take some of the young navy boys for long holidays on the estate. Some of the young men from the submarine Odin spent a holiday with me. They were a group of nice young boys, clean, neat, and tidy. The Odin was sunk, all the men lost at sea."

I said, "Neither Mr Bazley nor Johnny Walker ever used a car. They walked most of the time."

"I learnt to drive in a Baby Austin at the Botanical Gardens in Peradeniya," David told me, "in 1935. And I remember the Pathans in Kandy too. The moneylenders."

I remembered them too, leaning against the rails on the pavement near Elephant House, with their flaring turbans and billowing clothes, tall handsome men with wheat-coloured complexions. My father had a good friend among them, Mana Jhan. How many of his colleagues my father helped in the Railways. Those who were indebted to the Pathan moneylenders. He would arbitrate with them and persuade the Pathans to allow the railwaymen to take part of their wages home. It was a tough life for those Engine Drivers who liked drink and gambling; their salaries were not large, so they were sometimes in debt to the moneylenders.

Aunts Elsie and Ila.

Aunt Elsie (Solomons MBE) going to a Garden Party at Buckingham Palace, England.

XI

REBEL AUNTS
&
GENTEEL LADIES

Auntie Girlie (Solomons)

Cousin Lorna Grenier Jansz (M. Bert Albrecht)

Uncle Bertie (Grenier Jansz)

Auntie Tommy's Boarding House

During those war years, in between putting me into the Girls' High School hostel after the move from Kadugannawa to Anuradhapura and the final, for me, return to Kandy, my sister and I stayed with a friend of our mother's, Auntie Tommy. Miss Thomas, 'Auntie Tommy' as we called her, ran a boarding house. It was full for the most part of genteel Burgher ladies, retired teachers, spinsters, a divorcée or two, and widows. It was here that another set of my mother's relations also found themselves. There were two other children there too. The son and daughter of Mona de Saram were our playmates and so were our cousins. Lorna Albrecht spent a vacation there (Bert Albrecht was then working in a Firm in India) with her little daughter, Diana. It was here that I watched, observed and stored in my memory all the characters who walked across the stage of my childhood. Women like Miss Struys who played her endless games of solitaire in her bedroom; Suzy Toussaint knitting cardigans, jerseys, and twin-sets from English magazines to make a living; Mary Le Marchant from Galagedera; Doris Halliday, Aggie Samarasinghe, the Gillespie sisters.

Women, women, women. A world of women. It must have been an interim period in all our lives before we moved on, went away for ever, and Auntie Tommy herself disbanded her boarding house to become the chatelaine at the Suisse Hotel. My family revolved round aunts, uncles, and cousins. We found ourselves in the same boarding house, a strange concourse of women at Auntie Tommy's, who was an aunt not through real kinship, not blood-related, but an aunt all the same.

Cousin Myrtle, Auntie Ethel, Auntie Linda Redlich (Auntie Ethel's unmarried sister) had all moved into Auntie Tommy's boarding house. There must have been some sudden upheaval in their lives for them to move from Colombo to Kandy and to reside temporarily in the boarding house. There was no place for my Uncle Harry, Auntie Ethel's husband, in this house of women and he was at Sunnyside Gardens. There were Mona de Saram's young son and Mrs Gillespie's son (the mothers were both widows), but no married male could live here, however staid and respectable. There were many old Burgher ladies who found Auntie Tommy's home a refuge. There were young ones too like the beautiful Miss Poulier, an ivory-complexioned brunette. What was this woman, who looked like Helen of Troy, doing here, sharing a chaste bedroom with Auntie Tommy and myself? Who gently woke me up when I was late in getting up to go to school in the morning? This was no place for a child, with all these adults around.

I cannot remember even a place for my own books but I read all the books available in the boarding house, including Gene Stratton Porter's *Girl of the Limberlost*, and a memorable collection of Anglo-Indian verses with descriptions of Indian Maharajahs, Maharanis, Englishmen and their memsahibs seen through colonial eyes. Fascinated by drawings of men and women in the dress of that period, probably the Edwardian era, with wasp-waisted men being tightly laced in corsets and women in frills and lace and bustles riding on horseback or taking the air in open carriages on the maidan. The verses were satiric jingles mostly but I found them amusing, although at that time I was completely unconscious of anything connected with colonialism or the British Empire. I still have in my mind those black and white sketches of Babus, fakirs, Indian courtiers in all their regalia and wealthy Indian ladies bedecked in jewels, and drawings of the Empire builders and their ladies. I must have made myself at home there, free to do as I liked, playing in the stables in the garden below or curled up on the green cane settee, trying to play the phonograph which belonged to my dead brother Budgie, listening to the ghost of a voice on the cylindrical record – what was it, that tune, the words of that song, about time, about age? Was it, "I am twenty-one today?" Budgie died when he was eight years old. I knew him only from the memories of my mother.

I missed my mother, from whom I had never been separated before, and begged her to take me with her, back to Anuradhapura where there was only one school I could attend – the Roman Catholic Convent – but she was firm for perhaps once in her life and insisted that my education should continue at the private Methodist Girls' High School, which I was already attending. Until I became a boarder in the Hostel, I went to school from Auntie Tommy's, sharing a rickshaw every morning with my sister. Being at Auntie Tommy's was important for me I now realize. I was living with very special people, each of them survivors in an era where there was very little scope for women to express their uniqueness as individuals, retired teachers, widows, spinsters and those who were ageing with no homes of their own. Of course there was Mary le Marchant, who belonged to a Eurasian family, one of the off-shoots of colonialism, a woman who impressed me even at that young age with her gentleness of manner. Even at "Sunnyside" there were the two petite Eurasian teachers. Most of the Eurasian sons took to planting, like their European fathers, born of that inheritance of the blood. They became great teachers, principals of schools and colleges, priests. Their names were distinctly English or Scottish, unlike the Dutch Burghers many of whom had European names, not Dutch alone but German, Austrian and French. Names that came down from the seventeenth and eighteenth centuries and the Dutch East India Company. At Auntie Tommy's there were names that emerged out of a wide spectrum: Jansz, Redlich, Struys, Gillespie, Poulier, Thomasz. There were also the Samarasinghe sisters: Agnes, Aunt Aggie, whom I remembered so well, wearing court shoes with her saree which was neatly pinned up at the shoulder with a brooch; and then there was the beautiful, the exotic Sylvia Craighlaw whose father was Jewish I was told. And Mona de Saram, young and widowed with two children to bring up. Often lonely women. There was generally never an adult male in sight at the Boarding House except for the butler, Sinniah. Later on, with British servicemen billeted in Kandy, some of them used to drop in for conversation and a game of cards.

A way of life was maintained and preserved in this boarding house which was islanded in its own customs and rituals. Each room furnished according to individual taste with Chinese bedspreads, lace dressing-table runners, cretonne cushions and curtains – the lives in those beautifully neat and ordered rooms, so secret, so locked in, so closed and private. Meals served at the long dining table laid out with English crockery and cutlery. Serviettes crisply starched, folded into their ornamented silver and brass rings, polished cutlery gleaming beside each plate. Sinniah the butler dressed in white starched clothes, serving the consommé, the cutlets, the salad and vegetables, bread and butter with the soufflé omelettes full of strawberry jam for dessert... And all this in the heart of the town of Kandy where you could hear the drums and the horanewa from the great Temple of the Tooth, which stood beside the old palace of the Kandyan Kings. If you peered into the green waters of the lake you could feed the ancient tortoises and fish, with white porri from the cones of paper or even buy vadai from the 'lines' close to the bund where the Indian

Tamil community of workers lived. My mother described the
regattas on that lake where the Englishmen in Kandy sailed their
yachts.

At Auntie Tommy's one afternoon we children all had a very
special treat with a Punch and Judy show. It was my first
experience of puppets and I sat cross-legged on the floor with the
other children watching English puppets being cleverly
manipulated by their strings, with English voices speaking
invisibly from behind the scenes. Yes, we had our own
entertainment, our own ways of entertaining ourselves. The little
girl in the ASP's house called me to her home on a visit one day
and entertained me in a very dignified manner in her parent's
drawing room when they were out visiting. Sometimes I sat on
the settee and watched Sylvia waltz round the room with Captain
Desborough to gramophone music. Or helped Auntie Tommy to
choose one of her French silk, ninon or chiffon gowns to go dancing
with the lonely soldiers at a Church function. The ladies danced
so sedately to the music of Victor Sylvester and Charlie Kunz. Or
I waited for the ice-palam man as he trundled his green and white
striped cart packed with cardboard cones of lemon, strawberry
and orange water-ices.

Uncle Harry would come in the evenings to visit Auntie
Ethel. Ethel, Linda and Myrtle lived in one of the largest rooms at
Auntie Tommy's. Ethel spent most of her time in the big, four-
poster bed propped up against pillows, clad in a billowing white,
high-necked cotton nightgown, her soft white hair neatly braided
by her daughter, Myrtle, a placid expression on her fair-
complexioned face. Never a grumble or complaint emerged from
those patient lips. In her youth she must have been a typical rosy-
cheeked fraulein, descended no doubt from some German official
or mercenary in the Vereenidge Oost Indische Compaignie when

the Hollanders administered 'Zeilan' in the seventeenth and eighteenth centuries. Who were the ancestors of Ethel and Linda Redlich? Merchants, adventurers, burgomasters? She had the blue, blue Redlich eyes which all three children, Lorna, Myrtle and Ronald, inherited. Uncle Harry had blue eyes too. His eyes twinkled in his lively, jovial face. Every evening he would come visiting Auntie Ethel dressed to kill, like a young dandy visiting his sweetheart, wearing a full grey English worsted with silk waistcoat, twirling an elegant knobbed cane, smiling and joking, and Aunt Ethel would be brought out to the veranda to sit on the cushioned cane settee to chat with Uncle Harry. He always had a merry air about him and would trot in punctually every evening for their little tête-à-tête. My sister Rosemary and I would sing or chant a verse to amuse our fun-loving uncle:

Uncle Harry went to marry
In a donkey cart
Donkey died, Harry cried
Of a broken heart.

We were very fond of that uncle of ours. He must have felt sad and lonely away from Auntie Ethel whom he was devoted to, but there wasn't enough room for the whole family at "Sunnyside Gardens," nor could Uncle Harry stay at Auntie Tommy's.

All my memories grew from the faraway time of my childhood where everything was absorbed by me, even the very games I played until, with the passage of the years fantasy became reality. Those imaginary journeys my aunts traced on the large globe set on the dining table, before they went on Cunard liners to Great Britain, became the route which I took, beyond that childhood garden where I played during those endless hours with my ayah, Mungo. The garden where that mythology which became part of my psyche as I grew up. Here, at Auntie Tommy's there existed a different life, a life which somehow, to me, appeared to belong to a different plane of reality. I moved in a world of women who were, each in their own way, coping with the situations into which they had been plunged. They lived discreet lives, happy enough for the security that Auntie Tommy provided them with. They had their little rooms to which they retreated for privacy, emerging for meals or for an evening's conversation. There was no gossip and no peeping and prying into other people's affairs.

Myrtle's life revolved round her mother. Sometimes, in their bedroom she made nourishing soups for Auntie Ethel, thick vegetable soups with potato, carrots, leek, and lentils. My mother would insist that my sister and I drink cups of it some evenings, eating the vegetables with a teaspoon. Cousin Myrtle, so fresh-cheeked with her blue eyes and auburn curls, her Dutch and German blood making her look so much like a Gretel of the fairy tales. She was an enchanting cousin and a devoted daughter to her parents. After they moved to Colombo she kept house for her father until his death. Later on, Myrtle too, migrated to Australia where she was re-united with the rest of the family who were already there.

I would be invited into Miss Struys' room where she offered to teach me the card game of Patience. Her head swathed Maharaja-wise in green turban of chiffon she sat all alone in her little room and played Patience for hours on end. The cards lay face downwards on the green, gauze-covered table and were shuffled and dealt and arranged in their correct order – Kings and Queens, Jacks and Knaves, Clubs, Spades, Diamonds, and that elusive Jester who hid within the pack and emerged to somersault through my mind. I was at home in that old house with its green-painted cane chairs, the writing desk, with books and the old phonograph. Within the glass bell on the corner table was a wreath of waxen artificial flowers. I was reminded of the women in their beautifully ordered rooms living undisturbed each within a glass bell.

Hands shuffled out the cards, one by one, hour after hour to beguile the time. A game for a single, solitary person. No one to talk to in her lonely room. Miss Struys played games of Patience, giving herself surprises. A retired spinster teacher with that slight nervous tic that made one feel that an invisible metronome kept time to the chords and keys of memory. Years and years of teaching children in Private Missionary Schools of the past. A trained teacher who taught all subjects: poetry, parsing, reading and explaining English literature; the Idylls of the King. The Lady of Shallot, living in the Camelot of the Arthurian Court waiting for Sir Galahad or one of the knights of the Round Table. Perhaps an evening visit from an English soldier friend as lonely as herself, far from Blighty. Then the cards were put away and Miss Struys entertained herself with conversation.

Towards the end of the war the British soldiers, the Wrens, the ATS girls and the WAAFS, began to pack and prepare for departure to the distant battlefields and war zones. Would they return and go back to dear old Blighty with the scars, the wounds, and the mutilations of war? The soldiers, the sailors, the airmen were seen under the bright lights of "The Pink Elephant," a pub open on all sides, in the heart of the town of Kandy. They would go for wild rides in rickshaws through the gas-lit streets or walk arm in arm with the WAAFs and WAVEs and the ATS girls in their jaunty caps and khaki uniforms. The cinemas and theatre halls began to empty and "The White Cliffs of Dover" heard no more; the singing in the streets becoming silent.

Miss Struys was left alone again, shuffling her cards, readying herself for a game of Patience.

"Come, I'll teach you how to play Patience," she told me as I wandered into her room. But it was too difficult for me to arrange my life into that ordered pattern.

Shuffling the pack, each card came off her hands sliding like the hours, minutes, seconds. They fell with a silky pat onto the teapoy.

I did not like cards with hidden faces. I liked to build instead, out of those cards, mythical kingdoms, delicate structures, houses and palaces with storey upon storey, and extensions with maze after maze of rooms; to construct them you needed the most delicate touch. First the walls each supporting the other, then the roofs. The walls would collapse, falling inwards. They would be set up again. And so I built my palaces and my pavilions with kings and queens gazing at each other with solemn faces. My jester leapt over the wall, somersaulted through rooms, climbed stairways of air, and pouf! Escaped as perhaps one day I would need to escape the tumbling house of cards. Power lay in the dust, and into their coffins went reigning monarchs and their queens. Only the jester smiled and the magician put the cards away.

The turban came undone, unwound itself with soft grey strands, sprinkling its folds and blowing off, scattered in corners and crevices of the lonely room. Till the next day and the next, each card slipping out of the pack, spelling their own esoteric to her until evening came and the lonely companion sat with her in Camelot, in Xanadu, in Tartary.

Auntie Tommy's boarding house was Xanadu for the lonely ones. The transit travelers who had settled down there between their passage through life and death, through widowhood and divorce, through remarriage and temporary liaisons. That brief sojourn in the oasis of impermanency, unmoving for the moment, their suitcases packed and ready for imminent flight, with their crepe-de-chine pyjamas and silk kimonos.

My mother told me that Sylvia's father had fled from Germany. The old man used to drive around in an old Ford car. Sylvia was tall and slender, her movements feline, cat-like, her limbs smooth and sinuous. Her expression was like that of an odalisque. She was already married to Bubsy Direckse, fair-skinned, red-cheeked and blue-eyed, a cheerful and good-tempered railwayman who lived in Kadugannawa in one of the railway bungalows perched on a hill overlooking the Station where we had our memorable evening parties. During one of the big floods when it rained and rained, the Direckse family took shelter in our home in Kadugannawa and Sylvia had to borrow my mother's clothes. I remember how she brought the most delicious jam roly-poly with her, a pudding made with suet. It was a flavour I could never recapture for years and years however much I tried. Like Auntie May's Simnel Easter Cake. We were brought up on caramel custards and chocolate blancmange, as well as bread pudding with lots of fat plums; moss jelly and stewed fruit, stewed apples, pears and pineapple with custards flavoured with cinnamon and lemon rind.

Now Sylvia appeared flitting in and out of Auntie Tommy's boarding house. Here, she introduced her Captain to us, to the guests – small, perky, anxious-faced in his khaki uniform with its polished brass pips – and they waltzed away dipping and floating in the drawing room to the music of Strauss. Later on Sylvia left Bubsy, married the captain and vanished from our lives.

I watched Auntie Thomas getting ready to go to a social after the church service at St Paul's. St Paul's was an Anglican Church built in the nineteenth century.

"What shall I wear, the green chiffon, the lavender or the French ninon?" she asked me, opening her wardrobe. Soft draperies of semi-transparent materials were taken off their dress hangers and held up for me to view.

"Green, green, wear the green chiffon," I pleaded. It was cool to the touch like a spray of rainwater from a branch of shaken leaves.

"You will look beautiful, Auntie Tommy, like a queen."

Auntie Tommy stood before the mirror of the old-fashioned dressing table and patted Esther Dearborn mercolized wax tinged with pink on her soft cheeks. Then she dipped her powder puff with its little pink ribbon and fluffed her face with a cloud of pink powder. She delicately rouged her cheeks, touching her lips with the blossom lustre of red. Silk stockings and court shoes with glittering buckles, a pearl necklace and pearl ear-clips, a touch of lavender perfume, and Auntie Tommy was ready for the Church Service and a social afterwards in the community hall. Sometimes I would be taken too and would sit quietly like a mouse watching the ladies who took around tea and biscuits and slices of fruitcake to the guests. Many of them, both men and women, were British, from the army, the navy, and the air force. I wonder what they felt in these surroundings far from home, listening to sermons delivered by their own English priests in a red-brick church which architecturally was so similar to the ones in their own country. St Paul's had beautiful jewel-coloured stained-glass windows, the choir stalls, family pews and the organ loft. The hymns that were sung, the doxology, the psalms and Bible readings from the gospels of the Old and New Testaments, were all in English, "Standard English." During that period, it was the King James version that was used in the two churches I attended, the Anglican and the Methodist.

Sometimes I had no one to play with, no one to talk to. The house was empty. I too stood before the mirror and rouged my lips and cheeks, a very young, very naive, femme fatale who spoke a silent language of the mind, filled with symbols, addressed to the reflection of her persona. And then, it was all wiped away, washed off with Palmolive soap, and the ordinary image returned of a little girl who was very lost among all the women with their secret lives, the genteel ladies penned in within their rooms. In Kadugannawa too, I used to rummage in the big cabin trunk and try on my mother's dresses, particularly the lace wedding gown, while I draped her lace curtains to simulate long tresses. The other part of me was the little girl who wore taffeta and organdy or smocked Fuji silk or chintz or cotton and shoes and socks. We were never allowed to go barefoot, or even wear slippers in the house. Wooden clogs painted in different colours of red, yellow and blue were used when we had our baths, standing on the wet cement floors and pouring water over our heads.

I loved Diana, my cousin. She was the younger sister I longed to have. Diana was small, intense, with bright dark eyes, difficult to feed. So I would sit on the bed in their room and feed her with little morsels of cutlet and cubes of bread and butter pronged on a silver fork, telling her the fairy tales I knew. We went for long walks round the Kandy Lake where we fed the tortoise and fish with white porri from big baskets, emptying paper cones of it and fluttering the kernels into the water. The dark submerged shapes of fish surfaced suddenly to feed as they thrashed about with their fins and flippers. The tortoises would stretch out their throats to take sharp gurgling swallows of the porri and then they would disappear beneath the green almost-opaque water.

In the garden we crushed dry ice against our palms and sucked the orange and raspberry frozen sticks of ice-palam in their cardboard containers. We would go for walks past the railway lines, past Echelon Barracks which now housed the families of the police. I loved to peer in through the open windows with their glimpses of life and imagine what it must be to live in those small thick-walled rooms. My mother took me to our seamstress Mrs Alexander's house, to get home dresses, school uniforms and party dresses out of chintz and Riverina, sprigged organdy and taffetas. Delicate featherstitch was sewn on our smocked, yoked nightgowns and lingerie.

At Auntie Tommy's the dinner gong sounded every night. My sister and I sat at a separate table, circular, spread with damask, while the ladies sat at the long table with Auntie Tommy at the head. She had a little silver bell at hand to summon Sinniah the butler. Soup, a dish of cutlets, mashed potatoes, salad, stewed fruit and custard were served. Women sat at their rituals. Women who found her home a place of safety, a haven. Women who had chosen this way of life, to be independent of men. Women who lived, with apparent tranquility and peace, the turmoil of their emotions concealed from the rest of the world.

Suzy Toussaint, too, lived in one of those little corridor rooms of Auntie Tommy's boarding house. She looked so much like one of the characters in a book of English Nursery Rhymes, her cheeks rosily tinted with the same colour as the soft shades of wool she unwound from those great fluffy balls. She had silky white hair and the fashion of her dress never changed in all the years I knew her. She wore long ankle-length, full-skirted gowns, and stockings and buckled court shoes. She sat for hours in her little bedroom, her clicking needles weaving pattern after pattern from the English fashion journals, deciphering their esoteric codes to spin cocoons to enwrap and keep us warm. It was a way for her to earn a living too. Out of her knitting basket she lifted out the soft balls of wool, pink, blue, white, old rose, coral and russet, knitting from dawn to dusk to protect us from mists and chills and monsoon rains. Twin sets, jerseys, cardigans, sweaters were spun by this ageing Penelope. *Click, click, click* went the knitting needles – knit, plain, purl, knit, plain, purl, as she deciphered the Rosetta stone of this language. My mother and her friends "gave orders" for these warm garments, knitted in soft Angora and lambswool. It would seem as if we lived in a cold winter climate.

Muffled up in vests and coats, cardigans, mufflers and caps, we sallied forth on walks round the lake or jog-trotted in rickshaws to school. When the rains came, the damp khaki-coloured tarpaulin was fixed on hooks like a curtain across the front of the rickshaw, and we could peep out from its corners as we rode through the wet streets flashing by. We were warm and snug inside, buttoned up in Suzy's coats, our feet well protected in shoes and socks, white canvas on Drill days – while the sandaled or bare feet of the rickshawman, with his hooded canvas cape, sped along. The wheels churned up rainbow-coloured water in fountains and sometimes the rickshaws would leak. Perhaps the rickshaw puller would take a leisurely walk so that we could look around at the life that went on in the tea boutiques and hotels and shops. Hot tea was poured into glass tumblers from those samovar-like urns, or we saw elaborate iced cakes in the glass-fronted showcases – white sugar icing in flower garlands with tiny silver balls and bottles of sweets, hundreds and thousands, black and white striped candy, caramel toffees, liquorice all-sorts. The pingo bearers swung their fish baskets and fruits and vegetables, their clay pots and dolls furniture as they trotted along the road. My sister and I would sit together on the single seat, balancing our books on our laps or with our satchels knocking against our knees as we went to school.

A special rickshawman was hired to take us to Girls' High School from Auntie Tommy's before we became boarders at the Hostel. They were so trustworthy, those men, so kind and patient that we depended wholly on them. The rickshaw was our private carriage. To our shame we never questioned the manner in which it was drawn. The rickshawman, the water carriers, the sweepers (for there was no developed drainage system in Kandy in those days) were part of that life and of those times. Our own lives were comfortable, protected in every way. Even the clothes we wore were meant to protect us from fever and chills. "Keep your chest warm," "Keep your hat on or you'll get sunstroke" – which meant that we wore jerseys to school, and pith hats and sun helmets like Lilliputan Empire builders.

Auntie Thomas read tea-leaf fortunes. She, the mistress of the boarding house, chatelaine of the rooms where the chaste women dwelt, mystic juggler and reader of crystal balls, also peered deeply into our tea cups. The teapot stood perpetually on the table, the china pot in its thick, quilted tea cosy. I would quickly drink my cup of tea, drain it to the very dregs and plead, "Auntie Tommy, read my fortune." The sodden leaves looked like bees drowned and dead in their honey cells. What would my fortune reveal? A wedding? I had heard my mother talk of the Piachaud wedding, the bride with her alabaster complexion in oyster satin and champagne flowing at the reception. A surprise visit? My father? No, he never came to Auntie Tommy's. It was the house of women. And he was far away in some distant outpost a "malarial station" to which we couldn't be taken, unless it was during the vacation when we went to Anuradhapura and slept in wire-mesh-covered rooms. Would it be a gift? "You will have good fortune today," said Auntie Tommy. I gambled on my luck and found a stray puppy.

"No puppies here," said Auntie Tommy.

"I'll keep it down in the old stable," I pleaded.

"No, not even there. There is no one to look after it."

Auntie Tommy who loved me and denied me nothing was quite severe about it. How could she take on more responsibility? The puppy was spirited away. We went in search of it and found it in a nearby house. Auntie's heart eventually melted, and we kept the puppy. My mother took it back with her to Anuradhapura.

Auntie Tommy prepared for Christmas by making milk wine. The milk was boiled and the potent arrack spiced with crushed cardamoms, cloves and nutmeg added to it with burnt sugar syrup. It had to be filtered through fine muslin or filter paper for hours and hours. The entire paraphernalia was kept in her bedroom, the room which both of us shared, with the picture of the Guardian Angels above our bed. I tasted the wine as it seeped through drop by drop like hourglass time. I skipped in and out of the room sipping it as a bee sipped nectar. No one knew my secret. The guardian angels with great downy wings hovered over two children who were clinging to the edge of a dangerous-looking cliff.

"You too have a Guardian Angel," my mother always told me. The precipices were still to be encountered.

Auntie Daisy Was a Saint

After a visit to Uncle Hugh's home at Friedenheim one day, out of the blue my mother spoke her thoughts out aloud.

"Auntie Daisy was a saint."

"How did she die?" I asked, being curious since my uncle Hugh Jansz had married for a second time, the pale-complexioned, large-dark-eyed Amy. "Auntie Daisy ate a stale patty and died of food poisoning," said my mother, and I had to be satisfied with that explanation.

Auntie Murie, her sister, married Reggie Jansz. Two sisters, Muriel and Daisy married two brothers, Hugh and Reggie. Auntie Murie was very clever, she was at one time principal of Princess of Wales College at Moratuwa. All three of her sons were talented and brilliant. Beltran was a teacher at Royal College and we, his young cousins, found him extremely witty and amusing. He would amuse us by talking of the college tuckshop as "the café, the thé (tea) kadé," while Hereward, an excellent photographer, would also amuse us with his conversation. Hereward also worked with that great archetypal figure in the world of films, Lester James Peries and together they produced *Silhouettes* which now reposes in the archives. "Uncle Harry, Auntie Dolly, I've come for the Harrypera (perahera)," or he would say: "Uncle Harry let's not talk of the good old days. What about the bad new days?" Geoffrey, the third son, was a famed linguist. He was sent to London University to study languages. He returned to Ceylon after his studies, and the last time I met him was in the 1970s when he came for my mother's funeral armed with bibles in all the different languages and kept walking behind us as we were busying ourselves with the funeral arrangements, declaiming prophetic passages from the Old and New Testaments in Spanish, Russian, French, German Greek and Latin. He too was considered brilliant, a foil to Ronald, yet another cousin, who was considered very proper and was the epitome of dignity. Ronald would tell us how Geoffrey would walk along the Colombo pavements swirling his umbrella before and about him imagining that every passerby was about to attack him and needed to be warded off. Geoffrey was an intellectual who lived in a world of his own with his books in several languages, his translations, his writing.

The cousins were all left very well provided for by Uncle Reggie. He was very careful with his money. Saved, acquired property, built houses, but his sons were far more attached to their mother. His policy was 'spare the rod and spoil the child' and when he returned from work tired and out of temper, if Auntie Murie complained to him about the boys, he would thrash them, so said my mother.

When I visited Sunnyside I spent hours gazing at the framed photographs on the walls, on the what-not and side-board. So many photographs which reflected an epoch, an era of those times beginning from the early years of the twentieth century and running through the twenties, thirties and forties when Ceylon was still in its pre-Independence era. I was fascinated by the wedding photograph of Aunt Muriel and Uncle Reggie – she in a gown with a bustle, like one of the French Impressionist paintings and Reggie in full suit with waistcoat and spats and a carnation in his buttonhole; Auntie May with bobbed hair in a low-waisted twenties dress, sitting in an interior filled with period furniture and potted palms; my grandparents with part of their numerous offspring sitting at their feet, standing at their shoulders, products of a complacent civilization where you brought as many children as you desired into the world, with no thought of how many mouths there were to feed or that fecundity would bring early death to the beautiful Charlotte Grenier all I had of her was a semblance of that beauty in the faded daguerrotype in its oval frame, that too which is lost with time.

I would look deeply into the face of that grandmother married off at sixteen. "She tried to run away on the eve of her wedding," said my mother, "dressed in her white Victorian nightgown." Was it easier for my mother to create and fictionalize those historic episodes from memory than to read me the stories from books that my Solomons aunts gave as presents? Were all these snatches of stories, which began from no point of time, to surface from an unconscious that had suffered with the loss of her mother who had died so young. Three daughters were spinsters. All the sons married, and grandfather Jansz had the foresight to buy property and build a solid and substantial house, which stands even today on diminished acres, but it still, notwithstanding, stands with a lone descendant who refused to migrate from history.

So Auntie Daisy, Uncle Hugh's first wife was "a saint." It meant that she also endured, was a martyr and had to put up with unknown sufferings, chief of which from the point of view of the Janszs was that men were difficult especially as husbands. Aunt Murie withstood martyrdom. She had those three strong sons and "never gave in." Contrasting her as I knew her in later life, with spectacles, plain hairstyle, face devoid of the transparencies of make-up, I could not help but think of the bride with a chaste bouquet of Madonna lilies, swathed in yards of lace and wondered how she confronted all those Eleusian mysteries of marriage.

"Do you remember your mother?" I asked Auntie Daisy's daughter Evangeline, my cousin.

"No, not very well. I was fourteen years old when she died. David my brother was the brilliant one. He became a doctor. My mother used to sit by him and help him with his studies. He had the brains."

Auntie Daisy's son, David ended up as a lecturer in the Medical College. He married this girl with flaming red hair and had one son. We never saw this son who was supposed to be like his father. He was not allowed to mix with anyone. The wife, a white-faced, Titian-haired woman rarely met the Jansz relations. I saw her only once, at Aunt Nellie's funeral. Aunt Nellie was buried in beautiful silken garments sent by her niece Lorna from Australia. David's wife was so white, her hair dark red, an Italian Renaissance painting tucked away in a museum. As time went on, those minute hair-cracks of age on that canvas would be seen by no one. There would be no restoration of a masterpiece that slowly gathered cobwebs and dust. David had been a very eligible young Burgher bachelor doctor when he had passed out as a young House Officer, and on a hospital visit had been spotted by the parents. And so the daughter was married to this promising young man. Many years later, David, much married and jaded, fell madly in love with a young cousin, just out of university, seeing her as a tragic heroine from *Wuthering Heights*. And when she was about to be married all he could do was to clasp her hands in his and say, "Dearest darling," in a voice charged with emotion. David was a lecturer in anatomy at the Medical College, but he was more interested in Rosicrucianism and the mystical Cabaal, in Chaucer and the Romantics, and when he was at Cambridge University he bet on horses through astronomical calculations.

He was very particular about his manner of delivering lectures, and when he was staying at "Friedenheim" with Evangeline he used to rehearse his lectures before a mirror. He had his idiosyncrasies especially about the boiled eggs his sister gave him for breakfast. The egg had to be washed clean first of anything that adhered to it from its passage into the outside world.

"Do you know where this egg comes from?" he asked her one day, holding it under her nose. "It comes from…" Evangeline had to be very careful about 'The Egg' in future if she didn't want to get the full brunt of a very colourful description of its odyssey.

Evangeline herself had a chequered life. Evangeline was so beautiful with large dark eyes and curling lashes, always in search of a Utopian world, of ideal love and dreamy visions of romance unmarred and perfect. One of her admirers had been a very handsome Chinese Officer during the Second World War. She was very friendly with the Estonian artist and his wife the piano teacher, a couple with a Bohemian lifestyle. Both wooed her, in love and friendship, the artist painting enormous canvases, playing wildly exciting music on his violin, (while the wife accompanied him on the piano) and crying out to her in passionate voice, "Evangeline, Evangeline I luff you so much." Evangeline was the "leit motif" in this drama and most probably enjoyed her role, breaking away from the puritanical standards of her father and her saintly mother, but she could hardly emerge unscathed. Ultimately the music ceased, both of the violin and the piano, the couple lived apart, and another woman rapaciously, took not only the artist away but all his paintings to Europe. Karl Kassman went too and no one knows when and where this talented artist lived out his last days.

The wife lived alone giving piano lessons in a private missionary school where none of the students even wildly guessed at her secret life (nor the missionary principal either), and she continued teaching her pupils, the metronome ticking away beside her, Bach, Beethoven, Chopin as if her life were a passage of music with all its crescendos and diminuendos. Years later I used to see her at those charismatic church services listening to the harmonious voices ringing out in the well-trained choir. Her husband had long since died. No one either knew, remembered or cared about the paintings of that forgotten Estonian artist who played his gypsy Tzigane music as if evoking all the spirits of his faraway country in a drawing room dominated by an enormous canvas which covered the inner wall – a copy of some medieval world of courtiers, troubadours, women in long black gowns with coifed hair (or so it seems in my memory) and musicians with lutes and viols. All this drama took place in a two-storeyed house called "West End," which was very close to my old home so that I could not only hear the violin music but also see the painting in the evening illuminated by the lights. Bohemianism was a way of life which was accepted easily among that class of westernized Ceylonese. The music teacher was unconventional in her lifestyle, lived life the way she wanted to, converted it into a kind of Chelsea Arts Ball but also earned her bread and butter and supported her husband too by teaching music and letting out rooms. My two aunts (Solomons) also lived in one of the upper-storey rooms for some time. Evangeline got to know the couple when she too came to teach "Domestic Science" at Girls' High School, where she taught her students to make Garibaldi biscuits and Bachelors Buttons in the cookery class.

Once Evangeline sewed me a green linen dress for my parents twenty-fifth wedding anniversary, at which time she was also learning scientific dressmaking. The anniversary itself was to be a big occasion with the gathering of the clans. Trays of rich cake, which resembled wedding cake, were baked and iced with almond icing, and in the kitchen the fires were kept roaring for all the food prepared to feed uncles, aunts, cousins, friends. Evangeline I remember stuck pins all over me to get the perfect fit. It was a well-cut, meticulously stitched dress but it didn't suit my personality at all. Green was a colour I never wore and linen was hardly appropriate for the occasion I thought. It was all Evangeline's choice. I preferred rose pinks, reds, magentas with black lace to make my clothes as dramatic as possible. She caught hold of me one evening all unawares on the day of my brother's engagement to Iona Van Langenberg, when we were all staying at Uncle Elmer's at Stafford Place. Uncle Elmer was sharing his house with another family, the Van Burens who did the catering for him. What Evangeline did was shave me under the armpits, scraping and scraping away with a blunt blade. It was excruciating. I felt it was some kind of barbaric rite meant to initiate me into womanhood. I suffered. Felt sore, denuded. For Evangeline it was necessary, proper that one should be absolutely bare and hairless under the armpits, the ladylike thing do do.

Evangeline ultimately married a Prins. "My Prince Charming," she called him. "Now I am a princess," she added naively. My mother had been the matchmaker for they had met in our home. Evangeline was very well off. She was an heiress, owning a big house, "Friedenheim," shares in other houses in Colombo, and would also inherit money when she was twenty-one. Evangeline was a very special cousin.

Aunt Girlie's Banquets

She was christened Amelia, and she was yet another unmarried sister of my father's. You see her in my parents' wedding photograph with a picture hat and a chaste bouquet of flowers, sitting with the other bridesmaid, Aunt Norah. None of the protagonists of that marriage scene are now alive – the bride and groom, the bestman and groomsmen, the bridesmaids, the pageboy – but all of them, except one of the groomsmen, were to play an important part in my life.

Auntie Girlie worked for many years at Methodist College and very often her holidays were spent with her brothers and sisters. Auntie Girlie remained the eternal bridesmaid. She had a succession of dogs, all of which were called Bonzo – there was Bonzo the First, Bonzo the Second, and so on. So much so that I thought that no other name could be suitable for a dog. Perhaps Rover was another popular dog-name. But it was always Bonzo with Aunt Girlie. She too was a great Methodist like the rest of the family. With her sister Elsie, the Inspectress of Schools, she was Martha to Mary in the biblical sense. When Aunt Elsie entertained her special visitors it meant that Girlie would be standing at the stove, making her special pilau rice with plums, cadjunuts and green peas. Aunt Girlie's visit to her brother Harry (my father) was somewhat in the nature of an ordeal to my mother, because her main preoccupation was with food.

We had gargantuan and exotic meals when she was with us, and the already laden table groaned with an even greater weight. The whole carcass of an ox appeared to have disgorged its contents on the table, and my father himself went to his special beef stall in the Kandy market to get the choicest cuts of sirloin for beef-steaks, badun, crumb-chops, roasts and smoore. Then there were the other parts of the ox served up: liver badun or liver finkel curry or liver fried with bacon, potatoes, tomatoes and Bombay onions. Spleen curry and tripe too. My father insisted on the carrying out of the entire process by himself. If it were blanket tripe it was boiled for hours on the woodfire in a big earthenware chatty pot. Then it was fried in egg and breadcrumbs, or curried, served with home made chilli vinegar or stewed with vegetables – carrots, leeks, and potatoes. Brain cutlets were the piece-de-resistance. Auntie Girlie loved them. When she was boarded out in someone's home in Colombo as a working girl, she remembered how the boarding mistress and her family ate brain cutlets with their lunch – the cutlets were hidden in their plates of rice, she could see them peeping out. At her brother Harry's there was no such sense of deprivation. Sometimes trotters were stewed or made into a soup, gelatinous, rich and succulent trotters; or fried and curried prawns and crabs cooked into a red-hot curry with murunga leaves. A holiday at Harry's meant good food, rest and conversation.

Auntie Girlie spent hours sitting on the veranda, talking to my father as he rested on his lounger smoking his Havanas. We would sit and listen eagerly because we were fascinated by her endless desire for food – she ate several meals a day. She enjoyed her food and often went into the kitchen herself to make the most delicious dishes for us. My father felt a sense of pity for Girlie, who, unlike Elsie and Ila, never went globetrotting, never had the comfort of a husband and children, and so he wanted her to enjoy the choicest delicacies. Of course she ran the house for my grandfather at Karlsrhue Gardens – the house which was called "Morvan." She was in the end, when all had left home and my grandfather had died, forced to seek solace in food. Food gave her so much pleasure, such supreme delight. Even the ham-bone after all the ham had been sliced off, flavoured a green-gram curry.

And her soups were very special too – spicy with white cumin and sweet cumin, thick coconut milk, tempered with herbs and sliced red onions. There was also mulligatawny to be eaten with stringhoppers, egg rulang, and seeni sambol. She constantly needed her tastebuds to be titillated, after eating drab, insipid food in boarding houses. With all this rich food at home it is no wonder that I had "bilious attacks" or "acidosis" and had to drink bottles of Lucozade.

I needed simple food but we never had simple food at home, and after dinner we had chocolate pudding, or chocolate blancmange or caramel custard – and of course "Phla." Phla was the great event of Aunt Girlie's banquets. It was "a must" with her holiday visits, and we waited impatiently for this strange and exotic dish to be ready. It took hours of steaming, with the pudding bowl set in a pot of boiling water; the mouth tied with cloth. First, the best quality of kitul jaggery had to be bought and grated, mixed with thick coconut milk with dozens of eggs beaten into the mixture – it was flavoured with cardamom and nutmeg. In those days we bought the cadju straight off the man who sat with his basket of cadju nuts at a corner near Whiteways – the big haberdashery shop. It was bought at ninety cents a hundred. Slivers of cadju decorated the dark, creamy, porous, surface of the "Phla."

With Auntie Girlie's gradual fading into old age, there were no more Bonzos, no more "Phla," but she was cared for till the end by her sisters Ila and Elsie. As a family, the Solomons were a lively, loyal lot. They were strong, bonded by love, and steadfast, although they had their quirks and idiosyncrasies. "We must always stand by each other," Auntie Elsie would say. In the end it was Elsie who chose to go away, not be a burden to anyone, to die in the Victoria Home. She had a great sense of pride and self-reliance. And depended on no one but herself.

Sunnyside Aunts – Aunt Maud

Would I ever become like those aunts who were so much a part of my world, I wondered. The Sunnyside aunts who remained behind in the ancestral house were not married. Auntie Nellie, Auntie May and Auntie Maud. Auntie Nellie was part of the very conservative setup of that time. That conservatism was reflected even in her manner of dress. High-necked silk and linen gowns discreetly pinned at front openings with topaz and amethyst brooches set in gold; her virginal body entrapped, the curves restrained in corselets of whalebone, a kind of chastity-armour. Body shape was not something to be flaunted, however shapely the soft bosoms tucked away modestly beneath the silk gowns. Feminine women shapes that must not be too conspicuous, like the tinted illustrations in the fashion journals of those times. Auntie Maud had a voluptuous, Ruben's-like body and was always being exhorted to "push your bosoms in, Maud," as they attracted too much attention in what 'they,' the aunts, considered, the wrong way. Even during the day there was never a hair out of place on their well-coiffeured heads, their delicately powdered cheeks with their gently patted-in film of Pond's creams, their manicured nails and creaseless dresses.

They hardly ever spoke of their emotions, of childhood, of the past, while our household was always doing so. I wish my aunts told me of their lives more intimate details. How did Uncle Bertie live that life with his sisters, with all its constraints? There was at that time little inter-ethnic marriage in our families, and my Auntie May's sad spinster existence was due to that fact. The Grenier-Jansz family of Sunnyside clung to a separateness that created a fortress which they willed to be impregnable. They had history behind them. Their ancestors must have been a colourful lot, but the Sunnyside Janszs were so genteel, living with their roses and family portraits, their ordered households, their virgin rooms. Yet they had plenty of courage too. In the early years of the century my aunt Eleanor took over the responsibility of the family after their mother's death at 53.

Aunt Eleanor, Nellie to us, took her youngest sister Elsie Grenier all the way to the North to live by the sea for the sake of her health. Elsie with the long golden hair and the butterfly bow was not destined to live for long. Born in 1896. Died in 1922. The aunt I was never to know. Elsie Grenier in her high-yoked smocked dress looked out upon another era of nieces and nephews upon whom she gazed with her Alice-in-Wonderland look, a gentle smile illuminating her face from a framed photograph. What had she felt in that hot, dry climate, living alone with my aunt in Keerimalai, waiting patiently for the sun to heal her? Aunt Nellie devoted her whole life to her eleven brothers and sisters and her father, Edward Jansz. And when they were all grown up, a widower, Mr James, with children of his own, wanted to marry her, but by then she had perhaps purchased her freedom and declined the offer. My cousins twice removed, Ethel, May and Lou Grenier told me how proud Auntie Nellie was of Sunnyside and had often wondered whom it would go to. My cousin Iris spoke of the old oak door that my grandfather Jansz was so proud of. And that rosewood table at which the whole family sat down to meals.

Auntie Maud always dressed so elegantly even when she came on an evening's visit home. She was one of those early feminists and had pursued a professional career. She had been

Chief Supervisor at the Telephone Exchange in Kandy. She rode recklessly down steep inclines on a tandem cycle. She played tennis at the Garden Club wearing culotte-like divided skirts, swinging her Slazenger racquet with great élan as she nimbly dashed about the tennis court on her small feet –all Janszs had small feet, size three in shoes. Her curls tossed about in the breeze, her eyes blue grey sparkling, and an enchanting smile on her Cupid's bow lips. There were whispers, whispers. I listened. "Fell in love with a married man. He was the husband of her best friend. No one talked of divorce at that time. They were forbidden to ever see each other again." That was the time she came on a holiday to Kadugannawa – a peaceful haven for her to get over that passionate affair of the heart. She had to give in, move away, never see 'him' again. I spent hours in her company listening to the tales poured into my ears. Adult tales at that. She must have eventually recovered from the crise-du-coeur, that forbidden love affair, and enjoyed her freedom, or she went on holidays travelling all over the island.

We would love to visit Maud's bedroom at Sunnyside, fascinated by the Kodak photographs and snapshots that decorated the walls. I imagined her swinging her tennis racquet in a superb upsweeping gesture and cycling along shady roads by herself, and all this in the 1920s. She had amusing stories to tell of the messages that would come over the telephone exchange from the English planters – not only did they want their connections made as quickly as possible, but they also extended polite invitations to tea, invitations which, however, were politely declined. In those days Sunnyside was close to the home of the Piachaud cousins, in Katukelle, which was a wilderness, and my aunt stayed in town, a boarder in a Burgher home, as it was not thought safe to return home late in the evening.

When we were growing up, Auntie Maud used to give us children dire warnings about men: "They are butterflies. They will sip you, sip you." We listened fascinated, too young, too innocent to know what she meant. She never gave up her love of dancing for the sheer pleasure of its rhythm, lost in a dream world to the music. Those were the days of the big dances in Kandy at the Queen's Hotel: the New Year's Eve Dance, the Perahera Dance, the Easter Dance. The big bands would come up from Colombo with their trumpets and saxophones and double bass – the Grand piano belonged to the Queen's Hotel ballroom. I remember those names so clearly: Frosty Vanlangenberg on the double bass; Gazaali Amit on the electric guitar; Sonny Bartholomeusz at the piano; Peter Allon the pianist playing "In an Eighteenth Century Ballroom," "Jealousy," "Tales from the Vienna Woods," foxtrots, quicksteps, tangos, waltzes all 'by ear.' The ladies in ankle-length gowns with swishing skirts, and the men in coat-tails and dress suits gliding along the ballroom floor. They danced till dawn, and the band played on and on, not only their own varied repertoire but also the requests of the dancers.

Aunt Maud loved to be the chaperone for the grand dances held in the Hotel Ballroom. She was a delightful chaperone, as she herself loved floating on the dance floor with a blissful smile on her face.

Aunt Maud was always given to the grand gesture. When Queen Elizabeth made a State visit to the island in the 1950s with her consort, Prince Philip, Aunt Maud decided that she should greet her on the station platform in Kandy together with other distinguished guests, the Mayor of Kandy, the municipal councillors, and the august dignitaries who followed the Royal entourage. Aunt Maud wanted to hold her own. A Burgher woman who created her own drama on the stage of her own devising.

"Dolly," she told my mother, "I'm getting Banda tailor to make me an ankle-length gown with a train. Of old-gold velvet." Chamois gloves. A plumed picture hat, silk stockings, and gold high-heeled shoes of kid leather. Heirloom jewellery to complete the picture.

"All by yourself?" my mother asked. "What about a formal invitation?"

"Yes, I have been invited. Look," she said and drew the white envelope from her handbag. Maud Mabel Grenier Jansz was indeed invited to be in that small select gathering to meet the Queen of England. "And how will you go to the station in that fancy garb?" My mother was both amused and curious. "Oh, by rickshaw or taxi... never fear. In style of course, in style. I don't need any chaperone. I'm going on my own..." And go, she did. On the day the Royal couple stepped off the train onto the red-carpeted platform accompanied by the aides-de-congs, high-ranking British officials, Ladies-in-Waiting, in attendance on Royalty, and what not... Did the Queen ever carry in her mind a picture of a lady who resembled a Gainsborough painting curtseying to her on that station platform...? And yes, Maud carried a bouquet of Uncle Bertie's choicest flowers to present to the Queen.

Did she, I wondered, did she, the Queen of England, remember?

Bertanell

"This is Auntie Maud," my mother casually announced by way of introduction; the rest was left for us to discover. Aunt Maud was suddenly telling us a story, a fable, a myth, a fairytale, and the character, the protagonist she creates for us is 'Bertanell.' Bertanell begins to say and do the fantastical, to wave magic wands that transformed the ordinary world we lived in. The accustomed world of Railway bungalows and shunting engines, Dawson's tower and the hills of Belungala, the rubber estate on which the lonely English planter lives, all begin to change with the presence of Bertanell.

Bertanell appears in a chariot drawn by the fiery steeds of the sun racing through the clouds that hover over the Railway township above Jem Smith's house and the Barries' house, over the pini-jambu trees, the fruit so rosily pink, high above the swing beside the Railway Reading Room. Bertanell has the power to administer magical potions, elixirs; to give life and youth and immortal, eternal beauty. Yet, there was a darker side too, because Bertanell can banish you from the fairy kingdom if you transgress the laws; if you go against the wishes of the powerful fairy who rules that fabled territory. You ate of that luscious fruit, tempted by what was forbidden and you stretched out your hand to pick it, all golden and ripe from those laden branches. But the juice was too potent; it made you swoon and lose your senses. So Bertanell, the powerful androgynous fairy felt you must leave the magical kingdom for a space of time. Exile yourself in another less magical country, until your brain stopped sprouting those poisonous flowers and beneath your feet the moss black with mould and fungus became brilliant emerald green again.

"Bertanell, Bertanell, Bertanell says this and this and this." We lifted our faces to her as we sat on that flight of steps to know more and more about the powerful fairy. We knew about Fallada the Goose Girl and Rumpelstiltskin. We knew all about the ogres and giants, the witches and wizards, the good fairies and the bad fairies. We rubbed shoulders with the fabulous, the mythic. In the world of transformations, the magical beings lived alongside of the rakshas and rakshasas and the spirits that emerged out of the village of the exorcists that lay so close at hand. Aunt Maud was the banished fairy with eyes of changing colour. Amber, blue, grey, topaz? Shining, transparent jewels beneath that penumbra of brown curling hair, her skin like polished pippins. She who had to become an ordinary, suffering human for a space of time until Bertanell held the chalice of life and hope to her lips again.

"Who is Bertanell?" we asked our mother.

"Bertanell?" Our mother was confused for a moment. "Ah yes, she must mean Bertie and Nellie." Hubert and Eleanor, Auntie Maud's brother and sister with whom she lived at Sunnyside. Sunnyside with its garden of roses, carnations, dahlias, gladioli and hydrangeas, was the landscape of metamorphosis. Bertanell embodied both power and beauty. Male, female. Banishment. Why, what had she done? Her banishment was to remove her from her landscape of the imagination, but she brought to us the gift of her fables. She had found the secret cache, the love cache but within it she found the skeleton frame which haunted her. The treasure was tarnished. The love she longed for was far beyond her reach, bounded by the conventions and taboos of her times. My mother went about busying herself with her household work, seeing that the meals were cooked and served up, the beds arranged, linen changed, spreading her good Irish linen sheets on the French bed and on the fourposter. The furniture was meticulously dusted every day but we generally did not fill the Chinese vases with flowers. My father preferred that they should bloom and wither on the trees and bushes. "Old Boy, Podisingho," what was his real name? Lost in time. Renamed by the family that had adopted him as a child from the tea plantations, sat and polished the cutlery with bath brick, and the silver and brass with Brasso. Alwin, his hands stained with varnish, polished the furniture – the French-styled Louise Quartoze, the chairs and settees which were always covered with English cretonne cushions. What was this volatile substance that had transformed my aunt to make her more prone to tears than laughter? Did Herbert and Eleanor think that being with such young children in this ordered household would bring her back to the reality that she had escaped from?

When was I told the real story? I heard it as I heard all stories from my mother. Aunt Maud had had a love affair which ended in sadness and separation. How could she transgress the laws of friendship by a forbidden love? Romantic, passionate, love? Was that love reciprocated? – it had been, by all accounts. My beautiful fun-loving aunt had suffered that severance, for such love affairs would never be countenanced in the family. How had she met him? They had worked together in the General Post Office. But love affairs, forbidden or otherwise, could not be stopped, and life had to be lived in a heart-break house of loneliness.

Uncle Bertie and His Gallery of Dreams

As children we loved to go into Uncle Bertie's portrait gallery
where all the framed photographs of bridal couples hung on the
walls. The Bridal Studio, where he discussed his unique and
unusual creations to suit the individual tastes of those first colonial
brides, was housed in a gallery which was built behind
"Sunnyside." It was here that his imagination created bridal
bouquets, corsages and wreaths, with the flowers that not only
came by train from up-country but from his garden as well.

After we had finished playing under the biling tree, our
tongues cringing with the tart juices, we wandered in to watch
Uncle Bertie sitting beside tightly packed baskets of flowers lined
with evergreens, buckets of water in which the long-stalked
flowers stood, and all the paraphernalia of rolls of copper wires
and scissors.

The photographs captured those moments in personal
histories which would one day go back to England. Memories of
lives which belonged to that imperial era. Sometimes the brides
were photographed alone as if they were modelling bridal gowns
in those pre-war fashions. Sometimes they stood with arms tucked
securely in the crook of male elbows as if to establish that sense of
physical belonging. They fascinated me. I gazed at each portrait,
turning in my mind those fictional pages, into which I read those
unknown and mysterious histories of a virtually unknown and
alien breed of people whose complexions were different to mine,
so distanced, so different to those with whom I jostled shoulders
on the street.

Uncle Bertie's world in that gallery was a different world to that of "Sunnyside." "Sunnyside" was filled with his sisters and their friends, all admirable women – artists, teachers, and musicians among them. Women who had forged their own careers. Although they had never even left the country to travel like the Solomons aunts, their minds and imaginations had no inhibitions, no limitations. They would always be the remembered women who created their individual histories without a sense of feeling that they had missed out on life.

For me as a child, Uncle Bertie's gallery was the Gallery of Dreams. The room was filled with the fragrance of fresh flowers. Bunches of Ladies' Lace foamed like white sea-spray in the hands of mermaids. Cornucopias overflowed with arum lilies and agapanthus. The heavy gold signet ring glittered on his finger and his eyes blue as the hydrangeas, shaded by dark lashes, reflected the colour of the flowers as he bent over them. The fragrance of these flowers carried me away into other gardens far away where the air was chilly, misty, and limpid streams flowed through the valleys and the water was icy cold.

Gently, tenderly, the long-stalked flowers were lifted and arranged in a bouquet, the delicate maidenhair ferns enwrapping them. The carnations smelt the sweetest, like crushed cloves. The yellow, powdery pollen dust laid a pattern on my hands, gilding them.

Uncle Bertie grew roses especially imported from Holland in his garden. Hardy roses that proliferated and blossomed in blush-pink, creamy white, sunset orange and red.

The bridal portraits, many of them belonging to the past, were those of the wives of colonial administrators and planters who had married in St Paul's in Kandy. At these weddings the guests came attired in suits and gowns belonging to the fashions of the British empire. The receptions were held in the mirrored ballroom of the Queen's Hotel where champagne flowed with the toasts that were pronounced. After the wedding these English couples would set up homes in the big colonial-style bungalows with their phalanxes of servants – cooks and the appus, the local butlers, houseboys, nannies for the children, chauffeurs, gardeners – leaving far behind the suburban memories of their earlier lives. The English missionaries solemnized the ceremonies and delivered their homilies at St Paul's, the Anglican church which looked as if it had been lifted straight out of an English village or country town, with its stained-glass windows, marble memorial plaques, carved pews, organ loft, and its clock tower with a clock face that never told the correct time to passersby who wished to order their lives according to the hour. It was here that the reading of the King James' version of the Bible echoed sonorously from the pulpit, the organ pealed forth church music or played interludes from Handel and Bach. It was here that communion was solemnly partaken of. Every Sunday morning, togged up in silk and linen gowns, hats, shoes, stockings (with Uncle Bertie in his double-breasted worsted) my aunts and uncle would be driven by car to attend the High Church Anglican Service.

As a child taken to see the Sunnyside aunts, I gazed at these black and white photographs the framed mementos of consummations under a star-studded sky with the swooning scent of Queen of the Night creeping in through windows; of grand red-carpeted receptions, of wedding cake, wine and champagne at the Queen's Hotel ballroom.

The brides I saw wore gowns of slipper satin or lace, and one especially enchanted me with what my mother said was silver lamé, which sheathed her body making it as glittery as that of a mermaid. I saw nothing of the background against which they stood, as if the photographs had deliberately excluded a backdrop that was alien to their dress and stance. It was the bouquets that gave them away. The flowers came from a different landscape, grew from a soil that was fed with dew, rains and mist, soft, soft – never ice-hard, waiting for snows to melt and ice to thaw. They left their European seasons behind, and yet up-country the fireplaces were built just like at home, with the log fires burning to keep out the creeping chills and mist that swept over the tea-covered hills, while the planters' wives trained the cooks to roast their joints of beef and make their steaks and hot pots, suet puddings, custards and trifles, still dining off their surburbias.

When we were children, Uncle Bertie used to take us for drives, this being a big treat for us. We hardly ever sat but stood behind and held on gripping firmly to the upper edges of the front seats, looking at everything whizzing past us, or he put the hood down on his coupé so that we would feel the wind blowing through our hair. He loved "music, song, beautiful women," and gave lavish gifts to his girlfriends. He took it very much to heart when one of them ("gold digger" she was called by his elder sisters) took all the gifts and then, jilting him, married a police officer.

Uncle Bertie sometimes spoke of a special "Birthday treat," something looked forward to in his youth with so large a family of brothers and sisters, perhaps a special gift, a special birthday cake or new suit. Uncle Bertie certainly made up for it in later life with his iced Elephant House Rich cakes, his bottles of whiskey or wine, his collection of long-playing records which he so generously shared, but his generosity was prodigal and extravagant and he had later on to keep the home fires burning. By the time the car had been sold he needed a conveyance to take him into town or to church on Sundays. No one questioned how the money came. It was a world with its own social conventions that emerged from a colonial heritage. Unique in itself but difficult to maintain with his dwindling resources. Uncle Bertie somehow made it with his imported Dutch roses. We were too young and selfish to understand or even to help, and little by little the property dwindled, sold for a song. But his sisters stood by him. They were strong as a family, but the time had to come when Uncle Bertie was left all by himself; and Sunnyside, which was my mother's ancestral home, was growing bleak, although up to the very last Uncle Bertie had his Rich cake with almond icing for Christmas, the Christmas tree and the bonbons. He loved to speak of the "sweet, young things" and loved all the songs from *The Sound of Music*. At one stage he decided to put up a big Cross in the garden, a Cross as tall as one of his cypress evergreens – a grand gesture, a proclamation of his own faith, when he was left bereft and alone.

Uncle Bertie ultimately became lame and walked on crutches. It was the Cross he had to bear. His little room with its austere bed and chair and dressing table was his home for life

Later on, when his studio had been dismantled, Uncle Bertie sat just outside his room, surrounded by buckets of water filled with long-stalked gladioli and sweet-smelling carnations, while faithful Raman, his gardener, helped him to unpack the up-country flowers from their bed of ferns and cypress branches. He was the only florist of repute in Kandy at that time and each of his bouquets and wreaths, were in my mother's words, a "labour of love."

Everything had to be a celebration of life, a big celebration especially on Christmas day when he had taken charge of things at Sunnyside. The rosewood table had an iced and decorated cake, the wine, sherry and whiskey, the chocolates, nuts, bon-bons and gifts all laid out for us, with music from *My Fair Lady* and Christmas carols being played on his big radiogram for his nephew and nieces.

In the end Uncle Bertie was left alone at Sunnyside. He had to bury all his sisters. No one perhaps knew of his money problems and of how he had to maintain the big house. He loved the good things of life that belonged to his inheritance. He still continued making his wreaths and bouquets. The colonial brides had by that time departed or gone 'home' for good, and all the bridal portraits had been removed from the walls of his studio. I do not know what became of them. Even the family portraits were lost, never to be found again, only restructured in memory.

There are no longer rose trees growing in the garden at Sunnyside. The Cross too no longer exists. But Uncle Bertie's photograph remains, a black and white one. Yet the colour of his eyes, hair and complexion remain in my mind.

There is a quirky smile on his lips, a kind of wry mischief that lurks at their corners. His hair is beautifully brushed and combed in their brown waves, his blue eyes seem to twinkle, and his bow tie is set with a butterfly precision. We almost lost our inheritance because of him, but now, looking at the face of his passionate youth, I see the face of his romantic generation... And understand, at long last.

Aunt Elsie:
Family, Personal Missions and Free Masons

Right from the beginning I became conscious of my aunt Elsie as an indomitable woman, yet she never imposed her will on any of us. Perhaps it was by observing her that my own life began to search out that independent path. She had not adopted the traditional roles of her times which entailed marriage, children. But she adored "family" and turned her attention to my sister and myself, showering us with gifts of books, clothes, and toys. Always books more than toys. As for my brother Pat, she more or less felt he was her very own.

Spending a holiday in Karlsrhue Gardens when we were very young, the aunts looked through our wardrobe and found there was nothing suitable for church on a Sunday morning. My mother was in hospital, so my father had been helpless packing our clothes for the journey to Colombo.

"Where are your special dresses?" the aunts asked in consternation. They had not been taken off the hangers in the wardrobe, the pink frilled taffetas and organdies. "We shall have to ask the Crusz sisters to sew you something suitable." The new ensembles were to have Czechoslovakian folk embroidery on the blouses and would take time to complete. The designs were taken from the blouses that the aunts had brought from their travels in Europe.

Aunt Elsie, Girlie and Ila went to church one Sunday, while my sister and I were left behind, swinging on the garden gates wearing vests and rompers, proclaiming to everybody who asked us as they passed by, what we were doing clinging onto that gate:

"We can't go to Church today because our special Sunday dresses are being sewn for us. Lovely dresses with lots of embroidery. We'll be in church next Sunday."

All the good Christians wending their way through Karlsrhue Gardens were given our careful explanations to convince them of our complete innocence in the whole matter. Swinging on the gate and talking to all and sundry attired in their Sunday best was no doubt a more pleasurable pastime than listening to long sermons. There were lots of things to do in the house of our unmarried aunts. Experimenting with Aunt Ila's make-up, lipstick, rouge, cutex. And another little girl who was also visiting, saying: "Wait, I'll tell Auntie Ila what you did. She'll punish you. Sin for you. Sin for you." Sin? Guilt? Punishment? No, Aunt Ila would never punish me, but notwithstanding I hid behind the wardrobe in the huge cane linen basket until I was hauled out after an anxious time of searching for me.

The aunts were infinitely patient, bathing all of us collectively under showers as we romped about, being soaped with Palmolive soap, scrubbed, towelled vigorously, and dried. In the evenings being read to by Auntie Elsie.

"Would you like me to read you the story, or relate the story to you?" she would ask. "Relate the story," we told her. So Aunt Elsie would read each chapter of *Heidi* and then tell us the story in her own words. We would sit gathered closely round her, rapt, giving her all our attention. As children we had no inhibitions with those aunts. They were an accepted part of our childhood. It was just that as we grew older, we perhaps became more selfish about our own thoughts and emotions. It is only in the after years that their messages reach us, for us to encode as we become the narrators of our own stories…

Aunt Elsie always believed in "Family Loyalty, Trust." Always, her presence was felt in a crisis. Staunch Methodist. Like all the Solomons. My mother, an Anglican, after marriage, was no longer in the family pew of St Paul's Church in Kandy. Aunt Elsie and Aunt Ila sang Methodist hymns in their alto voices. Their brother, my father, had a strong bass. Aunt Elsie, like her father, was a scholar in classical languages, Greek, Latin and Hebrew. She had taught herself French and in Paris gave a speech in French at some academic Assembly. Aunt Elsie was a very strong personality till the very end. Her mind was always several leaps ahead of the others, so she was often impatient of those who wavered. But she had great love and loyalty to the family, and to the British Empire. All her life she openly admired British Royalty. She was awarded an MBE, which was framed behind glass and hung on the walls of our veranda among deer antlers and python skins. She planned her own commemoration ceremonies wherever she was. The same hymns that were sung at Westminster Abbey were sung in her room with her guests. An enormous Union Jack, specially brought down from Great Britain, adorned her walls. She sent gifts to the Royal family on important occasions, anniversaries, and Royal weddings. There were politely worded acknowledgements from Ladies-in-waiting on behalf of Buckingham Palace.

Aunt Elsie's Letter: "The Royal Sunlit Wedding"
My first Sunday in London coincided with Remembrance Day. For the first time in 55 years, remembrance service was held at St Margaret's and the Abbey, in addition to the traditional Cenotaph. As I had several anniversaries at the Cenotaph on my previous visits to England from 1927 to 1962, I plumped for St Margaret's

and the Abbey. Flaunting my medals and presenting my card (with MBE), I was led up to the front, the first row behind the Monarchy. I noticed the males in the front row, wives in the second. I was early, as soon as the doors opened, Choir rehearsal on. I enjoyed the special anthems interposed into the service – "A new heaven."

At 10.30 a.m. the males in the front row moved in procession to the grave of the unknown warrior in the Abbey next door. Our service continued. At 11.15 the service over. We moved out into the brilliant sunshine, and were in time for the dispersal of the bands at the Cenotaph. I stood apart – dreaming.

"Miss Solomons." – It was the principal of St Thomas', Bandarawela, and his wife. I hugged her.

The Abbey had been closed for days for security and for preparations. Rails were up all around. I wondered where I would stand for a ringside view. Ila and I had taken our wedding gift to Princess Anne and another for the Queen a few days before. On the 13th arrived a very sweet letter – just in time. We awoke at 5 a.m. Each carried a packet of ham sandwiches, and sweets to suck. We were at the Abbey by 7.20 a.m. Compared with the weddings of 1960, and the Coronation, all London was quieter, less exuberant. I donned my best saree and best silver grey fur coat, medals. Ila in slacks. Again flaunting my medals and brandishing the Queen's letter – we creep up to the railings and took a stand in front of the West gate. By 9.30 the grounds were densely crowded. All quiet till 10 a.m., then the limousines with guests drove past us to the West door. I shouted 'Ceylon-Lanka' as our flag appeared. Too fast – alas. Sometimes the cars halted by us. Fur hats chiefly. A few alighted and walked. Smart costumes. Some young guests hatless. All short frocks. By 10.30 the Horse Guards and cheers. The Queen's Party in a State Coach. The Queen, Queen

Mother, Prince of Wales, Prince Andrew. Second Coach - Princess Margaret, husband, son and Princess Alice (90 years). Third State Coach – Duke of Kent and family and Lady Helen Windsor. Fourth State Coach – Princess Alexandra and family. Then several State landaus with other members of royalty.

To our joy and surprise each carriage circled a column in front of us and then halted at the West door. We saw them all clearly. The Queen in bright peacock blue, the Queen Mother in gold and beige. Now excitement rises high. Sharp at 10.55.

'Here comes the bride.' Circled the column slowly, alighted at the West door. A vision in full white. She looked beautiful. Then silence. Alas, the service not broadcast. Thankfully all the hymns burst on the air. 'The Lord's my shepherd,' 'Glorious things of thee,' 'Immortal, invisible' 'Let all the world,' 'God be in my head,' and last Handel's 'Let their celestial concerts all unite.'

By now we had stood for six hours, demolished our sandwiches, sucked our sweets. Bells pealing, band playing a rollicking march. The Bride and Groom emerged. Cheers, shouts. They drove straight off – away from us. The empty coaches and landaus and limousines drove past us. I espied the Lanka Flag again. As on Sunday, dazzling sunshine blessing the wedding. The whole event was simple, elegant, human, natural. At 7 p.m. we watched the whole wedding from the emergence at Buck House; the ceremony inside; the departure, appearance on the balcony, departure for honeymoon at 4 p.m. The couple and the Royal family chatting during the long service. Little did they guess there were lip readers amongst the reporters. All reported in the papers. Sweet nothings. Harmless! Only from TV did we realize the vastness of the crowd, and yet 50% watched on TV only. The frock so simple – and yet unique – and a dream. I always shuddered in Ceylon at the ridiculous cumulus cloud frothing on the head of brides, eclipsing the elegant sarees and the dainty· features. Only the Kandyans and the Tamils with more sense ignored the Colonial-minded designers who still piled mountainous headgear – so out of place with the saree. Here the simple translucent veil held by an elegant tiara – enhanced the beauteous face and head of the radiant bride. The Little Maid – demure and serious in her mediaeval attire; the page looked a bewildered little Lord Fauntleroy. No bevy of bridesmaids – to eclipse the bride. The groom and bestman resplendent in scarlet and gold. All so splendiferous, the sea of heads along the route and around Buck House. At last the Royal Party withdrew from the crowd. Stayed on till 4 p.m. The couple in an open carriage. The bride in a dark suit – white collar and smart white hat. The secret was out – honeymooning at Richmond Park, home of Princess Alexandra.

All over – still – echoes 'Let all the world in every corner sing – and rejoice in only One world.'

P.S.

Before and after the wedding – Ceylonese and English I meet around ask, 'What brings you this time? 'The wedding.' *Which*? I then fish out the Queen's letter.

'More in me than meets the eye,' say I immodestly. 'I enjoy the libraries, music, and walks. Retired from the public eye.'

Elsie Solomons [date unknown]

And there was yet another letter, this time, written on behalf of Lady Diana Spencer from Rear-Admiral Sir Hugh Anion, KCVO, dated 21 July 1981 from Buckingham Palace. Aunt Elsie had sent Lady Diana one of her most precious possessions, the family prayer book. One can but wonder where that book reposes today and accept, rather than question, Aunt Elsie's need to forge that relationship with royalty and the Empire.

At the end of her life Aunt Elsie had no material possessions left. She had discarded or given away the few things that remained, but her strong, indomitable will and mind prevailed to the end, asking for nothing from anybody. All her life she had given: knowledge, donations generously to good causes, love and loyalty to family and friends. Sometimes we could not understand her. "She was too brilliant," "too clever," some of the relations pronounced; and her most caustic occasional comment "Born Fools." That was the only impatience she expressed when her point of view, difficult at times, could not be comprehended.

There was a stage when she was in her eighties (before she moved to the Methodist Home for Elders and the St Nicholas Home), when she stayed on a part of my brother's property in Maho. She lived alone, except for a young married couple who cooked for her, in the estate bungalow. In the past my brother used to spend his weekends there with family and friends. It was a coconut estate, and I remember how the gypsies used to encamp with their talipot-leafed abodes on the adjoining property. She was lonely and missed us and wanted us all, especially at Christmas time, to come and visit her. And we did have a big celebration one Christmas weekend when Aunt Elsie was there.

In one of her later postcards to me there was a barely veiled longing to see me and my family. She was very fond of my husband, who celebrated his birthday on the same day and month as herself. This is what she said: "The girls alone might be bored with their old aunt, but there's a lot of paints and books galore, the new magazines and journals and Pat's library. Since we broke up home, 'we girls' [what she always called Aunts Ila and Amelia and herself,] lived alone. So I am confined to my Trappist cloister. I am cutting out on extravagant Christmas cards and other trappings. Pat will have it all. I won't intrude, my inner circle all dead. I know how simple life is to the single especially retired from the public eyes. For a family daily living is so expensive. Old age has its advantages. Much love. Aunt Elsie."

But she was never forgotten by her old pupils at St John's, Panadura, which had been founded by another relative on my mother's side. She would always speak of her one-time pupils with love and affection, of the famous lawyer politician Colvin R. de Silva, and Wimala de Silva, Vice-Chancellor of Sri Jayawardenapura University.

She never settled for long wherever she went. In the latter stages she wanted to retrace her childhood roots, to go back to one of the small townships she lived in. But she was restless and moved on from one home to another, wanting to change, wanting to reform, wanting to radicalize her environment. She did not want to be a burden to anyone and finally died at the Victoria Home. She who had the most beautiful homes herself – sprawling acres at "Innisfree" in Pannipitiya, with her bedroom furnished in lavender and green. Surrounded by books. Always books. Church work. Guiding. YWCA. Travelling.

After the years had passed, one day I sat down and thought back on that remarkable, exceptional aunt of mine and wrote a play in which she was one of the main protagonists, Ethel Lorensz. The play was titled "Waiting for the Call." It is for the old, the forgotten Burgher ladies.

But first a poem by Aunt Elsie:

The Universe has come to me
I woke at 4 years in 1899 to the mystery of creation
And gradually that the Universe was mine
And all that's in it.
But only if I served it selflessly
As I did for eighty-seven years.
To discover that disabled, paralysed for life -
Bed-bound - the Universe has come to me,
Is all about and around me -
And I, joyfully dead to the world outside.
I saw Hayley's comet in 1909
And circled with it around our Universe
For 76 years and meet again
Linking it with Earth and Man.

A pile of letters lie spread before me, Aunt Elsie's letters which she sent to us, the various family members. Letters written when she was in her eighties:

"...when all's said and done all that counts at the end, is for each of the family to belong in heart and spirit, however scattered. My life's mission was that – helping individual after individual who was left alone, aged, ill, dying, for twenty-five years now. Not only in Ceylon. Mrs Ernst in London, I got her moved to hospital, was with her each time she collapsed. Mrs Van Dort, aged, crippled, blind, would not go to a Home. Only an oil stove for warmth and cooking (no central heating, no gas or electric hot plate even). Starving. After I left burned fatally. Died in hospital. Miss Spencer Shephard's sister, my friend for thirty-five years.

Lived alone in the same room. Crippled in 1970s. Would not go to a Home. I took her a meal every day. She left me her diamond ring but there was no diamond ring to be found! I befriended Tempy for thirty-five years. After I left England she was found dead in her locked room. Ila's neighbour in the next room, aged, crippled yet affluent. After I left she was found dead beside her door. I moved some to the Salvation Army hostel, said it was not their business. That was my life's mission. Several died in misery in their rooms in Wellawatte, Colpetty. Relatives left them alone. None penniless except one in the hostel. That is why I am concerned that Girlie and Elmer don't die alone."

Letter after letter in the latter years of her life spoke of her mission, her caring for those who were lost, lonely, abandoned, sick and dying. She was a totally selfless woman, very strong, self-sufficient, not propped up by any man. Her survival owed nothing to patriarchy.

She had as she called it "an acid wit" and the ability to see herself in the most uncompromising light, but she was one of the staunchest and most dependable of aunts, with great love for her two nieces, my sister Rosemary and myself, and her nephew, my brother Pat. In yet another letter she gave me the bare facts about herself and the family information that I had requested of her:

1. Don Solomon – from 1500 in Taprobane.

2. About 1800, two brothers fell out, one adopted 'Don,' the other 'Solomon.'

Today Dons and Solomons, cousins. Dons, rich businessmen. Solomons, more cultured and less rich.

Dons moved to England.

W.H.S. (William Henry Solomons), father, married Emilie Pereira. Father had two brothers – both died before we children were born. Dr Solomons one of the first colonial surgeons of Ceylon. Fredrick Solomons, Lawyer. WHS educated at St Thomas'. Became Head of Richmond College, Galle about 1885, Resigned in 1896 or so. I was born on Richmond Hill 22nd March 1895. Then WHS and family of seven moved to Anuradhapura. The eldest, Will, continued as a boarder at Kingswood. Came home on holiday at seventeen. All the family down with measles. The story is that he went for a bath to Nuwara Wewa, not knowing he had already contacted measles. It settled on his lungs, and died at nineteen. Buried at Anuradhapura. I was twelve years old.

In 1911 we left Anuradhapura and Ila, Elmer and I became boarders at St John's Panadura. I was there, a pupil, then teacher, then Head Mistress.

I left school at eighteen. Began teaching in January 1915. Private study for my matriculation, English, Latin, French, Elementary Maths, History. Saved up and went to King's College, London 1927-28 for Teachers Diploma.

In 1983 appointed Insprectess of Schools, MBE in 1953 from the Queen's Coronation years. Dedicated my gifts of Public Affairs and public speaking in UK, the European continents, USA and Canada. My private vocation, sanitation and anti-pollution wherever I was from 1933 to the present."

Her letters, the ones that were not morbidly obsessive thoughts and intimations of death – a preoccupation as she grew older – could even be quite witty, abrasively so of course. In one letter to me she said:

"Should have married an undertaker with similar vision. We both would have opened a Super Undertakers Firm.

a) Super Services, same for rich and poor. The rich pay; the poor only a token.

b) A Welfare Service–to the dying (again the rich pay, the poor a token).

c) Whatever their Faith– deaths and funerals prompt, and promote a sense of Mortality, Immortality and Eternity. Temporal and Spiritual, one."

Too, too funny. Here at home for Burgher elders, Elsie Solomons involved with four deaths; moved a rich inmate at midnight to hospital, dying. She died in hospital a few hours later. No matron, no one. I got Dr Vandergert, moved the ninety-year old dying, in one hour. Not dead yet. Only I sent a token of flowers, no one attends a funeral. Now, inmates sent to hospital by relatives. One on the day she was taken to hospital. Another moved two days ago.

So I know, God sent me to Matale, Badulla, Kandy and here (the Home for Elders). My destiny. And Elsie Solomons, wholly independent. Needs no one ill or well, or dying. The cat that walks by itself. The cat that walks in the night.

Iris, Louis B's wife died suddenly. She lived alone, in straitened circumstances, with two adult sons. Elsie again – Saturday to Monday. Not a hymn book in the house. Two padres did not know words of even 'The Lord's My Shepherd,' so Elsie Solomons - solo performance. Neither of the padres could begin the hymns at the cemetery. Elsie Solomons, solo performance again. I must repeat, too, too funny. Myself eighty-seven plus!! And I try to be unobtrusive. There's this comic element in funerals. To fulfill my welfare services. I should have been a millionaire. I had to find the money myself for all the trips from house (at Bambalapitiya flats) to cemetery and back. Took Quickshaws."

Free Masons

When Uncle Elmer died, the Grand Masters of the Free Masons had come prepared in all their regalia to carry out the burial rites. They had to, however, contend with Aunt Elsie, one of the pillars of the Methodist Church. She stepped forward at the graveside at Kanatte and confronted the Grand Masters with all the hymn sheets that had been printed for my grandfather Solomons' funeral almost half a century before. The Free Masons were completely confounded. My Aunt Elsie, small, indomitable, attired completely in black, said in her firm, very authoritarian voice:

"No Free Masons rites. My brother Elmer will be buried according to the rites of the Christian church. We are Methodists, have always been Methodists and will die Methodists. Step forward please."

She beckoned the Methodist padres forward. "Please continue with the obsequies."

The Free Masons were equally determined that their brother Free Mason who had held such high office in the Masonic Lodge both in his country and abroad should not be denied his rights. Where would poor Uncle Elmer's soul end with all these altercations? The mourners were silent until one brave soul began singing "Nearer my God to thee." Voices began to disturb the solemnity of the occasion.

"But Elmer Solomons was a Free Mason, the Grand Master, Head of the Masonic Constituencies of the Lodge," the Free Masons chorused.

"It is our duty," the Head intoned, "to carry out the rights and responsibilities due to his high standing."

The gravediggers with their spades suspended, ready for shovelling earth into the grave after the coffin was lowered, stood waiting expectantly among the piles of wreaths.

"A Christian burial according to the Methodist way. Distribute the hymn sheets," she ordered. When Aunt Elsie wanted something done, no one could gainsay her. The dignified Free Masons were equally determined. There was going to be a tussle.

"Let the Free Masons carry out their rituals and we'll carry out ours," piped up one of the relatives.

"What?" Elsie's tones were grim: "What, and Elmer's soul to be in jeopardy until Salvation Day? We Solomons must all be together when we stand before our Maker. On Judgement day we shall answer to God and God alone. Without the interference and the intercession of the Free Masons."

"We are staunch Methodists and we will do our duty. Harry," she called out to my father, "join me in singing the hymns. You sing bass. I'll sing alto with Girlie. The rest can sing soprano."

The Free Masons were equally adamant to have their way and resisted being dispersed by the Methodist prayers and the Methodist hymns. The Free Masons were expected to walk four times round the grave and place a sprig of acacia flowers in the center of the mound according to the ancient rites. No woman, as my mother told me was permitted to become a Free Mason, but she also told me the story of one woman who had been inquisitive about the goings-on in the Masonic lodge. It aroused her curiosity so much that somehow she had managed to secrete herself inside the hall before the august proceedings began, and was discovered once the assembly had gathered.

"And then what happened?" I asked.

"Well, they caught hold of her and made her a Free Mason too. The only woman to be made one," she answered. Things have changed since then. Women are also allowed to be Free Masons.

My father was later to report on the happenings that day at Kanatte: "The Masons were walking all over the grave, and Aunt Elsie and the Methodist church choir were valiantly singing all the funeral hymns."

With the crowds of mourners pressing in on all sides, it was possible that the Free Masons had no alternative but to carry out the rites in a rather unorthodox manner given the emotions of the moment.

(At any rate strange things happened to the Solomons family at funerals. In one instance my father had gone all dressed up in full mourning suit with the black tie and black armband to attend the funeral of a relative at Kanatte. Being a big, tall strong man he was very welcome at all times as pallbearer. Seeing the procession of pallbearers within the cemetery at a Burgher funeral staggering under the weight of the coffin, he had walked firmly up to them and helped take the load off their shoulders. Grateful as they were, a number of unfamiliar faces had turned to look at him. There was no recognition in their covert glances. "Are you related to the de Bruin family?" one of them asked in a tentative manner. All of them, my father said, were the Dutch Burgher Union type of Burghers with their well-documented genealogies. "No,"he answered, "Isn't this the Bartholomeusz funeral?" "No," answered the grateful pallbearer, "but you're welcome to join us." "Oh God, I'm carrying the coffin at the wrong funeral," my father had said, hastily shifting the load once more onto the de Bruin family mourners' shoulders and walked on at a rapid pace until he stood at the grave of his own family members. At any rate he took it all in his stride.)

One of the Methodist priests was already uttering the funeral prayers. Then the other delivered a peroration. The Free Masons had by this time recouped themselves from the initial disarray and carried on their rites and rituals. The Methodist choir was singing all the hymns that would be as appropriate as they were in the 1930s at my grandfather's funeral to the present day, to be preserved, from generation to generation. The entire gathering began to sing and make melody in their hearts to the Lord. Hymn after hymn followed and the mourners who were very familiar with both words and tune began to sing with great spirit, my father's deep bass and the contraltos of the sisters sounding sonorously in "Guide me O thou Great Jehovah," "Abide with Me," "Now the Day is Over," "In Heavenly Love Abiding."

The Free Masons tried their best to preserve the order and dignity of their own rites. Aunt Elsie, however, felt she had been victor and had won the day for Christianity and Methodism. Uncle Elmer's remains were interred with great solemnity. Both the Free Masons and the Methodists went their separate ways each with a deep sense of satisfaction of duty done. The hymn sheets were gathered once more to be used for the next funeral, which in 1982 would be that of my father's.

Safe Haven
Aunt Elsie was always searching for a safe haven. She could not rest for long in one place. At one time she decided she wanted to return to her childhood home in the provincial township of Matale. She probably felt that this had been one of the happiest times of her life. My mother's family too had shared that childhood in Matale and my mother remembers how tomboyish she herself was, playing in the freedom of gardens filled with fruit-laden guava trees, climbing the highest branches, rifling the guavas, my mother in those long-skirted dresses with frills, pin tucks and lace.

Both the Solomons and the Janszs belonged to large families so they had plenty of companionship among themselves.

The old house in which Aunt Elsie lived perhaps no longer stood there. She must have lived in rented out rooms. Long retired from her school inspectresship she had time on her hands. She looked around her and felt she must begin on a clearing-up campaign in the township. Part of her environmental planning entailed that the old sick, dying derelicts in the streets should be taken away to be cared for and tended in hospitals and not left to draw their last breath in public.

Aunt Elsie's desire to change the face of the world would also get her into trouble. In the township of Matale she began her cleaning up campaign. She gave summary instructions to high officials for the sick and dying to be taken off the streets to hospital. One such woman was found one day lying on the pavement, beside a drain, almost at death's door. Aunt Elsie compelled the authorities, much against their will to lift the woman into an ambulance and take her to hospital. It was against their rank and hierarchy to do so. But they had to do it under Aunt Elsie's stern eye. The authorities greatly resented this elderly woman's intrusion and interference.

She had to undergo a terrible ordeal on the 31st night when she was on her way to Watchnight Service. A group of people had been lying in wait for her knowing that she was a churchgoer and would not miss the midnight service. As she wended her way, all by herself, she heard the words "There she is," and they had surged out of a nearby house, where they had been keeping vigil, and beat her up, 'molested' this old lady, who was in her eighties at that time. The experience was traumatic for her, and she collapsed. Aunt Elsie was brought to the Kandy hospital where she was treated for shock. Then the Methodist padre and his wife Reverend Fernando and Ena, wonderfully kind people – gave her shelter in the Methodist Manse until she recovered.

Aunt Elsie had recognized her assailants but refused to take any steps to bring them to trial – they were important high-ups themselves, and she preferred to forget the incident. She had been happy in Matale as a child and perhaps wanted to recreate that happy past. Aunt Elsie had come in search of her roots – but it had all turned into tragedy for her.

It was her resilient spirit that brought her back to life. She did not retreat even after that experience but continued to engage in her environmentalist and community services, and she bore no grudge against those who had hurt her.

She lived until she reached her nineties, feeling she had accomplished the missions of serving others and maintaining family links which were so dear to her heart.

Auntie Elsie remains in my mind as an indomitable, valiant woman. She was idiosyncratic yet unselfish and very human. Reading her collection of the plays of Bernard Shaw as a young schoolgirl, I mused on the words inscribed from a friend, from an admirer in Cambridge: "Remembering those summer months…"

Memories of Sunnyside Gardens

My Grenier-Jansz aunts lived for many years at Sunnyside Gardens, sleeping in those spacious unchanging bedrooms until the day they died. Auntie Nellie, my spinster aunt, the eldest of the Jansz daughters, shared her room with "Elo dear," Elaine Walbeoff. She, too, was unmarried. Two of her sisters, Daisy and Muriel, had married Hugh and Reginald Jansz, both being brothers. Both Daisy and Muriel added their Walbeoff names to that of the Jansz and made it double-barreled.

Elaine did the most-exquisite embroidery and painted still-life's. She had so much talent. She had silky hair and skin like peaches and cream. My aunts were women who never raised their voices in anger or hysteria, so much so that one wonders how they ever contained their emotions. "Elo" dear wore beautiful ring-velvet coats, and her cheeks, with the pink tinge of a blush rose, were delicately powdered. Auntie Nellie was to give me one day, as a wedding present, an exquisite necklace of crystal beads, but I was so immature, so callow, that I thought it too old-fashioned and returned it.

Sunnyside was full of precious heirlooms, antique furniture, and photographs that would have illustrated a whole historical era. Nothing was preserved after Auntie Nellie's death; they remained for a short time while Uncle Bertie was alive. But before his death many things began to be sold off, furniture, crystal, cut glass, porcelain, and after his death, everything was lost, plundered. The rosewood dining table, the sideboards and what-not, the blue glass table with ebony frame and clusters of roses pressed between sheets of glass – no one knows where they are now or in whose possession. Even the only family portrait of my grandparents, and the cameo photogrph of my grandmoter, vanished.

It is easy to succumb to the pangs of nostalgia, sniff with longing at the pot-pourri of memories, but when you are young you are the least preoccupied with heritage, tradition, inheritance or the past. There are so many other preoccupations, especially the forming of one's own attachments. We had too little time for them, those aunts or that bachelor uncle of ours. Felt, perhaps, that their world was too sealed off and closed in from the one that we were newly exploring. It is only now, in this time, that we become explorers and discoverers in this crumbling anthill of the past, and it is historical necessity to re-enter those dark mazes, passages and labyrinths, to find out the source of our beginnings.

Spending an evening at Sunnyside was very different to life at home. I sat quietly in a corner of the drawing room, reading from the books neatly arranged on an occasional table, aware of the comforting presence of the objects around me; the piano on which the aunts played set beneath the arch which separated the living from the dining area, the glass-fronted cupboard just beside one of the doors that led to that whitewashed room where the two unmarried boarders lived, teachers at Kingswood College, Gertrude Thorpe and Millicent Clements. They were of Eurasian stock, came from the Uva province of tea plantations and had experienced the influence of missionary activity in that area through the evangelistic work that was carried on with so much fervour in the latter part of the nineteenth century.

There were many poignant, even tragic, stories that emerged from those colonial liaisons. Sometimes the offspring were sent off to Roman Catholic convents and colleges, where they were boarded, seldom going home even for holidays. Many of the sons became planters in turn or discovered their vocations as priests or teachers. We had both a teacher as well as a monk in the Roman Catholic College where I once taught, and when their father, a British planter, went back home on furlough he brought back an English wife. His children by the first alliance were not allowed to come to the Big House. Many of those Eurasians looked European, with brown or gold or red hair, fair skin and light eyes. They were a racial minority that had been created through colonialism. Many of them were provided for by their fathers and became planters on estates that they inherited. With death, migration and political changes the estates often changed hands and ceased to maintain any links with the colonial past.

To maintain Sunnyside must have been difficult. The piano was sold one day. Aunt Nellie, among her other accomplishments, gave piano lessons once upon a time. My mother's cousins, Ethel, May and Lou Grenier, once told me that Aunt Nellie was very proud of Sunnyside but she did not know who would ultimately inherit it, especially because grandfather Jansz had left a strange will. The last surviving heir would inherit everything – there again the will applied to his daughters and to Uncle Bertie, who was lame and could not go to work like the other brothers. But along the way so much happened. My mother never thought she would get "her share" of the property. Aunt Nellie needed a stable income and so she took almost sixteen perches of land and built a little cottage, which she rented out to a retired Anglo-Indian couple, the Alymores, who lived there with their Persian cats until they, too, went back 'home' to England to spend their last days. Finally, cousin Evangeline, inherited the house and now it is in the hands of the Lighthouse Church.

Aunt Nellie was a valiant woman but she really could not cope with children any more by the time we were born, although I am told she had longed to adopt me as a baby. When my mother had typhoid, and was in hospital, my father brought us all to Sunnyside. He was desperate as there was no one to care for us two little girls. On that day he took us out to lunch at Green Café where his friend, Cox Sproule's wife, ran the ménage. My sister and I sat at the table with platters of salad, lettuce and tomatoes and slices of fried seer fish before us, not even trying to eat, missing our mother and father who had gone to hospital, until a very kind unknown lady got up from her table, cut up everything on our plates to make it easy for us to eat... Yes, the kindness of strangers, an early memory, like so many others that remain in my mind.

Childhood had so many colours and flavours for me–fragrances too: Aunt Nellie's delicious guava jelly and Aunt May's Easter Simnel cake. Simnel cake – a flavour I tried to recapture many times over but never succeeded. At last, one day I tracked down the recipe in my mother's copy of Foulsham's Guest Entertainer. It lies before me as I write: "SIMNEL CAKE: 8 oz. Castor sugar, 6 oz. Butter, 4 oz. Margarine, 5 eggs, one pound flour, 4 oz. Ground almonds, 6 oz. Chopped mixed peel, half pound currants..." The cake remains a dream in my mind, together with chocolate Easter eggs in brilliant coloured foil from Millers, and Aunt Ila's hardboiled eggs, the shells dyed in cochineal, scarlet, green – yes, emerald or viridian – beautiful to look at but so mundane to eat. Even today, my cousin Diana Albrecht Atkins, who lives in Melbourne, recollects the unforgettable flavours of Aunt Nellie's guava jelly and chutneys.

My tongue too sampled and remembers these flavours. Somehow they belonged to those who created those poetic dishes out of imaginations that never had the opportunity to find other means of expression… Like my sister-in-law's mother's pol-kiri badun and caramel puddings. Rita Toussaint Vanlangenberg, my brother's mother-in-law, was lavish in everything she did. Her caramel puddings baked a lovely golden brown on the surface, were rich with eggs, milk, sugar and caramelized sugar syrup. The Vanlangenberg table was always laden with food: chicken, fish, beef, spiced sausage-lingus, salt beef, pickles, chutneys, fried brinjal and potato badun, and what not. When Ma Van bought dress materials, she bought many lengths at a time and her wardrobe was filled with neatly folded piles of materials. She herself was still full of life and vitality, but an invalid husband kept her at home in the latter years, housebound. When she went marketing she hired a taxi, which became filled with vegetables, fruits and everything under the sun, with enormous cabbages piled on the roof rack of the taxi…

So the past was remembered by taste, flavours which still lurk in the crevices of memory. It is I who now live in Sunnyside with my family, welcoming relatives who live abroad and returned home as on a pilgrimage. The garden is no longer filled with Uncle Bertie's roses and hydrangeas. I tried to preserve one last tree, that tree became gnarled and thorny. The delicate, spangled ferns still proliferate. The land has diminished, most of it sold off for a song. It is here that I returned 15 years after uncle Bertie's death. All I have of him is a single photograph, Auntie Maude's room is now my study. I sit facing the garden, at my writing table, watching the birds, squirrels, lizards as I write and think. A single parrot has appeared among all the other birds perched on the biling tree, enjoying the fruit juice… It is here that I scrutinize my identity, my inheritance and write my poems.

My Sunnyside aunts, uncles and cousins at the wedding of Aunt Ethel and Uncle Harry, Grenier Jansz, 1907.

XII

MIGRATIONS

My sister-in-law Iona Vanlangenberg Solomons, Dia Vanderwert Tsung as a child (my sister Rosemary's daughter), and my daughters Parvathi and Devi. Iona and Dia migrated to Australia and USA in the 1970s.

Migrations

The Burgher migrations are starting anew, take wing
Spread out their vari-coloured plumes, birds of a
Feather, flocking the clouds, feeding heavily on the way
Filling their beaks and pouches with silvery fish
That leap up from fecund waves.

Carrying their pillows with them this time – not their
Proven genealogies of European descent – stuffed
With kapok but the seeds are shrunk into dryness,
Won't take root in alien soil, the boll pods tossed
Away, the tight curling fleece unsnarled twining
Round your fingers, the fluff clings webbing your
Palm as you pack it tightly probing the tweaked
Out corners, into their cotton case, and as you lie
Pressing your head, on that softness, dreams
Burst open like cotton pods in sunlight, escaping
From the sun seared casing and falling onto earth
With its herbs and wild flowers and golden
Selalihinis that you will never see again, your
Lolling head whirring with currents of strange
New winds, sinking into uneasy slumber
In a country where your exploration just begins
Ducking your head against the boomerangs that are thrown
Around you as your walkabout starts, searching,
Searching for that dreamtime on street after crowded
Street, learning the new patois.

The pillows down under, you tell me, are stuffed
With feathers from the plucked blue-white bodies
Of slaughtered birds, their intrusive beaks tear
Your dreams apart and you see a naked goose,
Flesh all crinkled, stubbly with left over quill
Marks, dangling from its gibbet, it's your new
Psyche, you view a blue-white body in its chilled
Death, feathers gouged out into hieroglyphs
Of wounds, glazed eyes staring at nothing,
All trussed up for cooking, not the graceful hansa of
Temple frescoes and moonstones with delicate
Outstretched neck stalking now through the darkest
Nights of your loneliness; you learn the new folklore,
The legends of this habitation, inscribing their graffiti
On the cave walls of your mind, your voice takes on
The new rhythms and you lose the old cadences
Through which your thoughts sang; the iridescence
Of the violet blue peacocks flashburns the edges of
Your mind leaving you with the smell of singed leaves
In your hands as the forest smokes, smouldering in the
Dry season, the waterholes lingering with rust coloured
Moss and the wild boars rooting about with their
Sharp tushes;
But your head swims with dreams like a flurry
Of fish harpooned into bloodletting, they don't belong
Here, those fleece packed pillows that promised you
Argosies of dreams, yet you cling to them, hold them
Against your breast as tears drip soaking into them.
"It's all feathers," you remember they said, "of goose
Or swansdown, they tickle your pate and ears;

Your nostrils flare with sneezes, from pillows of feathers.
What have you come to seek here, the stories of your childhood,
The clutch of golden eggs wrested from threatening ogres?

So you take your kapok with you, to dream
Of a country left behind, the fire on the hearth,
The magpie on the branch, orioles, ripe yellow as jak pods
And selalihinis in gardens of bougainvillea and fern
Singing in your ears as you come home tired from assembly
Lines in factories, clipping tickets on station platforms,
Ironing baskets of laundry, bending over steaming piles
Of linen, stretching out starched sleeves, buttoning shirts,
Letting your heart drip down in beads of moisture
On the body of the garment, ironing sweat and tiredness
Into the fibres of the fabric which clothes the bodies
Of naked strangers, press doorbells to collect your dues,
Come back home, exhausted, to a supper of steak,
Chicken, fried fish fingers tasting your rice and curry
Like some old hangover... forgotten the evenings filled
With fireflies on the mugerine bush, the glow worms in your
Garden of jasmines and mango trees, you're the snail
travelling in the grass, the shell suddenly cracks and you're
Here, exposed, your moist flesh caught in the glare of sun
Shimmers like glass and then grows dull, hovering in shade;
Turns colour, flesh the colour of dark stone, no protection
Here, only a prefabricated cover hides you and you sniff
The threat of burning leaves and earth in crackling bush fires;
Your skin changes gradually, your voice too,
You're a snail, you can't escape like a gazelle or kangaroo
Away, swiftly across an ocean, back to this island,

You wait for a transmigration, a metamorphosis, as you cross
The Tropic of Capricorn into this new land where
The nuggets of gold feel hard against your palm.

You've come here to escape from what?
Genocide, refugee camps, fear of unemployment,
Social disturbances, communal clashes, an uncertain
Future or because of the children.

And now you come back, re-visit me, your hair
Lorna, that was once waist length, gold brown
Flecked with burnished tint now wreath of ebon curls.
Your lips carmine bright and you, Malcolm, unchanging;
You both look so young as if you've re-entered Paradise.
You look at me and say, "There's no place
Like home"; but what was home to you and me?
Eating Christmas puddings and rich cake, keeping salt
On the table, putting up the Christmas tree, fragrant
Evergreens; now you show me albums, interiors,
Tables laden with food, trimmed perfect lawns,
A daughter in a bridal gown.

We look at each other for perhaps the last time.
Home is now a place where the bombs go off
Almost at our doorstep and the waterways thick
With salmon shoals of blood red.
I shall put up a wreath of blood-red Hollyberries,
Remembering you, remembering you.

Diasporic Travellers

(These are excerpts from letters from my niece Dia Vanderwert Tsung, in Colorado, USA; followed by a poem by Devi, my daughter living in Toronto, Canada.)

"I did a lot of work on my garden this summer, and still managed to not damage the sense of wildness conferred by my ancient apple tree and small plum grove, which are all overgrown by two unrestrained grape vines. I have two clay firepots in the back yard and two wood piles, and have barbecues and meals at the picnic tables under the apple tree. At night I hear the crickets, and the train whistles, and the light traffic on the front street. In many ways, both inside and out, I feel that this house, with its fruit trees and books and old furniture, resembles 321, Peradeniya Road. I regret that none of this can be shared with you, and that I was not able to share any of it with Grandpa. When I look back, I see that he and all of us have always lived solitary lives, whether or not we lived in close proximity with other people. As I hear you describe your sense of solitariness, I wonder if we feel this way only because we are conscious and aware, and it is only those who are not who manage to evade the realization of essential aloneness. I experience a sense of connection with some of the writers whose books I read, which at times seems more real than the flesh and blood connections of my friends.

I have always felt that some part of you got internalized in me because I found them in your bookshelves. Looking up from my desk I see *Justine, Balthazar, Mountolive, Clea* (the Alexandria quartet, by Lawrence Durrell), *Seven Japanese Tales, The White Pony, An Anthology of Asian Literature* (with its translation of the Gita

Govinda by George Keyt), and many others. I listen to Fado (Amalia Rodriguez) and Cuban music (did you have a record by Juan Serrano?) and Jean Sablon, etc. My international taste in music came directly from you, as did my fondness of Lieder, and Ella Fitzgerald. You bought the first radio (the old Grundig) and the first record player I ever saw. Now I listen to everything from Maria Callas to Carnatic and Hindustani music, of which I have a huge collection.

I remember all the books you bought me, *Amal Biso, Hasan of the Desert, Chendru,* and the art classes you took me to with Cora Abrahams, and your friends from "The Young Artists Group," and I still love Goya (from the cover of one of your records) and Modigliani. I remember your Matisse-like paintings, and your plant still-lifes, and the objects you returned with from your trips to Italy and India and Iran – ashtrays, my brown cotton skirt with the little mirrors, your brass lamp, your flowered wool rug... I remember the bus trips we took to old temples (Degaldoruwa) and the concerts at St Anthony's (Maria Goretti). Your influence on me was profound and enduring, and I feel that I was shaped by you in so many indelible ways. I read a lot of history (Roman and Greek) and recognize the early evidence of declining empire that America cannot or will not see. I love good poetry and good writing, and a literary sensibility that came directly from you."

"...but the question I am pondering on is, who or what is the me you love. I don't know how important it is to know of someone in order to know him or her... Perhaps we connect to each other on some essential level built upon memory and impression, and perhaps once the seeds of love have been planted in infancy, the incidents of our natures came to have no bearing on the reasons that inspire others to love us.

I am now thinking of Grandpa's love, which was indeed the single anchor of my childhood. I know beyond a doubt that were he alive today, he would love me in the way he always did and perhaps in a way resembling how you love me now. I was a very happy child when I lived with him at 321. I had a home and friends and books and toys. Grandpa used to take Cluny [pet dog] and me for walks up the hill and teach me the names of the trees and plants, the names of the stars and the Greek alphabet, which was probably how I taught myself to read Greek. I don't remember what you refer to as 'my miraculous escape crossing Peradeniya Road.' What happened?"

(*My niece was about three years old when she opened the gate of our house at 321 Peradeniya Road and, since at that hour the main road was clear, toddled across onto the other side. Then she decided to return, and as she began that saga journey to her safe haven, the screech of traffic being brought to a halt was heard and voices screamed out at the jeopardizing of the child's safety. We, her young carer Menike and myself, rushed out to rescue her, and were roundly berated by those who had applied their brakes. The child was safe. We castigated ourselves on our negligence, especially Menike, who was preparing her milk at that time. It was a miraculous escape crossing.*)

"I remember Grandma had my clothes sewn out of your old skirts by the dhoby's daughter Cecily in Deiyangewela. I remember the toys you brought me from India – a bullock cart and toy acrobats, and the brown skirt with kutch work which I wore all the time. I remember brightly coloured flowered pyjamas and a dark green corduroy pair of pants you had the tailor sew for me. I remember a pair of shorts with leopard spots and a purple blouse. I remember coming home from school and bringing melted sweets from the tuck shop, in the front pocket of my school uniform.

I think now that this was the fabric which supported my later life and helped me survive and become who I am.

I find stories written by southerners (I mean the American south) to have a ring of familiarity, because they echo the themes of interiority and gentility tenaciously retained within straitened circumstances that I got a sense of growing up in Ceylon. I think that Burghers have something in common with the immediately following generations of confederate families that survived the US civil war. Then there is also the sense of strongly demarcated social distinctions which separate and define people of different classes, as they live side by side and forever divided from each other in the lush green humidity of their environment. Do you know the Solomons woman (now living in Australia) who recently wrote a novel about life in Ceylon?

Here in the southwest, in sight of the Rocky Mountains, we have an airier and more open climate, with distinct seasons, and varied terrain. Americans are fast losing their geographical and cultural distinctions, but the east coast and west coast and south produced very different types of people, and different sorts of writers. I think that having lived more than half my adult life here in the southwest, I have been influenced by my surroundings, and perhaps it is this influence that you refer to as my 'strength.' It was hard won, because we all grew up with the continuing sense of social insecurity which is a great hindrance to developing personal independence. Even as an American 'hybrid,' I cannot imagine living with a curtailment of my autonomy at all..."

(Dia Vanderwert Tsung, Colorado, USA)

Four Cobras

Four cobras follow me stalking as I
dream in dread orange
black designed hood
everywhere I turned

at home I would have
drifted to the kitchen cups
of coffee in blue-white delicate
aromas china tell them

awaiting their interpretations
danger's sometimes good
how I miss it sometimes
as someone scrapes coconuts

slivers of white sweet and
moulds red balls of flame chillies
hot fire in kitchens kitten
paws rasping on glass windows

wet paw marks fur occasionally
floats into open dishes
as dogs yawn with impatience
the hedge today is full

hibiscus plants thrive in wet
rubbish heap the trees are full
of knife wounds hurting endearing
it for more fruit which appear
as tears sticky in red
and white appear on its trunk.

(Devi Arasanayagam, Maine, USA, 1989)

Early Migrants

Stories are also revelations about other people's lives in which there were intimations of joy and sorrow. The beautiful Belle Mills once opened her suitcase, packed and ready with her trousseau to take to Australia in those early days of emigration. Folded in among the carefully packed clothes in the suitcase was a cardboard box with her wedding gown and long tulle veil wrapped in folds of tissue. The embroidered scalloped veil would drift from her shoulders into a billowing train to be borne by flower girls in flounced and frilled ankle-length dresses and silver hair-bands. Belle's fiancé, a Burgher boy who had migrated earlier, was going to marry her in Australia. Belle was beautiful, with soft brown clusters of curls tumbling on her shoulders and amber-coloured eyes. I looked at her with admiration at that time. I still didn't know why people were migrating to Australia. It was a world I knew nothing of.

Then one day whispers were heard. Belle's fiancé had married an Australian girl and "let her down," jilting her. It was a sad story. She had gone to Australia and then discovered his perfidy. "Sue him for breach of promise. You have all his love letters," the elders advised her. Belle was inconsolable but was against going to Courts. Eventually the entire family emigrated to Australia and became lost among the other emigrants. Belle's mother was a lively woman, full of vitality. Mrs Mills was a fervent follower of the new charismatic churches, which were making their presence felt in our township. She would often invite us to the Hall where the Pentecostal assemblies were held, to view lantern slides presented by visiting American missionaries. Mrs

Mill's father had been a famous British sportsman and planter, Harry Storey. My father had his autobiography, and Mrs Mills was very proud to point out his photograph to us, a black-and-white plate showing him in sportsman's clothes, a pith helmet and hunting gear, his gun upright beside him, standing over the game he had bagged. He had long drooping moustaches too. His daughter had wanted that book. Perhaps my father did give it to her. Had he known Harry Storey just as he had known so many planters and administrators during the British Raj? Soon those families, too, the offspring of sometimes indigenous alliances would all emigrate, and only then stories would be recorded through memory and recollection in the mind of someone who had felt the touch of those lives on her own sensibilities.

And what were the other stories I recorded on the yet unwritten script of my mind? That of a brother and sister belonging to a Dutch-Burgher family, in which the son had been given away for adoption to foster parents. The brother and sister were not to meet until years later when they were adults. Both of them were exceptionally good-looking. Totally unknowing they both fell in love with each other. They had a passionate love affair. Their greatest wish was to marry. It was then that the thunderbolt fell. If they married it would be an incestuous affair. Too late, too late to break off that intense and powerful bonding. No, they could never marry, nor could they break away from each other. I remember the girl with her beauty, her vibrant personality, dark curling hair, and perfectly shaped features. Were they twins even? I can't remember. They loved each other with great intensity. Perhaps those kinship bonds were instinctual and inherent within them. She eventually did marry someone else. I do not know whether he ever married, but brother and sister had lived together and no other relationship could replace what they had lost. They are both long gone out of my life, but legends remain and are still remembered.

Some of the Burgher girls married servicemen during the war. Dr Anthonisz's daughter was one, the other was Doreen La Brooy. At the Variety entertainments staged in the Trinity College Hall for servicemen, Doreen was famous for her snake dance. Draped in black, her supple body and graceful arms simulated all the sinuousities of a snake uncoiling from its basket. Sheila de Zylva, a young teacher, married an Anglo-Indian soldier named Viyera and died in childbirth. The doctor was unfortunately blamed for her death, as it was said the Caesarian operation had been tragically unsuccessful.

Olga Anthonisz and many other Burgher girls married British Army officers and emigrated to England, their connections with the island severed for all time. Dr Anthonisz's son Brian was another left-behinder, who stayed on in the old house. As far as I know, Brian never followed a profession but did his own thing, without any pressure being exerted on him by his parents. He had his romantic affairs of the heart, he was both charming and handsome, as well as a wonderful conversationalist. He would talk for hours on end on every subject under the sun. I remember him telling me all about the Ancien Regime in France, a kind of mini lecture, after reading one of my history examination papers. He was, by the way a nephew of Warden de Saram of St Thomas' College, Colombo. It was sad in the end seeing, Brian who used to be a habitué of the Queens Hotel, Kandy, living it up in grand style, having a lonely cup of tea at Paiva's Café, almost all his Burgher contemporaries having emigrated.

Brian was one of the left-behinders like Valerie Winn, who was sent to England to do a course in catering and hoteliering. She was an only child, the daughter of Dr and Mrs Winn. One of the highlights of her sojourn in England was that, as a lovely young debutanté, she was presented to the Queen at Buckingham Palace. She returned to Ceylon where she eventually married and had a family. I used to meet her in Colombo and she told me of her great desire to write a narrative of her Burgher recollections. It was a wish that was never realized. We each went our own ways. Valerie died shortly afterwards, tragically. I remember her as a lovely, soft-spoken young woman with a genteel upbringing in Kandy. I also remember her as a child performing an elfin dance with my cousin Yvonne Jansz. They both belonged to that world. The imaginary childlike world of fantasy and enchantment, recapturing a world of innocent belief in magic and the supernatural. When we were hostel boarders at Girls' High School, the big girls used to help us create Fairy Gardens which we filled with silver wands, stars, miniature chalices, strewing them among the flowers and ferns we planted. The next morning we would find 'signs' that the fairies had visited these gardens, discovering magic circles or fairy rings of a white powdery substance. In our imaginations a fairyland really existed in the country of our dreams.

Emigrant Voices: Evangeline

My cousin Evangeline had married a handsome bachelor quite smitten by her charms (and she certainly was charming with her beautiful eyes, dark curling hair, ivory complexion). They had a lovely wedding at St Paul's Church in Kandy, Evangeline all dressed in white lace, with white tulle frothing from a tiara, and carrying one of Uncle Bertie's Bouquets. After she went to Australia, one of the many Burgher emigrants, the couple lived apart, as her husband preferred life in Ceylon. Evangeline went across because her children were already there. She loved ballroom dancing and took part in competitions where she excelled in waltzes, tangos, fox-trots, the rhumbas and other Latin American dances. After Evangeline and her Prince Charming parted amicably, she married John, English-Australian. When she returned on one of her visits she was full of stories of her "Second Marriage."

"Did I show you my wedding video with John, my second husband?"

"No," we chorused, "only the photographs."

"You should have seen the video – the flowers, the cake the buffet – the whole house was videoed. My friend Bonnie was also there."

"Bonnie," I asked, "Who's she?"

"Yes, Bonnie. Did I tell you how I stood up for her among those bitchy Australian women? We were all having tea together at our workplace when I heard them talking about her behind her back. I heard whispers, Bonnie this and Bonnie that. I was sipping my cup of tea with my head down. Then I heard: '...man mad.' I couldn't stand it; I sat up. Then I got onto a chair so that I could command their attention and shouted above their chatter. 'How dare you say these things about Bonnie behind her back. Say them to her face.' Just then Bonnie walks in. 'What is it, Evangeline?'

"'Bonnie, you know what these women are saying about you? They're saying terrible things about you. Yes, talking behind your back.' People can be pretty bitchy there. 'Piss off,' they say. Using four-letter words. One of the nurses told me, 'Get stuffed.' Yes, I defended Bonnie because she was my friend."

Courage was a typical characteristic of Evangeline, integrity part of her make up. Evangeline continued her story: "Bonnie stopped coming to see me after some time. She had a reason. 'I've found the real thing!' she told me. 'I've found the correct man.' Of course that means living together. When John suggested that we should live together, I put my foot down, 'Nothing doing,' I said. 'I'm a Seventh Day Adventist and it's only marriage for me. No living together. You'll have to bear with my religion.' Six months before his wife had left him. 'Everything was *tittha*, bitter, for him,' she said, making a wry mouth.

"It was Bonnie who suggested we go to the Singles Club for dancing. You know me, my feet are always tapping out rhythms... 'I'll bring you a partner,' said Bonnie. 'I don't want any beer bellies,' I said.

"Well, gradually, John and I became closer. Give me two years, I said, and I'll make my decision. One day he told me to keep my feet up and he went into the pantry and did all the washing up... 'No curry lunches this time,' he said. 'We'll have roast pork, roast ham, roast chicken, roast turkey and varieties of salad.' And John prepared it all himself."

"And the roses, Evangeline, tell, us about the roses," we pleaded.

"Yes, when I went back to Australia there was a huge bouquet of red roses from John placed on our bed. Ah, at last I have love. Love. I am loved from top to toe."

Evangeline was the eternal romantic. She searched for, she believed in true love perhaps because she had lost her mother at a very young age. Her father had been stern with strict moral values. One day, her mother had called Evangeline to her bedside when she was ill. She must have been concerned about Evangeline's future, her sense of vocation. "What do you want to be when you grow up?" she asked her daughter.

"I want to be a ballet dancer," she said, lifting herself on her toes. "Think again," Aunt Daisy said without much enthusiasm. "I want to go to Hollywood and become a film star." "You want to be the cynosure of all eyes," Aunt Daisy had said even more disapprovingly.

Evangeline continued: "Nobody thought I was beautiful. I used to stand before the mirror and say, 'I'm beautiful, no? I'm beautiful, no? I have beautiful eyes, a flawless complexion, long legs, a high waist and perfect teeth. A lovely smile too.' And Auntie Dolly, I can't forget her; I might have also been a spinster if it hadn't been for her. But I am beautiful am I not? And my figure, it's still good. And at last I have love. Love. John gives me all the love."

Lucky, lucky Evangeline to feel that illusion was reality, to forget the hurt she felt at any barbs aimed at her. Was Romance the El Dorado these Janszs pursued? Did they read all those romantic novels that were in fashion during those times they lived in? To those who imagined that marriage was the be-all and end-all of life: spinsterhood was something to be dreaded. Evangeline read out the fictions of her life as she spoke to us. We were her audience, her Third World cousins, and to us she unfolded those great sagas of her journeys on the continent of her life.

"One of my nieces approached me one day," Evangeline told us. "'Auntie Evangeline I want to ask you a question.' 'Ask, child.' 'Do you still… at sixty-five? And which was better, your first or your second honeymoon?' 'Child, my first was a disaster. Why child, it was over in five minutes." Evangeline gave a tinkling bubbling laugh. Champagne bubbles bursting in the air, floating about like miniature festive balloons. "Tick, tuck, tuk!" She snapped her fingers. Her face softened. She smiled with a beatific expression on her face.

"My second – beautiful, natural, love… bathed in love I must say," she uttered in a satisfied manner. "But I can't forget. I met my husband at Auntie Dolly's and Uncle Harry's. Prince Charming. I still feel for him you know. After all, he is the father of my children, the children who filled my life. Children I adore."

The courtship had been a romantic one and Evangeline had made a radiant bride. Evangeline's wedding photograph had appeared in the Girls' High School magazine.

Her husband once went to Melbourne on a holiday. He couldn't stay there for his full three months. "Some holiday!" he told us. "Not a soul in the streets after everyone has gone out to work. Dead silence. I had offers for babysitting. Pocket money, and to keep myself occupied, reliable too. Babysitting? Not for an elderly man like myself. Mornings were so lonely. Not a human voice to be heard. You could be murdered and who would know? What could I do, shut up in a silent, lonely room, gazing at the precise angle of cushions which Evangeline arranged in her ordered apartment – talk to myself? Of course I had a wonderful time when I first got there. Everybody wanted to give me a good time. They took me here and there, parks, zoos, picnics, promised me an allowance, monthly of course, if I'd stay. My son too wanted me to babysit. I wish I could have, I loved my grandchild but would I have coped? Evangeline took the responsibility in Ceylon when I was working outstation. Well, I had to refuse gracefully. 'Not for me,' I said, 'I'll come back one day.' I was happy to return. No place like home."

Fortunately Willie had a home in Ceylon to return to. He came back to stay in Evangeline's house, "Bethel," the one she had inherited later from Aunt Norah. Her first home was "Friedenheim," built by her father, my uncle Hugh, on grandfather Jansz's property. My grandfather had also given Hugh Jansz right of way on his own land, as there was no other access to the house. Colonel Piachaud did not want his private road used. Evangeline had reserved a special room for her beloved husband where he could be completely himself, whenever he did come home, from the outlandish parts where he was stationed on Excise duty at one stage in wild elephant country among the sugar cane plantations.

After Evangeline sold "Friedenheim," the Light House Mission Church was built there. Evangeline's second house "Bethel," which was built by Auntie Nellie, was also eventually sold to the church. She was very generous-hearted to various charities and relations. Her first husband did not live long after he moved out and lived in Hettipola with relatives. He died soon afterwards. Evangeline went back to Australia and planned a world cruise with John. She enjoyed her money while in Sri Lanka.

"I have breakfasted at the Queen's Hotel, dear," she said, "I don't eat bacon and eggs now – fruit juice, toast, marmalade, butter, fruit, a pot of tea, and I fancied pancakes and maple syrup for breakfast at the Ramada." Evangeline eating kiribath at a planter's house years before was told not to use her fingers – kiribath with a fork, western style. "'You have to have standards,' the pukka Sahib of the tea estates said, 'You can't let yourself down before the servants. They're used to European masters'."

"No pockets in our shrouds," she said to me, "Dine with me at the 'Flower Song.' I'm sixty-five now and I'm going to enjoy life. When John gets his superannuation fund we're going to visit England and fly to Canada."

Uncle Hugh had been careful. He saved. "He made me return the pair of shoes I bought for my twenty-first birthday. I had to take it back to the shop in Matara. I cried my heart out. He said it was too expensive. I went through hard times in Melbourne too. I was out of job, 'redundant.' So I went for a TV audition, dear. Paid my hard-earned savings, three hundred dollars. You know, we were tested for talent for TV ads and so on, to see whether we were photogenic. It was one big swindle. The man who was in charge of the audition was a con-man. There were all these Australian women sitting there, so excited, thinking they were potential TV stars. Then the man said, 'I want people to go upstage and introduce themselves.' Some of them mumbled; others could hardly express themselves, stumbling over the words. Then I walked up with confidence, back straight, head held up high. My English clear, my voice rang out like a bell: 'I come from the beautiful island called Sri Lanka. I was educated in English in a private missionary school. I was a teacher of Domestic Science. I have a beautiful house in Sri Lanka with maids to do my work. I know I can be a success on TV.' I felt confident of being chosen.

"What a fraud! The man who was in charge of the audition visited me in my flat one day. I was alone. He wanted to peer through the front opening of my dress to see whether I had the correct TV figure. I wasn't having any of it. And then there was that big convention at the hotel I was working in – some Peace and Friendship Convention. A tall handsome man was the chairperson. A real Valentino. He came into the room when I was making the bed and he just swooped on me and gave me a lingering kiss. Yes, child, that's exactly what he did. I'd never been kissed like that before in all my life. He kept phoning me up from wherever he moved on to. Then I didn't hear from him for a long time. I phoned him up at his last address. A woman's voice answered. It was curt, cold: 'Oh, so you're another of them. He's had so many calls.' I hung up."

When my cousin Evangeline came visiting with tins of Australian cheese, International Roast coffee and local chocolates, she told us of a friend's plight in Melbourne.

"What do you think happened one day? She's in a home for senior citizens, a young man entered the premises, went upstairs and, would you believe it, stripped the old ladies to the buff! – It's a wonder they didn't die of chills. Then he came downstairs, raided the fridge and ate everything inside – you know there's food in such quantities, pans of soup just emptied the next day, and hundreds of boiled eggs. I used to make sandwiches, how can you waste dozens and dozens of them, all to be thrown away into the garbage bins... Anyway, thank goodness my friend wasn't upstairs at the time, didn't know a thing had happened. Poor soul. At least she wasn't subjected to such indignities.

"I open the door of my apartment, silently enter my room, peer into my wardrobe, and look into every nook and cranny. Dear, you don't know who could be lying in wait for you and you must be careful returning late from work. A man stalked me one night. I was so afraid Anyway I switch on the light, tip-toe up to the wardrobe, open the doors. I say a little prayer and breathe a sigh of relief. 'Safe,' I whisper under my breath."

Evangeline had always loved ballroom dancing. Won all the gold medals at home – tangoing, rhumbaing and waltzing through life. "She took me," my brother Pat recounts, "to one of those dance halls, not like the ballrooms at the Queens and the Grand, elderly people doing the most elaborate steps, stretching out across the floor. Entertainment at three dollars for the privilege, but for me it certainly wasn't. Pure agony it was."

Cousin Lorna, writes in her elegant fist from her Private Nursing Home: "I'm seventy-seven but I am growing old gracefully. I still love life and people and I am young at heart." For me cousin Lorna would never age. In my mind, in my memory I preserved her Reynold's – like portrait, for ever.

Evangeline wrote: "Well, I'm a fair dinkum Ausssie now. The moment I stepped onto this land I felt I belonged. But I've had hard times. You know, at one of the places I worked, a home for geriatrics, I was beckoned by the Sister-in-Charge. 'Come here,' she ordered. Her expression was supercilious. Had a firm mouth. 'What are you doing? Go immediately and perform a manual.' 'What's a manual?' I asked curiously. 'All these old men whose bowels are stuffed with laxatives, Agarol and what not. You have to insert two fingers and pull the stuff out.' There were reports about me. 'Nurse,' the sister says, 'you don't work hard enough. Look, you've not even trained but you're drawing a large salary.' Oh, those old men. 'Nurse,' his feeble voice was always calling out, 'give me a thrill.' I do a back sponge. Take a wet towel and rub all over. The sister put me out of the room, locked the door. I heard his feeble voice going on and on... 'Nurse, give me a thrill.' He was 85 years old."

Let's Go Down Under

What did the Burghers fear that compelled many of them to give up a lifestyle they had been privileged to enjoy for years, to emigrate from Sri Lanka to Australia in the 1950s? It should be clarified that not all Burghers enjoyed a privileged lifestyle. I myself recollect the Burgher brother and sister who did the rounds of certain houses in Colombo armed with a basket of homemade chutneys and jams, with a teaspoon to sample the product first before purchasing it. And there were those who came home regularly every month for their 'monthly allowance.' The grandmother who stood at the gate to collect the charity given by my father to take home – so the grandchildren would not have to beg. It was a matter of pride that the young girls should not be sent out to service – domestic service. And there were the others, too, to whom we would 'pass down' clothes: good strong coats and trousers of twill and tussore, party dresses, home frocks, for the poor but respectable families we knew. There were also Christmas hampers packed with Christmas cheer for those who looked forward to the celebration of festivities. They were all part of that life we lived, and from an early age I was aware of Mrs Cramer's work-worn hands, of Peterson, the Portuguese-Burgher shoemaker who hand made all my father's shoes, and a myriad others to whom a rupee or two would in those days make a vast difference.

For the Burghers who emigrated to Australia, a new lifestyle opened out. We were always listening to stories of how "they now owned property, possessing their own house, perhaps two or more,' each family member had their own car, good jobs, education, plenty of money, could go on holidays and cruises, return to the island in their distinctive clothes, their trolleys in the supermarkets filled with all the luxury articles, staying in posh hotels. That was, of course, one side of the matter. There was the other: coping with the rat-race, racism, a permissive society, meeting the payments of the 'never-never,' stress, the loneliness of old age.

However, my own visits to the homes of my nieces Romaine and Rhona in Melbourne gave me a glimpse of what the Burghers could achieve to enjoy a satisfactory lifestyle in Australia. They were still making 'sacrifices' for the sake of the family – and they still preserved their Sri Lankan identity of family unity, hospitality and generosity, reflected in the way they all got together. My sister-in-law and my nieces with their husbands and children welcomed me warmly whenever I arrived in Melbourne, and my sister-in-law would entertain me lavishly to stringhoppers, chicken curry, cutlets, seeni sambol and a variety of other home-cooked dishes. In my niece's home we ate, drank and talked, as we would have in our own island. 'For the sake of the children's education' was one of the reasons that compelled the Burghers to emigrate. The hope of greener pastures yet another.

Then there were the left-behinders who chose to stay back. Those who did not take part in the growing Burgher diaspora to Australia. Those who did not go into exile to sit down by the Waters of Babylon and weep. Each one had their reasons for emigration, and each one will find individual justification for voluntary displacement in the act of 'going away.' The Burghers, considered themselves western-oriented, their first language – 'however it was spoke' – was English. With the gradual drying up of the 'English stream' in the schools and colleges, many

Burghers felt they could not adapt to the changes. However, change and the transformation of society were inevitable after gaining Independence. The upsurge of nationalist feelings after years of colonial subjugation was still to be understood. The post-independence era of the 1950s saw the passing of the Sinhala-Only Bill of 1956. English became the prerogative of a privileged class of society. The language led to divisiveness among the haves and the have-nots. The majority of the Burghers perhaps felt threatened by the displacement they felt they would have to suffer through the political changes. Perhaps they could have made a valuable contribution to the country that had given them so much if only they had decided to remain behind and be part of that great resurgence of nationalism. Each one now became conscious of a Burgher identity, and if that identity could help you to get across to another continent – Australia was the Canaan land 'flowing with milk and honey,' to those who had still to learn of the displacement and the dispossession of the 'Dreamtime People,' the Aboriginal people.

Within the Burgher community too there were differences – the 'pure Dutch Burghers' as they called themselves and 'the other.' There were pure Dutch Burghers with their documented genealogies and wapenherauts preserved by the Dutch Burgher Union. Tombstones and family vaults too. Also, the colour of skin, fair complexioned, blue-eyed, blond, auburn or titian haired, perhaps the 'purer' of the lineage. But what about 'the other'? They too had their Burgher names derived from the period of Dutch occupation in the island in the seventeenth and eighteenth centuries. 'Hybridity,' an indigenized bloodline, showed their differences.

To get to Australia with its "White Australia" policy in those days, the would-be emigrant had to prove that they had a European ancestor. My parents had no intention of emigrating. They were quite satisfied and content with their lives in Ceylon. Some of the first family members to emigrate from my mother's side was a cousin, Lorna and her husband Bert Albrecht, the cousin whose romantic courtship I remembered beneath the flowering thumbergia bower in Kadugannawa.

The Burghers who did not have their recorded genealogies had to seek out information in churches, kirks and the graveyards round the churches. Some of the graveyards were overgrown, in the heart of the city, in Colombo, in the Fort and Pettah areas. In Pettah, near Kayman's gate there was a large patch of land, a no-man's land which stood beside the busy hub of the shopping centre. The shops were on either side of Main Street, which was in turn cut into segments by Cross Street, First, Second, Third and Fourth. In the midst of the teeming mass of Indian and Muslim shops, the streets congested with hundreds of bullock carts, overloaded lorries carrying gunnysacks of vegetable and other commodities of trade; the clanging of trams piled with people wending their way through a mass of humanity in the humid, steaming air –lay a peaceful plot of ancient history surrounded by an old thick wall with a rusty iron gate which was permanently locked. The interior of the old Dutch graveyard could be glimpsed as you travelled in the trams. It was a neglected graveyard, some tombstones in ruins, their monuments awry – the artifacts of history, time and oblivion. They were of granite and so the monuments endured. Until the explorations began (and there were monuments and graveyards in Galle, Matara, Jaffna, Trincomalee, Batticaloa, and other areas of the maritime provinces where the

Hollanders had once held sway), these graveyards were a haven for wild birds and even reptiles. There was no human intrusion there. With the burning need to find that forgotten European ancestor, the new invasions began.

The peace and tranquility was shattered as the Burghers began their search – scrutinizing the monuments of the past. They could be seen clearing the wilderness of weeds and grass that surrounded the ruined monuments with their Latin inscriptions, to take down names, dates, and establish connections to help them construct the family tree. Sometimes a discovery would lead to perplexity and confusion as descendants, who had gone a long way from that original ancestor, faced each other across the sacred but neglected territory with all the signs of hybridity clearly writ all over them. Sometimes they would even grow irate as they laid claim to a supposedly common ancestor.

"Who are these people?" one dignified old Burgher gentleman demanded, looking at another family taking down notes from the inscriptions.

"I don't know them from Adam, papa," the daughter reiterated.

"This is our great-great-grandfather's grave. We are the famous Van Imhoffs. Who are you, may I know?" Mr Van Imhoff persisted.

"We are the Van Imhoffs too," said the other party. "Well, what do we do? Share the ancestor of course. That's the only thing that will help us get across, reach Down Under… We do look different, but this is not the time to argue about pedigrees. Let's get on with the job…"

Hoe Lang is Eeuigheyt
– How Long is Eternity

After the 1950s when the rest of my relatives, cousins aunts, uncles, began to emigrate to England, Canada, the United States and Australia, I would only see them again on their brief returns to the island when they came on holidays or to sell their inherited properties and houses for which they no longer had use.

Some of them relinquished everything, never returned, were never seen or heard of again. We had been so close within that Burgher enclave. Now its territory began to shrink, enclosing shadows and emptinesses. Auntie Ila decided to settle down permanently in England. Auntie Elsie continued her globe-trotting, though she was one who always returned to her roost. Some of the cousins had dreams of coming back from self-imposed exile, building small houses and having a place where they could return at will to recapture a spacious past. These were only pipe-dreams. Their gifts and talents, their quirks and idiosyncrasies, their family ties and connections became legends. Legends that no one wanted to be ever reminded of even.

To prove their European ancestry, the Jansz and Grenier genealogies were resurrected from the Dutch Burgher Union Journals where they had been documented and preserved. Copies of those genealogies fell into my hands by chance. It was the eighteenth-century ancestor, Adriaan Jansz, whose genealogy was the first I was to see. The bloodline on my maternal grandfather's side. This was the document that was produced by the first Grenier and Jansz emigrants to Australia, the relations on my mother's side. The Solomons too had to prove their colonial connections when they emigrated.

At first it was merely historical curiosity which made me read those documented genealogies, uncovering connection after interconnection with those heterogeneous often eclectic forebears. Later I began to question an identity that was forged out of those mixed genes. I was very much a navigator on uncharted oceans like my ancestors. I had to rub off the accumulated dust of centuries with its layers of fact and surmise and discover my self – germinating within that fertile soil. Fertile all right because those ancestors left their progeny behind so that those genealogies still have continuity. I began to see myself in a different light. Here I was, married outside that safe and predictable enclave, creating all kinds of adventures for myself. Sometimes the terrain was harsh and inhospitable but I created my own landscape, I created a history of my own and an identity for myself out of both genealogies and personal narratives. Many of the family portraits were lost or misplaced, but the oral narratives of my parents, remained. Moreover, historian after historian had recorded the western conquests of the island under the Portuguese, Dutch and British.

I was reminded of a game I had once played as a child when I had gathered together all the quicksilver globules from a broken glass thermometer, which had recorded my soaring fevers or the return to normal body temperature. The mercury lay in the palm of my hand and I gently moved the silvery fluid till it coalesced into one large globule. I could shake it at will, the forms would separate and under my scrutiny I saw each shape and form individually.

Hybridity became a passport for my relatives, giving them a legitimate right to enter countries as emigrants. They did not have to be smuggled out as human contraband. I wonder whether they felt complacent about it once they settled into a new culture.

I was never to exploit that part of my ancestry. I chose to remain close to my roots so firmly entrenched in the fertile soil of the country of my birth. I created extensions to those genealogies, extensions which did not entail the exploitation of an inheritance for either exile or escape. It did not mean that I was often easy in my mind in the place which I inhabited. I sometimes felt a sense of unease, a sense of being one of history's hybrid excrescences on that ancestral tree. I was condemned to loneliness, rejection and unacceptance. The pearl that wasn't perfectly shaped and formed. My mother's strands of Japanese Ciro pearls were all perfect in shape... That would never be me.

Turning over the pages of Adriaan Jansz's history my curiosity was aroused. His name had given credibility through the inheritance, to the new emigrants. Who then was that man Adriaan Jansz? He left no legacies. No documentation of his everyday life. On 16 February 1794 he had married Elazabet de Zielwe at the Dutch Reformed Church in Galle, during the period of governor J.G. Anglebeek's administration (1794-1796). He had by her, as it was stated, four sons. Gerard Wilhelm, Hendrick Constantyn, Peter and Adriaan. Two years after his marriage to Elazabet, Adriaan faced an uncertain future at the surrender of the Galle Commandary to the British.

That he served in the civil and administrative services is apparent after the British took over the maritime provinces. He stayed on in the island while other Dutch countrymen were sent off. The historian priest Father S.G. Perera described the surrender of Trincomalee (1795), and of Colombo and Galle (1796):

> *All the Dutch officials were permitted to remain on the island as private individuals with reasonable means of subsistence subjected to the approval of the government of Fort St George. Those who wished to leave the island could do so with all their possessions free of all duties, the military were to be prisoners of war and to be sent to Madras at British expense. The clergy were to be retained, continue their functions and to be paid by the British.*

No doubt Adriaan Jansz's services would continue to be utilized with the experience he had acquired in the administrative setup of the Dutch. Even the children born to him after the British took over, continued to have Dutch names and were baptized in the Dutch Reformed Church. Their descendants, however, showed the influence of British missionary activities, took on anglicized names and were baptized in Wesleyan and Anglican churches. They were later to enter the British Civil Service and Legal Services, study at British universities, Cambridge, Oxford and London, and even take Holy Orders at Oxford House, Bethnal Green, London.

Who was that man Adriaan Jansz? And the woman Elazabet? And what did they look like, that couple? Their faces are imaged out of the canvases of those Dutch portrait painters of the seventeenth and eighteenth centuries in the illustrations from books and art galleries which dealt with that period of colonization. That was what I imagined.

Adriaan must have set sail in one of those Dutch Merchant vessels which took the route to the Indies, embarking from the seaport of Amsterdam. It was here perhaps that he had heard stories from the seafarers who had returned from their fabled explorations, setting his mind and imagination afire with visions of amassing a fortune out of those silks, spices, ivory and gems which were said to abound in the Orient. Untold wealth. Trade. Barter. Commerce. Revenues. All he had perhaps in his sea chest when he set sail from Amsterdam were a few sparse possessions. How long would those European clothes have lasted in this tropical climate anyway – tall hats with tilted brims, ruffles of linen at the throat, long-sleeved coats, breeches which billowed out below the knees, thick woolen hose, and leather boots? Yes, how long would the linen and wool of that temperate climate last in this island? The buttons and buckles soon to tarnish with sea spray; rents appearing and patches roughly darned. The accoutrements of a Burgher of Amsterdam gradually abandoned.

And the colour of hair, eyes, skin? His complexion would soon change. That beard, moustache, hair grow grizzled, bleached in the strong sun; the skin lose its paleness and become bronze, ruddy. His tastebuds would savour the flesh, fruit and vegetables, the chicken roasted on spits, the fish wrapped in thick coconut milk with country herbs, and the platters of rice. And where did he dwell with his wife Elazabet? In one of those dwellings in Leyn Baan or Zeeberg or Lighthouse straat with the steps leading up to the pillared veranda, slaap kamers, the zaal, the keuken, the shragggery – the storeroom with its rice and coconuts, over which Elazabet would preside. But all that would come later.

He first established his history in the fort wrested from the hands of the Portuguese in a bloody battle amidst scenes of terrible carnage. By the time Adriaan reached Punte-de-Galle, the map drawn by the cartographist Resende de Barreto had already been changed. Punte-de-Galle had possessed all the features of a

Portuguese fort. It had a fortalessa, freitoria or factory, the water pass and its water tower or guarita, its Cathedral and monasteries of St Pedro, St Domingo, St Antonio. It is a map that fascinates me. On it is drawn a picture of a fish market and a man chopping fish. Galle was the headquarters of the Dutch in the island, described as a "formidable structure erected of solid stone and lime-bounded rampart." It controlled extensive cinnamon lands with an entire mahabadde or cinnamon department to control the cinnamon trade. The Dutch renamed the bastion of St Jago, the Sun Bastion or Hoofdwatch, the mainguard being there. St Antonio was named Zee Punt or Star Bastion, and Conceycao became Middle Punt.

Adriaan's mind must have been stored with all the island stories from the descriptions of men like Guyon le Fort, who together with Joris Van Spilbergen and Cornelis Speck had undertaken expeditions fitted out by the House of Mucheron in three ships, the *Schaap*, the *Ram* and the frigate *Lam*. And what had he heard? Of its gems, rubies and sapphires, the ammonium scents, the marshes and cinnamon, the forests, that the most common plants furnish precious perfumes, and that elephants run there in herds as the wild boar do in the forests of Europe, while the brilliant peacocks and the Bird of Paradise occupy the place as the rooks and swallows of Europe.

For Adriaan it must have been a long voyage of several months, sailing through the Oceanis Orientalis. Feeling the heave and swell of that vessel as it ploughed through those deep furrows of the ocean. Night after night pacing the deck or snatching a few winks of sleep, breathing in the smell of sea and brine, his clothes damp from sea spray, as he longed for the taste of fresh meat and fruit awaiting arrival at the "insula Indici." Taprobane. Had he made promises to anyone to return to the Netherlands – parents, brothers, sisters? To return, to tell them of his whereabouts, bring home a fortune? Who knows? Gazing day after day at an unending expanse of water, watching the fish swirl out of the spray, the dolphins spearing the air with the silver slant of their bodies, he must have felt an overpowering sense of loneliness. Where he would go there would be no European seasons, only the hot sun, great shell-backed turtles, trees that were different to those that grew in his own land, fruit that he had never tasted before. And a new race of people he would walk among, whose language he would learn, whose riches and commodities of trade he would enter in the great ledgers of the VOC, the Dutch East India Company.

What did his mind dwell on? Of the descriptions in the new maps? An island surrounded by the sea, the details of its terrain drawn and the maritime possessions of the Hollanders marked out precisely. The cartographist had drawn pictures of the people in whose midst they lived, whose lives they changed by their laws, religion, language, taxes and impositions. Whose territory they claimed as their own. In those maps Adriaan's people too were shown wearing their wide-brimmed hats and long tunics and capes of linen, the bounty of the land piled up around them. Behind the cartographers' drawings and markings on those parchments, other images swirled in his mind: elephants, ivory tusks, gems, spices, chank, dyes, elephants for princes, rubies, smooth-lustred pearls, palm trees, clusters of ripe fruit overhanging from their branches… He had only a few guilders in his pocket, no woman yet, and a lineage to establish.

He must have had mixed thoughts on that day, 23 February 1796, at 12 noon when Commander Fretz "shedding tears," handed over the keys of the different gates of the garrison on a large silver salver to Lachlan Macquarie. Macquarie had marched from Colombo with a formidable contingent of troops, 30 artillerymen, 7 companies of Madras sepoys (each company 100 strong) and 3 subalterns, to Galle after the signing of the treaty capitulating to the British. Lachlan Macquarie was at that time an officer in His Majesty's 77th Regiment of Foot. In Galle, his detachment having been stationed outside the Fort, he was conducted formally to Government House and met by Commander Fretz. For the Dutch it was the end of one of their most valuable colonial possessions in the East, but for the native inhabitants of the island it heralded once more over a hundred years of colonialism and subjugation. For me, a part of that heritage, it meant a long and painful investigation engendered by colonization. However, on that day, 23 February 1796, for the British it was a scene of triumph:

> *The British detachment then marched in through the main gate to the Grand Parade in the middle of the Fort, drums beating, colours flying. The 650 Dutch Troops already assembled, saluted. The Dutch guards were relieved, the Dutch flag struck, formal possessions were taken in the name of His Britannic Majesty and a Royal Salute fired.*

Adriaan and Elazabet lived and died in Galle. Their remains were buried in a vault in the Dutch Reformed Church.

Their grandson, Joseph, the son of Susan Johnston, who was the only child and only daughter of the famous Captain Arthur Johnston, was to return to the Fort one day well over a century later, to take up his duties as postmaster in Galle. My mother as a child recollects a house in the Fort in which she lived. On the second floor of the house dwelt an invalid lady who spent hours and days in loneliness. Between her and the little girl grew a deep and abiding friendship. The invalid lady would make small packages wrapped in brown paper with gifts in them - dolls, finely sewn dolls dresses, tea sets, spinning tops, homemade sweets - and lower them down to where the child played. Messages would pass between the two of them. In a family where there were many children and her own mother, delicate and frail with so much childbearing, Charlotte did not have much pampering. The lonely Burgher lady who never came down the stairway was her friend until Charlotte left Galle.

Visit to a Dutch Church – Galle

I climb the old stone steps and
feel I've entered another time,
the silence filtering in sun wedges
on empty wooden pews
cold memorials studded with dust
grey walls engraved with names,
dates, events, "Lost at sea"
"Faithful to his Heavenly Father."
I see names that live on in
descendants of this undeniable
past,
names we share,
and tread gently this long sleep
never to be disturbed
except in thought.

A man, death's caretaker
points to the stone slabs engraved
upon the floor. "These people
came
from the Dutch and the English
communities."
I wonder how many times he
repeated
these lines.

Outside unrelenting
the heat is unending
on the silent cobbled road
Soldiers in camouflage uniforms
guard forgotten ghosts.

Parvathi Arasanayagam (Kandy)

Postscript

Recently a relative of mine, another Solomons connection married to an Israeli, had begun investigating yet another strand of her ancestry, her researches carried on in the Hague and on the Internet. What she wants to confirm is the truth of the existence of a Jewish ancestor, an identity now important to her children through their patriarchy. On one of her visits to my home she brought family photographs, early family records and letters from a great-grand-aunt which spoke of Isaac Solomon. The story was that he had embarked on a Dutch sailing vessel in Amsterdam, came out to the Orient, and somewhere near the southern coast of Ceylon, jumped ship and swam ashore. He had then disappeared, leaving only this historical trail to be explored centuries later.

One day I had a telephone call from Israel from my cousin telling me that a famous Israeli TV director was visiting Sri Lanka to make a television series on those who had any Jewish affiliations in Sri Lanka. He wanted an interview with me, which I granted, an interview which turned out to be like many others, which I was never to see or hear, travelling across different worlds, sometimes in different languages, my thoughts, feelings, ideas floating in an extraterrestrial world.

Eitan Oren, invaded my home one day with his cameraman and TV crew. We went through an interminable interview where I had to answer a barrage of questions. There seemed to be no time limit to restrict us. "Do you known you have a Jewish ancestor?"

Well, in my youth I was once told I resembled Lola Montez, the dancer who was a Spanish Jewess. Her colourful portrait had been painted by one of the Impressionist artists. Others had named me with different identities, from Marjorie Morningstar to Anna Magnani, to a Portuguese Jewess from Gibraltar to a Waugh heroine in Point Counterpoint, and others... I can barely recall, there were so many personae to be summoned. I listened to Eitan, read identity poems to him, and talked of the political scenario I inhabited (under the vigilant eyes of two very charming officials from the Film corporation sent by Tissa Abeysekera).

Eitan continued: "Your ancestor probably emigrated from Spain during the time of the Spanish Inquisition to escape the religious persecution of the Jews..." Well, I had, a French ancestor whose people were Huguenots...

For me, mythmakers like my cousin Jennifer, who still held on to her Dutch name, Van der Greft, needed to establish specific identities for specific purposes. We all inhabited a colonial gameboard. There were the victors, there were the defeated. Jennifer would carry on with her research, which might even end in the library of the University of Peradeniya in the Ceylon Room where historical documents were preserved. We were all searchers because we were cast adrift on perilous oceans.

For me, who remained behind, it was responsibility, confessional and expiation. I would never be a migrant seeking to lose an identity and assume a new one. The variegated strands of a colonial identity offered endless scope for my viewing life through a different lens. Out of subjugation of that historical self, I would find my individual freedom and a rationale for survival.

Patterns of Migration

(Bellagio, Como, Italy, 2003)

I have come here to Bellagio, a writers' and artists' and academics' retreat in Italy, to complete my manuscript. Looking at the exhibits of the visual artist Patricia McKenna's packages of soil ranged on the marble floors of the Villa, I observe the meticulously designed labels with their important landmarks from the different counties, in Ireland. I am especially interested in the package from County Clare where Lt Col. Arthur Johnston came from. He fits into what I see as the martial migrations of those times.

His martial routes led to the founding of a bloodline which flourished within the colonial context which in turn led to a different kind of migration, the migrations of those of his descendants who left the island and spread all over the globe in search of greener pastures. They are the hidden witnesses to that period of colonization, but their journeys are diasporic, exiles of a different time and lineage.

I will begin here in these gardens of the Villa Serbelloni as I walk along the pebbled pathways, Camminare sul Sentiore, the pleasant promenades that many have taken and will take to command a view of the lakes Como and Lecco with the rugged Swiss Alps towering above them. I have time on these walks to ponder and think on my inheritance. Here perhaps is that space I need in which to make certain connections. Have I come so many thousands of miles away from home to explore the complex strands of that inheritance? Across the snow-covered Alpine peaks I look out on the history of the past. These places have all known the conflicts between warring tribes, powerful monarchical dynasties and Renaissance Popes, leading to feuds and political turbulence. It was a way of life that those faraway ancestors had been accustomed to. They had wanted to extend the frontiers of their existence as well as of their nation-states, which meant embarking on voyages of discovery and exploration for trade, barter, acquisition of wealth and territory. I wonder whether they ever thought of the progeny they begot on those martial migrations. That they paused somewhere along the way and encountered women with whom they shared some part of their lives. Of those ancestors whom I know of, it was only the Dutchman who ultimately became a householder, while the others took different routes once they felt that the more important missions, the martial missions, had been accomplished. Those routes led to that European inheritance and I am reminded of those connections.

From this garden which Fillipo Meda describes, I look out on the snowy Alps which seem to enclose us in this valley. Yes, I have come thousands of miles away from home to ask myself unanswered questions. Is it only myself who scrutinizes these colonial inheritances? Patricia McKenna provides pointers and clues to this search. This visual artist's packages of Irish earth embody patterns of migration and this is one important connection that makes me think of my inheritance. Those were the early colonial migrations but more than a century or two later, the descendants of those soldiers of fortune embarked on new migrations, peaceful ones. Strand after strand of migration unknotted themselves, the people leaving houses and gardens desolate. Many of them do not want to be reminded of their past. Leave letters unanswered. One whole branch now living in Melbourne who once occupied the railway bungalows of Mount

Mary, the children of my mother's twin brother Joshua, with their new personae, have detached themselves completely from the family history. Others like Diana Albrecht Atkins, yet another cousin, brought mementos, framed family photographs, when she visited me in Melbourne, while Frances Prins was happy to attend our reunion at the tea party planned by my niece Romaine.

As I read the history of the Castle Keep of the Villa Serbelloni, the history of the Stangas, the Sfondrati, the Serbellonis, I wonder what connections we have – but of course there are connections. A whole lot of European names in our genealogy show that conquest brought in new races, new ethnic groups, new cultural patterns, and new identities.

The endless stretches of water. The mountains, snow covered. Sometimes there is no other definition but outline. The waters of Como are half-obscured, gathered into a sheath of silver.

Beside the sculpture of Carlo Sfondrati there is another sculptured in very classical lines of a boy playing a flute with the pelt of a young lion draped about his shoulders. I seem to hear that haunting melody in the wind. A tune runs through my head very delicate with soft trills like the music David Simons, the American composer/performer, creates from his theremin standing before that electronic instrument, moving his body and limbs before it to evoke his compositions.

In the gardens of the Villa I see my childhood garden of Eden but in that faraway garden I was too young to interpret those intimations of violence in the games I played with Mungo. The pebbles I played with then were to remain embedded in my consciousness to grow into the images of violence and upheaval in the year 1983 just as the earthquake which disturbed the natural order of things threw our childhood world in turmoil with its unenvisaged dangers. Safety was only imagined. The thornless roses vanished with my childhood. The roses I plucked later on drew blood, left wounds that took time to heal.

Every day I walk through the gardens. Dominating the knoll beside the veduta I observe a brutal stone carving of a lion and two tigers. The lion is being mauled by the two tigers. What warning signals did this sculpture intimate amidst these flowering trees and ordered flowerbeds, the threatening branches of lofty trees lopped off or pollarded? In the past there must have been great dangers on this wooded promontory, enemies that could overpower you. There were the lake pirates, the cavargnoni who in 1537 had burned down to the ground the Marchesino Stanga's palace, leaving it in ruins until it came into the possession of Count Francesco Sfondrati of Milan. "Wicked and unbridled," those cavargnoni had been described as. Here on this promontory then, those violent deeds had taken place.

I keep musing on that sculpture. Who first began the attack: was it the lion in all its power and strength? Two to one, the lion was being overpowered, the final act, death. Reminders of the past, the violent past in which we have all been involved. Presagements of the future. Down in the village the Peace banners proclaim their message. There are Peace protests in almost every Italian city and township. At breakfast there are earnest and serious discussions and dialogues on the impending war against Iraq. Bellagio too has known Nazi occupation. The Princess was requested to leave the Villa and to hand it over to the Nazis. Italian smugglers led her to the Swiss border through the mountain passes. Looking at those rugged snow-covered mountains I marvelled at her indomitable will and resilience at her age. She was no longer in her first youth, yet she made the journey and returned to the Villa after the war was over. Mussolini and his mistress had been shot and killed by the Italian Partizans by then. The Principessa, Ella Walker, American heiress to the Walker Bourbon whiskey fortunes, had spent the greater part of her life in Europe – survived the Nazi Occupation and lived out the rest of her days in the Villa, ultimately bequeathing this great treasure to the Rockefeller Foundation.

While I think of the connections and connecting threads of the book I have come to complete, my thoughts go to the Irishwoman Patricia McKenna. Her packages of earth are ranged in an orderly fashion against the walls of corridors which are covered with tapestries and oil paintings from the past. "Plant a seed in each lump of soil," I say, "make history sprout." What would the Principessa herself have thought? Finally Patricia did add another package, that of earth from the garden of the Villa Serbelloni, to the visual art collection. The themes of Patricia's art are embodied in those packages. Migration, departure, abandonment. Earth of different colours, ranging from burnt umber to brown sienna, from khaki to yellow ochre. What was her vision? Loss, migration, displacement – it was not worth fighting and shedding blood, a kind of unique vision of the unifying forces of a soil lived on and shared.

The Grey House in Ireland of which Patricia shows a videoclip is transformed by her imagination. She fills it with her sculptures and with the memorabilia of the past, the walls covered with symmetrically arranged pairs of shoes, and envelopes with their addresses to people everywhere in the world. Movement, travel, mobility, going away, departure – everything that we are part of in her imagination. In what she shows us, the insights she gives us, I find the connecting links with migration and Diaspora.

Not only did my European ancestors embark on their martial migrations and conquest expeditions, but their descendants too follow the migration routes, some of them not only to the colonies that were once part of the British Empire, like Australia and Canada, but also to the United States and to the former mother country. None of them ever followed the ancestral routes to the Netherlands or to France or to Ireland. Where I was concerned, there was no search for roots, except for my personal investigations into the past that engendered us. Those descendants had found new homelands where they settled down. They never returned to the island. The houses they had lived in, the properties they had owned, now had new occupants, or were abandoned, sold, razed to the ground. They returned with their memories to the past, but the new generation had severed all connections. What impelled them to go away? Was their search rewarded? From time to time their voices reach me. I preserve their letters with care.

Yes, time to ponder, to contemplate as I walk on these pebbled pathways and climb higher and higher through the woods to reach the Castle Keep.

One morning, the 20th of February, I came upon the statue of Pliny seated in his protected niche with a stone scroll in his hands. In that historical narrative of Bellagio and the Villa Serbelloni, as it is recorded by John Marshall (1970) in "The Castle Keep," I had read of Pliny. It was said that he owned several Tuscan villas and acres of productive farmland, land rich in olives and grapes. Vineyards and orchards abounded, laden in spring with cherries, oranges, quinces, olives and grapes.

Pliny's statue bears the inscription:
'Hic Tragedia'
But why?

What has Pliny to do with my search for an inheritance, for ancestors, for an identity engendered out of colonial forebears, for my self questioning my investigation of a history which was unpredicted and unplanned? Sheldon Segal and his wife Harriet (the distinguished Ella Wheeler Scholars) asked me one evening, "And what is a nice Burgher girl doing here in the Villa Serbelloni?" It is here that I can find at least some of the answers to that question. At any rate I have to find answers to many questions about myself. No one here at the Villa – and they were scholars, writers, artists, musicians, photographers, singers, dancers from all over the world – knew who the Sri Lankan Dutch Burghers were, and since I was making a presentation on my work (together with the new poems I was writing inspired by the Bellagio experience), I had to offer some explanation about this special identity. The explanations also entailed the history of western colonization in Ceylon – and the resultant 'miscegenation' of blood and the hybridity of the Dutch Burgher lineage. My friend Ann Markusen came up eventually with this description of me (I was "one of her favourites,"she said):

"Jean Arasanayagam, a Sri Lankan poet, Methodist, Dutch Burgher (meaning some European and some Sri Lankan parentage) who writes wonderful short stories and poems."

Yes, some part of that complex inheritance had been understood. And why was this inheritance so important then? Had it become a kind of political identity, which gave me a rationale to go by, being, as I now was, a left-behinder without any prospect of taking the migratory route out of the context of my birthright? I was one of the last of the floricans anyway, the floricans I had tracked down in Reed Hall. An almost, probably by now extinct species, of that bird that had provided those colonial hunters with sport and game for the table.

Again, back to the question, "What has all this to do with Pliny?" I came upon him through the routes I discovered as I explored these gardens. He had belonged to the Oufantina tribe. Who were the descendants of that tribe and where did they come from? History could explain that to those who wanted to know. And who was I? That's what this narrative sets out to discover. My interwoven narrative being distinguished, not for any exoticism, but significant for the identity of the survivor.

My ancestors' lives, except for a few, were perpetually migratory. Why would they want to stay back? Once their martial expeditions were over, they embarked on new voyages, made new lives elsewhere, forgot their descendants. They fought for imperial policies, not personal stakes. What they fought to possess was never to be theirs. Everything belonged to the Crown, to Monarchs, to Nations, States and Empires. Those ancestors all had other lives. Other countries to which they returned, if their voyage took them safely back across the ocean. The artist Patricia McKenna's themes contained the germinal seed of truth. Identity, migration, departure, loss.

I would leave my island home again and again but always return to the only home I know, the country of my birth where I possess my own complex inheritance.

Colonizer/Colonized

The blood of the colonizer that runs
In my veins is also the blood of the
Colonized, an island invaded
An island raped
Subjugated/victim
Conqueror/victimizer.

Where is there room here
For the ancient gods, the ancient
Goddesses?

No conquest can destroy them
Those who still inhabit the springs
The rivers, the trees of this earth.

History cannot exorcise them
They still breathe in water, air, leaf.
The earth is still theirs, the field,
The threshing floor where flame eats
Flame and the sacrifice and offerings
Still go on, food laid out for the deities
And god-language, incantations streaking
Into the night.